WILLIAM WORDSWORTH
SELECTED POEMS

WORDSWORTH

SELECTED POEMS

Edited with an Introduction
and Notes by

H. M. MARGOLIOUTH

COLLINS
LONDON AND GLASGOW

GENERAL EDITOR: J. B. FOREMAN, M.A.

First published in this form 1959
Latest reprint 1987

The publishers wish to thank the Clarendon Press, Oxford for permitting the use of sections of the 1805 *Prelude*. Readers are referred to the Editor's Note on page 76.

ISBN 0 00 420228 7 (Souvenir)
ISBN 0 00 424710 8 (Gift)

Printed and bound in Great Britain by
William Clowes Limited,
Beccles and London

CONTENTS

An asterisk in this list of contents marks any volume or poem that is not printed here in its entirety.

[1] References in brackets are to the Books and lines of the 1805 text.

WILLIAM WORDSWORTH

A BIOGRAPHICAL AND CRITICAL STUDY BY H. M. MARGOLIOUTH

WILLIAM WORDSWORTH

COCKERMOUTH is just outside the Lake and Mountain district. It belongs to West Cumberland and looks towards that region of farm and mine. Yet Skiddaw is hourly visible from its windows, the shores of Bassenthwaite are within easy walking distance, and the small child travelling to Penrith to visit his grandparents could gaze up in awe at the great green slope of Blencathra.

The grandfather was a substantial tradesman who, like Gray's mother, kept a mercer's shop. His daughter had married John Wordsworth, attorney and estate-manager to the chief local magnate, Lord Lonsdale, who provided him with the biggest house in Cockermouth but left it to his successor to pay his charges. John Wordsworth's second son, William, was born 7 April 1770. The only daughter Dorothy followed on Christmas Day 1771; John in 1772; Christopher in 1774; all these, and even the eldest, Richard, born in 1768, are of importance in William's biography. Never was a poet so knit with his family. He was a man of deep and lasting affections.

The Birth of a Poet's Mind (1770–1783)

Mrs. Wordsworth was no worrier, though she recognized—and wondered about—William's passionate character. She let him spend long summer days alone with nature, at the bottom of the garden, bathing, and romping through a forest of tall ragwort, a naked savage five years old. She died when he was eight. Next year he, like his brothers, was sent away to Hawkshead School, near Esthwaite Lake west of Windermere, an old foundation at which the sons of farmers and local gentry received an excellent education. The boys were boarded in cottages and were perfectly free out of school hours. William acquired great affection for his old 'dame', Anne Tyson, who also was no worrier. She only insisted that he should wear his oldest clothes for rambling over rough country. His activities were those of the completely natural country boy, but his senses of sight and hearing, and perhaps touch, were more acute, and his powers of interior visualization were altogether beyond the ordinary. His visual memories were prolonged, vivid and clearly defined. The light of his dreams was brighter than day. Such a phrase as 'The glory and the freshness of a dream' is most revealing.

He was the natural boy but something more. The 'gentle shock of mild surprise' which followed the 'mimic hootings' hardly does justice to the skill and sensitiveness with which Wordsworth describes the first beginnings of that still receptiveness of what seemed to be impulse from without but was really motion of the soul within. This grew, as we shall see, fostered by beauty and by fear.

But against the merely fearsome he was armoured. He was a great reader, within doors and without. His abridged *Arabian Nights,* his Spenser and *Don Quixote* and other imaginative lore led him almost to expect the uncommon. When in his first days at Hawkshead he saw a drowned man lifted vertically from the lake, he recognized his reading.

Early Adolescence (1783–1787)

Wordsworth's father died just after Christmas 1783. The boys had barely got home for the holidays. The irony of William's eager watch for the horses to take them home was something he never forgot. The death was a shock and a bereavement rather than a great grief. The silent man of business was no domestic tyrant and left no legacy of reaction against authority. He had given his sons the priceless gift of the run of his library, and he gave them a much-loved home, but no intimacy of affection. The home was now gone. The Christmas holidays at the end of the first half-year were in future spent with a paternal uncle and guardian at Whitehaven. The longer summer holidays after the second half-year were spent with the maternal relations at Penrith. The grandfather and uncle there were not congenial to three exceptionally intelligent and sensitive boys (Richard soon left school for London) whose clannishness was thereby intensified. The poet's mind in William was growing fast, John was a poet in all but words, Christopher—destined to have a distinguished career at Cambridge—was as keen as William on books and on noting natural appearances. Their sister they did not know. On her mother's death she had been sent at the age of six to live with relations at Halifax.

The uncomfortable summer holidays cast no shadow over school. There is no trace of bullying or of any other vices which can spring from too close confinement, and from 1781 to 1786 Hawkshead and Wordsworth were fortunate in a young headmaster named William Taylor, a man who 'loved the poets'. The loss of his father's library was more than made up to William by that of his headmaster, and from his headmaster he received encouragement in both the study and the writing of poetry. His reading now included modern poets, Beattie, for example, and Chatterton. Verse composition in English was regularly set as a school task. Wordsworth's Popian couplets on the Hawkshead bicentenary in 1785 have survived. They are, of course, very good for a boy of fifteen, and they led him on to compose verses for the first time not as a school task but of his own initiative. Yet what he wrote at school left out much that was going on in his mind and that would mature later.

What was going on was twofold but not unconnected, observation and experience.

While in the west the robe of day,
Fades, slowly fades, from gold to gray,
The oak its boughs and foliage twines
Mark'd to the view in stronger lines,
While every darkening leaf between
The sky distinct and clear is seen.

Wordsworth was seventeen when he wrote this in a poem he called *The Vale of Esthwaite,* part 'nature' and part 'Gothic'. Even at that age his descriptions were the product of repeated observation, of mental images preserved and lovingly dwelt upon, and of reflexion. Of this particular observation, subsequently incorporated, but not improved, in *An Evening Walk,* he said long afterwards—'I recollect distinctly the very spot where this first struck me. It was in the way between Hawkshead and Ambleside, and gave me extreme pleasure. The moment was important in my poetical history; for I date from it my consciousness of the infinite variety of natural appearances which had been unnoticed by the poets of any age or country, so far as I was acquainted with them; and I made a resolution to supply, in some degree, the deficiency. I could not have been at that time above 14 years of age.'

The qualifications 'so far as I was acquainted with them' and 'in some degree' are the old man's, nor was the old man always accurate about dates: '14' may not be right. But the enthusiastic boy's realization of the infinite scope for new descriptive poetry was indeed a landmark. And what a width and carefulness of reading is revealed in the conviction that the appearance had been hitherto unrecorded. Reading (even 'infinite variety' shows he knew Enobarbus on Cleopatra) did indeed stimulate observation to the point where observation outpaced reading.

The boys studied not only the poets but the guidebooks. Gray had written a *Journal of a Tour in the Lakes,* West's *Guide* was published in 1778, Clarke's *Survey* in 1787; Gilpin's more famous *Guide* not till later (1789). The guide-writers described the scenery from 'stations', i.e. viewpoints: the boys verified what was written, and saw more from other stations of their own. So in *The Recluse,* l. 19, when young William first saw Grasmere

The Station whence he look'd was soft and green.

Here, as with poetry, books provided a stimulus and a starting-point. That led, among other things, to Wordsworth's own *Guide to the Lakes,* first written as an anonymous introduction to one Joseph Wilkinson's *Select Views in Cumberland, Westmorland, and Lancashire* (1810), reprinted in the same volume as the Duddon sonnets (1820) and then in three editions as an independent work.

Poets invariably begin by imitating other poets in both matter and form. There was nothing original about Wordsworth's form until the famous 'experiments' of *Lyrical Ballads* in 1798. He was then twenty-eight, and a late developer in that respect. Original observation of nature, however, began, as we have seen, in adolescence and is found in his poetry almost from the beginning. Something much more fundamental and important, which I have called experience, also began then. The main record is in some of the *Prelude* passages included in this selection under 'Hawkshead Schooldays'. The man looking back may have understood more vividly and consciously than the schoolboy the character of these experiences, but there is no reason whatever to suppose that he imported into them a vividness not originally there. They are too much of a piece for that, too purely spiritual sensation, free at the time from the reflexion which became habitual with the later man, and they start from the thoroughly boyish. Probably most children have experienced the garden going round, or something of that sort, when they have suddenly stopped rapid motion. William 'oftentimes' stopped his skating, became the solitary that for his poetry he had to be, and then

the solitary Cliffs
Wheeled by me, even as if the earth had roll'd
With visible motion her diurnal round;
Behind me did they stretch in solemn train
Feebler and feebler, and I stood and watch'd
Till all was tranquil as a dreamless sleep.

The apparent motion gradually ceases. The boy stands stockstill. Then everything is still. This is the climax of the experience, the object of it all, the semi-trance of rest and silence after motion and after the din with which before 'the precipices rang aloud'. This, not the wheeling cliffs, is the pure spiritual sensation.

It should be noted that the reflexion 'as if the earth had roll'd' &c is not given as part of the original experience. It is the later man's reflexion when the lines were written in Germany at the end of 1798 at the same time as 'A slumber did my spirit seal'. Critics have pointed out the near-identity of language—'Rolled round in Earth's diurnal course'.

The pure spiritual sensation here, in the Owl passage, in *Nutting* and elsewhere, may be called a mystical experience or not according to the meaning we decide to give to the word 'mystical'. It is fundamental to Wordsworth's poetry. Failure to realize this means failure to understand his poetry and life. He is a poet of Nature, that is to say of observation, it is true, but he is much more a poet of experience, of

the Mind of Man—
My haunt, and the main region of my song.

This known dominance of the mind dates from his adolescence, with its 'Fallings from us, vanishings' of the outside world. On his half-mile walk from Anne Tyson's to the school he often had to grip something solid such as a gate to bring himself back. It frightened him. Observation had ceased. The light of sense was extinguished, but an invisible world, the unplumbed depth of Mind, was revealed.

These were special experiences, but, when the boy returned to the normal life of observation and bodily activity, they had their influence. From them came the 'gleam'—

> *An auxiliar light*
> *Came from my mind which on the setting sun*
> *Bestow'd new splendor.*

No Obvious Progress (1787–1791)

Wordsworth went up to St. John's College, Cambridge, in the Michaelmas Term of 1787. He took his B.A. degree in January 1791. He could, like his brother Christopher after him, have worked for and obtained a fellowship, become a good academic scholar and a clerical don with a safe and distinguished career. He could, but he could not. Something much stronger than the instinct of safety first (and Wordsworth had that instinct) or the desire for public applause (which he had not) impelled him to forgo immediate and obvious satisfactions. He had little to show for over three years at the University. What he had gained, more in the vacations than in the terms, was stored up for superb future use.

He did compose *An Evening Walk,* published in 1793. Its 446 lines of decasyllabic couplets contain his observations of nature at Hawkshead and elsewhere.

In the vacation before he went up to Cambridge he met his sister Dorothy for the first time for nine years. The child of six was at fifteen almost a young woman. Her letters to a girl friend in Halifax survive. She had been recalled to help in the house and shop at Penrith. She found the Wordsworths were treated as poor relations, but the reunion with her brothers was a delight to them and her. She reminded William of his mother. This first reunion was a matter of some five weeks only. When the new school half-year began in the first week of August, William, though he had finished with school, was packed off to Hawkshead with John and Christopher—the grandparents and uncle treated him like that. He returned to Penrith for three weeks before going to Cambridge, while Dorothy performed a mother's part in getting his clothes ready. Though she was younger than William and always remained younger in mind, this maternal aspect of her relation to him is worth remembering.

William, Dorothy reported, 'wishes very much to be a Lawyer if his health will permit, but he is troubled with violent headaches and a pain in his side.' The wish to be a lawyer was a seventeen year old boy's purely temporary idea of following in the footsteps of his father and elder brother, but the headaches were presumably a form of migraine with which a pain in the side can be an associated symptom. This trouble recurred frequently in Wordsworth's maturity. One critic, writing of his maturity, has even argued that it indicated inhibition and a divided mind. Its occurrence so early, when there is no question of mental stress or inhibition—on the contrary a glad looking forward to Cambridge —is enough to refute the suggestion.

As in the seventeenth century, undergraduates from distant homes still remained in Oxford or Cambridge during the shorter vacations. It was in the Long Vacation of 1788, though he spent part of it at Hawkshead and Whitehaven, that William rejoined Dorothy. There were long walks and long talks, and the foundation was laid of the later vital companionship. Then Dorothy went to live with a more congenial uncle in Norfolk, where she was loved by uncle and aunt and the babies as they came. William visited her there.

Dorothy's friends at Penrith were the Hutchinson girls, Mary, Margaret ('Peggy'), Sarah and Joanna, parentless like the Wordsworths. Their father had been the Penrith tobacconist. Mary was the same age as William. With Mary and, one may be sure, Peggy (the next in age) at least, William went long walks in the 1789 vacation. Later, when married to Mary, he looked back with pleasure to the 'blessed season', but there is little reason to suppose that he was then in any sense in love with her. The beginnings of that date from 1797, when she paid a long visit to Racedown.

The change to Cambridge threw into brilliant relief the two vacations spent in the north. The undergraduate with his fine clothes and powdered hair might dance at the house of farmer or squire and enjoy 'slight shocks of young love-liking' with 'frank-hearted Maids of rocky Cumberland', but in the presence of lake and mountain, sunrise or the public road at night, stillness and trancelike vision came over him with power:

On I walk'd
In blessedness, which even yet remains.

For at the University there was less scope and freedom than there had been at school. Mathematics, it is true, might be neglected in favour of Italian which had no examination value, but the College gate had fixed hours for opening and shutting, there were compulsory chapels to attend (he nearly missed one evening through drinking silent 'libations' to Milton) and there was too much unstimulating companionship. Characteristically and almost pathetically Wordsworth tried in his College bedroom to recreate his attic at Anne Tyson's. At Anne Tyson's he had been able to lie in bed and

watch
The moon in splendour couch'd among the leaves
Of a tall ash, that near our cottage stood,
Had watch'd her with fix'd eyes, while to and fro
In the dark summit of the moving Tree
She rock'd with every impulse of the wind.

A new observation, and an oft-repeated experience. So at Cambridge by moving his bed he could look through the open door (there was no bedroom window) at the moonlight: just opposite was the antechapel window and he could think of, but not see, the statue of Newton below it.

The chapel window was a poor substitute for the ash, but there was an ash in the College grounds through which he could look up and see the moon. Moreover, as novelty wore off, old habits were resumed. He left his companions, as he had left the skaters, and 'walked along the fields, the level fields' (a thing nobody did), and found that the absence of familiar scenery made his mind not less but more active. The mystical experiences were deeper. He felt

Incumbencies more awful, visitings
Of the Upholder, of the tranquil Soul,
Which underneath all passion lives secure
*A steadfast life.**

Of all such experiences the deepest and most lasting was in the Alps. Thither in July 1790, his last Long Vacation, Wordsworth had set out on 'a pedestrian tour' with a College friend, Robert Jones from North Wales. It is difficult for us to realise what a bold, unprecedented action this was. It was, of course, an 'open slight

* I have no authority for the comma after 'Upholder', but it seems to me to make a more impressive and more Wordsworthian sense. Wordsworth admitted he was 'no adept at punctuation'.

of College cares and study', but the mere hardihood of it appalled all prudent souls and brought prophecies of disaster. Goldsmith, it is true, had had his vagabondage on the Continent and supported himself by his flute, but this of Wordsworth and Jones was a serious tour in search of the picturesque and the grand. Some sort of conveyance would have been considered essential by anyone else, but these two mountain-bred youths neither desired nor could afford one. William told none of his relations beforehand, not even Dorothy. With a few pounds in their pockets and their 'bundles' on their heads they marched across France in a fortnight, fraternizing delightedly with the groups returning home from celebrating the first anniversary of the fall of the Bastille, but with no serious political interest. Through Switzerland they went to the Italian lakes (which made a very different sensuous impression) and back through Switzerland: then in 'a little Bark' down the Rhine to Cologne and home by Belgium.

'The impressions of three hours of our walk among the Alps will never be effaced', he wrote to Dorothy: 'I had not a thought of man, or a single created being; my whole soul was turned to Him who produced the terrible majesty before me.'

The darkness and the light
Were all like workings of one mind, the features
Of the same face, blossoms upon one tree,
Characters of the great Apocalypse,
The types and symbols of Eternity,
Of first and last, and midst, and without end.

So, years later, the experience finally found full expression.

It conformed to type. Like the boyish skating experience it followed on a relaxation of physical effort and tension. The Alps had just been crossed and the downward journey begun.

The wonderful and strenuous holiday was followed by a year of marking time. Uncle William Cookson, at whose rectory Dorothy now lived, expected William to be ordained, but not till April 1793 would he reach the canonical age. He could still draw modestly on such ready money as his father had left or on advances from the Whitehaven uncle. After taking his B.A. in January 1791 he spent four months in London, observing humanity and growing up a little. Then till September he was with Robert Jones at his father's parsonage in Denbighshire. This probably cost him nothing except when, as was natural, they went off together for another 'pedestrian tour'. Then, again with Jones and again on a mountain, came one of his greatest experiences which, if not then at any rate later, was also an apocalypse or revelation of Mind. The slackening is not on this occasion quite so obvious, but it is there. The hour of steady plodding with head down was followed by silent standing and gazing at the island-studded ocean of mist and the blue chasm.

In September he returned to Cambridge. Uncle William, noticing perhaps that, though his nephew had not paid too particular attention to Latin and Greek, he seemed to be keen enough on learning Italian, suggested that he should study 'the oriental languages': Hebrew would be useful for a clergyman. There is no evidence that he even made a beginning, but he thought of something else. He would go to France, learn the language thoroughly, and so qualify for a travelling tutorship. He reached Dieppe from Brighton on 28 November 1791. He was back in London about the middle of December 1792. He was away longer than he had intended, he learnt French, and he had a year of utterly unforeseen experiences.

Admiration, Hope and Love (1792)

The 'march of military speed' through France in 1790 had shown to the two young men a country *en fête*. Only the doom impending over the Chartreuse suggested the other side. Differences since then had widened. At Orleans, where Wordsworth was living very comfortably on less than a pound a week, political divisions were obvious. His landlord was strongly opposed to the Revolution as were most of the army officers, three of whom lodged in the house. When, in about March, he moved to Blois, he again had anti-Revolutionary fellow-lodgers. He could now understand their talk better: it was all for privilege. Wordsworth, though a not wholly impecunious member of a middle class, found himself against privilege. He had been brought up in an almost egalitarian society of small land-owning farmers, petty gentry, shopkeepers and professional men. Snobbery, caused by the uprush of the trading classes, had not arrived there.* At Cambridge (ignoring the nonsense of the gentleman-commoners) he had found a similar academic democracy. His only contact with the English aristocracy was not favourable. Lord Lonsdale was using all the law's delays

* As late as 1836 my own great-great-great-uncle in West Cumberland left money to five nieces whose husbands are described respectively as gentleman, gentleman, draper, millwright and bricklayer.

to avoid paying several thousand pounds owed to his late agent's heirs.

This, however, did not amount to a passion for the Revolution. In mid-May Wordsworth can write fairly coolly to a friend. War between France and Austria had opened disastrously for the 'patriot army', whose general Dillon had then been murdered by the mob—

> "An ignominious flight, the massacre of their general, a dance performed with savage joy round his burning body, the murder of six prisoners, are events which would have arrested the attention of the reader of the annals of Morocco, or of the most barbarous of savages. The approaching summer will undoubtedly decide the fate of France. It is almost evident that the patriot army, however numerous, will be unable to withstand the superior discipline of their enemies. But suppose that the German army is at the gates of Paris, what will be the consequence? It will be impossible to make any material alteration in the Constitution, impossible to reinstate the clergy in their antient* guilty splendour, impossible to give an existence to the noblesse similar to that it before enjoyed, impossible to add much to the authority of the King."

From this cool partisanship Wordsworth was roused by one man, Michel Beaupuy or Beaupuis, the single democrat among the officers Wordsworth met. An aristrocrat by birth, free from personal ambition, with a strong intellect and wide sympathies but no fanatic, thirty-seven years old to Wordsworth's twenty-two, he won the latter's deep admiration and affection. This personal attachment, not any previous interest in politics, led Wordsworth to listen enthusiastically to Beaupuy's exposition of the philosophy of government for the good of the people. The dry subject of constitutional law and practice took on the 'attraction of a Country in Romance'. Reason was assisted by compassion. The only words of Beaupuy which Wordsworth actually records had a profound effect on him: "Tis against *that* Which we are fighting'† was Beaupuy's agitated exclamation at the sight of 'a hunger-bitten Girl'.

Wordsworth's admiration for Beaupuy led him to admire the whole revolutionary mood and activity, in particular the young men whom he saw leaving their homes to join the patriot army. It may perhaps have been Beaupuy (of whom, as well as of John

* After six months in France, Wordsworth already uses this word in the French sense equivalent to 'former'.

† The rather un-English translation suggests *C'est contre ça que nous combattons.*

Wordsworth and Nelson, Wordsworth was thinking when he later wrote *The Character of the Happy Warrior*) who inspired Wordsworth for a time with the thought of being not a lawyer or a clergyman but a soldier. This admiration, not of mountains but of men, was something new in Wordsworth. With it went something else new, Hope—not the hope for their own future which animates all young people, but a hope for mankind—in fact the youthful belief with which we used to be so familiar that the millennium is just round the corner. Its power in an ardent nature like Wordsworth's is almost inexpressible.

Bliss was it in that dawn to be alive,
But to be young was very heaven.

He would have no old man's mere Pisgah-sight of the happy world to come, but would live in it for years. Monarchy, aristocracy, privilege would go. And had not England shown the way to republicanism? So now he turned to read, perhaps in French translations which abounded, the English republicans, Milton, Ludlow, Harrington. He came to share the French reverence for Algernon Sidney as a republican martyr.

Meanwhile what of the poet Wordsworth? He had still in him much of the naïve eighteenth century romanticism which his early reading had induced. Even as he walked with Beaupuy along the wooded Loire, his mind sometimes strayed from the 'earnest dialogues' to thoughts of the romantic past, to the hermits (who still survive in the opening passage of *Tintern Abbey*), to the heroines of Ariosto and Tasso and Spenser, to the former chivalric splendours and gallantries of the châteaux. The early Wordsworth always aimed at connecting his reading and his observation.

Here by the Loire he wrote *Descriptive Sketches*, a long poem of the same type as *An Evening Walk* but without its absolute genuineness. *Descriptive Sketches* describes the pedestrian tour of 1790 but makes much use of a French account of Switzerland, and it gives a melancholy origin of the tour which is completely belied both by his contemporary account to Dorothy and by the later account in the *Prelude*.

Me, lur'd by hope her sorrows to remove,
A heart, that could not much itself approve,
O'er Gallia's wastes of corn dejected led.

Wordsworth was not yet engaged in writing the *Prelude*. in that definite, difficult and completely sincere adventure of spiritual autobiography—an adventure which had its wonderful trial trip with *Tintern Abbey*. If, then, in writing a poem, of which the main purpose perhaps was that it should be written, that the poet-to-be should be doing something to justify his vocation, he chose to adopt the eighteenth century convention of melancholy as seen, for example, in Goldsmith's *Traveller,* he need not be blamed too severely. Moreover the 'heart that could not much itself approve' did exist, though not in 1790. It is in 1791, when Wordsworth was at a loose end and wrote to his friends about it with a rather unhappy flippancy, that this lack of self-approval is evident (and Wordsworth's moral sense was always strong). It may well have had something to do with his going to France at the end of 1791.

The melancholy and self-disapproval, as far as they existed, were certainly in the past only. In the present he was in an ecstasy of Admiration and Hope, and also of Love. It must have been while she was on a visit to Orleans that he met Annette Vallon, probably in December 1791, but her home was at Blois, and that was why Wordsworth moved there. (If he had not done so, he might never have met Beaupuy). The child Caroline was born in December 1792.

Annette was four years older than William. She was passionate, affectionate, loyal and courageous. She overwhelmed him, but he was ready to be overwhelmed. Alone for the first time in his life in a foreign country, passionate in his own way, needing affection and companionship, with no mastery of the nuances of the French language, he passed into a new experience. How far the long story of Vaudracour and Julia* in the ninth book of the *Prelude* is factually autobiographic, one cannot say: some of it certainly is not, but the lover's emotions were Wordsworth's. That was why he included it in 'The Growth of a Poet's Mind'.

> *Earth liv'd in one great presence of the spring*
> *. . . all paradise*
> *Could by the simple opening of a door*
> *Let itself in upon him.*

Throughout 1792 there was no slackening in the attachment on either side. Why did they not marry?

In its early stages the affair had moved too swiftly. After that,

* It was subsequently modified into a separate poem published in 1820, but the 1805 *Prelude* version should be read.

if it had been in England, they certainly would have married. Neither was a light-o'-love, but it was a time in which mere custom was being called in question. On the other hand the customary deference in France to the wishes of the family was very powerful. What were the Vallons, an old-established family of the professional classes (Annette's father had been a surgeon and so was her step-father), Catholics, French, not too happy about the Revolution, to think of a penniless Protestant foreigner, an enthusiastic 'democrat'? Yet it seems almost certain that an agreement was reached that Wordsworth should marry her when he could show that he could support a wife.

In the autumn Annette returned to Orleans to prepare for her confinement away from home. Wordsworth left for England by way of Paris. There he delayed for two months, probably hoping to get into journalism and so make a living which would justify the marriage. If, as stated on her tombstone, Caroline was born on 6 December*, he heard the news before finally leaving for England.

Paris had been something of a shock. The news of the September massacres had reached Orleans before Wordsworth left, but the grand news of the first success of the patriot army at Valmy on 20 September had followed. Immediately afterwards monarchy was abolished and the Republic proclaimed. It was celebrated in Orleans by a civic feast. Wordsworth arrived in Paris 'enflam'd with hope', but he could not banish the thought of the massacres and of the neurosis they portended. Soon the party strife began: he was living in a city of denunciation and counter-denunciation. The days of the 'unjust Tribunals' were at hand. Yet a 'paramount mind' could make the Republic what it was meant to be. If only he, William Wordsworth, could solve the national problem and his personal problem together by writing the articles which would convince and heal. But the only paramount mind which emerged, a few years later, was that of Napoleon Bonaparte.

The Treble Shock (1793)

What finally brought Wordsworth back was that he had no money. Evidently neither his uncles nor his brother Richard, the

* She was baptized in Orleans Cathedral on 15 December, Wordsworth being named the father and represented by a proxy. The baptismal certificate stated that she was born on the same day. It seems improbable that, especially in December, a baby would be taken out to the Cathedral when only a few hours old.

lawyer in London, would remit more: but he would find bed and board with Richard. His first act was to get *An Evening Walk* and *Descriptive Sketches* published by Johnson, the progressive bookseller by St. Paul's. They were out in a month, and, though they brought him neither fame nor fortune, they meant that he had definitely appeared as a poet: Coleridge now knew of Wordsworth's existence and found much to admire.

If they had brought Wordsworth wealth, it would not have helped him to marry Annette. In January the Revolutionaries beheaded Louis XVI. The dismissal of the French Ambassador from London was followed on the first of February by a declaration of war by France. Some letters still got through, but reunion was impossible. Two very long letters of Annette's, one to William, and one to Dorothy who was ready to welcome her with open arms, were held up in March in the post-office at Blois, to be discovered there in 1922. They reveal her character, warm-hearted and voluble, with no intellectual interests. The women who helped Wordsworth the poet were his sister and the Hutchinsons. The cruel circumstances which kept William and Annette apart were kind to English poetry.

To Wordsworth it was agony, and so was the war with France. He had obviously never thought of the possibility. Completely out of touch in France with the body of opinion in England which was hardening against the Revolution, he was struck to the heart when his beloved native land was at war with the hope of the world. Excesses, mistakes, party strife there were, but the Golden Age could come if not forcibly prevented. Wordsworth could only hope for French victories, and indeed for the whole of this war, which lasted until 1802, the British army made no impression on the French. It was different at sea.

Wordsworth always maintained that Pitt's government was in the wrong and that we could and should have kept out of this war, and the Whig party as a whole took the same view. Wordsworth at this time went much further. He wrote a fervid pamphlet entitled *A Letter to the Bishop of Llandaff on the Extraordinary Avowal of his Political Principles . . . by a Republican.* The circumstances which called it forth are unimportant, and Wordsworth failed to find a publisher (Johnson was always careful: in 1791 he had changed his mind about publishing Blake's *French Revolution*). It is a good piece of writing and valuable evidence of Wordsworth's mind at this time. He was no doubt particularly interested in the Bishop who had a large estate on the shores of Windermere and who had

had a reputation for liberal opinions, but had now roundly declared that the British Constitution and way of life were the best possible. Wordsworth replies as a republican. It is simply not true that monarchy and aristocracy provide the best possible system. He is all for the changes which have taken place in France. He is not in favour of bringing them about by violence. Wordsworth never thought that ends justified means not in themselves justifiable. He was always for immediate human values. His horror at the cruelties and internecine passions of which he had seen the beginning in Paris was to be terribly augmented in this year 1793, when the Reign of Terror began. Not until the joyful moment in the summer of 1794 when he heard of the death of Robespierre did his full confidence in the Revolution return.

It is impossible to exaggerate the violence and steady duration of the treble shock felt by this young man of twenty-three. He was separated from his beloved, his country was at war on the wrong side, the Revolution was becoming a bloodbath. Three mighty rifts had opened in his life. A minor problem was that of his own livelihood. We hear no more of ordination. His sense of poetic vocation, though at the moment almost drowned by politics, was still there. He stayed with Richard all the first half of 1793. He could not visit Dorothy: Uncle William was displeased with him. A casual love affair would no doubt have been reprehended and pardoned: it was a common enough occurrence for a young man to have a natural child. But to marry the woman! As it happens, Uncle William was right, though for reasons he did not know.

Wordsworth's reason or excuse for going to France had been to qualify himself as a tutor. The war meant that there was no demand for travelling tutors, but he might still support himself as a tutor in England. 'He is looking out,' wrote Dorothy in June 1793, 'and wishing for the opportunity of engaging himself as tutor to some young gentleman, an office for which even friends less partial than I am allow him to be particularly well qualified.' He obtained no tutorship, but a young man of property named William Calvert, who had been with Wordsworth at Hawkshead, invited him to tour the west of England, Calvert paying all expenses. Wordsworth accepted, though, in order not to be entirely penniless, he obtained an advance of five pounds from Richard. But for that five pounds what happened on Salisbury Plain and in the Wye valley might have been impossible. Another important and unexpected consequence of this tour, which was no tour, was a small but invaluable legacy eighteen months later.

The 'tour' started with a month or so in the Isle of Wight, which Wordsworth found 'delightful': but the sound each evening of the 'sunset cannon' from the fleet off Spithead 'overcast' his spirit. The tour began in earnest in August in a light carriage called a whiskey, which before very long disintegrated in an accident on Salisbury Plain. The joint tour had to be abandoned, but Wordsworth continued it on foot. 'Having found myself so happy alone (such blessing is there in perfect liberty!) I walked off'—those were Coleridge's words just ten years later when he parted from the Wordsworths in Scotland. Wordsworth might have used them now of himself, though 'happy' in one sense only. He must indeed have been happy to be for the first time in years in the exact environment that spoke to his inmost soul. He was alone, in a wide landscape, not desert but deserted, the great sky above and all around, the rolling plain in every direction. For three days he was in the wilderness, and he was restored to poetry. He saw Stonehenge and, out of the bogus antiquarianism of his eighteenth century reading, pictured the Druids. But the impending horrors of the War and the Terror were with him also: as in childhood, his imagination projected a vision externally—of armed Britons, and prisoners sacrificed in wicker cages, as he had read in Caesar.

It was a vision that Blake might have had. Indeed this whole phenomenon of external visualization by men of great imaginative power deserves an examination yet to come. Coleridge experienced it too: he called such visions 'ocular spectra'. It is common in religious history and goes back at least to the Hebrew prophets. Wordsworth did not cultivate it. What he did cultivate was the clear inner picturing of memorable scenes.

Soon he began a poem about Salisbury Plain which was with him for many years. In its original form it was a poem about the Plain itself with the single traveller (Wordsworth) upon it. Then he added a woman, or more probably he combined the Salisbury Plain poem with another poem about a Cumbrian woman—the sufferer from the American War who first made her appearance in *An Evening Walk*. The traveller was now no longer Wordsworth but an unfortunate to whom the woman told her tale. He too was a war victim: he had been pressed for the navy, deprived of his pay or prize money, and in desperation had committed a murder. The whole poem was not published till 1842 and was then called *Guilt and Sorrow*, but part of it, containing the woman's story, was included in *Lyrical Ballads* in 1798 as *The Female Vagrant*.

'Salisbury Plain' was the first unpublished poem which Wordsworth showed to Coleridge (in 1796). Its genesis, not in the characters but in the Plain, is worth noting. Exactly the same is true of another poem, which started in 1795 with experiences in a ruined cottage. Then a woman whose husband had been lost in the American war was added: then a male character, a pedlar, who tells her story to the poet. Known at different times as 'The Ruined Cottage', 'The Story of Margaret' and 'The Pedlar', it was eventually used as Book I of the *Excursion.*

Wordsworth now left the Plain, crossed the Severn estuary and made his first acquaintance with the Wye. He was nature-hungry, but he also wanted to escape from harrowing thoughts. He was right, of course. There was nothing he could do about Annette or the War or the Revolution. There was much to make up. His poetry had indeed suffered from politics. Now

like a roe
I bounded o'er the mountains, by the sides
Of the deep rivers, and the lonely streams,
Wherever nature led; more like a man
Flying from something that he dreads, than one
Who sought the thing he loved . . .
. . . the tall rock,
The mountain, and the deep and gloomy wood,
Their colours and their forms, were then to me
An appetite.

His interest in human nature had reawakened also—in individual human characters, not just in generalized humanity or excited patriot regiments. At Goderich on the Wye he had an unforgettable meeting with the little girl who very naturally did not think of the two who slept in the churchyard as no longer part of her family. This questioning of children, and others, became habitual with him until he received the striking lesson recorded in *An Anecdote for Fathers.* Much further up, near Builth, he fell in with a 'wild rover' who became the original of Peter Bell and accompanied him down stream to Hay, more than twenty miles by the windings of the river. When they first met they were terrified of each other, for Wordsworth also looked a 'wild rover'—he had probably slept out for a week or more.

Now, however, he sought a friendly house, that of Robert Jones in the Vale of Clwyd. In three out of four successive summers these two young men were together. We do not know how long he stayed or where else he was until at Christmas he was with his friendly relations at Whitehaven.

On 7 October 1793 a Girondin deputy named Gorsas was guillotined at Paris. Nearly half a century later Wordsworth, according to Carlyle, told Carlyle that he had seen it. Did Carlyle misunderstand Wordsworth? Did Wordsworth's memory deceive him? He was often wrong in his old age about dates, but it is not like him to be wrong about such a hard fact of experience—actually seeing a deputy guillotined. Did he then manage to slip across to France in the autumn of 1793? provided with money by whom? hoping to be of some political use to the Girondins? hoping to see, or even bring back, Annette and Caroline? If so, did he in fact see them? And, if he did, was it somehow the beginning of disillusion, for Annette was against the Revolution? Perhaps some day documentary evidence will turn up to show either that he was in England on 7 October or that he was not.

Dorothy and Racedown (1794–7)

The shocks Wordsworth had endured made him examine the bases not only of political but of moral life. Godwin's *Political Justice*, published early in 1793 and widely read, is as much concerned with morals as with politics. It is uncompromisingly rationalist. Conduct must not depend in any way on feeling, and some feelings, e.g. gratitude, are irrational and should be discouraged altogether. Such premises and conclusions were alien to Wordsworth's deepest instincts. That for a time he fell for them shows how shaken and shocked and warring with each other his feelings were, and how, in spite of Salisbury Plain, his imagination had lost its supremacy. Yet it was impossible for one of Wordsworth's make-up to find satisfaction or an answer to his problems in such a philosophy. He ended by yielding up 'moral questions in despair'. Nor would it have been possible for him to find refuge in an escapist hedonism like Omar Khayyám's.

The beginning of the answer appeared in 1794 when the intellectual struggle was in full blast, for he spent the whole of that year in the north, about four months of it with Dorothy. Yet the rationalist preoccupation was strong. Far from looking on the child as father of the man in political as in imaginative life, he still held to the fallacy of the clean slate. When Robespierre fell, the millenium could still come. And rationalism led to an excessive interest in the picturesque as such. It is true that as a boy he had based his systematic study of the landscape on views from 'stations' recommended by the guidebooks, but its value lay in feeling and imagination. Now, partly perhaps because William Gilpin had recently produced a new book on the picturesque, he was in some danger of becoming a connoisseur rather than a poet. The picturesque, of course, is that which will make a picture, but to look at landscape not imaginatively but according to 'rules of mimic art' was treason. It was bound up with the contemporary fashion of 'comparison of scene with scene', of evaluating instead of enjoying, and it increased a danger to which Wordsworth knew he was liable, of letting sense, that is the eye, predominate over imagination. Wordsworth, like Blake, knew that one must look not with but through the eye. And he was never conquered. Nature, that is in effect Wordsworth's nature,

> *when the spirit of evil was at height*
> *Maintain'd for me a secret happiness.*

He drew even then on the 'spots of time', notable past experiences of the imagination whose potency was literally inexhaustible. To return again and again in thought to some person or place or experience means that the returner finds something there, of admiration or hope or love, which he does not exhaust. It goes on feeding him and giving him spiritual life. This fact is at the basis of religion and poetry (It can also, if the 'spots of time' are of contempt or despair or hate, lead to hell). Wordsworth came to understand it fully and to see and feel, even in a new present experience, 'life and food For future years'.

The beginning of 1794 found Wordsworth in Cumberland, by mid-February he was at Halifax reunited with Dorothy for the first time since 1791, and in April the two left for Keswick where Calvert was lending them a house called Windy Brow. They had hardly any money and lived with incredible frugality, but it was a preliminary realization of the dream of a cottage together. Originally it had been William's parsonage that Dorothy would share, then a cottage with William and Annette and the child. The dream was still of that. Some letters got through from Annette at least as late as November 1795, and at Windy Brow Wordsworth wrote a poem *Septimi Gades* in which a 'Mary', whose

> *arms shall be my home*
> *My only bed thy breast,*

William Wordsworth (1770–1850) as portrayed by Henry William Pickersgill in 1840.
By courtesy of the National Portrait Gallery, London

The house in Cockermouth where William Wordsworth was born on 7 April 1770 and where he lived until after his mother's death in 1778. It is now a museum and under the care of the National Trust. By courtesy of the English Tourist Board, London

is to live with him, perhaps by the Rhône, but failing that a Grasmere. It is quite impossible that, as has been supposed, 'Mary is his future wife Mary Hutchinson, who was at this time not very much more than an acquaintance. It was Wordsworth's custom to change actual Christian names in his poems. Dorothy becomes Emmeline, little Basil Montagu is Edward, of Lucy I shall speak later. There had been more than one 'Mary' in his schoolboy poems. This 'Mary' (unless the poem, which has little value, is a mere exercise—it is based on an Ode of Horace) can only be Annette, and Mary scans more easily than Annette.

At Windy Brow Wordsworth finished 'Salisbury Plain' and took long walks with Dorothy, much to the disgust of the aunt-by-marriage in Penrith who also objected to Dorothy's 'unprotected situation'. Dorothy wrote a spirited reply. Like Richard II she pointed out that she was 'now twenty-two years of age. . . . Besides I not only derive much pleasure but much improvement from my brother's society. I have regained all the knowledge I had of the French language some years ago, and have added considerably to it, and I have now begun reading Italian.' So William had found one pupil.

It must not be supposed that Wordsworth was unintermittently miserable during the years of stress from 1793 to 1797. There had been three great shocks and there was the ceaseless intellectual striving along the wrong lines. But he was young: cheerfulness and hope would break in. There were journalistic possibilities, though he examined them without enthusiasm. He had to find his way to poetry and had a firm ally here in Dorothy.

There came also an unexpected duty which helped him to feel of use to someone. From Windy Brow they went to Whitehaven. When they parted, they had been together for at least four months. He spent a month in late summer with cousins at Rampside opposite Peele Castle, in wonderful weather: even Wordsworth, the storm lover, felt that no poet could ask more. He recalled it years later—

I was thy Neighbour once, thou rugged Pile!
Four summer weeks I dwelt in sight of thee.

Before that he had been back at Keswick and there he spent the rest of the year. William Calvert's younger brother Raisley had developed consumption. He had also become an ardent believer in Wordsworth as a poet. He wanted Wordsworth's company, and he could give him modest financial help to enable him to live for poetry and poetry only. For months Wordsworth was his almost hourly companion. He was twenty-one when he died in January 1795. He left Wordsworth £900. It was not a great deal, it was a long time before it was all paid over, and Wordsworth was not particularly wise in his method of investing it: but now that there was something, he and Dorothy could live together and poetry, poetry only, could be his profession.

From February to August 1795 he lived again in London, not this time with Richard but with Basil Montagu who was reading for and teaching for the bar. He probably did not intend to stay so long in London, but some of the legacy had to be obtained, the arrangement for a home with Dorothy could not be made in a day, and Montagu, who was in much personal distress, needed him. Wordsworth's 'healing power' lay not only where Matthew Arnold meant but in his personal character. He was a comfort to Raisley Calvert, to Basil Montagu, to Dorothy, to Coleridge: a man so different from him as Robert Jones enjoyed his company. With his great imaginative power and intellectual activity there went also solid commonsense (see his letters to William Mathews) and an interest in other people which can only be called tender (consider the Discharged Soldier and Simon Lee).

In London Wordsworth made Godwin's acquaintance and visited him several times. He was in the full tide of Godwinism. 'Godwin on Necessity' became his gospel, and indeed fatalism can bring its own consolation. Yet the fate-driven sailor now introduced into a revised 'Salisbury Plain' is a comforting character only to those who have lost all, even hope. Of more lasting importance was the friendship he struck up with two of Montagu's law pupils, John and Azariah ('Aza') Pinney. Their father, a wealthy Bristol sugar-merchant, owned a small country house called Racedown Lodge in Dorset. It was little used, and the sons easily persuaded him to let it to Wordsworth and Dorothy. Not till the following year did he learn that the rent was nil: however he was easily appeased.

Wordsworth stayed for a few weeks with the Pinneys in Bristol. There he first met Coleridge. Then he walked in two or three days to Dorset, met Dorothy's coach, presumably at Chard or Crewkerne, and together they arrived at Racedown Lodge at midnight on Saturday, 26 September, 1795, as Joseph Gill the resident caretaker and factotum recorded. The dream of a 'cottage' together had been realized. The household was soon increased by

Basil Montagu's motherless three year old child Basil (to be immortalized as Edward in *An Anecdote for Fathers*) and a faithful local maid named Peggy, who two years later accompanied the Wordsworths and Basil to Alfoxden. Somewhere in the background Joseph Gill, who was quite friendly, kept an eye on Mr. Pinney's interests, such as the inventory of glass and tableware and the hedges. It is a little hard on him that this latter activity was combined with a story of Erasmus Darwin's to produce (*Goody Blake and Harry Gill*). But Wordsworth was always interested to discover in real life an analogue or partial analogue of something he had read.

They stayed at Racedown for a year and three quarters. When they left, Wordsworth had recovered his poetic balance. He had some sharp times to go through, as *Incipient Madness*, the first account of the actual ruined cottage, indicates. But he had a double anchor, his home and his sister, and above all he had his own fundamental strength and perseverance. He won through, through Godwinism which he exposed in the drama he wrote at Racedown, *The Borderers*, through excessive concern with mere politics which petered out in attempts at satire, and, surely, through Annette, whose letters ceased to arrive and who, he must have realized, could not be a life-mate for a poet

the Gods approve
The depth, and not the tumult, of the soul.

He was in touch with Coleridge, to whom ne sent the revised version of 'Salisbury Plain' and who admired him as *the* coming poet. He had Dorothy who believed in him utterly and to whom he was willing to give the credit for restoring him finally to poetry. He had hill and meadow at his door and the simplest of peasantry, a low and rustic life in which he found elementary feelings in full reality, unspoilt and unhid by sophistication. He was himself achieving a simpler style and diction: elevation could come at any moment, but not on linguistic stilts. The opening passage of the *Prelude* and the originally final passage of 'The Ruined Cottage' both belong to 1795.

In the spring of 1797 Mary Hutchinson paid them a long visit. Wordsworth was not then in love with her, or he would not, very shortly after her arrival, have gone off for about three weeks to Bristol, Bath and finally Nether Stowey where he found Coleridge much dejected. Coleridge returned the visit in June. He and

Dorothy discovered each other, and so indeed did he and William. The great triple alliance sprang up. Between the poets currents flowed. In the ensuing twelve months, the *annus mirabilis* 1797–8, Coleridge was to be stimulated into writing his most memorable poetry, *Kubla Khan, The Ancient Mariner*, the first part of *Christabel, Frost at Midnight, The Nightingale:* Wordsworth was to make, not one more beginning, but immortal verse culminating in *Tintern Abbey.*

For Coleridge took them both back with him for a visit to Stowey and immediately found for them a large furnished house in a park, Alfoxden House, unoccupied because the owner was a minor. It was to let for the nominal rent of £2 a month. Wordsworth took it until the following June quarterday, for eleven months and a half. They moved in on Sunday, 16 July, 1797 and Basil and Peggy followed.

Coleridge and Alfoxden (1797–8)

The detailed story of the wonderful year which produced that landmark in English poetry *Lyrical Ballads* has often been told. There is plenty of information about it from surviving letters, Dorothy's journal (January to May), Coleridge's account in *Biographia Literaria,* the reminiscences of Joseph Cottle who published *Lyrical Ballads,* and also from Thomas Poole, Coleridge's friend at Nether Stowey, Thelwall the revolutionary who visited Coleridge and Wordsworth the very day after the move into Alfoxden House, the Wedgwoods, and even the Home Office archives—for, on information received, a detective was sent from London to look into the queer people at Alfoxden. Their north-country accent was taken for foreign, they hung out the washing on a Sunday, above all they rambled about the district with notebooks. Were they French spies? No, reported the detective, but 'democrats'. Thelwall's arrival was, in fact, unfortunate. It helped to give them a bad name and to prevent a renewal of the lease for another year. In March, when this became clear, a plan to go to Germany was discussed. They would acquire another language and Coleridge would gather material for a book on Lessing. The plan materialized in September 1798.

Meanwhile, Alfoxden and Nether Stowey being only three miles apart, there was almost daily intercourse except during some absences, e.g. when the Wordsworths went to London in December and when Coleridge preached in Shropshire in January. There were great walks together, such as that to Lynton in November which saw the genesis of *The Ancient Mariner*. To begin with, Wordsworth and Coleridge thought of actual collaboration, but that did not work. Wordsworth's contributions to *The Ancient Mariner* consisted of a few lines and important suggestions about the story. Joint authorship of a prose tale had previously come to nothing.

Not collaboration but division of labour was the solution. Coleridge's account in *Biographia Literaria* is as follows:

"During the first year that Mr. Wordsworth and I were neighbours our conversations turned frequently on the two cardinal points of poetry, the power of exciting the sympathy of the reader by a faithful adherence to the truth of nature, and the power of giving the interest of novelty by the modifying colours of imagination. The sudden charm which accidents of light and shade, which moonlight or sunset diffused over a known and familiar landscape, appeared to represent the practicability of combining both. These are the poetry of nature. The thought suggested itself (to which of us I do not recollect) that a series of poems might be composed of two sorts. In the one, the incidents and agents were to be, in part at least, supernatural; and the excellence aimed at was to consist in the interesting of the affections by the dramatic truth of such emotions as would naturally accompany such situations, supposing them real. And real in this sense they have been to every human being who, from whatever source of delusion, has at any time believed himself under supernatural agency. For the second class, subjects were to be chosen from ordinary life; the characters and incidents were to be such as will be found in every village and its vicinity where there is a meditative and feeling mind to seek after them, or to notice them when they present them selves.

In this idea originated the plan of the *Lyrical Ballads;* in which it was agreed that my endeavours should be directed to persons and characters supernatural, or at least romantic; yet so as to transfer from our inward nature a human interest and a semblance of truth sufficient to procure for these shadows of imagination that willing suspension of disbelief for the moment, which constitutes poetic faith. Mr. Wordsworth, on the other hand, was to propose to himself as his object to give the charm of novelty to things of every day, and to excite a feeling analogous to the supernatural, by awakening the mind's attention from the lethargy of custom and directing it to the loveliness and the wonders of the world before us; an inexhaustible treasure, but for which, in consequence of the film of familiarity and selfish solicitude, we have eyes yet see not, ears that hear not, and hearts that neither feel nor understand."

Such poems as *The Thorn* or *Simon Lee* or *The Last of the Flock* or *Old Man Travelling* contain scenes from 'ordinary life' observed by 'a meditative and feeling mind'. They are also, in the words of the *Advertisement* or preface, 'experiments' in the use of simple language for poetry. The poetic diction of the eighteenth century (from Pope through Gray to Cowper) is found in Wordsworth's earlier poems and he is liable to slip back into it, but he had come to the opinion that a special kind of language could not be necessary for poetry, and he was now experimenting on that basis. Not all the poems in *Lyrical Ballads* are among the experiments, not Coleridge's four contributions (*The Ancient Mariner*, *The Nightingale* and two excerpts from a play), not *Tintern Abbey* which was an afterthought. That contains much elevated language: 'on a wild secluded scene impress Thoughts of more deep seclusion' is not 'the language of conversation in the middle and lower classes of society', but neither is it poetic diction. Gray's schoolboy cannot bowl a hoop, he has 'to chase the rolling circle's speed', and Gray overdoes personification just as the young Wordsworth could in *An Evening Walk:*

With Hope Reflexion blends her social rays
To gild the total tablet of his days.

That sort of thing is not found in *Lyrical Ballads.*

Most of the *Lyrical Ballads* are simple psychological studies. Wordsworth is interested in Betty Foy as showing maternal affection at its simplest, in little Edward and the child of *We Are Seven* as showing the child's mind at work, in Harry Gill because of the action of the curse, in the Old Man Travelling because his mind is reduced to its simplest elements. Combined with this, in some but not all these poems, we see the social reformer who has thought things out for himself. The Female Vagrant and the owner of the Last of the Flock suffer because they are reduced to a propertyless poverty. Goody Blake is poorer than anyone ought to be. The Convict ought not to be imprisoned but transported to a colony or plantation ('plant thee') where he could make a fresh start (Transportation to America had, in fact, been customary until the revolt of the colonies made it impossible: Australia was substituted a few years before Wordsworth wrote this poem).

There is among the poems another group in which Wordsworth rejects the philosophy of books for the immediate impulse of the stimulating and beautiful natural environment in which man is placed ('impulse' is a technical philosophical word—power from without 'impels All thinking things'). Living the right kind of life, subjecting ourselves to the right influences (or impulses) can literally teach us more and better philosophy than books because we shall be rightly attempered.

One moment now may give us more
Than fifty years of reason.

The whole theory, based on Wordsworth's intimate experience deeply considered and on his sense of what was life indeed, is presented in *Tintern Abbey*—a poem composed without a written note during four days of walking up and then down the Wye Valley and finished as he and Dorothy re-entered Bristol on their return.

Wordsworth in this year did more than *Lyrical Ballads.* He began *Peter Bell,* not published till 1819, and he about doubled the length of 'The Ruined Cottage'. Above all, in January and before *Lyrical Ballads,* he began what was to be a blank verse *opus magnum.* Coleridge admired Wordsworth as both poet and thinker, and he wanted him to write a grand philosophical poem. It was to be called 'The Recluse; or Views of Nature, Man and Society.' It would thus cover the whole of life. It was much too vast a subject. It is too vast a subject for any poem and it is the wrong sort of subject. Into a long poem a poet may indeed put his whole personality, but he cannot do that if he gives excessive prominence to a philosophical exposition. So Coleridge's suggestion was unfortunate in that it weighed upon Wordsworth with a sense of duty left undone, especially in later years when it was evident that 'The Recluse' would not be completed. On the other hand from this suggestion sprang the *Prelude,* the *Excursion, Home at Grasmere* and many unpublished or incomplete passages of much interest and value. It is not clear exactly what (apart from 'The Ruined Cottage') was written in the early months of 1798 before it was laid aside for *Lyrical Ballads,* but it included, at least in a first draft, the magnificent passage beginning

On Man, on Nature and on Human Life

with which *Home at Grasmere* concludes and which was used in 1814 as a 'Prospectus' to the *Excursion.* It is not inferior to *Tintern Abbey.*

The Poet Blossoms in a German Winter (1798–9)

In mid-September, 1798 the Wordsworths and Coleridge (leaving Mrs. Coleridge and the two infants at Nether Stowey) sailed from Yarmouth to Hamburg, over a British-controlled sea to a neutral port. The two to three weeks in Hamburg are fully described by Coleridge in *Satyrane's Letters* and by Dorothy in her journal. Coleridge's diary-notebooks published in 1957 add some details, e.g. 'Wordsworth & Sister determined to go on, & seek, lower down, obscurer & cheaper Lodgings without boarding'. They separated, which, from the point of view of learning German, was a wise move. Coleridge went first to Ratzeburg and early next year to the University of Göttingen. The Wordsworths went—not lower down, but higher up—to an old town called Goslar, not intending to stay there longer than they felt inclined. They did not know how bitter winter can be in the central European plain or how primitive were German means of transport. After a few autumnal walks they found themselves weatherbound till nearly the end of February. After that they moved about, twice seeing Coleridge, but they were glad to get back to England in May.

They had learnt little German. At Goslar they met no one interesting. They could not afford to accept hospitality which they would be expected to return. It was an embarrassment that 'sister' turned out to be a German euphemism for mistress. In any case for much of the time the exceptional cold kept them within doors. There they told each other about the childhood which they had lived apart. To William it came back with an extraordinary vividness: his present inertia and lack of achievement seemed a painful contrast. 'Was it for this?' he asked again and again in verses that were to become part of the first book of the *Prelude*, 'was it for this?' that I had those early raptures and deep experiences. He went on to describe them. In a letter to Coleridge they sent the Nutting, Skating and Stolen Boat passages, selected 'from the mass of what William has written'. In effect he wrote a poem on his childhood and concomitantly on the poetic character: most of it eventually found a home in the first two or later books of the *Prelude.*

Nor was this all. Of the poems published in the second volume of *Lyrical Ballads,* dated 1800, at least a dozen were written in Germany. They include *A Poet's Epitaph, The Two April Mornings The Fountain, Ruth* in its first and shorter form, *Lucy Gray,* and four which form a group—'A Slumber did my spirit seal', 'She dwelt among th'untrodden ways', 'Strange fits of passion I have known' and 'Three years she grew in sun and shower'. This group, with one other poem not written till 1801, comprises what are known as the Lucy poems, though the name Lucy does not occur in the first or last of the four. In all except 'Strange fits of passion' Lucy is dead: in that poem the poet fears she may be dead and in a final unpublished stanza hints pretty strongly that she did die before the poem was written.

The habit of calling them the Lucy poems is misleading. The name of Lucy is not peculiar to them. It is found in *Lucy Gray,* obviously a different girl. It is found in a rejected part of *Nutting* where Lucy is anything but a retiring violet: she has a 'keen look Half cruel in its eagerness' and almost seems 'An enemy of nature' (This Lucy, even apart from her description, cannot, of course, be Dorothy who never had a chance of going nutting with Wordsworth the schoolboy). It is found in the published version of *The Glowworm* ('Among all lovely things my love had been'), a poem which does record an incident connected with Dorothy; but Wordsworth originally wrote 'Emma', he then tried changing the name to 'Mary' and finally to 'Lucy'. The fact is that the *name* Lucy means nothing at all, just as in *Septimi Gades* and earlier *juvenilia* the *name* Mary means nothing at all. Let us speak of the group of five poems as the poems on the Dead Girl, the fifth being 'I travell'd among unknown men'.

To identify the dead girl is not of primary importance. To understand how she got into the poems is. Wordsworth was now a professional poet. He neither had nor intended to have any other profession. He wanted to write poems which were both beautiful and true. Since he was thirteen his ears had been

> *open to the charm*
> *Of words in tuneful order, found them sweet*
> *For* their own sakes, *a passion and a power.*

He had thought and felt, and continued to think and feel, long and deeply about the art of poetry. We must not in our biographical and psychological research and speculation forget to think of the poems as conscious artistic creations of the imagination. Wordsworth wanted them to be true, and the beginning of this was to base them on selected fact, fact which had appealed to his emotion and imagination: but that was a beginning only. The truth must be psychological truth. *The Affliction of Margaret*, for example, is beautiful as an artistic creation; it was based on an actual woman in Penrith; but its truth lies in its reproduction of the state of mind not absolutely of that woman but of a woman so situated, not knowing whether she is bereaved or not.

So the Dead Girl poems are beautiful artistic creations. They take their origin from a real girl who died. The truth which each poem tells is a psychological truth. In 'A Slumber did my spirit seal' we have in the first stanza the dreamlike certainty of 'I' (who is not necessarily the poet, but is the 'I' of the drama*) about 'She' who seems pure spirit not subject to mortality. In the second stanza the dream is shattered. She seems only body, dead body, part of a merely material world. There is no more to it than that, but who has not felt the unmeasurable difference between the living person and the dead? and has any poet ever reproduced the feeling of that difference more simply, more beautifully, and more completely?

'I', in fact, was not William but Dorothy. In March 1796 Peggy Hutchinson, the second of the sisters, died of a galloping consumption. 'Last year at this time', Dorothy wrote, 'we were all together and little supposed that any one of us was so near death.' Of course she said the same to William at Racedown, and three years later her words took on the beauty of 'I had no earthly fears.' William knew Peggy. He is certain to have felt affection for her as he felt for all the Hutchinsons, having indeed an affectionate nature. He may even have felt something more than affection. We cannot say, for the poems are poems and do not, except at a far remove, contain autobiography. They doubtless reflect Peggy's character and situation as seen imaginatively by Wordsworth. It may be otherwise with mere incident. Wordsworth did use actual incident in whatever way suited his poetic purpose. The three years of 'Three years she grew in sun and shower' need not apply to Peggy. The incident in 'Strange fits of passion' has been conjectured to have

* A very clear example is in *The Solitary Reaper* where 'I' was not Wordsworth but his friend Wilkinson.

happened in connexion with Dorothy. Perhaps: but why the unpublished final stanza?

> *I told her this; her laughter light*
> *Is ringing in my ears;*
> *And when I think upon that night,*
> *My eyes are dim with tears.*

Only Peggy can be the original of the Dead Girl. She appears finally in the fifth poem of the group, written two years after the others and sent to Mary Hutchinson in a letter ending in strong emotion.

> *Thy* (i.e. England's) *mornings showed, thy nights conceal'd,*
> *The bowers where Lucy play'd;*
> *And thine is, too, the last green field*
> *Which Lucy's eyes survey'd!*

Mary Hutchinson, now William's beloved, knew he was writing of her sister.

A Poet Living in Retirement (1799–1802)

On returning from Germany in May 1799 the Wordsworths went straight to Sockburn-on-Tees to stay at the Hutchinsons' farm, and there, except for brief absences, they stayed till a week before Christmas. They would have gone back to Somerset if a house could have been found for them. At Sockburn Wordsworth's first concern was financial, the fate of that anonymous volume *Lyrical Ballads* and the temporarily unsatisfactory state of his small capital. But tidying up, copying out and perhaps continuing the poetry of the German winter occupied much of the summer and autumn, and then he was unwell. Racedown, Alfoxden and even Germany seem to have suited him, but on his return to and settlement in the north we hear more of the rather mysterious ailments —now in the form of stomach trouble, inability or at least physical reluctance to perform the act of writing, and finally eye trouble. We cannot say of him, as we can say of Coleridge, that settling in the north was a mistake, but his native climate did not altogether suit him.

Coleridge did not return from Germany till the end of July.

At Nether Stowey he was desolated at the loss of Wordsworth, though he still had in Tom Poole a staunch friend, helper and believer. In October, hearing that Wordsworth was ill, he dashed up to Sockburn. Wordsworth had recovered, and the two had a grand walking-tour in Cumberland and Westmorland, part of it with John Wordsworth home for a time from the sea. The tour had two momentous results. It made Coleridge in love with the north country. It showed Wordsworth a vacant cottage, once an inn, at Grasmere. He took it. On Tuesday, 17 December, 1799 he and Dorothy left Sockburn. After some miles on horseback they walked most of the way, and at dark on Friday they arrived at the cottage. Coleridge meanwhile had made a beginning at Sockburn of his stimulating, embarrassing, comforting and really rather odd love affair with Sarah Hutchinson.

At Grasmere the winter, though hard, must have seemed mild compared with their experience the year before. Furnishing and home making were on a modest scale. Molly Fisher from a neighbouring cottage came in to help for two or three hours a day for two shillings a week, which was sixpence more than she had asked. Wordsworth got on with *The Recluse*. He wrote a whole book, concluding it with the passage 'On Man, on Nature and on Human Life' first drafted two years before. He never published anything but excerpts from it. It gives us a perfect picture of the poet and his sister during the first months in their first real home.

In the spring Coleridge came for a visit. In July Coleridge and his family came to live at Greta Hall, Keswick. The two poets were now thirteen miles apart instead of three as in Somerset. It meant that they slept more often at each other's houses: the intimate intercourse was fully resumed.

It at once had a definite object. *Lyrical Ballads* was now sold out: a second edition was called for. It was decided to have two volumes, the first being a reprint of the original volume with a few changes, the second containing new poems. Wordsworth had plenty of material and he also set about adding to it.

The new edition was to be in Wordsworth's name with an acknowledgment that some poems had been provided by a friend. The only new poem of Coleridge's was *Love,* inspired by Sockburn and Sarah Hutchinson, which was inserted into the first volume, *Lines written near Richmond* and *The Complaint of a forsaken Indian Woman* being removed to the second. The printing was done as before at Bristol, where their young scientific friend Humphry Davy undertook to help with the proof-reading. Many changes were made as the book went through the press. Originally *Christabel,* to which Coleridge had now added Part II but which was still uncompleted, was to be included. In October a contrary decision was made: it might, if completed, make a separate book together with Wordsworth's 'Ruined Cottage' now known as 'The Pedlar'. Wordsworth himself was at work until December on a poem always referred to in the correspondence as 'The Sheepfold' but finally entitled *Michael.* Reaching the printer so late it had, of course, to come at the end of the second volume, but in any case Wordsworth would have thought that a fitting place for it. He liked to put a specially important poem first or last in a volume. The 1798 volume had opened with *The Ancient Mariner* (now, owing to unfavourable criticism, put last but one, *Expostulation and Reply* being given the place of honour at the beginning), and it had closed with *Tintern Abbey,* like *Michael* a late arrival at the press.

The opening poem of the new volume was *Hart-Leap Well,* the scene of which William and Dorothy had visited on their walk to Grasmere in the previous December. The volume thus opens with Wordsworth's tenderness to animals

Never to blend our pleasure or our pride
With sorrow of the meanest thing that feels,

as it concludes with his tenderness to suffering man

There is a comfort in the strength of love.

The *Advertisement* of 1798 was superseded by a much longer *Preface.* Wordsworth wrote it, but every detail of it was discussed with Coleridge. It is a very important document. Its only weakness lies in Wordsworth's inability to explain fully why he wrote in verse rather than prose. He gives four reasons— (1) He has tried to 'superadd' the acknowledged 'charm' of metre. (2) The regularity of metre prevents the excitement aroused from being unbearable. (3) The reader is accustomed to 'feelings of pleasure' from metre, and will therefore enjoy the poem more. (4) The managed variations of metre provide 'similitude in dissimilitude', which is a fundamental element in all pleasurable activity. This last reason he doubtless derived from Coleridge, and none of the four reasons is negligible, but the modern reader is surprised to find no apparent understanding that a poem is an artistic whole, in which matter and manner, subject and form, story and style, thought and feeling and language are chemically combined*. The same matter in prose might also be an artistic whole, but it would be a different one.

The question 'why write in verse' arises naturally from Wordsworth's explanation why he has abandoned 'poetic diction', an explanation admirably summed up in his criticism of Gray's sonnet on West.

Wordsworth's battles have long been won, not only about 'poetic diction' but also about subject-matter—'the human mind is capable of excitement without the application of gross and violent stimulants'. The best known passage in the *Preface* describes the origin of poetry, or at any rate of Wordsworth's poetry: 'it takes its origin from emotion recollected in tranquillity.' The process is then carefully described. Wordsworth does *not* say that poetry is emotion recollected in tranquillity. A very simple example of the process will be found in Wordsworth's own words in his poem on the daffodils, 'I wandered lonely as a Cloud'.

Wordsworth did find his arguments about diction and metre difficult to get across. In 1802 another edition of *Lyrical Ballads* was called for. He made some modifications in the *Preface* and he also introduced for the first time some grand passages about poetry. 'Poetry is the breath and finer spirit of all knowledge; it is the impassioned expression which is in the countenance of all Science . . . Poetry is the first and last of all knowledge—it is as immortal as the heart of man.' In the 1802 version also there appears for the first time the revealing phrase 'the grand elementary principle of pleasure', which is implicit in all Wordsworth's poetry and is at least as important as the 'worthy purpose'.

After the effort and output of 1800 the poet in Wordsworth lay fallow for most of 1801, but the lover awoke. Mary Hutchinson paid long visits both to her native Penrith and to Grasmere. It may have been John Wordsworth rather than William who first thought of her in the way of marriage, but by the end of the year it was understood that William and Mary would marry if and when they could. For about six years nothing had been heard of or from Annette. During those years William's mind had known much turmoil, much comfort old and new, great accesses of poetry. Dorothy had become his permanently; so, it seemed, had Cole-

* A recent newspaper review expatiated on the opening lines of Vaughan's *Retreat*

Happy those early days! when I
Shin'd in my Angel-infancy,

but misquoted 'Shin'd' as 'Shone', thereby ruining the couplet by bringing in wrong vowel.

ridge; and his deep capacity for affection took in the Hutchinsons and especially Mary. The 'gross and violent stimulant' of his year in France was long past, and so was the chill solitude of Germany.

'Tis past, that melancholy dream!

So he told Mary in the poem he sent to her. She was the poet's bride, not the passionate foreigner whom he had loved so passionately when little more than a boy. But only if Annette released him, could he and Mary marry. There was a possibility of renewed communication. The war was at a standstill from the autumn, though the treaty of Amiens was not signed till March 1802. On 21 December came a letter from France. It must have assumed no change in William, for a month later Dorothy is sad because Mary has no chance of happiness. But William wrote, there was a mysterious Frenchman in London with whom Coleridge was there in touch, and by the end of March 1802 William and Dorothy decided to go to France and see Annette. They went in August. There is no evidence at all whether Annette, who had adopted the style of 'Veuve Williams', was deeply disappointed or was relieved. Perhaps both. She too had been through years of stress and development. As the Revolution grew in violence and in extreme measures, she had become a determined Royalist. As a hundred and fifty years later Frenchwomen were to hide and succour escaping British prisoners of war, so for years she hid and succoured escaping royalists. For this in 1816 she received recognition and reward. She too may have looked back and seen the year of passion with a young man of alien birth and mind as something strange and not permanently continuable—even though passion should temporarily flame from its ashes.

Marriage and Duty (1802–4)

The spring of 1802 saw another memorable outburst of Wordsworth's poetry. Having once more finished 'The Pedlar' and seen the fair copy transcribed and stitched by Dorothy, he wrote *Personal Talk, The Sailor's Mother, Alice Fell* (where once more 'I' is not Wordsworth), *Beggars, To a Butterfly, The Emigrant Mother* ('Once in a lonely Hamlet') and *The Rainbow* ('My heart leaps up'). No longer is there any idea of a revolutionary break with the past. The child is father of the man each day is father of the next and the man of each day should look back to the man of the former day with that natural dutifulness and affection which is the proper meaning of the word 'piety'. Indeed the child may be more and greater than the man. It may take all a man's efforts to live up to the child he was and he may not quite succeed. Wordsworth wrote *The Rainbow* in the evening of the last Friday in March. Next day he began an Ode:

There was a time when meadow, grove, and stream.

He wrote four stanzas which were finished in May, ending

Where is it now, the glory and the dream?

They are complete in themselves, and there is no evidence that he thought otherwise, though two years later he added a great deal and introduced fresh ideas. Neither now nor when published in 1807 had the poem any title but *Ode.*

In *The Rainbow* the heart of the man leaps up just as the heart of the child had. In the *Ode* something had been lost, the 'gleam'. Does this mean that Wordsworth's 'more than usual organic sensibility' was declining? He did eventually develop eye trouble, though the first mention of it is not till 1804 and there was nothing serious about it for ten years or so after that. Or does it mean that his inner visualization was so exceptionally bright, as his dreams certainly were, that in memory he added a 'light that never was, on sea or land' to the scenes recalled? It cannot be altogether that, for in 1818 in a poem *Composed upon an Evening of Extraordinary Splendour and Beauty* he celebrates a late return of the gleam,

of the light
Full early lost, and fruitlessly deplored.

Or was he in 1802 merely pessimistic? A poet's senses cannot always be at their acutest. At any rate it was a magnificent spring, he could enjoy it to the uttermost, yet something had gone—'the visionary gleam'.

Is it possible that his approaching marriage, with its responsibilities other than poetic, had something to do with it? Certainly it was the cause of one or two quite different misgivings apparent in 'The Leech-Gatherer', later called, rather tiresomely, *Resolution and Independence.* In that poem clean and attractive natural description, grandeur of imagery, and a representation of the poet's trance-like experience are shot through with a prudential misgiving about the future ('how can He expect that others should Build for him?') and an even more deadly misgiving that poetic vision and inspiration may fail.

It is not only that the 'gleam' has gone. What has happened to Coleridge? Wordsworth had shown Coleridge his *Ode* in April. Coleridge was thinking of it, and making actual reference to it, in the poem which in its final form he called *Dejection: An Ode.* In that poem Coleridge was dejected both because of his marital unhappiness and because of the apparent drying-up of his poetic inspiration. The 'dejection' in *Resolution and Independence* is a direct reference to Coleridge. May not he, Wordsworth, suffer the same fate? The example of the leech-gatherer supplies him with a sturdy answer.

Poetic exaltation is matched by corresponding dejection,

As high as we have mounted in delight
In our dejection do we sink as low

but of course it can be looked at the other way round. What great moments of delight there are! And there are other times of quiet happiness. That is charmingly evident in *Stanzas Written in my Pocket Copy of Thomson's 'Castle of Indolence'*, which was written in May between the first draft of 'The Leech-Gatherer' and its revision. It describes Coleridge, the 'noticeable Man with large grey eyes', and Wordsworth who had his times of stress and his times when 'happier soul no living creature has'.

So the time passed until William and Dorothy went away for their strange visit to Calais, where they spent all August. Wordsworth for the first time (unless he *did* get across in 1793) saw his daughter Caroline, now nine and a half. They walked with her and her mother by the shore. It was 'a beauteous Evening, calm and free', and Caroline frisked about 'untouch'd by solemn thought'. At other times William and Dorothy walked without the others. There is no record of any of the conversation. There is a record in Wordsworth's 'Sonnets Dedicated to Liberty' of the impact on him of France after nearly ten years. France had betrayed the Revolution. England, for all its faults, was now the upholder of liberty. The Whigs, and others, who were hurrying to Paris to see Bonaparte, 'the new-born Majesty', were 'Men of prostrate mind'. How different it had been

Jones! when from Calais southward you and I
Travell'd on foot together.

He would not despair, but he was glad to be back in England, even though England was 'a fen of stagnant waters'. And what beauty it had! On their way out they had crossed Westminster Bridge on the coach in the early morning light. On their way back, on 3 September, 1802*, Wordsworth composed his famous sonnet. No mountains or lakes were more beautiful.

Earth has not any thing to shew more fair.

They paid a visit to Uncle William at Windsor, and so on to Gallow Hill in Yorkshire where one of the Hutchinsons now had a farm. William and Mary were married at Brompton Church on Monday, 4 October. They and Dorothy then went by chaise to Grasmere.

The first year of married life was not prolific in poetry, but the prudential misgivings must have been allayed by the death of Lord Lonsdale and the payment by his successor of his debt to the Wordsworths. With nearly twenty years' interest this amounted to about £8,500, so that William and Dorothy got £1,700 apiece.

The first child was born in June 1803. In August William, Dorothy and Coleridge set out for the famous tour in Scotland so fully described in Dorothy's *Recollections*. The tour was made with the help of an Irish jaunting-car which caused amusement in places like Carlisle and discomfort to Coleridge who hated sitting in it and being rained on. He was a sick man and was taking part in the tour as an 'experiment'. After a fortnight the Wordsworths persuaded him to leave them and to set out for home. But the weather cleared and Coleridge cleared, and it was only after a strenuous fortnight on his own—not without vomiting and foot-soreness—that he worked round to his coach at Edinburgh. The Wordsworths meanwhile in the Highlands spent passionate weeks among loch and mountain and mist, finding stations for wonderful views, sleeping in primitive cabins and finding beauty and simplicity in low and rustic life. There must have been many returns of the gleam, and many visionary memories were stored up to emerge in poems written sooner or later after the return home.

* On publication in the first of the 1807 volumes the sonnet was dated, by author's slip or by misprint, 1803. This has caused some trouble, but in the 1838 and subsequent editions Wordsworth corrected it to 1802.

The strangeness of it all comes out in *Stepping Westward.* When Wordsworth lamented the passing of the gleam, was he at all forgetting that the gleam in childhood is partly a matter of strangeness, of newness? As Traherne wrote

A Stranger here
Strange Things doth meet, strange Glories See;
Strange Treasures lodg'd in this fair World appear,
Strange all, and New to me.
But that they mine should be, who nothing was,
That strangest is of all, yet brought to pass.

At the beginning of the tour they had visited Burns's grave and passed through the Burns country. Wordsworth, who knew Burns's Kilmarnock volume (1786) soon after it was published, always had a fellow-feeling for him. At the end of the tour they visited Scott who became a lifelong friend. The first of the three Yarrow poems, *Yarrow Unvisited,* was the immediate result.

They got home a fortnight after Coleridge. The winter was saddened by their leave-taking of him. He was to go to Malta in search of health. He was taken ill in their house at Grasmere and had to stay there over the New Year. When he reached London and eventually Portsmouth, he had to wait till April before he could find passage in a ship to be escorted through enemy-infested waters. The war had started again in May 1803, and Trafalgar was not yet.

During those early months of 1804 Wordsworth was hard at work, mainly on the *Prelude* of which later, but he also added seven more stanzas to his *Ode* and wrote the *Ode to Duty.* This poem, which shocked Coleridge, marks the real turning point in Wordsworth's life and character. Hitherto he had been the poet only, henceforth he is the poet *and* the married man with family responsibilities. 'Jesus', Blake had written, 'was all virtue, and acted from impulse, not from rules.' Wordsworth had taken the same line. Love was 'an unerring light, And joy its own security.' That was still the ideal life, but in his life as it was he must submit to law and duty, regularity and control. That is how the universe is governed, by law—'Thou dost preserve the Stars from wrong', a line of which the critics, with their eighteenth century limitations, could make nothing.

The turning-point was inevitable. Coleridge saw that it threatened a loss to poetry. Wordsworth hoped to have it both ways, as indeed for some years he did. He had the English poetic imagination at its highest, and he also had the solid English sense of duty. He was always a moral man. Hitherto his duty had seemed to be to poetry only, now it both seemed and was to others also. That included his country, and here there had for years been no divided mind. Illusion about France had entirely disappeared. The subjugation of Switzerland in 1798 had been enough, but Calais in 1802 during the short peace clinched the matter. Now, with invasion threatening, he was a volunteer and a 'determined hater of the French'. He was happy in his country and his home and his married life shared by Dorothy, the predestined and devoted aunt. He had enough imaginative capital to live on for years. His imaginative income would decline.

'*The Growth of a Poet's Mind*' *and* '*The Waggoner*' (1804–6)

The *Prelude* was never so called by Wordsworth. An elaborate title-page, the work of Mrs. Wordsworth's brother George, to a manuscript copy of 1806 reads 'Poem/Title not yet fixed upon/by/ William Wordsworth/Addressed to S. T. Coleridge'. When Mrs. Wordsworth published the poem shortly after the poet's death in 1850 she called it *The Prelude/Or/Growth of a Poet's Mind;/An Autobiographical Poem*. The shorter and in some ways misleading title has stuck, but it is far, far more than a prelude. The point, however, is that it was considered to be a prelude to '*The Recluse*', that vast poem-to-be of which the *Excursion* is the chief monument.

It did not start as such a prelude. It started with the childhood reminiscences written in Germany and sent in part to Coleridge at Ratzeburg. More were added, and, when at home in 1799 Wordsworth thought of addressing a poem to Coleridge, it seems clear that these passages were to be the nucleus. Such a poem would correspond to the prose account of his own childhood which Coleridge had written in a series of letters to Tom Poole and with which Wordsworth was undoubtedly acquainted. Coleridge was delighted and wanted it to be part of 'The Recluse', not a prelude but a 'tail-piece'. If Wordsworth temporarily concurred, we can properly suppose (as there are good reasons for supposing) that a part of 'The Recluse' written in 1803 was really part of the introductory half of *Prelude*, Book I. But not till early in 1804 did Wordsworth really get going again. Then he was stimulated by the prospect of Coleridge's departure to get on with the 'poem on my own earlier life' which was also the 'poem to Coleridge'. He finished it, five Books, and a fair copy was made and sent to Coleridge just before he left.

The poem (no title) went as far as the end of Wordsworth's first year at Cambridge. There was no particular point in stopping there, and so, though he had not meant it, he went on. The work had, indeed, gripped him. Moreover he had omitted from the first five Books some of his ready material, e.g. the *Nutting* passage (which he never did include) and the Penrith Beacon and Waiting for the Ponies passages now found in Book XI.

The writing went on through 1804 and well into 1805, with an interval when the heavy blow of John Wordsworth's death stopped all composition. When it was finished, at least two fair copies were made, one for presentation to Coleridge to whom it was addressed. It was read to him first, in January 1807. It affected him deeply and brought forth the poem *To William Wordsworth Composed on the Night after his Recitation of a Poem on the Growth of an Individual Mind,* the last of Coleridge's poems that really matter.

It is this form of the poem, as read to Coleridge, and known in the family as the 'poem to Coleridge', from which extracts (amounting to nearly a quarter of the whole) are given in the present volume. It was first published in 1926, edited by E. de Selincourt for the Oxford University Press. It is divided into 13 Books. The version published in 1850 was divided into 14 Books, the long original Book 10 being split in two, and was the result of many revisions, the last in 1839. In these revisions Wordsworth made changes which are discussed by de Selincourt under six headings in the introduction* to his edition. (1) Some changes of phraseology improve by tightening up loosenesses of style. (2) Some changes of phraseology are an unfortunate return to 'poetic diction'. (3) Some changes in the text were made because the 'poem to Coleridge' was being prepared for the public: many little details of person and place were omitted as not of general interest. (4) Fourthly he was concerned that his own neglect of set studies at Cambridge should not be described with an approval that might mislead the contemporary undergraduate. (5) Though his original attitude to the French Revolution had already been modified by 1804, he inserted later passages expressing political views which he held neither during the Revolution nor when he was writing the *Prelude.* (6) Finally, while opinion on the extent of his

* That introduction wrongly ascribes the second part of the *Ode* and the *Ode to Duty* to 1805: de Selincourt's own later researches set them back to early 1804.

Christianity in 1804–5 depends very much on one's definition of Christianity, he could certainly not then be called a Churchman: gradually he became a Churchman, and this is reflected in many of the later changes or additions.

It is worth noting that two of the most famous lines of the *Prelude* were not written till 1832 at the earliest. They follow the 'St. John's College' excerpt in the present volume. After 'Newton, with his Prism and silent Face' he went on

> *The marble index of a mind for ever*
> *Voyaging through strange seas of Thought, alone.*

In spite of this and some other improvements found in the 1850 text, that of 1804–5 must be preferred as a mirror of Wordsworth's mind at the time and as a consistent poem. A poet has every right to change his opinions. He may even change them for the better, but change demands a new poem rather than the patching of an old one.

Doubt has sometimes been cast on the complete genuineness of Wordsworth's account of his childhood experiences. It has been suggested that it is coloured by his mature experiences. It is of course true that we are often more fully conscious of our feelings and even thoughts when we look back than we were at the time, but clearer knowledge (which makes possible more exact description) does not delude. There is no suggestion in the childhood experiences, as recorded, of such mature experience as we find in *Tintern Abbey*. Nor was their recounting occasioned by the mature experience: it was occasioned simply by the talk of William and Dorothy when they were shut in together by the Goslar winter.

So, on the French Revolution and after, Wordsworth gives a faithful account of his thoughts and feelings. He does inevitably bring into it thoughts on 'Nature, Man and Society', which might otherwise have found a place in that improbable, and even undesirable, work, the projected 'Recluse': that so much good material had gone into 'the poem of my own life' made the completion of the projected poem even more unlikely.

Nevertheless the immediate result of finishing the *Prelude* was stimulus to get on with 'The Recluse'. It turned out to be the *Excursion,* which will be considered in its place. Meanwhile he took a busy holiday writing something quite different, that jolly poem *The Waggoner,* which dates from the first fortnight of 1806*.

* Not from 1805 as stated in the modern editions. Wordsworth himself said 1806, and, though his dates can be wrong, this one is corroborated by correspondence in the spring of 1806 in which *The Waggoner* or 'Benjamin' is alluded to and is obviously a new poem.

The Waggoner is the longest and latest of the poems in which Wordsworth shows his affection for the lively rascal. This is a side of the moral poet not always remembered. Rascal is, however, too strong a word for Benjamin (except from his employer's point of view). He had a taste for good liquor and good company which made him heedless of time and of other people's anxieties. He had no difficulty in passing the former inn now inhabited by 'A simple water-drinking Bard', he safely passed the Swan, a storm came on and his kind heart could not refuse a lift to a woman and her baby, and at the Cherry Tree his good intentions gave out. The arrival of the sailor with his model of a Man-of-war completed his downfall. That was all. He was wonderful with the horses, and his employer (who was Coleridge's generous landlord) probably made a mistake in dismissing him. When we remember Wordsworth's fondness for Burns, we can see in *The Waggoner* Wordsworth's *Tam o'Shanter* with a more lovable character as the hero and, of course, with no supernatural element.

The poem was not published until 1819 and was then dedicated to Charles Lamb, who had thirteen years before heard it with delight when read from manuscript. The published version is shorter than the original, but the spirit is the same—tender and tolerant enjoyment of Benjamin's enjoyment.

With this we may class *The Farmer of Tilsbury Vale* written in 1800 and published in that year in the 'Morning Post', but not in book form until Wordsworth's first collected edition in 1815. The farmer had farmed for thirty years, loving his farm, over-generous to many and robbed by the rest. Finally after a not too honest bankruptcy he fled to London, maintained himself as he could, was as jolly as ever but thinking always of his beloved Tilsbury Vale. The poem was 'founded on fact', as *Poor Susan* was apparently not. Since its first appearance in *Lyrical Ballads* in 1800 this latter poem has been without its final stanza, removed at Lamb's earnest entreaty. But poor Susan originally was no mere exile from the north; she was an unfortunate, a 'Poor Outcast' who is urged to return home.

In *Beggars*, written in 1802 and included in one of the 1807 volumes, it is the superb handsomeness of the woman and the versatile energy of the little boys which attract the poet. He has never a thought of morals, but morals reappear—and in no conventional form—in *Gipsies*, published in one of the 1807 volumes and written not long before. There it is not on rascality but on sheer absence of energy, idleness, that he fastens:

oh better wrong and strife,
Better vain deeds or evil than such life!
The silent Heavens have goings on;
The stars have tasks—but these have none.

He must have written this soon after seeing the gipsies, but more often the experience worked in him for some time before demanding release in poetry. In the *Prelude* Wordsworth described himself as one 'not used to make A present joy the matter of my Song', and in the epilogue to *The Waggoner* there are some informative lines which should be set beside the better known and more detailed passage in the 1800 *Preface.*

Nor is it I who play the part,
But a shy spirit in my heart
That comes and goes—will sometimes leap
From hiding-places ten years deep;
Or haunts me with familiar face,*
Returning, like a ghost unlaid,
Until the debt I owe is paid.

'*Poems in Two Volumes*' and '*The White Doe of Rylstone*' (1806–8)

Coleridge had returned in the summer of 1806, a changed and broken man, to resume intimacy with the Wordsworths who loved him as much as ever but were shocked at the change. Before Christmas he parted from his wife and joined the Wordsworths at Coleorton in Leicestershire, where their friend Sir George Beaumont had lent them a house for the winter. Here Wordsworth was engaged in preparing for the press *Poems in Two Volumes,* which were published in May 1807. They include poems recording two great griefs, of which one, *The Complaint*, was a late addition and was occasioned by Coleridge's changed behaviour. He needed Wordsworth as much as ever, but he seemed no longer to be a giver also. His perpetual and varied illnesses, his domestic estrangement and his self-accusations at not producing anything had led to too much brandy and too much opium. The old geniality and forthcomingness had gone. He accepted love. The Wordsworths, who had spent two anxious years over letters and news from Malta,

* This unrhymed line is the modified survivor of a rather poor couplet. Wordsworth made the change for the better in the 1827 collected edition.

Sicily and Italy which too seldom arrived, could only hope that there was still 'A Well of love' in spite of the 'silence and obscurity'.

The other great grief had been the loss of the beloved brother John Wordsworth, when his ship went down off Portland in February, 1805. Sir George Beaumont's painting of Peele Castle in a storm brought only too keenly the thought of the storm in which John had perished. In these *Elegiac Stanzas* the poet, who at that very time was recounting in the *Prelude* how he had advanced through love of Nature to love of Man, knows that he cannot exist without love of Man, 'at distance from the Kind'. His happiness must be tempered by a stoic fortitude which shuns no reality: if it is a Christian Stoicism, 'not without hope', it is still Stoicism.

Many mistakes have been made about Wordsworth. None is more wide of the mark than the idea that he lived in an ivory tower. From 1792 onward his interest in all that was going on was keen, too keen sometimes for the necessary canalization of thought and energy which poetry can demand.

The 1807 volumes are more varied than *Lyrical Ballads,* even though 'with Pastoral and other Poems' is part of the full title of the latter. The high lights of the two new volumes include, besides poems such as *The Affliction of Margaret* and *Resolution and Independence* already mentioned, so many others that choice is difficult. 'She was a Phantom of delight', written two years after marriage, is Wordsworth's tribute to his wife. In three stanzas he describes successively his, perhaps idealized, memory of the young girl at Penrith, his closer view of her as a visitor in 'virgin liberty' at Racedown and Grasmere, and finally his intimate knowledge of the 'machine'—and, if the old fashioned use of that word here and in *The Waggoner* pulls the modern reader up, he has only to remember Hamlet, 'while this machine is to him'. This poem describing quiet, competent, loving Mary should be compared with those about Dorothy with her eagerness and her tenderness.

The *Character of the Happy Warrior* was written in 1806. The immediate occasion was Nelson's death at Trafalgar on 21 October 1805, but it is based on thoughts more intimate and deep-rooted, on the character of John Wordsworth, master-mariner, and of Beaupuy, and perhaps on what Wordsworth himself would have aimed at if he had adopted a military career. Indeed Wordsworth was himself now a soldier of sorts in two senses. He was an active volunteer in the local force, and he was, as we have seen, attempting a Stoic fortitude amid the shocks of life. The Stoic creed was *vita est militare.*

The sonnets which occupy the last third of the first volume were in 1802 a new departure for Wordsworth, though the *Personal Talk* sonnets in a familiar style must belong to earlier in the same year. His exemplar and stimulus was Milton, and, though Coleridge had published sonnets in newspapers several years before, Wordsworth is the first since Milton to make extensive and effective use of the form. He had once despised it as artificial, thought it, indeed, 'egregiously absurd', but now in the *Prefatory Sonnet* he recognizes a value based on experience, a value not altogether unconnected with the new philosophy of the *Ode to Duty* and the sad knowledge that there can be 'too much liberty'. In another sonnet ('Scorn not the sonnet') not published till 1827 he defended the form and glorified Milton's use of it—'the thing became a trumpet'.

So here in the *Sonnets Dedicated to Liberty* Wordsworth emerged as the poet not only of Nature and of Man and of Moods of my own Mind but also of the Society in which he lived, a Society of much corruption but worth saving, the only bulwark, however imperfect, against French imperialism.

The second volume opened with the poems inspired by, though mostly not written during, the 1803 tour in Scotland. Nothing is more characteristic of Wordsworth than *The Solitary Reaper*. Here is the single human being in the landscape of hill and field. Here are Wordsworth's characteristic words with their romantic overtones, 'profound', 'haunt', 'Cuckoo', 'silence'. Here is the voice which, like the Cuckoo's, becomes disembodied and even when unheard is still a ditty of no tone. Here the 'discerning intellect of Man' has found beauty the 'simple produce of the common day'. Yet Wordsworth himself tells us that his imagination was fired not by the actual sight and sound of the 'Highland Lass' but by reading a friend's account of a different tour in Scotland, 'the last line being taken from it *verbatim*'. The friend was Thomas Wilkinson who lived by Ullswater and whose spade Wordsworth addressed in this same volume.

The place of honour at the end of the second volume was given to the *Ode* which had no other title. Not until 1815 was a sub-title added—*Intimations of Immortality from Recollections of Early Childhood.* The *Ode* affirms pre-existence (which implies post-existence) and it speaks of the grave as a place of waiting, but it does not contain any direct 'Intimations' of immortality in the sense of future personal life. It does delight in the primacy of the spiritual over the material—a primacy most evident to Wordsworth from his

'Recollections of Early Childhood', though later evidence such as that of the 'blessed mood' of Tintern Abbey could bear it out. On the whole the sub-title has done more harm than good to the understanding of the poem, and the now common reference to it as the Immortality Ode is a harmful convenience: it blurs the main subject of the poem, the 'gleam'.

The seven new stanzas added in the spring of 1804 take up the question of the lost 'gleam'. The answer is that the child is nearer his divine home. The attractions of the world into which he is born gradually wean him from the heaven which lay about him in his infancy. The poet looks at a particular child (Hartley Coleridge) and sees him playing at all the goings-on of our life,

As if his whole vocation
Were endless imitation.

Yet the little child is on his 'Being's height'. Custom will bring him down. Now comes the song of thankfulness for the 'recollections' which are the source of our conviction of spiritual primacy. Therefore, so fortified, we can bear the present loss of the gleam. We know it did exist and was real. There remain primal sympathy, faith, and the philosophic mind. There remains a love of nature as strong as ever, and with it is intertwined a profound and tender love of man.

Connected with the *Ode* are the two stanzas *To H.C., Six Years Old* in the same metrical form. They read like an overflow from the *Ode* in which the 'four year's Darling' was later changed to 'six'. Hartley was six in September 1802, but he was only four in the spring of 1801 when he paid the Wordsworths a long visit and attended Grasmere school. He was the wonder child whom they all loved, and it is like Wordsworth to base his imaginative vision on a real child—and also to do as he pleases about the child's age.

After the publication of *Poems in Two Volumes* Wordsworth settled down to write *The White Doe of Rylstone*, a long poem (nearly 2,000 lines in its present form) occasioned by a visit to Bolton Abbey in Yorkshire. Like *The Waggoner* it is divided into cantos in clear imitation of Scott's *Lay of the Last Minstrel*, and the metre was influenced by that and by Coleridge's still unpublished *Christabel*. The real point of the poem lay in a problem in Wordsworth's mind. How is suffering to be accepted and yet subdued? This problem lurks dimly in *Resolution and Independence* and the *Ode to Duty*. It is explicitly referred to in two lines, which can baffle or mislead, in the great *Ode*,

In the soothing thoughts that spring
Out of human suffering.

Whose suffering? Our own, or that of others, or both? It emerges starkly in the Peele Castle *Elegiac Stanzas*. Indeed the dreadful blow of John Wordsworth's death was a direct cause of *The White Doe*.

A comparison with Scott is purely superficial. Wordsworth's own statement in 1843 explains that 'Sir Walter pursued the customary and very natural course of conducting an action, presenting various turns of fortune, to some outstanding point on which the mind might rest as a termination or catastrophe. The course I attempted to pursue is entirely different. Everything that is attempted by the principal personages in "The White Doe" fails, so far as its object is external and substantial. So far as it is moral and spiritual it succeeds. The heroine of the Poem knows that her duty is not to interfere with the current of events, either to forward or delay them, but

To abide
The shock, and finally secure
O'er pain and grief a triumph pure.

. . . The anticipated beatification, if I may so say, of her mind, and the apotheosis of the companion of her solitude [the white doe] are the points at which the Poem aims.'

The poem describes the failure of the Rising of the North in 1569, the destruction therewith of the Norton family, especially one son, Francis, who was torn between family loyalty and disapproval of the rebellion. The sister Emily is left, her only companion being the white doe. It is in her that the problem of suffering is worked out,

there oft she sate
Forlorn, but not disconsolate.
And, when she from the abyss returned
Of thought, she neither shrunk nor mourned;
Was happy that she lived to greet
Her mute Companion as it lay
In love and pity at her feet.

Emily belongs to the company of Wordsworth's solitary, suffering women—the woman in *An Evening Walk* who had lost her husband at Bunker's Hill, the Female Vagrant, Margaret of 'The Ruined Cottage', Ruth, Margaret of *The Affliction of Margaret.* She is more spiritual than any of them, and she attains a consolation denied to them. Yet the poem is perhaps a gallant failure rather than a success. There is so much narrative of action, and yet action is admittedly not what the poem is really about. Emily, dear creature, finds consolation and strength: but if she had been a man, and a man with Wordsworth's own power of intellect and power of suffering, would the means have been adequate?

The White Doe was completed in 1808, shown to Lamb, Hazlitt and Coleridge, and intended for publication. Yet Wordsworth had his misgivings. *Poems in Two Volumes* had not been well received by the critics. He feared that *The White Doe* would be a failure, and jumped at the delay implicit in criticisms and suggestions to come from Coleridge. Eventually, after revision, it was published in quarto in 1815.

At Allan Bank and Grasmere Rectory (1808–13)

In May 1808 the Wordsworths left the cottage at Town End, Grasmere, which was now much too small for them. There were three children and a fourth on the way besides William, Mary, Dorothy and, very often, Sarah Hutchinson. From its four small rooms they moved to a newly built house, Allan Bank, whose chimneys were soon found to smoke so badly that rooms were often entirely unusable. There were, however, plenty of them, and Coleridge was given a bedroom and a 'parlour' and stayed most of the time till May 1810. It proved the last and saddest period of daily intimacy between him and Wordsworth.

However much the causes may excite our compassion, there is no denying that Coleridge was now a difficult and selfish house-mate. The great talker had never bored, but the sullen addict, who fled to his parlour as soon as meals were over, indeed justified *A Complaint.* Yet the twenty months were not unfruitful. A periodical, *The Friend,* had its first issue in June 1809 and ran, with some irregularities, till 15 March 1810, twenty-eight numbers in all. Then the devoted assistance of Sarah Hutchinson as amanuensis came to an end, and so, without notification or design, did *The Friend.* It contains much of Coleridge's most interesting prose and contributions in both prose and verse from Wordsworth.

Wordsworth's main literary occupations at this time were his pamphlet on the Convention of Cintra and, latterly, resumed work on 'The Recluse', i.e. the *Excursion.* Under the Convention of Cintra the British government and supreme military commanders had permitted the French, defeated by Wellesley at Vimiero, to evacuate Portugal with all their equipment and booty. This spineless action, which prolonged the Peninsular War till 1814, aroused much indignation. Wordsworth, who was living in retirement but was certainly not a recluse, was more deeply moved than by any political or military happening since at least the French occupation of Switzerland in 1798. As in 1792–3 and in 1802, outward events led him to penetration of character and to examination of first principles. His pamphlet is a massive appraisement, in prose worthy of Milton, of the fundamentals for a healthy national life. One can even see in it the same mind as that of the 1793 *Letter to the Bishop of Llandaff.* It is by greatness of soul that a nation is great.

The return to 'The Recluse' was made at much the same time as the writing of the three Essays on Epitaphs for *The Friend.* The middle books of the *Excursion* contain accounts of those whose graves are in the churchyard, and Wordsworth was now at this stage. He was writing regularly, about 50 lines a day in February 1810, but this is a sinister change from the 'kindling' of earlier years when a poem seized him and he could not eat or finish dressing till its demands were met.

Coleridge left in May 1810 just before the Wordsworths' fifth child was born. He went back to Keswick and his wife for five months, and then with Basil Montagu to London. As they passed through Grasmere in the carriage on the way to London, they looked up Wordsworth. He wanted to explain to Montagu that nearby lodgings for Coleridge might work better than having Coleridge under his roof. By some Hardyesque crass circumstance the explanation had to be hurried. In a week Montagu discovered his guest's weak points, and blurted out that Wordsworth had warned him. The famous Wordsworth-Coleridge quarrel began. Coleridge in London complained bitterly, but Wordsworth knew nothing about it till next spring: he had long ceased to expect letters. After that it took a year till a reconciliation was affected, and it was not complete till 1828 when the two went together on a continental tour.

In 1811 the Wordsworths left Allan Bank and its diabolical chimneys for the old Rectory at Grasmere. Here they spent two years in which the *Excursion* was nearly finished. The year 1812 was one of bitter grief. In June Catherine, the child born in May 1808, died, and in December Thomas who was six and a half. Coleridge failed, in spite of the reconciliation, to show adequate sympathy over Thomas. Wordsworth, the loving father and man capable of deep suffering, records the common experience of forgetting for a moment that the dead are dead in the sonnet about Catherine

Surprised by joy—impatient as the Wind.

On the first of May 1813 they left the Rectory for the house and grounds of Rydal Mount, where they were to stay for the rest of their lives.

The Distributor of Stamps, 'Laodamia', and 'The Excursion' (1813–4)

In 1812 Wordsworth had applied through Lord Lonsdale for a post which would help him to meet the current inflation—'the unexpected pressure of the times, falling most heavily upon men who have no regular means of increasing their income in proportion.' He wanted one which would leave him time for study and would 'place me in a situation where, with better hope of success, I might advance towards the main object of my life, I mean the completion of my literary undertakings; and thereby contribute to the innocent gratification, and perhaps the solid benefit of my countrymen.' The 'grand elementary principle of pleasure' and the 'worthy purpose' both remain valid.

The upshot was that in 1813 he was appointed Distributor of Stamps for Westmorland and part of Cumberland. His district was afterwards twice enlarged, and he held the post till 1842. A good deal of nonsense has been written about it. It was not a sinecure, nor was the work all done by a clerk. He did not even have an office. The stamps (revenue stamps, there were no postage stamps in those days) had to be kept at his own house and there all the correspondence about them came. His large district was organized into sub-districts under sub-distributors, who had to be appointed, visited and kept up to the mark. I have gone into the whole matter elsewhere at some length.* It is enough to say two things here. First the varying and never large income from the office was enough, with other sources, to keep Wordsworth and his family free of financial worries though they never approached opulence: it was because of this appointment that they were able to take Rydal Mount. It was a victory for the prudence which is first seen emerging in *Resolution and Independence,* or, shall we say?, for the responsible head of a family. Secondly, this sort of work, which must often have had to take first place, must have been bad for his poetry. To have plenty of time is not enough for a poet: he must be free to give first place at any time and, if necessary, all the time to poetry and to the imaginative experiences which will lead to poetry. Otherwise he will miss the heights and depths.

Except for the Hundred Days and Waterloo the years at Rydal Mount from 1814 onwards were years of international peace in Europe. There had been many French prisoners of war in England. One, Eustace Baudouin, had written to Wordsworth from Oswestry in 1812. By October 1814 his brother was engaged to Caroline. The coming of peace had reopened communication with Annette. In this year Wordsworth wrote *Laodamia*:

the Gods approve
The depths, and not the tumult, of the soul.

It is a majestic poem with a Miltonic richness of classical basis. Protesilaüs, first Greek on Trojan soil, was killed as prophesied. From his tomb outside Troy grew a clump of trees which withered whenever their height equalled the city walls and then grew again. This 'incident of the trees', Wordsworth said in 1843, 'put the subject into my thoughts'. No doubt it did, but there was something about the story of Protesilaüs and Laodamia which was specially apt to his thoughts in 1814 when news came once more of Annette (and of his marriageable daughter for whom he accepted full responsibility). Laodamia, according to one ancient version, had been married for only one day to Protesilaüs. After his death the gods granted her prayer that he should return. It was for three hours only. William and Annette had had their passionate year in 1792, and in 1802 had met again for a month. How did Annette then greet him? Not, we may be sure, with twentieth century English casualness. She must have thrown her arms round him. He must for four months have been dreading just this. However

* *Wordsworth and Coleridge, 1795–1834* (1953), pp. 179–82.

Penrith, Looking South by Peter de Wint (1784–1849). After the deaths of their parents, William and his brothers spent their summer holidays in Penrith, and it was here that he renewed his friendship with Mary Hutchinson who later became his wife.
By courtesy of Abbot Hall Art Gallery, Kendal

Windermere from Troutbeck 1803 by Julius Caesar Ibbetson (1759–1817). During his happy schooldays at nearby Hawkshead, William and his fellows would frequently row on the lake at Windermere.
By courtesy of Ferens Art Gallery, Hull

much Annette accepted, perhaps even welcomed, the abandonment of a marriage without which she had got on for nearly ten years, did her passionate nature suggest some resumption of old delights however shadowy? Had Wordsworth to be careful to be chaperoned? 'We walked by the seashore almost every evening with Annette and Caroline, or William and I alone,' wrote Dorothy. Certain it is that the 'worthy purpose' of the poem is to put passion in its place. In the last stanza, as originally published in 1815, there is a tenderness which goes beyond the classical sources. In later editions Laodamia's Elysian happiness is changed for a doom, permanent in one version, for 'her appointed time' in another. We may suppose that he was then thinking only of the legend, and that the hidden spring of personal experience had dried up, whether or not that experience belonged only to 1792.

The year in which *Laodamia* was written saw the publication of the *Excursion*, the longest and most ambitious poem published by Wordsworth in his lifetime, yet offered as a mere section of 'The Recluse'. In spite of Coleridge's disappointment and of Jeffrey's 'This will never do', it did much to establish Wordsworth's reputation. Book 1 is our old friend 'The Ruined Cottage'. Most of Books 2–4 belong to Wordsworth's great decade, though they include later revisions. Books 5–9 are not dull and contain fine passages and lines. If, as a whole, they are Wordsworth and water, that may have helped to make them acceptable to contemporaries. Yet it was not Wordsworth and water that made young Keats class the *Excursion*, along with Haydon's pictures and Hazlitt's 'depth of Taste', among 'three things to rejoice at in this Age'. Wordsworth was becoming a vital influence on the next generation of poets. Keats did not much take to the man Wordsworth, and it was probably the *Excursion* which sent Keats back to Wordsworth's early poems. He discovered *Tintern Abbey*. 'We feel the "burden of the Mystery", to this Point was Wordsworth come, so far as I can conceive, when he wrote 'Tintern Abbey' and it seems to me that his Genius is explorative of those dark Passages . . . Here I must think Wordsworth is deeper than Milton.'

That was in 1818 and struck a very different note from young Byron's cheeky and amusing satire, nine years before, in *English Bards and Scotch Reviewers*, of the 'simple Wordsworth'

Who, both by precept and example shows
That prose is verse, and verse is merely prose.

Even Byron, however, began to feel Wordsworth's influence. It is visible in the later cantos of *Childe Harold*.

The *Excursion* describes an excursion. After the Wanderer (formerly the Pedlar) has on the first day told Wordsworth the story of Margaret in Book 1, the two set out on a walking tour. Since the scene of Book 1 (really Somerset) is not located, two days suffice to bring them to Cumberland—not that any place names are given. On the fourth day (Books 2, 3, 4) they walk up Langdale and cross the ridge to Blea Tarn where they find the Solitary, a disappointed man who has retired into a cynical but not unkindly isolation. The three walk about in the neighbourhood of the cottage where the Solitary lodges and talk: 'Despondency' and 'Despondency Corrected' are the titles of Books 3 and 4. All spend the night at the cottage. On the fifth day (Books 5–9) they leave the valley and arrive, defying geography, at Grasmere where they meet the Pastor, who gives them the life histories of many of those buried in the churchyard. In Book 8, after a discussion on industrialism, all go to the parsonage and meet the pastor's delightful family. In Book 9 they walk to the lake, row across, climb Loughrigg and see a wonderful sunset. They row back, and the Solitary leaves them and sets out on his walk home.

This simple framework contains Wordsworth's mature thoughts on life and the inner conflicts from which those thoughts grew. The Solitary is what Wordsworth's disappointments and disillusionments might have made of him. The Wanderer is what he might have become if his origin had been in 'low and rustic life' at its simplest and best. The Pastor, though he has never been a 'suffering man', is Wordsworth as a meditative observer of human life. It is, however, Book 4, before the Pastor is introduced, which is doctrinally central.

We live by Admiration, Hope, and Love.

That line, more than the emphasis on God and Duty and 'things eternal', shows both where Wordsworth had arrived and where he had always been. It completely sums up the ecstasies of 1792. It was when Admiration or Hope or Love had seemed to fail or conflict that he had been unhappy. He got them all back at Alfoxden and Grasmere. He never again lost them or objects for them. Whatever failings of power supervened, there was no failing in this triple source of spiritual life.

The *Excursion*, like any long poem, has its dull passages. It also has its high lights as seen in the extracts in this volume. What Blake might have called two 'Contraries' are summed up in

> *central peace subsisting at the heart*
> *Of endless agitation.*

Recognition Grows as Inspiration Lessens (1814–43)

The mere fact that early in 1815 Wordsworth published his first collected edition shows that recognition had come. It was dedicated to Sir George Beaumont who had been a steady friend and patron since 1803. The leading reviewers now all paid attention to Wordsworth's work. If their remarks were often unfavourable, attention was nevertheless attention: he was not neglected. The commonest complaint was that, though a poet of great genius, he was often wrongheaded. 'Why', asked Jeffrey in the Edinburgh Review in 1814, 'should Mr. Wordsworth have made his hero a superannuated Pedlar? What but the most wretched affectation, or provoking perversity of taste, could induce any one to place his chosen advocate of wisdom and virtue in so absurd and fantastic a condition?' 'It should be held in mind,' wrote John Wilson in Blackwood's in 1817, 'by Mr. Wordsworth's admirers, among whom are to be found every living Poet of any eminence, that, with all the fearlessness of original genius, he has burst and cast away the bonds which were worn very contentedly by many great writers. Mr. Wordsworth is a man of too great power not to have very often written ill. . . . He has brought about a *revolution* in Poetry; and a revolution can no more be brought about in Poetry than in the constitution, without the destruction or injury of many excellent and time-hallowed establishments. I have no doubt that, when all the rubbish is removed, and free and open space given to behold the structures which Mr. Wordsworth has reared in all the grandeur of their proportions, that Posterity will hail him as a regenerator and a creator . . . if he has often written ill, Milton and Shakespeare have done so before him.'

The White Doe of Rylstone ('the very worst poem we ever saw imprinted in a quarto volume', said Jeffrey in the Edinburgh Review) was published separately two months after the two volumes of the collected edition. Wordsworth was now forty-five. From 1815, revision, classification and frequent republication were to take up much of his time. In 1842 he was even to publish for the first time two very old works, *Guilt and Sorrow* and *The Borderers*. There was also much new writing but, with some grand exceptions, it was of less value than the old. In the main Wordsworth had by 1815 had his say. It would have been better for his ultimate reputation, and therefore for the reception of the beauty and truth he has to offer, if he had refrained from a repetition which often seems to come by rote rather than from the old imaginative depths.

The majority of the poems written after 1815 fall into two categories, sonnet sequences and poems written during or after returning from tours.

The sonnet, which Wordsworth had discovered in 1802, became a favourite medium after he had finished with the *Excursion*. In 1820 he published *The River Duddon*, a series of thirty-four (originally thirty-three) of which more than half were written in 1818. They trace the little river from source to sea. The idea probably goes back to the stream at Alfoxden, the brook which set Coleridge planning a poem in which the various arts and types of life would be described while a great river was followed in verse, an early idea, in fact, for 'The Recluse'. The Duddon sonnets are pleasant and meditative and mature, but too self-conscious.

Ecclesiastical Sonnets, mostly composed in 1821, were published in 1822 as *Ecclesiastical Sketches*. This is an enormous series of 132 divided into three parts, (1) From the Introduction of Christianity into Britain to the Consummation of the Papal Dominion, (2) To the Close of the Troubles in the Reign of Charles I, (3) From the Restoration to the Present Times. The third part includes the magnificent *Mutability* (where 'unimaginable' takes us back to the poet's early days) and *Inside of King's College Chapel;* but the sonnet is hardly the ideal medium for a history of the Christian Church in England, nor, though the subject undoubtedly touched Wordsworth's imagination, can it be said to have fired it.

The tours began in 1820 when four months were spent on the Continent. After all the years of war Wordsworth was travel-hungry, but there had been difficulties about going earlier. Now he went with his wife and Dorothy and other relations, saw Annette and Caroline and her husband, visited the field of Waterloo, and Germany and Switzerland, and the Italian Lakes with their memories of 1790. Dorothy at last saw the scenes described to her when William and Jones saw them. *Memorials of a Tour on the Continent 1820* was also published in 1822. How much better it might have been if the poet had waited to see whether anything leaped from hiding-places ten years deep.

In the summer of 1828 Wordsworth went on a continental tour for several weeks with his daughter Dora and Coleridge. It was a happy reunion of two ageing men. It bore no poetic fruit, and that is a tribute to the quantity and quality of the conversation.

Tours in Scotland in 1831 and 1833 produced *Yarrow Revisited, and other Poems* and *Poems composed or suggested During a Tour, in the summer of 1833* (mostly sonnets) both published in 1835. The first of these two volumes contained *On the Power of Sound,* which is among the very best of the later poems. Another long continental tour in 1837 resulted in 'Memorials of a Tour in Italy', published in 1842 in *Poems Chiefly of Early and Late Years.* It was his only visit to Italy except for the lakes. The long *Musings near Aquapendente* and *The Cuckoo at Laverna* show the authentic mellow Wordsworth at his best. After that there were no more long tours, though plenty of moving about. In 1841 he revisited Alfoxden and places in the west country which he had made famous for ever. 'These,' he wrote, 'were farewell visits for life, and, of course, not a little interesting.'

That was the year before 1842 when Tennyson's *Poems* brought fame to him and a decline in relative popularity to Wordsworth. But from the death of Byron in 1824 until 1842 Wordsworth was generally recognized as the greatest living English poet. Oxford gave him an honorary doctorate in 1839. In that same decade he was at Cambridge 'established in possession of the minds of all who profess to care for poetry'. So Matthew Arnold wrote, confirming a similar statement by Macaulay. Visitors from at home and America sought him out at Rydal Mount.

At Rydal Mount, in this same decade of unquestioned fame, Dorothy's health failed. There were some years of sharp attacks of illness and of recovery, but from 1835 to her death in 1855 she was a permanent invalid, often difficult and distressing, always tended with an unremitting and uncomplaining care which is one of the most attractive characteristics of Wordsworth and his family. 'The tale of her days of insensibility or mental vagary is more properly regarded as a part of the lives of those who suffered the greater torture of witnessing her wreck, and who, through the long years of hope and sorrow, repaid to her in full measure the love which she had lavished upon them."*

The Wordsworth whose climax of recognition coincided with this sorrow was a Tory and a Churchman. It is customary to hold this against him as if a poet has no right to be a Tory and a

* E. de Selincourt, *Dorothy Wordsworth* (1933), p. 394.

Churchman. The primary justification for treating it as a crime is that the gradual change from being a Whig and what we may perhaps call a free-thinking Christian did undoubtedly coincide with a gradual decline in poetic power. There is no reason whatever to suppose that one caused the other. If there is a connexion other than coincidence, it must be that both sprang from a common cause. If there is a common cause, it can be summed up in one word—prudence.

Wordsworth was never a real Conservative in the sense of wanting to keep the whole of the existing order for its own sake. Even in 1806 he was found to be 'strongly disposed towards Republicanism'. Late in life he said to a Chartist 'there is nothing unreasonable in your Charter: it is the foolish attempt at physical force, for which many of you have been blamable.' Less than is usually supposed had he abandoned his youthful position as exhibited in the 1793 *Letter to the Bishop of Llandaff,* in which he was already opposed to violence. The lesson of the French Revolution remained. Unleash violence and anything may happen, especially the opposite of the desired reforms. Nowadays we give in to agitation. Agitation preceded the passing of the Reform Bill in 1832. The agitation was enough to confirm Wordsworth as an anti-Reformist. He was half a Chartist: the half he was not was the violent, agitational half.

The trauma in Wordsworth's life was inflicted in 1793, the year of the treble shock. It was accentuated by the subsequent course of the French Revolution, culminating in Napoleonic despotism in France and aggression abroad. That eventually made him a Conservative and a Churchman—a Churchman because he believed more and more in firm institutions as a safeguard against the 'red fool fury of the Seine', as Tennyson called the Paris revolution of 1830. He had never been an anti-Christian, though he had at first refused to discuss Christianity with Coleridge, but the 'poem to Coleridge' shows no doubt about God. It is the more specifically Christian doctrines which come in later. Here the predominating influence was probably his wife, and he sometimes envied her her certainty. There is a difference between the immortality of the great *Ode,* an eternal spiritual existence which we now have as well as our earthly life, and the survival of personality. In 1824 he addressed to Mary that revealing poem which begins

O dearer far than light and life are dear.

That was a cry from the heart, and a fine poem.

Perhaps there is no need to do so much connecting and explaining about the poetic decline. Why should a poet not have said his say by the time he is forty-five? Shakespeare retired to Stratford when not much older, and wrote no more. Wordsworth's mistake was to write, and publish, so much more. Unfortunately, from posterity's point of view, he now had a public. In 1808 he had been inhibited by the unpopularity of his poetry from publishing *The White Doe*. No such unpopularity inhibited the publication in 1822 of *Ecclesiastical Sketches*. Moreover Wordsworth had a conscience, a strong sense of duty, as we have seen. He was the dedicated poet and felt he must go on. Yet the really memorable fraction of what he wrote after 1815 would go into a 'slim volume'.

For 1815 is the dividing year. There has been much discussion of a decade beginning in 1797 or 1798, and no doubt the core of the creative Wordsworth is to be found there. But core is not everything. The *Excursion* is a great work, and *Laodamia* alone would mark a poet as memorable. The wars with France and Wordsworth's poetic achievement almost coincide.

The Aged Laureate (1843–50) *and Afterwards*

Southey, who had been Poet Laureate since 1810 but whose mind failed in 1839, died in March 1843. Within a fortnight Wordsworth had succeeded him. He refused at first on the ground of age and inability to perform the customary duties. The Prime Minister, Sir Robert Peel, and the Lord Chamberlain assured him that it was intended as an honour only and that no duties would be required. He then accepted. In 1847 he composed, with the assistance of his nephew Christopher, an *Ode on the Installation of His Royal Highness Prince Albert as Chancellor of the University of Cambridge,* but in general the terms of the appointment were kept. In that same year he lost his daughter Dora.

Wordsworth died in April 1850, shortly after his eightieth birthday. Dorothy survived him for five years, Mary for nine.

In 1851 his nephew Christopher published the first biography, the *Memoirs*. But for it we should lack much valuable information. There is no mention of Annette. That, in 1851, was right and proper. The Wordsworth whose biography was wanted was the Sage of Rydal, the elderly subject of the Pickersgill portrait, the advocate of the religious philosophy of the *Excursion,* the respected author of many later pieces. A youthful indiscretion was not merely unedifying and incongruous, not merely the sort of thing which it would be indecent for a dutiful nephew to mention, it was irrelevant. It had always been known to Wordsworth's family and intimate friends. Knowledge of it remained after his death, though only to a few, and it lingered not always accurately. By the end of the nineteenth century the tradition in the Coleridge family was of an illegitimate son, not daughter.

Professor Harper, working on his life of Wordsworth published in 1916, rediscovered the incident from Dorothy's letters, then unpublished. Emile Legouis found out more. It came as a shock to the old-fashioned Wordsworthians, and it threw the new critics off their balance. They found Annette writ large in Wordsworth's poetry and Annette explaining all his mental history after 1792. We have got over that now. She is interesting and not unimportant, but Wordsworth's mental history is to be found where he wrote it, in the *Prelude*. This does not mean that the *Prelude* is to be read uncritically: it does mean that it is to be read as the honest product of a highly gifted poet writing for his most intimate friend.

Before Harper's life there were two principal landmarks—first Matthew Arnold's Preface to the Golden Treasury *Poems of Wordsworth* which he selected and edited in 1879, secondly Emile Legouis's *La Jeunesse de William Wordsworth* of which the English translation appeared in 1897. Matthew Arnold, who in his youth had known Wordsworth, aimed at disentangling the poetry from the 'philosophy' beloved of contemporary Wordsworthians. He put Wordsworth above all modern European poets except Dante, Shakespeare, Milton, Molière and Goethe—'not only is Wordsworth eminent by reason of the goodness of his best work, but he is eminent also by reason of the great body of good work which he has left to us'. He did not include the *Excursion* and the *Prelude* among Wordsworth's best work. It was Legouis who first did justice to the *Prelude*. Since he wrote its greatness has been recognized.

* * *

It seems clear now that Wordsworth is a poet for all time, if not for all persons at all times. His manly moral philosophy may appeal most to one, his rendering of the 'feeling for nature' to another, his 'mysticism' to another, his reading of the human heart to another, the modulations of his song surely to all. It sums up to this, he was 'a man speaking to men.' And he did away with the strange and widespread delusion that the basic human affections can be really felt only by the refined. It is no longer true that

There are who think that strong affection, love
Known by whatever name, is falsely deemed
A gift, to use a term which they would use,
Of vulgar nature; that its growth requires
Retirement, leisure, language purified
By manners studied and elaborate;
That whoso feels such passion in its strength
Must live within the very light and air
Of courteous usages refined by art.

from

THE GROWTH OF A POET'S MIND

posthumously called

THE PRELUDE

EDITOR'S NOTE TO THE PRELUDE

WORDSWORTH referred to this poem as the 'poem to Coleridge' or in some such way as 'the poem on my own life' or 'the poem on the growth of my own mind' or 'the poem on the growth of an individual mind'. The emphasis on 'growth' and 'mind' tends to be lost in the more compact title *The Prelude* given to the poem on publication in 1850.

The extracts here given are from the text completed in manuscript in 1805 and first published by The Clarendon Press, Oxford in 1926, and in 1933 in the Oxford Editions of Standard Authors. The Clarendon Press has generously permitted the reprinting of what follows.

The extracts are not given in the order in which they appear in the complete poem but have, as far as possible, been arranged in biographically chronological order. Although *The Prelude* is in a sense autobiographical and chronological, the incidents in it do not appear in the strictly correct sequence. For example the incidents I have headed 'Penrith Beacon' and 'The day before the holidays' both appear in Book XI of *The Prelude*, being chosen as examples of 'spots of time'. Yet the first happened when Wordsworth was 'not six years old', the second when he was 'nearly fourteen'.

The headings are mine, not Wordsworth's. I have included *Nutting* here, though it is not part of *The Prelude*. It was, however, written at the same time as other childhood passages. It was published in the 1800 *Lyrical Ballads*.

THE PRELUDE

'MY HONOUR'D MOTHER'

EARLY died
My honour'd Mother; she who was the heart
And hinge of all our learnings and our loves:
She left us destitute, and as we might
Trooping together. Little suits it me
To break upon the sabbath of her rest
With any thought that looks at others' blame,
Nor would I praise her but in perfect love.
Hence am I check'd: but I will boldly say,
In gratitude, and for the sake of truth,
Unheard by her, that she, not falsely taught,
Fetching her goodness rather from times past
Than shaping novelties from those to come,
Had no presumption, no such jealousy;
Nor did by habit of her thoughts mistrust
Our Nature; but had virtual faith that he,
Who fills the Mother's breasts with innocent milk,
Doth also for our nobler part provide,
Under his great correction and controul,
As innocent instincts, and as innocent food.
This was her creed, and therefore she was pure
From feverish dread of error or mishap
And evil, overweeningly so call'd;
Was not puff'd up by false unnatural hopes;
Nor selfish with unnecessary cares;
Nor with impatience from the season ask'd
More than its timely produce; rather lov'd
The hours for what they are than from regards
Glanced on their promises in restless pride.
Such was she; not from faculties more strong
Than others have, but from the times, perhaps,
And spot in which she liv'd, and through a grace
Of modest meekness, simple-mindedness,
A heart that found benignity and hope,
Being itself benign.

INFANCY AT COCKERMOUTH

WHEN, having left his Mountains, to the Towers
Of Cockermouth that beauteous River came,
Behind my Father's House he pass'd, close by,
Along the margin of our Terrace Walk.
He was a Playmate whom we dearly lov'd.
Oh! many a time have I, a five years' Child,
A naked Boy, in one delightful Rill,
A little Mill-race sever'd from his stream,
Made one long bathing of a summer's day,
Bask'd in the sun, and plunged, and bask'd again
Alternate all a summer's day, or cours'd
Over the sandy fields, leaping through groves
Of yellow grunsel, or when crag and hill,
The woods, and distant Skiddaw's lofty height,
Were bronz'd with a deep radiance, stood alone
Beneath the sky, as if I had been born
On Indian Plains, and from my Mother's hut
Had run abroad in wantonness, to sport,
A naked Savage, in the thunder shower.

PENRITH BEACON

At a time
When scarcely (I was then not six years old)
My hand could hold a bridle, with proud hopes
I mounted, and we rode towards the hills:
We were a pair of horsemen; honest James
Was with me, my encourager and guide.
We had not travell'd long, ere some mischance
Disjoin'd me from my Comrade, and, through fear
Dismounting, down the rough and stony Moor
I led my Horse, and stumbling on, at length
Came to a bottom, where in former times
A Murderer had been hung in iron chains.
The Gibbet-mast was moulder'd down, the bones
And iron case were gone; but on the turf,
Hard by, soon after that fell deed was wrought

Some unknown hand had carved the Murderer's name.
The monumental writing was engraven
In times long past, and still, from year to year,
By superstition of the neighbourhood,
The grass is clear'd away; and to this hour
The letters are all fresh and visible.
Faltering, and ignorant where I was, at length
I chanced to espy those characters inscribed
On the green sod: forthwith I left the spot
And, reascending the bare Common, saw
A naked Pool that lay beneath the hills,
The Beacon on the summit, and more near,
A Girl who bore a Pitcher on her head
And seem'd with difficult steps to force her way
Against the blowing wind. It was, in truth,
An ordinary sight; but I should need
Colours and words that are unknown to man
To paint the visionary dreariness
Which, while I look'd all round for my lost guide,
Did at that time invest the naked Pool,
The Beacon on the lonely Eminence,
The Woman, and her garments vex'd and toss'd
By the strong wind.

HAWKSHEAD SCHOOLDAYS

THE DROWNED MAN

Well do I call to mind the very week
When I was first entrusted to the care
Of that sweet Valley; when its paths, its shores,
And brooks, were like a dream of novelty
To my half-infant thoughts; that very week
While I was roving up and down alone,
Seeking I knew not what, I chanced to cross
One of those open fields, which, shaped like ears,
Make green peninsulas on Esthwaite's Lake:
Twilight was coming on; yet through the gloom,
I saw distinctly on the opposite Shore
A heap of garments, left, as I suppos'd,
By one who there was bathing; long I watch'd,
But no one own'd them; meanwhile the calm Lake
Grew dark, with all the shadows on its breast,
And, now and then, a fish up-leaping, snapp'd
The breathless stillness. The succeeding day,
(Those unclaimed garments telling a plain Tale)
Went there a Company, and, in their Boat
Sounded with grappling irons, and long poles.
At length, the dead Man, 'mid that beauteous scene
Of trees, and hills and water, bolt upright
Rose with his ghastly face; a spectre shape
Of terror even! and yet no vulgar fear,
Young as I was, a Child not nine years old,
Possess'd me; for my inner eye had seen
Such sights before, among the shining streams
Of Fairy land, the Forest of Romance:
Hence came a spirit hallowing what I saw
With decoration and ideal grace;
A dignity, a smoothness, like the works
Of Grecian Art, and purest Poesy.

SNARING

FAIR seed-time had my soul, and I grew up
Foster'd alike by beauty and by fear;
Much favour'd in my birthplace, and no less
In that beloved Vale to which, erelong,
I was transplanted. Well I call to mind
('Twas at an early age, ere I had seen
Nine summers) when upon the mountain slope
The frost and breath of frosty wind had snapp'd
The last autumnal crocus, 'twas my joy
To wander half the night among the Cliffs
And the smooth Hollows, where the woodcocks ran
Along the open turf. In thought and wish
That time, my shoulder all with springes hung,
I was a fell destroyer. On the heights
Scudding away from snare to snare, I plied
My anxious visitation, hurrying on,
Still hurrying, hurrying onward; moon and stars
Were shining o'er my head; I was alone,
And seem'd to be a trouble to the peace
That was among them. Sometimes it befel
In these night-wanderings, that a strong desire
O'erpower'd my better reason, and the bird
Which was the captive of another's toils
Became my prey; and, when the deed was done
I heard among the solitary hills
Low breathings coming after me, and sounds
Of undistinguishable motions, steps
Almost as silent as the turf they trod.

BIRDSNESTING

NOR less in springtime when on southern banks
The shining sun had from his knot of leaves
Decoy'd the primrose flower, and when the Vales
And woods were warm, was I a plunderer then
In the high places, on the lonesome peaks
Where'er, among the mountains and the winds,
The Mother Bird had built her lodge. Though mean

My object, and inglorious, yet the end
Was not ignoble. Oh! when I have hung
Above the raven's nest, by knots of grass
And half-inch fissures in the slippery rock
But ill sustain'd, and almost, as it seem'd,
Suspended by the blast which blew amain,
Shouldering the naked crag; Oh! at that time,
While on the perilous ridge I hung alone,
With what strange utterance did the loud dry wind
Blow through my ears! the sky seem'd not a sky
Of earth, and with what motion mov'd the clouds!

'MIMIC HOOTINGS'

THERE was a Boy, ye knew him well, ye Cliffs
And Islands of Winander! many a time
At evening, when the stars had just begun
To move along the edges of the hills,
Rising or setting, would he stand alone
Beneath the trees, or by the glimmering Lake,
And there, with fingers interwoven, both hands
Press'd closely, palm to palm, and to his mouth
Uplifted, he, as through an instrument,
Blew mimic hootings to the silent owls
That they might answer him.—And they would shout
Across the watery Vale, and shout again,
Responsive to his call, with quivering peals,
And long halloos, and screams, and echoes loud
Redoubled and redoubled; concourse wild
Of mirth and jocund din! And when it chanced
That pauses of deep silence mock'd his skill,
Then sometimes, in that silence, while he hung
Listening, a gentle shock of mild surprize
Has carried far into his heart the voice
Of mountain torrents; or the visible scene
Would enter unawares into his mind
With all its solemn imagery, its rocks,
Its woods, and that uncertain Heaven, receiv'd
Into the bosom of the steady Lake.

Nutting[1]

It seems a day,
(I speak of one from many singled out)
One of those heavenly days which cannot die,
When forth I sallied from our Cottage-door,*
And with a wallet o'er my shoulder slung,
A nutting crook in hand, I turned my steps
Towards the distant woods, a Figure quaint,
Tricked out in proud disguise of Beggar's weeds
Put on for the occasion, by advice
And exhortation of my frugal Dame.
Motley accoutrement! of power to smile
At thorns, and brakes, and brambles, and, in truth,
More ragged than need was. Among the woods,
And o'er the pathless rocks, I forced my way
Until, at length, I came to one dear nook
Unvisited, where not a broken bough
Drooped with its withered leaves, ungracious sign
Of devastation, but the hazels rose
Tall and erect, with milk-white clusters hung,
A virgin scene!—A little while I stood,
Breathing with such suppression of the heart
As joy delights in; and with wise restraint
Voluptuous, fearless of a rival, eyed
The banquet, or beneath the trees I sate
Among the flowers, and with the flowers I played;
A temper known to those, who, after long
And weary expectation, have been blessed
With sudden happiness beyond all hope.—
Perhaps it was a bower beneath whose leaves
The violets of five seasons re-appear
And fade, unseen by any human eye;
Where fairy water-breaks do murmur on
For ever, and I saw the sparkling foam,
And with my cheek on one of those green stones
That, fleeced with moss, beneath the shady trees,
Lay round me, scattered like a flock of sheep,
I heard the murmur and the murmuring sound,

[1] See Editor's Note to *The Prelude*, page 76
* The house at which I was boarded during the time I was at School.

In that sweet mood when pleasure loves to pay
Tribute to ease; and, of its joy secure,
The heart luxuriates with indifferent things,
Wasting its kindliness on stocks and stones,
And on the vacant air. Then up I rose,
And dragged to earth both branch and bough, with crash
And merciless ravage; and the shady nook
Of hazels, and the green and mossy bower,
Deformed and sullied, patiently gave up
Their quiet being: and, unless I now
Confound my present feelings with the past,
Even then, when from the bower I turned away
Exulting, rich beyond the wealth of kings,
I felt a sense of pain when I beheld
The silent trees and the intruding sky.—

Then, dearest Maiden! move along these shades
In gentleness of heart; with gentle hand
Touch,——for there is a Spirit in the woods.

'THE DAY BEFORE THE HOLIDAYS'

ONE Christmas-time,
The day before the holidays began,
Feverish and tired, and restless, I went forth
Into the fields, impatient for the sight
Of those two Horses which should bear us home;
My Brothers and myself. There was a crag,
An Eminence, which from the meeting-point
Of two highways ascending, overlook'd
At least a long half-mile of those two roads,
By each of which the expected Steeds might come,
The choice uncertain. Thither I repair'd
Up to the highest summit; 'twas a day
Stormy, and rough, and wild, and on the grass
I sate, half-shelter'd by a naked wall;
Upon my right hand was a single sheep,
A whistling hawthorn on my left, and there,
With those companions at my side, I watch'd,
Straining my eyes intensely, as the mist
Gave intermitting prospect of the wood

And plain beneath. Ere I to School return'd
That dreary time, ere I had been ten days
A dweller in my Father's House, he died,
And I and my two Brothers, Orphans then,
Followed his Body to the Grave. The event
With all the sorrow which it brought appear'd
A chastisement; and when I call'd to mind
That day so lately pass'd, when from the crag
I look'd in such anxiety of hope,
With trite reflections of morality,
Yet in the deepest passion, I bow'd low
To God, who thus corrected my desires;
And afterwards, the wind and sleety rain
And all the business of the elements,
The single sheep, and the one blasted tree,
And the bleak music of that old stone wall,
The noise of wood and water, and the mist
Which on the line of each of those two Roads
Advanced in such indisputable shapes,
All these were spectacles and sounds to which
I often would repair and thence would drink,
As at a fountain.

THE STOLEN BOAT

One evening (surely I was led by her)
I went alone into a Shepherd's Boat,
A Skiff that to a Willow tree was tied
Within a rocky Cave, its usual home.
'Twas by the shores of Patterdale, a Vale
Wherein I was a Stranger, thither come
A School-boy Traveller, at the Holidays.
Forth rambled from the Village Inn alone
No sooner had I sight of this small Skiff,
Discover'd thus by unexpected chance,
Than I unloos'd her tether and embark'd.
The moon was up, the Lake was shining clear
Among the hoary mountains; from the Shore
I push'd, and struck the oars and struck again
In cadence, and my little Boat mov'd on
Even like a Man who walks with stately step

Though bent on speed. It was an act of stealth
And troubled pleasure; not without the voice
Of mountain-echoes did my Boat move on,
Leaving behind her still on either side
Small circles glittering idly in the moon,
Until they melted all into one track
Of sparkling light. A rocky Steep uprose
Above the Cavern of the Willow tree
And now, as suited one who proudly row'd
With his best skill, I fix'd a steady view
Upon the top of that same craggy ridge,
The bound of the horizon, for behind
Was nothing but the stars and the grey sky.
She was an elfin Pinnace; lustily
I dipp'd my oars into the silent Lake,
And, as I rose upon the stroke, my Boat
Went heaving through the water, like a Swan;
When from behind that craggy Steep, till then
The bound of the horizon, a huge Cliff,
As if with voluntary power instinct,
Uprear'd its head. I struck, and struck again,
And, growing still in stature, the huge Cliff
Rose up between me and the stars, and still,
With measur'd motion, like a living thing,
Strode after me. With trembling hands I turn'd,
And through the silent water stole my way
Back to the Cavern of the Willow tree.
There, in her mooring-place, I left my Bark,
And, through the meadows homeward went, with grave
And serious thoughts; and after I had seen
That spectacle, for many days, my brain
Work'd with a dim and undetermin'd sense
Of unknown modes of being; in my thoughts
There was a darkness, call it solitude,
Or blank desertion, no familiar shapes
Of hourly objects, images of trees
Of sea or sky, no colours of green fields;
But huge and mighty Forms that do not live
Like living men mov'd slowly through the mind
By day and were the trouble of my dreams.

SKATING

—All shod with steel,
We hiss'd along the polish'd ice, in games
Confederate, imitative of the chace
And woodland pleasures, the resounding horn,
The Pack loud bellowing, and the hunted hare.
So through the darkness and the cold we flew,
And not a voice was idle; with the din,
Meanwhile, the precipices rang aloud,
The leafless trees, and every icy crag
Tinkled like iron, while the distant hills
Into the tumult sent an alien sound
Of melancholy, not unnoticed, while the stars,
Eastward, were sparkling clear, and in the west
The orange sky of evening died away.

Not seldom from the uproar I retired
Into a silent bay, or sportively
Glanced sideway, leaving the tumultous throng,
To cut across the image of a star
That gleam'd upon the ice: and oftentimes
When we had given our bodies to the wind,
And all the shadowy banks, on either side,
Came sweeping through the darkness, spinning still
The rapid line of motion; then at once
Have I, reclining back upon my heels,
Stopp'd short, yet still the solitary Cliffs
Wheeled by me, even as if the earth had roll'd
With visible motion her diurnal round;
Behind me did they stretch in solemn train
Feebler and feebler, and I stood and watch'd
Till all was tranquil as a dreamless sleep.

FIRST LOVE OF POETRY

Thirteen years
Or haply less, I might have seen, when first
My ears began to open to the charm
Of words in tuneful order, found them sweet
For *their own sakes,* a passion and a power;
And phrases pleas'd me, chosen for delight,
For pomp, or love. Oft in the public roads,

Yet unfrequented, while the morning light
Was yellowing the hill-tops, with that dear Friend
The same whom I have mention'd heretofore,
I went abroad, and for the better part
Of two delightful hours we stroll'd along
By the still borders of the misty Lake,
Repeating favourite verses with one voice,
Or conning more; as happy as the birds
That round us chaunted. Well might we be glad,
Lifted above the ground by airy fancies
More bright than madness or the dreams of wine,
And, though full oft the objects of our love
Were false, and in their splendour overwrought,
Yet, surely, at such time no vulgar power
Was working in us, nothing less, in truth,
Than that most noble attribute of man,
Though yet untutor'd and inordinate
That wish for something loftier, more adorn'd,
Than is the common aspect, daily garb
Of human life. What wonder then if sounds
Of exultation echoed through the groves!
For images, and sentiments, and words,
And everything with which we had to do
In that delicious world of poesy,
Kept holiday; a never-ending show,
With music, incense, festival, and flowers!

BOATING ON WINDERMERE

But ere the fall
Of night, when in our pinnace we return'd
Over the dusky Lake, and to the beach
Of some small Island steer'd our course with one,
The Minstrel of our troop, and left him there,
And row'd off gently, while he blew his flute
Alone upon the rock; Oh! then the calm
And dead still water lay upon my mind
Even with a weight of pleasure, and the sky
Never before so beautiful, sank down
Into my heart, and held me like a dream.

EARLY MORNING WALKS

My morning walks
Were early; oft, before the hours of School
I travell'd round our little Lake, five miles
Of pleasant wandering, happy time! more dear
For this, that one was by my side, a Friend
Then passionately lov'd; with heart how full
Will he peruse these lines, this page, perhaps
A blank to other men! for many years
Have since flow'd in between us; and our minds,
Both silent to each other, at this time
We live as if those hours had never been.
Nor seldom did I lift our cottage latch
Far earlier, and before the vernal thrush
Was audible, among the hills I sate
Alone, upon some jutting eminence
At the first hour of morning, when the Vale
Lay quiet in an utter solitude.
How shall I trace the history, where seek
The origin of what I then have felt?
Oft in these moments such a holy calm
Did overspread my soul, that I forgot
That I had bodily eyes, and what I saw
Appear'd like something in myself, a dream,
A prospect in my mind.

'I WALKED WITH NATURE'

'Twere long to tell
What spring and autumn, what the winter snows,
And what the summer shade, what day and night,
The evening and the morning, what my dreams
And what my waking thoughts supplied, to nurse
That spirit of religious love in which
I walked with Nature. But let this, at least
Be not forgotten, that I still retain'd
My first creative sensibility,
That by the regular action of the world
My soul was unsubdu'd. A plastic power
Abode with me, a forming hand, at times
Rebellious, acting in a devious mood,

A local spirit of its own, at war
With general tendency, but for the most
Subservient strictly to the external things
With which it commun'd. An auxiliar light
Came from my mind which on the setting sun
Bestow'd new splendor, the melodious birds,
The gentle breezes, fountains that ran on,
Murmuring so sweetly in themselves, obey'd
A like dominion; and the midnight storm
Grew darker in the presence of my eye.
Hence my obeisance, my devotion hence,
And hence my transport.

'MAN ENNOBLED'

A RAMBLING Schoolboy, thus
Have I beheld him, without knowing why
Have felt his presence in his own domain,
As of a Lord and Master; or a Power
Or Genius, under Nature, under God,
Presiding; and severest solitude
Seem'd more commanding oft when he was there.
Seeking the raven's nest, and suddenly
Surpriz'd with vapours, or on rainy days
When I have angled up the lonely brooks
Mine eyes have glanced upon him, few steps off,
In size a giant, stalking through the fog,
His Sheep like Greenland Bears; at other times
When round some shady promontory turning,
His Form hath flash'd upon me, glorified
By the deep radiance of the setting sun:
Or him have I descried in distant sky,
A solitary object and sublime,
Above all height! like an aerial Cross,
As it is stationed on some spiry Rock
Of the Chartreuse, for worship. Thus was Man
Ennobled outwardly before mine eyes,
And thus my heart at first was introduc'd
To an unconscious love and reverence
Of human Nature; hence the human form
To me was like an index of delight,
Of grace and honour, power and worthiness.

CAMBRIDGE AND VACATIONS

ST. JOHN'S COLLEGE

THE Evangelist St. John my Patron was,
Three gloomy Courts are his; and in the first
Was my abiding-place, a nook obscure!
Right underneath, the College kitchens made
A humming sound, less tuneable than bees,
But hardly less industrious; with shrill notes
Of sharp command and scolding intermix'd.
Near me was Trinity's loquacious Clock,
Who never let the Quarters, night or day,
Slip by him unproclaim'd, and told the hours
Twice over with a male and female voice.
Her pealing organ was my neighbour too;
And, from my Bedroom, I in moonlight nights
Could see, right opposite, a few yards off,
The Antechapel, where the Statue stood
Of Newton, with his Prism and silent Face.

'A SINGLE TREE'

ALL winter long, whenever free to take
My choice, did I at night frequent our Groves
And tributary walks, the last, and oft
The only one, who had been lingering there
Through hours of silence, till the Porter's Bell,
A punctual follower on the stroke of nine,
Rang with its blunt unceremonious voice,
Inexorable summons. Lofty Elms,
Inviting shades of opportune recess,
Did give composure to a neighbourhood
Unpeaceful in itself. A single Tree
There was, no doubt yet standing there, an Ash
With sinuous trunk, boughs exquisitely wreath'd:
Up from the ground and almost to the top
The trunk and master branches everywhere

Were green with ivy; and the lightsome twigs
And outer spray profusely tipp'd with seeds
That hung in yellow tassels and festoons,
Moving or still, a Favourite trimm'd out
By Winter for himself, as if in pride,
And with outlandish grace. Oft have I stood
Foot-bound, uplooking at this lovely Tree
Beneath a frosty moon. The hemisphere
Of magic fiction, verse of mine perhaps
May never tread; but scarcely Spenser's self
Could have more tranquil visions in his youth,
More bright appearances could scarcely see
Of human Forms with superhuman Powers,
Than I beheld, standing on winter nights
Alone, beneath this fairy work of earth.

CHAUCER, SPENSER AND MILTON

Beside the pleasant Mills of Trompington
I laugh'd with Chaucer; in the hawthorn shade
Heard him (while birds were warbling) tell his tales
Of amorous passion. And that gentle Bard,
Chosen by the Muses for their Page of State,
Sweet Spenser, moving through his clouded heaven
With the moon's beauty and the moon's soft pace,
I call'd him Brother, Englishman, and Friend.
Yea, our blind Poet, who, in his later day,
Stood almost single, uttering odious truth,
Darkness before, and danger's voice behind;
Soul awful! if the earth has ever lodg'd
An awful Soul, I seem'd to see him here
Familiarly, and in his Scholar's dress
Bounding before me, yet a stripling Youth,
A Boy, no better, with his rosy cheeks
Angelical, keen eye, courageous look,
And conscious step of purity and pride.

Among the band of my Compeers was one
My class-fellow at School, whose chance it was
To lodge in the Apartments which had been,
Time out of mind, honor'd by Milton's name;

The very shell reputed of the abode
Which he had tenanted. O temperate Bard!
One afternoon, the first time I set foot
In this thy innocent Nest and Oratory,
Seated with others in a festive ring
Of common-place convention, I to thee
Pour'd out libations, to thy memory drank,
Within my private thoughts, till my brain reel'd
Never so clouded by the fumes of wine
Before that hour, or since. Thence forth I ran
From that assembly, through a length of streets,
Ran, Ostrich-like, to reach our Chapel Door
In not a desperate or opprobrious time,
Albeit long after the importunate Bell
Had stopp'd, with wearisome Cassandra voice
No longer haunting the dark winter night.
Call back, O Friend! a moment to thy mind,
The place itself and fashion of the rites.
Upshouldering in a dislocated lump,
With shallow ostentatious carelessness,
My Surplice, gloried in, and yet despised,
I clove in pride through the inferior throng
Of the plain Burghers, who in audience stood
On the last skirts of their permitted ground,
Beneath the pealing Organ. Empty thoughts!

AFTER THE DANCE

In a throng,
A festal company of Maids and Youths,
Old Men, and Matrons staid, promiscuous rout,
A medley of all tempers, I had pass'd
The night in dancing, gaiety and mirth;
With din of instruments, and shuffling feet,
And glancing forms, and tapers glittering,
And unaim'd prattle flying up and down,
Spirits upon the stretch, and here and there
Slight shocks of young love-liking interspers'd,
That mounted up like joy into the head,
And tingled through the veins. Ere we retired,
The cock had crow'd, the sky was bright with day.

Two miles I had to walk along the fields
Before I reached my home. Magnificent
The morning was, in memorable pomp,
More glorious than I ever had beheld.
The Sea was laughing at a distance; all
The solid Mountains were as bright as clouds,
Grain-tinctured, drench'd in empyrean light;
And, in the meadows and the lower grounds,
Was all the sweetness of a common dawn,
Dews, vapours, and the melody of birds,
And Labourers going forth into the fields.
—Ah! need I say, dear Friend, that to the brim
My heart was full; I made no vows, but vows
Were then made for me; bond unknown to me
Was given, that I should be, else sinning greatly,
A dedicated Spirit. On I walk'd
In blessedness, which even yet remains.

THE DISCHARGED SOLDIER

A FAVOURITE pleasure hath it been with me,
From time of earliest youth, to walk alone
Along the public Way, when, for the night
Deserted, in its silence it assumes
A character of deeper quietness
Than pathless solitudes. At such an hour
Once, ere these summer months were pass'd away,
I slowly mounted up a steep ascent
Where the road's watery surface, to the ridge
Of that sharp rising, glitter'd in the moon,
And seem'd before my eyes another stream
Creeping with silent lapse to join the brook
That murmur'd in the valley. On I went
Tranquil, receiving in my own despite
Amusement, as I slowly pass'd along,
From such near objects as from time to time
Perforce, intruded on the listless sense
Quiescent, and dispos'd to sympathy,
With an exhausted mind, worn out by toil,
And all unworthy of the deeper joy
Which waits on distant prospect, cliff, or sea,

The dark blue vault, and universe of stars.
Thus did I steal along that silent road,
My body from the stillness drinking in
A restoration like the calm of sleep,
But sweeter far. Above, before, behind,
Around me, all was peace and solitude,
I look'd not round, nor did the solitude
Speak to my eye; but it was heard and felt.
O happy state! what beauteous pictures now
Rose in harmonious imagery— they rose
As from some distant region of my soul
And came along like dreams; yet such as left
Obscurely mingled with their passing forms
A consciousness of animal delight,
A self-possession felt in every pause
And every gentle movement of my frame.
While thus I wander'd, step by step led on,
It chanc'd a sudden turning of the road
Presented to my view an uncouth shape
So near, that, slipping back into the shade
Of a thick hawthorn, I could mark him well,
Myself unseen. He was of stature tall,
A foot above man's common measure tall,
Stiff in his form, and upright, lank and lean;
A man more meagre, as it seem'd to me,
Was never seen abroad by night or day.
His arms were long, and bare his hands; his mouth
Shew'd ghastly in the moonlight: from behind
A milestone propp'd him, and his figure seem'd
Half-sitting, and half-standing. I could mark
That he was clad in military garb,
Though faded, yet entire. He was alone,
Had no attendant, neither Dog, nor Staff,
Nor knapsack; in his very dress appear'd
A desolation, a simplicity
That seem'd akin to solitude. Long time
Did I peruse him with a mingled sense
Of fear and sorrow. From his lips, meanwhile,
There issued murmuring sounds, as if of pain
Or of uneasy thought; yet still his form
Kept the same steadiness; and at his feet
His shadow lay, and mov'd not. In a Glen

Hard by, a Village stood, whose roofs and doors
Were visible among the scatter'd trees,
Scarce distant from the spot an arrow's flight;
I wish'd to see him move; but he remain'd
Fix'd to his place, and still from time to time
Sent forth a murmuring voice of dead complaint,
Groans scarcely audible. Without self-blame
I had not thus prolong'd my watch; and now,
Subduing my heart's specious cowardise
I left the shady nook where I had stood,
And hail'd him. Slowly from his resting-place
He rose, and with a lean and wasted arm
In measur'd gesture lifted to his head,
Return'd my salutation; then resum'd
His station as before: and when, erelong,
I ask'd his history, he in reply
Was neither slow nor eager; but unmov'd,
And with a quiet, uncomplaining voice,
A stately air of mild indifference,
He told, in simple words, a Soldier's tale,
That in the Tropic Islands he had serv'd,
Whence he had landed, scarcely ten days past,
That on his landing he had been dismiss'd,
And now was travelling to his native home.
At this, I turn'd and looked towards the Village
But all were gone to rest; the fires all out;
And every silent window to the Moon
Shone with a yellow glitter. 'No one therc,'
Said I, 'is waking, we must measure back
The way which we have come: behind yon wood
A Labourer dwells; and, take it on my word
He will not murmur should we break his rest;
And with a ready heart will give you food
And lodging for the night.' At this he stoop'd,
And from the ground took up an oaken Staff,
By me yet unobserved, a traveller's Staff;
Which, I suppose, from his slack hand had dropp'd,
And lain till now neglected in the grass.

Towards the Cottage without more delay
We shap'd our course; as it appear'd to me,
He travell'd without pain, and I beheld

With ill-suppress'd astonishment his tall
And ghastly figure moving at my side;
Nor, while we journey'd thus could I forbear
To question him of what he had endur'd
From hardship, battle, or the pestilence.
He, all the while, was in demeanour calm,
Concise in answer; solemn and sublime
He might have seem'd, but that in all he said
There was a strange half-absence, and a tone
Of weakness and indifference, as of one
Remembering the importance of his theme
But feeling it no longer. We advanced
Slowly, and, ere we to the wood were come
Discourse had ceas'd. Together on we pass'd,
In silence, through the shades, gloomy and dark;
Then, turning up along an open field
We gain'd the Cottage. At the door I knock'd,
Calling aloud 'my Friend, here is a Man
By sickness overcome; beneath your roof
This night let him find rest, and give him food,
If food he need, for he is faint and tired.'
Assur'd that now my Comrade would repose
In comfort, I entreated that henceforth
He would not linger in the public ways
But ask for timely furtherance and help
Such as his state requir'd. At this reproof,
With the same ghastly mildness in his look
He said 'my trust is in the God of Heaven
And in the eye of him that passes me.'
The Cottage door was speedily unlock'd,
And now the Soldier touch'd his hat again
With his lean hand; and in a voice that seem'd
To speak with a reviving interest,
Till then unfelt, he thank'd me; I return'd
The blessing of the poor unhappy Man;
And so we parted. Back I cast a look,
And linger'd near the door a little space;
Then sought with quiet heart my distant home.

PENRITH WITH DOROTHY OR MARY

In summer among distant nooks I rov'd
Dovedale, or Yorkshire Dales, or through bye-tracts
Of my own native region, and was blest
Between these sundry wanderings with a joy
Above all joys, that seem'd another morn
Risen on mid noon, the presence, Friend, I mean
Of that sole Sister, she who hath been long
Thy Treasure also, thy true friend and mine,
Now, after separation desolate
Restor'd to me, such absence that she seem'd
A gift then first bestow'd. The gentle Banks
Of Emont, hitherto unnam'd in Song,
And that monastic Castle, on a Flat
Low-standing by the margin of the Stream,
A Mansion not unvisited of old
By Sidney, where, in sight of our Helvellyn,
Some snatches he might pen, for aught we know,
Of his Arcadia, by fraternal love
Inspir'd; that River and that mouldering Dome
Have seen us sit in many a summer hour,
My sister and myself, when having climb'd
In danger through some window's open space,
We look'd abroad, or on the Turret's head
Lay listening to the wild flowers and the grass,
As they gave out their whispers to the wind.
Another Maid there was, who also breath'd
A gladness o'er that season, then to me
By her exulting outside look of youth
And placid under-countenance, first endear'd,
That other Spirit, Coleridge, who is now
So near to us, that meek confiding heart,
So reverenced by us both. O'er paths and fields
In all that neighbourhood, through narrow lanes
Of eglantine, and through the shady woods,
And o'er the Border Beacon, and the Waste
Of naked Pools, and common Crags that lay
Expos'd on the bare Fell, was scatter'd love,
A spirit of pleasure and youth's golden gleam.

WALK THROUGH FRANCE

When the third summer brought its liberty
A Fellow Student and myself, he, too,
A Mountaineer, together sallied forth
And, Staff in hand, on foot pursu'd our way
Towards the distant Alps. An open slight
Of College cares and study was the scheme,
Nor entertain'd without concern for those
To whom my worldly interests were dear:
But Nature then was sovereign in my heart,
And mighty forms seizing a youthful Fancy
Had given a charter to irregular hopes.
In any age, without an impulse sent
From work of Nations, and their goings-on,
I should have been possessed by like desire:
But 'twas a time when Europe was rejoiced,
France standing on the top of golden hours,
And human nature seeming born again.
Bound, as I said, to the Alps, it was our lot
To land at Calais on the very eve
Of that great federal Day; and there we saw,
In a mean City, and among a few,
How bright a face is worn when joy of one
Is joy of tens of millions. Southward thence
We took our way direct through Hamlets, Towns,
Gaudy with reliques of that Festival,
Flowers left to wither on triumphal Arcs,
And window-Garlands. On the public roads,
And, once, three days successively, through paths
By which our toilsome journey was abridg'd,
Among sequester'd villages we walked,
And found benevolence and blessedness
Spread like a fragrance everywhere, like Spring
That leaves no corner of the land untouch'd.
Where Elms, for many and many a league, in files,
With their thin umbrage, on the stately roads
Of that great Kingdom, rustled o'er our heads,
For ever near us as we paced along,
'Twas sweet at such a time, with such delights

On every side, in prime of youthful strength,
To feed a Poet's tender melancholy
And fond conceit of sadness, to the noise
And gentle undulations which they made.
Unhous'd, beneath the Evening Star we saw
Dances of liberty, and, in late hours
Of darkness, dances in the open air.
Among the vine-clad Hills of Burgundy,
Upon the bosom of the gentle Saone
We glided forward with the flowing stream:
Swift Rhone, thou wert the wings on which we cut
Between thy lofty rocks! Enchanting show
Those woods, and farms, and orchards did present,
And single Cottages, and lurking Towns,
Reach after reach, procession without end
Of deep and stately Vales. A lonely Pair
Of Englishmen we were, and sail'd along
Cluster'd together with a merry crowd
Of those emancipated, with a host
Of Travellers, chiefly Delegates, returning
From the great Spousals newly solemniz'd
At their chief City in the sight of Heaven.
Like bees they swarm'd, gaudy and gay as bees;
Some vapour'd in the unruliness of joy
And flourish'd with their swords, as if to fight
The saucy air. In this blithe Company
We landed, took with them our evening Meal,
Guests welcome almost as the Angels were
To Abraham of old. The Supper done,
With flowing cups elate, and happy thoughts,
We rose at signal giv'n, and form'd a ring
And, hand in hand, danced round and round the Board;
All hearts were open, every tongue was loud
With amity and glee; we bore a name
Honour'd in France, the name of Englishmen,
And hospitably did they give us hail
As their forerunners in a glorious course,
And round, and round the board they danced again.
With this same throng our voyage we pursu'd
At early dawn; the Monastery Bells
Made a sweet jingling in our youthful ears;
The rapid River flowing without noise,

And every Spire we saw among the rocks
Spake with a sense of peace, at intervals
Touching the heart amid the boisterous Crew
With which we were environ'd. Having parted
From this glad Rout, the Convent of Chartreuse
Received us two days afterwards, and there
We rested in an awful Solitude;
Thence onward to the Country of the Swiss.

CROSSING THE ALPS

Upturning with a Band
Of Travellers, from the Valais we had clomb
Along the road that leads to Italy;
A length of hours, making of these our Guides
Did we advance, and having reach'd an Inn
Among the mountains, we together ate
Our noon's repast, from which the Travellers rose,
Leaving us at the Board. Ere long we follow'd,
Descending by the beaten road that led
Right to a rivulet's edge, and there broke off.
The only track now visible was one
Upon the further side, right opposite,
And up a lofty Mountain. This we took
After a little scruple, and short pause,
And climb'd with eagerness, though not, at length
Without surprise, and some anxiety
On finding that we did not overtake
Our Comrades gone before. By fortunate chance,
While every moment now increas'd our doubts,
A Peasant met us, and from him we learn'd
That to the place which had perplex'd us first
We must descend, and there should find the road
Which in the stony channel of the Stream
Lay a few steps, and then along its banks;
And further, that thenceforward all our course
Was downwards, with the current of that Stream.
Hard of belief, we question'd him again,
And all the answers which the Man return'd
To our inquiries, in their sense and substance,

Translated by the feelings which we had
Ended in this; *that we had crossed the Alps.*

Imagination! lifting up itself
Before the eye and progress of my Song
Like an unfather'd vapour; here that Power,
In all the might of its endowments, came
Athwart me; I was lost as in a cloud,
Halted, without a struggle to break through.
And now recovering, to my Soul I say
I recognise thy glory; in such strength
Of usurpation, in such visitings
Of awful promise, when the light of sense
Goes out in flashes that have shewn to us
The invisible world, doth Greatness make abode,
There harbours whether we be young or old.
Our destiny, our nature, and our home
Is with infinitude, and only there;
With hope it is, hope that can never die,
Effort, and expectation, and desire,
And something evermore about to be.
The mind beneath such banners militant
Thinks not of spoils or trophies, nor of aught
That may attest its prowess, blest in thoughts
That are their own perfection and reward,
Strong in itself, and in the access of joy
Which hides it like the overflowing Nile.

The dull and heavy slackening that ensued
Upon those tidings by the Peasant given
Was soon dislodg'd; downwards we hurried fast,
And enter'd with the road which we had miss'd
Into a narrow chasm; the brook and road
Were fellow-travellers in this gloomy Pass,
And with them did we journey several hours
At a slow step. The immeasurable height
Of woods decaying, never to be decay'd,
The stationary blasts of water-falls,
And every where along the hollow rent
Winds thwarting winds, bewilder'd and forlorn,
The torrents shooting from the clear blue sky,
The rocks that mutter'd close upon our ears,

Black drizzling crags that spake by the way-side
As if a voice were in them, the sick sight
And giddy prospect of the raving stream,
The unfetter'd clouds, and region of the Heavens,
Tumult and peace, the darkness and the light
Were all like workings of one mind, the features
Of the same face, blossoms upon one tree,
Characters of the great Apocalypse,
The types and symbols of Eternity,
Of first and last, and midst, and without end.

'INDEPENDENT SPIRIT OF PURE YOUTH'

Oh! most beloved Friend, a glorious time
A happy time that was; triumphant looks
Were then the common language of all eyes:
As if awak'd from sleep, the Nations hail'd
Their great expectancy: the fife of War
Was then a spirit-stirring sound indeed,
A Blackbird's whistle in a vernal grove.
We left the Swiss exulting in the fate
Of their near Neighbours, and when shortening fast
Our pilgrimage, nor distant far from home,
We cross'd the Brabant Armies on the fret
For battle in the cause of Liberty.
A Stripling, scarcely of the household then
Of social life, I look'd upon these things
As from a distance, heard, and saw, and felt,
Was touch'd, but with no intimate concern;
I seem'd to move among them as a bird
Moves through the air, or as a fish pursues
Its business, in its proper element;
I needed not that joy, I did not need
Such help; the ever-living Universe,
And independent spirit of pure youth
Were with me at that season, and delight
Was in all places spread around my steps
As constant as the grass upon the fields.

ASCENT OF SNOWDON

In one of these excursions, travelling then
Through Wales on foot, and with a youthful Friend,
I left Bethgelert's huts at couching-time,
And westward took my way to see the sun
Rise from the top of Snowdon. Having reach'd
The Cottage at the Mountain's foot, we there
Rouz'd up the Shepherd, who by ancient right
Of office is the Stranger's usual guide;
And after short refreshment sallied forth.

It was a Summer's night, a close warm night,
Wan, dull and glaring, with a dripping mist
Low-hung and thick that cover'd all the sky,
Half threatening storm and rain; but on we went
Uncheck'd, being full of heart and having faith
In our tried Pilot. Little we could see
Hemm'd round on every side with fog and damp,
And, after ordinary travellers' chat
With our Conductor, silently we sank
Each into commerce with his private thoughts:
Thus did we breast the ascent, and by myself
Was nothing either seen or heard the while
Which took me from my musings, save that once
The Shepherd's Cur did to his own great joy
Unearth a hedgehog in the mountain crags
Round which he made a barking turbulent.
This small adventure, for even such it seemed
In that wild place and at the dead of night,
Being over and forgotten, on we wound
In silence as before. With forehead bent
Earthward, as if in opposition set
Against an enemy, I panted up
With eager pace, and no less eager thoughts.
Thus might we wear perhaps an hour away,
Ascending at loose distance each from each,
And I, as chanced, the foremost of the Band;
When at my feet the ground appear'd to brighten,
And with a step or two seem'd brighter still;

Nor had I time to ask the cause of this,
For instantly a Light upon the turf
Fell like a flash: I looked about, and lo!
The Moon stood naked in the Heavens, at height
Immense above my head, and on the shore
I found myself of a huge sea of mist,
Which, meek and silent, rested at my feet:
A hundred hills their dusky backs upheaved
All over this still Ocean, and beyond,
Far, far beyond, the vapours shot themselves,
In headlands, tongues, and promontory shapes,
Into the Sea, the real Sea, that seem'd
To dwindle, and give up its majesty,
Usurp'd upon as far as sight could reach.
Meanwhile, the Moon look'd down upon this shew
In single glory, and we stood, the mist
Touching our very feet; and from the shore
At distance not the third part of a mile
Was a blue chasm; a fracture in the vapour,
A deep and gloomy breathing-place through which
Mounted the roar of waters, torrents, streams
Innumerable, roaring with one voice.
The universal spectacle throughout
Was shaped for admiration and delight,
Grand in itself alone, but in that breach
Through which the homeless voice of waters rose,
That dark deep thoroughfare had Nature lodg'd
The Soul, the Imagination of the whole.

A meditation rose in me that night
Upon the lonely Mountain when the scene
Had pass'd away, and it appear'd to me
The perfect image of a mighty Mind,
Of one that feeds upon infinity,
That is exalted by an underpresence,
The sense of God, or whatsoe'er is dim
Or vast in its own being, above all
One function of such mind had Nature there
Exhibited by putting forth, and that
With circumstance most awful and sublime,
That domination which she oftentimes
Exerts upon the outward face of things,

So moulds them, and endues, abstracts, combines,
Or by abrupt and unhabitual influence
Doth make one object so impress itself
Upon all others, and pervade them so
That even the grossest minds must see and hear
And cannot chuse but feel. The Power which these
Acknowledge when thus moved, which Nature thus
Thrusts forth upon the senses, is the express
Resemblance, in the fulness of its strength
Made visible, a genuine Counterpart
And Brother of the glorious faculty
Which higher minds bear with them as their own.
That is the very spirit in which they deal
With all the objects of the universe;
They from their native selves can send abroad
Like transformations, for themselves create
A like existence, and, whene'er it is
Created for them, catch it by an instinct;
Them the enduring and the transient both
Serve to exalt; they build up greatest things
From least suggestions, ever on the watch,
Willing to work and to be wrought upon,
They need not extraordinary calls
To rouze them, in a world of life they live,
By sensible impressions not enthrall'd,
But quicken'd, rouz'd, and made thereby more apt
To hold communion with the invisible world.
Such minds are truly from the Deity,
For they are Powers; and hence the highest bliss
That can be known is theirs, the consciousness
Of whom they are habitually infused
Through every image, and through every thought,
And all impressions; hence religion, faith,
And endless occupation for the soul
Whether discursive or intuitive;
Hence sovereignty within and peace at will
Emotion which best foresight need not fear
Most worthy then of trust when most intense.
Hence chearfulness in every act of life
Hence truth in moral judgements and delight
That fails not in the external universe.

BOOKS: A DREAM

While he was sitting in a rocky cave
By the sea-side, perusing, as it chanced,
The famous History of the Errant Knight
Recorded by Cervantes, these same thoughts
Came to him; and to height unusual rose
While listlessly he sate, and having closed
The Book, had turned his eyes towards the Sea.
On Poetry and geometric Truth,
The knowledge that endures, upon these two,
And their high privilege of lasting life,
Exempt from all internal injury,
He mused; upon these chiefly: and at length,
His senses yielding to the sultry air,
Sleep seiz'd him, and he pass'd into a dream.
He saw before him an Arabian Waste,
A Desart; and he fancied that himself
Was sitting there in the wide wilderness,
Alone, upon the sands. Distress of mind
Was growing in him when, behold! at once
To his great joy a Man was at his side,
Upon a dromedary, mounted high.
He seem'd an Arab of the Bedouin Tribes,
A Lance he bore, and underneath one arm
A Stone; and, in the opposite hand, a Shell
Of a surpassing brightness. Much rejoic'd
The dreaming Man that he should have a Guide
To lead him through the Desart; and he thought,
While questioning himself what this strange freight
Which the Newcomer carried through the Waste
Could mean, the Arab told him that the Stone,
To give it in the language of the Dream,
Was Euclid's Elements; 'and this,' said he,
'This other,' pointing to the Shell, 'this Book
Is something of more worth.' And, at the word,
The Stranger, said my Friend continuing,
Stretch'd forth the Shell towards me, with command

That I should hold it to my ear; I did so,
And heard that instant in an unknown Tongue,
Which yet I understood, articulate sounds,
A loud prophetic blast of harmony,
An Ode, in passion utter'd, which foretold
Destruction to the Children of the Earth,
By deluge now at hand. No sooner ceas'd
The Song, but with calm look, the Arab said
That all was true; that it was even so
As had been spoken; and that he himself
Was going then to bury those two Books:
The one that held acquaintance with the stars
And wedded man to man by purest bond
Of nature, undisturbed by space or time;
Th' other that was a God, yea many Gods,
Had voices more than all the winds, and was
A joy, a consolation, and a hope.
My friend continued, 'strange as it may seem,
I wonder'd not, although I plainly saw
The one to be a Stone, th' other a Shell,
Nor doubted once but that they both were Books.
Having a perfect faith in all that pass'd.
A wish was now ingender'd in my fear
To cleave unto this Man, and I begg'd leave
To share his errand with him. On he pass'd
Not heeding me; I follow'd, and took note
That he look'd often backward with wild look,
Grasping his twofold treasure to his side.
—Upon a Dromedary, Lance in rest,
He rode, I keeping pace with him, and now
I fancied that he was the very Knight
Whose Tale Cervantes tells, yet not the Knight,
But was an Arab of the Desart, too;
Of these was neither, and was both at once.
His countenance, meanwhile, grew more disturb'd,
And, looking backwards when he look'd, I saw
A glittering light, and ask'd him whence it came.
'It is,' said he, 'the waters of the deep
Gathering upon us,' quickening then his pace
He left me: I call'd after him aloud;
He heeded not; but with his twofold charge

Beneath his arm, before me full in view
I saw him riding o'er the Desart Sands,
With the fleet waters of the drowning world
In chase of him, whereat I wak'd in terror,
And saw the Sea before me; and the Book,
In which I had been reading, at my side.

THE YEAR IN FRANCE

THE NATURAL DEMOCRAT

For, born in a poor District, and which yet
Retaineth more of ancient homeliness,
Manners erect, and frank simplicity,
Than any other nook of English Land,
It was my fortune scarcely to have seen
Through the whole tenor of my School-day time
The face of one, who, whether Boy or Man,
Was vested with attention or respect
Through claims of wealth or blood; nor was it least
Of many debts which afterwards I owed
To Cambridge, and an academic life
That something there was holden up to view
Of a Republic, where all stood thus far
Upon equal ground, that they were brothers all
In honour, as in one community,
Scholars and Gentlemen, where, furthermore,
Distinction lay open to all that came,
And wealth and titles were in less esteem
Than talents and successful industry.
Add unto this, subservience from the first
To God and Nature's single sovereignty,
Familiar presences of awful Power
And fellowship with venerable books
To sanction the proud workings of the soul,
And mountain liberty. It could not be
But that one tutor'd thus, who had been form'd
To thought and moral feeling in the way
This story hath described, should look with awe
Upon the faculties of Man, receive
Gladly the highest promises, and hail
As best the government of equal rights
And individual worth. And hence, O Friend!
If at the first great outbreak I rejoiced
Less than might well befit my youth, the cause

In part lay here, that unto me the events
Seemed nothing out of nature's certain course
A gift that rather was come late than soon.

BEAUPUY

I

Among that band of Officers was one
Already hinted at, of other mold,
A Patriot, thence rejected by the rest
And with an oriental loathing spurn'd,
As of a different caste. A meeker Man
Than this liv'd never, or a more benign
Meek, though enthusiastic. Injuries
Made him more gracious, and his nature then
Did breathe its sweetness out most sensibly
As aromatic flowers on alpine turf
When foot hath crush'd them. He thro' the events
Of that great change wander'd in perfect faith,
As through a Book, an old Romance or Tale
Of Fairy, or some dream of actions wrought
Behind the summer clouds. By birth he rank'd
With the most noble, but unto the poor
Among mankind he was in service bound
As by some tie invisible, oaths profess'd
To a religious Order. Man he lov'd
As Man; and to the mean and the obscure
And all the homely in their homely works
Transferr'd a courtesy which had no air
Of condescension, but did rather seem
A passion and a gallantry, like that
Which he, a Soldier, in his idler day
Had pay'd to Woman; somewhat vain he was,
Or seem'd so, yet it was not vanity
But fondness, and a kind of radiant joy
That cover'd him about when he was bent
On works of love or freedom, or revolved
Complacently the progress of a cause,
Whereof he was a part; yet this was meek
And placid, and took nothing from the Man

That was delightful: oft in solitude
With him did I discourse about the end
Of civil government, and its wisest forms,
Of ancient prejudice, and chartered rights,
Allegiance, faith, and law by time matured,
Custom and habit, novelty and change,
Of self-respect, and virtue in the Few
For patrimonial honour set apart,
And ignorance in the labouring Multitude.
For he, an upright Man and tolerant,
Balanced these contemplations in his mind
And I, who at that time was scarcely dipp'd
Into the turmoil, had a sounder judgment
Than afterwards, carried about me yet
With less alloy to its integrity
The experience of past ages, as through help
Of Books and common life it finds its way
To youthful minds, by objects over near
Not press'd upon, nor dazzled or misled
By struggling with the crowd for present ends.

But though not deaf and obstinate to find
Error without apology on the side
Of those who were against us, more delight
We took, and let this freely be confess'd,
In painting to ourselves the miseries
Of royal Courts, and that voluptuous life
Unfeeling, where the Man who is of soul
The meanest thrives the most, where dignity,
True personal dignity, abideth not,
A light and cruel world, cut off from all
The natural inlets of just sentiment,
From lowly sympathy, and chastening truth,
Where good and evil never have that name,
That which they ought to have, but wrong prevails,
And vice at home. We added dearest themes,
Man and his nobler nature, as it is
The gift of God and lies in his own power,
His blind desires and steady faculties
Capable of clear truth, the one to break
Bondage, the other to build Liberty
On firm foundations, making social life,

Through knowledge spreading and imperishable,
As just in regulation, and as pure
As individual in the wise and good.
We summon'd up the honourable deeds
Of ancient Story, thought of each bright spot
That could be found in all recorded time
Of truth preserv'd and error pass'd away,
Of single Spirits that catch the flame from Heaven,
And how the multitude of men will feed
And fan each other, thought of Sects, how keen
They are to put the appropriate nature on,
Triumphant over every obstacle
Of custom, language, Country, love and hate,
And what they do and suffer for their creed,
How far they travel, and how long endure,
How quickly mighty Nations have been form'd
From least beginnings, how, together lock'd
By new opinions, scatter'd tribes have made
One body spreading wide as clouds in heaven.
To aspirations then of our own minds
Did we appeal; and finally beheld
A living confirmation of the whole
Before us in a People risen up
Fresh as the morning Star: elate we look'd
Upon their virtues, saw in rudest men
Self-sacrifice the firmest, generous love
And continence of mind, and sense of right
Uppermost in the midst of fiercest strife.

2

And when we chanc'd
One day to meet a hunger-bitten Girl,
Who crept along, fitting her languid gait
Unto a Heifer's motion, by a cord
Tied to her arm, and picking thus from the lane
Its sustenance, while the girl with her two hands
Was busy knitting, in a heartless mood
Of solitude, and at the sight my Friend
In agitation said, ' 'Tis against *that*
Which we are fighting,' I with him believed
Devoutly that a spirit was abroad

Which could not be withstood, that poverty
At least like this, would in a little time
Be found no more, that we should see the earth
Unthwarted in her wish to recompense
The industrious, and the lowly Child of Toil,
All institutes for ever blotted out
That legalised exclusion, empty pomp
Abolish'd, sensual state and cruel power
Whether by edict of the one or few,
And finally, as sum and crown of all,
Should see the People having a strong hand
In making their own Laws, whence better days
To all mankind.

HOPE FOR MAN

O PLEASANT exercise of hope and joy!
For great were the auxiliars which then stood
Upon our side, we who were strong in love;
Bliss was it in that dawn to be alive,
But to be young was very heaven; O times,
In which the meagre, stale, forbidding ways
Of custom, law, and statute took at once
The attraction of a Country in Romance;
When Reason seem'd the most to assert her rights
When most intent on making of herself
A prime Enchanter to assist the work,
Which then was going forwards in her name.
Not favour'd spots alone, but the whole earth
The beauty wore of promise, that which sets,
To take an image which was felt, no doubt,
Among the bowers of paradise itself,
The budding rose above the rose full blown.
What temper at the prospect did not wake
To happiness unthought of? The inert
Were rouz'd, and lively natures rapt away:
They who had fed their childhood upon dreams,
The Play-fellows of Fancy, who had made
All powers of swiftness, subtlety, and strength
Their ministers, used to stir in lordly wise
Among the grandest objects of the sense,

And deal with whatsoever they found there
As if they had within some lurking right
To wield it; they too, who, of gentle mood
Had watch'd all gentle motions, and to these
Had fitted their own thoughts, schemers more mild,
And in the region of their peaceful selves,
Did now find helpers to their hearts' desire,
And stuff at hand, plastic as they could wish,
Were call'd upon to exercise their skill,
Not in Utopia, subterraneous Fields,
Or some secreted Island, Heaven knows where,
But in the very world which is the world
Of all of us, the place in which, in the end,
We find our happiness, or not at all.

LOVE

He beheld
A vision, and he lov'd the thing he saw.
Arabian Fiction never fill'd the world
With half the wonders that were wrought for him.
Earth liv'd in one great presence of the spring,
Life turn'd the meanest of her implements
Before his eyes to price above all gold,
The house she dwelt in was a sainted shrine,
Her chamber-window did surpass in glory
The portals of the East, all paradise
Could by the simple opening of a door
Let itself in upon him, pathways, walks,
Swarm'd with enchantment till his spirit sank
Beneath the burthen, overbless'd for life.
This state was theirs, till whether through effect
Of some delirious hour, or that the Youth,
Seeing so many bars betwixt himself
And the dear haven where he wish'd to be
In honourable wedlock with his love
Without a certain knowledge of his own,
Was inwardly prepared to turn aside
From law and custom, and entrust himself
To Nature for a happy end of all;
And thus abated of that pure reserve

Congenial to his loyal heart, with which
It would have pleas'd him to attend the steps
Of Maiden so divinely beautiful
I know not, but reluctantly must add
That Julia, yet without the name of Wife
Carried about her for a secret grief
The promise of a Mother.
To conceal
The threaten'd shame the Parents of the Maid
Found means to hurry her away by night
And unforewarn'd, that in a distant Town
She might remain shrouded in privacy,
Until the Babe was born. When morning came
The Lover thus bereft, stung with his loss
And all uncertain whither he should turn
Chafed like a wild beast in the toils; at length,
Following as his suspicions led, he found
O joy! sure traces of the fugitives,
Pursu'd them to the Town where they had stopp'd,
And lastly to the very House itself
Which had been chosen for the Maid's retreat.

PARIS

THIS was the time in which enflam'd with hope,
To Paris I returned. Again I rang'd
More eagerly than I had done before
Through the wide City, and in progress pass'd
The Prison where the unhappy Monarch lay,
Associate with his Children and his Wife
In bondage; and the Palace lately storm'd
With roar of cannon, and a numerous host.
I crossed (a black and empty area then)
The Square of the Carrousel, few weeks back
Heap'd up with dead and dying, upon these
And other sights looking as doth a man
Upon a volume whose contents he knows
Are memorable, but from him lock'd up,
Being written in a tongue he cannot read,
So that he questions the mute leaves with pain
And half upbraids their silence. But that night

When on my bed I lay, I was most mov'd
And felt most deeply in what world I was;
My room was high and lonely, near the roof
Of a large Mansion or Hotel, a spot
That would have pleased me in more quiet times,
Nor was it wholly without pleasure then.
With unextinguish'd taper I kept watch,
Reading at intervals; the fear gone by
Press'd on me almost like a fear to come;
I thought of those September Massacres,
Divided from me by a little month,
And felt and touch'd them, a substantial dread;
The rest was conjured up from tragic fictions,
And mournful Calendars of true history,
Remembrances and dim admonishments.
'The horse is taught his manage, and the wind
Of heaven wheels round and treads in his own steps,
Year follows year, the tide returns again,
Day follows day, all things have second birth;
The earthquake is not satisfied at once.'
And in such way I wrought upon myself,
Until I seem'd to hear a voice that cried,
To the whole City, 'Sleep no more.' To this
Add comments of a calmer mind, from which
I could not gather full security,
But at the best it seem'd a place of fear
Unfit for the repose which night requires,
Defenceless as a wood where tigers roam.

IN ENGLAND AGAIN

THE WAR WITH FRANCE

AND now the strength of Britain was put forth
In league with the confederated Host,
Not in my single self alone I found,
But in the minds of all ingenuous Youth,
Change and subversion from this hour. No shock
Given to my moral nature had I known
Down to that very moment; neither lapse
Nor turn of sentiment that might be nam'd
A revolution, save at this one time,
All else was progress on the self-same path
On which with a diversity of pace
I had been travelling; this a stride at once
Into another region. True it is,
'Twas not conceal'd with what ungracious eyes
Our native Rulers from the very first
Had look'd upon regenerated France
Nor had I doubted that this day would come.
But in such contemplation I had thought
Of general interests only, beyond this
Had [never] once foretasted the event.
Now had I other business for I felt
The ravage of this most unnatural strife
In my own heart; there lay it like a weight
At enmity with all the tenderest springs
Of my enjoyments. I, who with the breeze
Had play'd, a green leaf on the blessed tree
Of my beloved country; nor had wish'd
For happier fortune than to wither there,
Now from my pleasant station was cut off,
And toss'd about in whirlwinds. I rejoiced,
Yea, afterwards, truth most painful to record!
Exulted in the triumph of my soul
When Englishmen by thousands were o'erthrown,
Left without glory on the Field, or driven,

Brave hearts, to shameful flight. It was a grief,
Grief call it not, 'twas anything but that,
A conflict of sensations without name,
Of which he only who may love the sight
Of a Village Steeple as I do can judge
When in the Congregation, bending all
To their great Father, prayers were offer'd up,
Or praises for our Country's Victories,
And 'mid the simple worshippers, perchance,
I only, like an uninvited Guest
Whom no one own'd sate silent, shall I add,
Fed on the day of vengeance yet to come?

SALISBURY PLAIN

Also, about this time did I receive
Convictions still more strong than heretofore,
Not only that the inner frame is good,
And graciously composed, but that, no less,
Nature for all conditions wants not power
To consecrate, if we have eyes to see,
The outside of her creatures, and to breathe
Grandeur upon the very humblest face
Of human life. I felt that the array
Of outward circumstance and visible form
Is to the pleasure of the human mind
What passion makes it, that meanwhile the forms
Of Nature have a passion in themselves
That intermingles with those works of man
To which she summons him, although the works
Be mean, have nothing lofty of their own;
And that the genius of the Poet hence
May boldly take his way among mankind
Wherever Nature leads, that he hath stood
By Nature's side among the men of old,
And so shall stand for ever. Dearest Friend,
Forgive me if I say that I, who long
Had harbour'd reverentially a thought
That Poets, even as Prophets, each with each
Connected in a mighty scheme of truth,

Have each for his peculiar dower, a sense
By which he is enabled to perceive
Something unseen before; forgive me, Friend,
If I, the meanest of this Band, had hope
That unto me had also been vouchsafed
An influx, that in some sort I possess'd
A privilege, and that a work of mine,
Proceeding from the depth of untaught things,
Enduring and creative, might become
A power like one of Nature's. To such mood,
Once above all, a Traveller at that time
Upon the Plain of Sarum was I raised;
There on the pastoral Downs without a track
To guide me, or along the bare white roads
Lengthening in solitude their dreary line,
While through those vestiges of ancient times
I ranged, and by the solitude overcome,
I had a reverie and saw the past,
Saw multitudes of men, and here and there,
A single Briton in his wolf-skin vest
With shield and stone-axe, stride across the Wold;
The voice of spears was heard, the rattling spear
Shaken by arms of mighty bone, in strength
Long moulder'd of barbaric majesty.
I called upon the darkness; and it took,
A midnight darkness seem'd to come and take
All objects from my sight; and lo! again
The desart visible by dismal flames!
It is the sacrificial Altar, fed
With living men, how deep the groans, the voice
Of those in the gigantic wicker thrills
Throughout the region far and near, pervades
The monumental hillocks; and the pomp
Is for both worlds, the living and the dead.
At other moments, for through that wide waste
Three summer days I roam'd, when 'twas my chance
To have before me on the dreary Plain
Lines, circles, mounts, a mystery of shapes
Such as in many quarters yet survive,
With intricate profusion figuring o'er
The untill'd ground, the work, as some divine,

Of infant science, imitative forms
By which the Druids covertly express'd
Their knowledge of the heavens, and imaged forth
The constellations, I was gently charm'd,
Albeit with an antiquarian's dream,
I saw the bearded Teachers, with white wands
Uplifted, pointing to the starry sky
Alternately, and Plain below, while breath
Of music seem'd to guide them, and the Waste
Was chear'd with stillness and a pleasant sound.

DEATH OF ROBESPIERRE

O FRIEND! few happier moments have been mine
Through my whole life than that when first I heard
That this foul Tribe of Moloch was o'erthrown,
And their chief Regent levell'd with the dust.
The day was one which haply may deserve
A separate chronicle. Having gone abroad
From a small Village where I tarried then,
To the same far-secluded privacy
I was returning. Over the smooth Sands
Of Leven's ample Æstuary lay
My journey, and beneath a genial sun;
With distant prospect among gleams of sky
And clouds, and intermingled mountain tops,
In one inseparable glory clad,
Creatures of one ethereal substance, met
In Consistory, like a diadem
Or crown of burning Seraphs, as they sit
In the Empyrean. Underneath this show
Lay, as I knew, the nest of pastoral vales
Among whose happy fields I had grown up
From childhood. On the fulgent spectacle
Which neither changed, nor stirr'd, nor pass'd away,
I gazed, and with a fancy more alive
On this account, that I had chanced to find
That morning, ranging thro' the churchyard graves
Of Cartmell's rural Town, the place in which

An honor'd Teacher of my youth was laid.
While we were Schoolboys he had died among us,
And was borne hither, as I knew, to rest
With his own Family. A plain Stone, inscribed
With name, date, office, pointed out the spot,
To which a slip of verses was subjoin'd,
(By his desire, as afterwards I learn'd)
A fragment from the Elegy of Gray.
A week, or little less, before his death
He had said to me, 'my head will soon lie low;'
And when I saw the turf that cover'd him,
After the lapse of full eight years, those words,
With sound of voice, and countenance of the Man,
Came back upon me; so that some few tears
Fell from me in my own despite. And now,
Thus travelling smoothly o'er the level Sands,
I thought with pleasure of the Verses, graven
Upon his Tombstone, saying to myself
He loved the Poets, and if now alive,
Would have loved me, as one not destitute
Of promise, nor belying the kind hope
That he had form'd, when I at his command,
Began to spin, at first, my toilsome Songs.

Without me and within, as I advanced,
All that I saw, or felt, or communed with
Was gentleness and peace. Upon a small
And rocky Island near, a fragment stood
(Itself like a sea rock) of what had been
A Romish Chapel, where in ancient times
Masses were said at the hour which suited those
Who crossed the Sands with ebb of morning tide.
Not far from this still Ruin all the Plain
Was spotted with a variegated crowd
Of Coaches, Wains, and Travellers, horse and foot,
Wading, beneath the conduct of their Guide
In loose procession through the shallow Stream
Of inland water; the great Sea meanwhile
Was at safe distance, far retired. I paused,
Unwilling to proceed, the scene appear'd
So gay and chearful, when a Traveller
Chancing to pass, I carelessly inquired

If any news were stirring; he replied
In the familiar language of the day
That, *Robespierre was dead.* Nor was a doubt,
On further question, left within my mind
But that the tidings were substantial truth;
That he and his supporters all were fallen.

IMAGINATION IMPAIRED AND RESTORED

THE GODWINIAN

I

This was the time when all things tending fast
To depravation, the Philosophy
That promised to abstract the hopes of man
Out of his feelings, to be fix'd thenceforth
For ever in a purer element
Found ready welcome. Tempting region that
For Zeal to enter and refresh herself,
Where passions had the privilege to work,
And never hear the sound of their own names;
But, speaking more in charity, the dream
Was flattering to the young ingenuous mind
Pleas'd with extremes, and not the least with that
Which makes the human Reason's naked self
The object of its fervour. What delight!
How glorious! in self-knowledge and self-rule,
To look through all the frailties of the world,
And, with a resolute mastery shaking off
The accidents of nature, time, and place,
That make up the weak being of the past,
Build social freedom on its only basis,
The freedom of the individual mind,
Which, to the blind restraints of general laws
Superior, magisterially adopts
One guide, the light of circumstances, flash'd
Upon an independent intellect.

2

Thus I fared,
Dragging all passions, notions, shapes of faith,
Like culprits to the bar, suspiciously
Calling the mind to establish in plain day
Her titles and her honours, now believing,

Now disbelieving, endlessly perplex'd
With impulse, motive, right and wrong, the ground
Of moral obligation, what the rule
And what the sanction, till, demanding *proof,*
And seeking it in everything, I lost
All feeling of conviction, and, in fine,
Sick, wearied out with contrarieties,
Yielded up moral questions in despair.

FALLACY OF THE CLEAN SLATE

This History, my Friend, hath chiefly told
Of intellectual power, from stage to stage
Advancing, hand in hand with love and joy,
And of imagination teaching truth
Until that natural graciousness of mind
Gave way to over-pressure from the times
And their disastrous issues. What avail'd,
When Spells forbade the Voyager to land,
The fragrance which did ever and anon
Give notice of the Shore, from arbours breathed
Of blessed sentiment and fearless love?
What did such sweet remembrances avail,
Perfidious then, as seem'd, what serv'd they then?
My business was upon the barren sea,
My errand was to sail to other coasts.
Shall I avow that I had hope to see,
I mean that future times would surely see
The man to come parted as by a gulph,
From him who had been, that I could no more
Trust the elevation which had made me one
With the great Family that here and there
Is scatter'd through the abyss of ages past,
Sage, Patriot, Lover, Hero; for it seem'd
That their best virtues were not free from taint
Of something false and weak, which could not stand
The open eye of Reason. Then I said,
Go to the Poets; they will speak to thee
More perfectly of purer creatures, yet
If Reason be nobility in man,
Can aught be more ignoble than the man

Whom they describe, would fasten if they may
Upon our love by sympathies of truth.

Thus strangely did I war against myself;
A Bigot to a new Idolatry
Did like a Monk who hath forsworn the world
Zealously labour to cut off my heart
From all the sources of her former strength;
And, as by simple waving of a wand
The wizard instantaneously dissolves
Palace or grove, even so did I unsoul
As readily by syllogistic words
Some charm of Logic, ever within reach,
Those mysteries of passion which have made,
And shall continue evermore to make,
(In spite of all that Reason hath perform'd
And shall perform to exalt and to refine)
One brotherhood of all the human race
Through all the habitations of past years
And those to come, and hence an emptiness
Fell on the Historian's Page, and even on that
Of Poets, pregnant with more absolute truth.
The works of both wither'd in my esteem
Their sentence was, I thought, pronounc'd; their rights
Seem'd mortal, and their empire pass'd away.

FALSE ATTITUDE TO NATURE

Oh! soul of Nature, excellent and fair,
That didst rejoice with me, with whom I too
Rejoiced, through early youth before the winds
And powerful waters, and in lights and shades
That march'd and countermarch'd about the hills
In glorious apparition, now all eye
And now all ear; but ever with the heart
Employ'd, and the majestic intellect,
Oh! Soul of Nature! that dost overflow
With passion and with life, what feeble men
Walk on this earth! how feeble have I been
When thou wert in thy strength! Nor this through stroke
Of human suffering, such as justifies

Remissness and inaptitude of mind,
But through presumption, even in pleasure pleas'd
Unworthily, disliking here, and there,
Liking, by rules of mimic art transferr'd
To things above all art. But more, for this,
Although a strong infection of the age,
Was never much my habit, giving way
To a comparison of scene with scene,
Bent overmuch on superficial things,
Pampering myself with meagre novelties
Of colour and proportion, to the moods
Of time and season, to the moral power
The affections, and the spirit of the place,
Less sensible. Nor only did the love
Of sitting thus in judgment interrupt
My deeper feelings, but another cause
More subtle and less easily explain'd
That almost seems inherent in the Creature,
Sensuous and intellectual as he is,
A twofold Frame of body and of mind;
The state to which I now allude was one
In which the eye was master of the heart,
When that which is in every stage of life
The most despotic of our senses gain'd
Such strength in me as often held my mind
In absolute dominion.

NATURE AS COUNTERPOISE

Long time hath Man's unhappiness and guilt
Detain'd us; with what dismal sights beset
For the outward view, and inwardly oppress'd
With sorrow, disappointment, vexing thoughts,
Confusion of opinion, zeal decay'd,
And lastly, utter loss of hope itself,
And things to hope for. Not with these began
Our Song, and not with these our Song must end:
Ye motions of delight, that through the fields
Stir gently, breezes and soft airs that breathe
The breath of Paradise, and find your way
To the recesses of the soul! Ye Brooks

Muttering along the stones, a busy noise
By day, a quiet one in silent night,
And you, ye Groves, whose ministry it is
To interpose the covert of your shades,
Even as a sleep, betwixt the heart of man
And the uneasy world, 'twixt man himself,
Not seldom, and his own unquiet heart,
Oh! that I had a music and a voice,
Harmonious as your own, that I might tell
What ye have done for me. The morning shines,
Nor heedeth Man's perverseness; Spring returns,
I saw the Spring return, when I was dead
To deeper hope, yet had I joy for her,
And welcomed her benevolence, rejoiced
In common with the Children of her Love,
Plants, insects, beasts in field, and birds in bower.
So neither were complacency nor peace
Nor tender yearnings wanting for my good
Through those distracted times; in Nature still
Glorying, I found a counterpoise in her,
Which, when the spirit of evil was at height
Maintain'd for me a secret happiness.

'SPOTS OF TIME'

There are in our existence spots of time,
Which with distinct pre-eminence retain
A vivifying Virtue, whence, depress'd
By false opinion and contentious thought,
Or aught of heavier or more deadly weight
In trivial occupations, and the round
Of ordinary intercourse, our minds
Are nourished and invisibly repair'd,
A virtue by which pleasure is enhanced
That penetrates, enables us to mount
When high, more high, and lifts us up when fallen.
This efficacious spirit chiefly lurks
Among those passages of life in which
We have had deepest feeling that the mind
Is lord and master, and that outward sense
Is but the obedient servant of her will.

Such moments worthy of all gratitude,
Are scatter'd everywhere, taking their date
From our first childhood.

DOROTHY

I

Then it was
That the belovèd Woman in whose sight
Those days were pass'd, now speaking in a voice
Of sudden admonition, like a brook
That did but cross a lonely road, and now
Seen, heard and felt, and caught at every turn,
Companion never lost through many a league,
Maintained for me a saving intercourse
With my true self; for, though impair'd and chang'd
Much, as it seemed, I was no further chang'd
Than as a clouded, not a waning moon:
She, in the midst of all, preserv'd me still
A Poet, made me seek beneath that name
My office upon earth, and nowhere else.

2

Child of my Parents! Sister of my Soul!
Elsewhere have streams of gratitude been breath'd
To thee for all the early tenderness
Which I from thee imbibed. And true it is
That later seasons owed to thee no less;
For, spite of thy sweet influence and the touch
Of other kindred hands that open'd out
The springs of tender thought in infancy,
And spite of all which singly I had watch'd
Of elegance, and each minuter charm
In nature and in life, still to the last
Even to the very going out of youth,
The period which our Story now hath reach'd,
I too exclusively esteem'd that love,
And sought that beauty, which, as Milton sings,
Hath terror in it. Thou didst soften down

This over-sternness; but for thee, sweet Friend,
My soul, too reckless of mild grace, had been
Far longer what by Nature it was framed,
Longer retain'd its countenance severe,
A rock with torrents roaring, with the clouds
Familiar, and a favourite of the Stars:
But thou didst plant its crevices with flowers,
Hang it with shrubs that twinkle in the breeze,
And teach the little birds to build their nests
And warble in its chambers. At a time
When Nature, destined to remain so long
Foremost in my affections, had fallen back
Into a second place, well pleas'd to be
A handmaid to a nobler than herself,
When every day brought with it some new sense
Of exquisite regard for common things,
And all the earth was budding with these gifts
Of more refined humanity, thy breath,
Dear Sister, was a kind of gentler spring
That went before my steps.

REALITY FOUND IN LOW AND RUSTIC LIFE

I LOVE a public road: few sights there are
That please me more; such object hath had power
O'er my imagination since the dawn
Of childhood, when its disappearing line,
Seen daily afar off, on one bare steep
Beyond the limits which my feet had trod
Was like a guide into eternity,
At least to things unknown and without bound.
Even something of the grandeur which invests
The Mariner who sails the roaring sea
Through storm and darkness early in my mind
Surrounded, too, the Wanderers of the Earth,
Grandeur as much, and loveliness far more;
Awed have I been by strolling Bedlamites,
From many other uncouth Vagrants pass'd
In fear, have walk'd with quicker step; but why
Take note of this? When I began to inquire,
To watch and question those I met, and held

Familiar talk with them, the lonely roads
Were schools to me in which I daily read
With most delight the passions of mankind,
There saw into the depths of human souls,
Souls that appear to have no depth at all
To vulgar eyes. And now convinced at heart
How little that to which alone we give
The name of education hath to do
With real feeling and just sense, how vain
A correspondence with the talking world
Proves to the most, and call'd to make good search
If man's estate, by doom of Nature yoked
With toil, is therefore yoked with ignorance,
If virtue be indeed so hard to rear,
And intellectual strength so rare a boon
I prized such walks still more; for there I found
Hope to my hope, and to my pleasure peace,
And steadiness; and healing and repose
To every angry passion. There I heard,
From mouths of lowly men and of obscure
A tale of honour; sounds in unison
With loftiest promises of good and fair.

There are who think that strong affections, love
Known by whatever name, is falsely deem'd
A gift, to use a term which they would use,
Of vulgar Nature, that its growth requires
Retirement, leisure, language purified
By manners thoughtful and elaborate,
That whoso feels such passion in excess
Must live within the very light and air
Of elegances that are made by man.
True is it, where oppression worse than death
Salutes the Being at his birth, where grace
Of culture hath been utterly unknown,
And labour in excess and poverty
From day to day pre-occupy the ground
Of the affections, and to Nature's self
Oppose a deeper nature, there indeed,
Love cannot be; nor does it easily thrive
In cities, where the human heart is sick,
And the eye feeds it not, and cannot feed:
Thus far, no further, is that inference good.

Yes, in those wanderings deeply did I feel
How we mislead each other, above all
How Books mislead us, looking for their fame
To judgments of the wealthy Few, who see
By artificial lights, how they debase
The Many for the pleasure of those Few
Effeminately level down the truth
To certain general notions for the sake
Of being understood at once, or else
Through want of better knowledge in the men
Who frame them, flattering thus our self-conceit
With pictures that ambitiously set forth
The differences, the outward marks by which
Society has parted man from man,
Neglectful of the universal heart.

COLERIDGE

I

I, TOO, have been a Wanderer; but, alas!
How different is the fate of different men
Though Twins almost in genius and in mind!
Unknown unto each other, yea, and breathing
As if in different elements, we were framed
To bend at last to the same discipline,
Predestin'd, if two Beings ever were,
To seek the same delights, and have one health,
One happiness. Throughout this narrative,
Else sooner ended, I have known full well
For whom I thus record the birth and growth
Of gentleness, simplicity, and truth,
And joyous loves that hallow innocent days
Of peace and self-command. Of Rivers, Fields,
And Groves, I speak to Thee, my Friend; to Thee,
Who, yet a liveried School-Boy, in the depths
Of the huge City, on the leaded Roof
Of that wide Edifice, thy Home and School,
Wast used to lie and gaze upon the clouds
Moving in Heaven; or haply, tired of this,
To shut thine eyes, and by internal light
See trees, and meadows, and thy native Stream
Far distant, thus beheld from year to year
Of thy long exile. Nor could I forget
In this late portion of my argument
That scarcely had I finally resign'd
My rights among those academic Bowers
When Thou wert thither guided. From the heart
Of London, and from Cloisters there Thou cam'st,
And didst sit down in temperance and peace,
A rigorous Student. What a stormy course
Then follow'd. Oh! it is a pang that calls
For utterance, to think how small a change
Of circumstances might to Thee have spared

A world of pain, ripen'd ten thousand hopes
For ever wither'd. Through this retrospect
Of my own College life I still have had
Thy after sojourn in the self-same place
Present before my eyes; I have play'd with times,
(I speak of private business of the thought)
And accidents as children do with cards,
Or as a man, who, when his house is built,
A frame lock'd up in wood and stone, doth still,
In impotence of mind, by his fireside
Rebuild it to his liking. I have thought
Of Thee, thy learning, gorgeous eloquence
And all the strength and plumage of thy Youth,
Thy subtle speculations, toils abstruse
Among the Schoolmen, and platonic forms
Of wild ideal pageantry, shap'd out
From things well-match'd, or ill, and words for things,
The self-created sustenance of a mind
Debarr'd from Nature's living images,
Compell'd to be a life unto itself,
And unrelentingly possess'd by thirst
Of greatness, love, and beauty. Not alone,
Ah! surely not in singleness of heart
Should I have seen the light of evening fade
Upon the silent Cam, if we had met,
Even at that early time; I needs must hope,
Must feel, must trust, that my maturer age,
And temperature less willing to be mov'd,
My calmer habits and more steady voice
Would with an influence benign have sooth'd
Or chas'd away the airy wretchedness
That batten'd on thy youth. But thou hast trod,
In watchful meditation thou hast trod
A march of glory, which doth put to shame
These vain regrets; health suffers in thee; else
Such grief for Thee would be the weakest thought
That ever harbour'd in the breast of Man.

2

With such a theme,
Coleridge! with this my argument, of thee

Shall I be silent? O most loving Soul!
Placed on this earth to love and understand,
And from thy presence shed the light of love,
Shall I be mute ere thou be spoken of?
Thy gentle Spirit to my heart of hearts
Did also find its way; and thus the life
Of all things and the mighty unity
In all which we behold, and feel, and are,
Admitted more habitually a mild
Interposition, and closelier gathering thoughts
Of man and his concerns, such as become
A human Creature, be he who he may!
Poet, or destined for a humbler name;
And so the deep enthusiastic joy,
The rapture of the Hallelujah sent
From all that breathes and is, was chasten'd, stemm'd
And balanced by a Reason which indeed
Is reason; duty and pathetic truth;
And God and Man divided, as they ought,
Between them the great system of the world
Where Man is sphered, and which God animates.

3

Whether to me shall be allotted life,
And with life power to accomplish aught of worth
Sufficient to excuse me in men's sight
For having given this Record of myself,
Is all uncertain: but, beloved Friend,
When, looking back thou seest in clearer view
Than any sweetest sight of yesterday
That summer when on Quantock's grassy Hills
Far ranging, and among her sylvan Combs,
Thou in delicious words, with happy heart,
Didst speak the Vision of that Ancient Man,
The bright-eyed Mariner, and rueful woes
Didst utter of the Lady Christabel;
And I, associate with such labour, walk'd
Murmuring of him who, joyous hap! was found,
After the perils of his moonlight ride
Near the loud Waterfall; or her who sate
In misery near the miserable Thorn;

When thou dost to that summer turn thy thoughts,
And hast before thee all which then we were,
To thee, in memory of that happiness
It will be known, by thee at least, my Friend,
Felt, that the history of a Poet's mind
Is labour not unworthy of regard:
To thee the work shall justify itself.

The last and later portions of this Gift
Which I for Thee design, have been prepared
In times which have from those wherein we first
Together wanton'd in wild Poesy,
Differ'd thus far, that they have been, my Friend,
Times of much sorrow, of a private grief
Keen and enduring, which the frame of mind
That in this meditative History
Hath been described, more deeply makes me feel;
Yet likewise hath enabled me to bear
More firmly; and a comfort now, a hope,
One of the dearest which this life can give,
Is mine; that Thou art near, and wilt be soon
Restored to us in renovated health;
When, after the first mingling of our tears,
'Mong other consolations we may find
Some pleasure from this Offering of my love.
Oh! yet a few short years of useful life,
And all will be complete, thy race be run,
Thy monument of glory will be raised.
Then, though, too weak to tread the ways of truth,
This Age fall back to old idolatry,
Though men return to servitude as fast
As the tide ebbs, to ignominy and shame
By Nations sink together, we shall still
Find solace in the knowledge which we have,
Bless'd with true happiness if we may be
United helpers forward of a day
Of firmer trust, joint-labourers in a work
(Should Providence such grace to us vouchsafe)
Of their redemption, surely yet to come.
Prophets of Nature, we to them will speak
A lasting inspiration, sanctified
By reason and by truth; what we have loved,

Others will love; and we may teach them how;
Instruct them how the mind of man becomes
A thousand times more beautiful than the earth
On which he dwells, above this Frame of things
(Which, 'mid all revolution in the hopes
And fears of men, doth still remain unchanged)
In beauty exalted, as it is itself
Of substance and of fabric more divine.

THE DEDICATED POET

Oh! who is he that hath his whole life long
Preserved, enlarged, this freedom in himself?
For this alone is genuine Liberty:
Witness, ye Solitudes! where I received
My earliest visitations, careless then
Of what was given me, and where now I roam,
A meditative, oft a suffering Man,
And yet, I trust, with undiminish'd powers,
Witness, whatever falls my better mind,
Revolving with the accidents of life,
May have sustain'd, that, howsoe'er misled,
I never, in the quest of right and wrong,
Did tamper with myself from private aims;
Nor was in any of my hopes the dupe
Of selfish passions; nor did wilfully
Yield ever to mean cares and low pursuits;
But rather did with jealousy shrink back
From every combination that might aid
The tendency, too potent in itself,
Of habit to enslave the mind, I mean
Oppress it by the laws of vulgar sense,
And substitute a universe of death,
The falsest of all worlds, in place of that
Which is divine and true. To fear and love,
To love as first and chief, for there fear ends,
Be this ascribed; to early intercourse,
In presence of sublime and lovely forms,
With the adverse principles of pain and joy,
Evil as one is rashly named by those
Who know not what they say. By love, for here
Do we begin and end, all grandeur comes,
All truth and beauty, from pervading love,
That gone, we are as dust. Behold the fields
In balmy spring-time, full of rising flowers
And happy creatures; see that Pair, the Lamb
And the Lamb's Mother, and their tender ways
Shall touch thee to the heart; in some green bower

Rest, and be not alone, but have thou there
The One who is thy choice of all the world,
There linger, lull'd and lost, and rapt away,
Be happy to thy fill; thou call'st this love
And so it is, but there is higher love
Than this, a love that comes into the heart
With awe and a diffusive sentiment;
Thy love is human merely; this proceeds
More from the brooding Soul, and is divine.

This love more intellectual cannot be
Without Imagination, which, in truth,
Is but another name for absolute strength
And clearest insight, amplitude of mind,
And reason in her most exalted mood.
This faculty hath been the moving soul
Of our long labour: we have traced the stream
From darkness, and the very place of birth
In its blind cavern, whence is faintly heard
The sound of waters; follow'd it to light
And open day, accompanied its course
Among the ways of Nature, afterwards
Lost sight of it bewilder'd and engulph'd,
Then given it greeting, as it rose once more
With strength, reflecting in its solemn breast
The works of man and face of human life,
And lastly, from its progress have we drawn
The feeling of life endless, the great thought
By which we live, Infinity and God.
Imagination having been our theme,
So also hath that intellectual love,
For they are each in each, and cannot stand
Dividually.—Here must thou be, O Man!
Strength to thyself; no Helper hast thou here;
Here keepest thou thy individual state:
No other can divide with thee this work,
No secondary hand can intervene
To fashion this ability; 'tis thine,
The prime and vital principle is thine
In the recesses of thy nature, far
From any reach of outward fellowship,
Else is not thine at all. But joy to him,

Oh, joy to him who here hath sown, hath laid
Here the foundations of his future years!
For all that friendship, all that love can do,
All that a darling countenance can look
Or dear voice utter to complete the man,
Perfect him, made imperfect in himself,
All shall be his: and he whose soul hath risen
Up to the height of feeling intellect
Shall want no humbler tenderness, his heart
Be tender as a nursing Mother's heart;
Of female softness shall his life be full,
Of little loves and delicate desires,
Mild interests and gentlest sympathies.

LYRICAL BALLADS, 1798

WITH

A FEW OTHER POEMS

EDITOR'S NOTE

THIS section contains the whole of the 1798 *Lyrical Ballads* with the exception of the four poems contributed by Coleridge, viz., *The Rime of the Ancyent Marinere, The Foster-Mother's Tale, The Nightingale, A Conversational Poem,* and *The Dungeon.*

The order of Wordsworth's contributions to *Lyrical Ballads* is here retained, as is the text of 1798, which differs in certain respects from later versions.

LYRICAL BALLADS, 1798

ADVERTISEMENT

It is the honourable characteristic of Poetry that its materials are to be found in every subject which can interest the human mind. The evidence of this fact is to be sought, not in the writings of Critics, but in those of Poets themselves.

The majority of the following poems are to be considered as experiments. They are written chiefly with a view to ascertain how far the language of conversation in the middle and lower classes of society is adapted to the purposes of poetic pleasure. Readers accustomed to the gaudiness and inane phraseology of many modern writers, if they persist in reading this book to its conclusion, will perhaps frequently have to struggle with feelings of strangeness and awkwardness: they will look round for poetry, and will be induced to enquire by what species of courtesy these attempts can be permitted to assume that title. It is desirable that such readers, for their own sakes, should not suffer the solitary word Poetry, a word of very disputed meaning, to stand in the way of their gratification; but that, while they are perusing this book, they should ask themselves if it contains a natural delineation of human passions, human characters, and human incidents; and if the answer be favorable to the author's wishes, that they should consent to be pleased in spite of that most dreadful enemy to our pleasures, our own pre-established codes of decision.

Readers of superior judgment may disapprove of the style in which many of these pieces are executed: it must be expected that many lines and phrases will not exactly suit their taste. It will perhaps appear to them, that wishing to avoid the prevalent fault of the day, the author has sometimes descended too low, and that many of his expressions are too familiar, and not of sufficient dignity. It is apprehended, that the more conversant the reader is with our elder writers, and with those in modern times who have been the most successful in painting manners and passions, the fewer complaints of this kind will he have to make.

An accurate taste in poetry, and in all the other arts, Sir Joshua Reynolds has observed, is an acquired talent, which can only be produced by severe thought, and a long continued intercourse with the best models of composition. This is mentioned not with so ridiculous a purpose as to prevent the most inexperienced reader from judging for himself; but merely to temper the rashness of decision, and to suggest that if poetry be a subject on which much time has not been bestowed, the judgment may be erroneous, and that in many cases it necessarily will be so.

The tale of Goody Blake and Harry Gill is founded on a well-authenticated fact which happened in Warwickshire. Of the other poems in the collection, it may be proper to say that they are either absolute inventions of the author, or facts which took place within his personal observation or that of his friends. The poem of the Thorn, as the reader will soon discover, is not supposed to be spoken in the author's own person: the character of the loquacious narrator will sufficiently shew itself in the course of the story. The Rime of the Ancyent Marinere was professedly written in imitation of the *style*, as well as of the spirit of the elder poets; but with a few exceptions, the Author believes that the language adopted in it has been equally intelligible for these three last centuries. The lines entitled Expostulation and Reply, and those which follow, arose out of conversation with a friend who was somewhat unreasonably attached to modern books of moral philosophy.

Lines

LEFT UPON A SEAT IN A YEW-TREE WHICH STANDS NEAR THE LAKE OF ESTHWAITE, ON A DESOLATE PART OF THE SHORE, YET COMMANDING A BEAUTIFUL PROSPECT

—Nay, Traveller! rest. This lonely yew-tree stands
Far from all human dwelling: what if here
No sparkling rivulet spread the verdant herb;
What if these barren boughs the bee not loves;
Yet, if the wind breathe soft, the curling waves,
That break against the shore, shall lull thy mind
By one soft impulse saved from vacancy.

—————————Who he was
That piled these stones, and with the mossy sod
First covered o'er, and taught this aged tree,
Now wild, to bend its arms in circling shade,
I well remember.—He was one who own'd
No common soul. In youth, by genius nurs'd,
And big with lofty views, he to the world
Went forth, pure in his heart, against the taint
Of dissolute tongues, 'gainst jealousy, and hate,
And scorn, against all enemies prepared,
All but neglect: and so, his spirit damped
At once, with rash disdain he turned away,
And with the food of pride sustained his soul
In solitude.—Stranger! these gloomy boughs
Had charms for him; and here he loved to sit,

His only visitants a straggling sheep,
The stone-chat, or the glancing sand-piper;
And on these barren rocks, with juniper,
And heath, and thistle, thinly sprinkled o'er,
Fixing his downward eye, he many an hour
A morbid pleasure nourished, tracing here
An emblem of his own unfruitful life:
And lifting up his head, he then would gaze
On the more distant scene; how lovely 'tis
Thou seest, and he would gaze till it became
Far lovelier, and his heart could not sustain
The beauty still more beauteous. Nor, that time,
Would he forget those beings, to whose minds,
Warm from the labours of benevolence,
The world, and man himself, appeared a scene
Of kindred loveliness: then he would sigh
With mournful joy, to think that others felt
What he must never feel: and so, lost man!
On visionary views would fancy feed,
Till his eye streamed with tears. In this deep vale
He died, this seat his only monument.

If thou be one whose heart the holy forms
Of young imagination have kept pure,
Stranger! henceforth be warned; and know, that pride,
Howe'er disguised in its own majesty,
Is littleness; that he, who feels contempt
For any living thing, hath faculties
Which he has never used; that thought with him
Is in its infancy. The man, whose eye
Is ever on himself, doth look on one,
The least of nature's works, one who might move
The wise man to that scorn which wisdom holds
Unlawful, ever. O, be wiser thou!
Instructed that true knowledge leads to love,
True dignity abides with him alone
Who, in the silent hour of inward thought,
Can still suspect, and still revere himself,
In lowliness of heart.

The Female Vagrant

By Derwent's side my Father's cottage stood,
(The Woman thus her artless story told)
One field, a flock, and what the neighbouring flood
Supplied, to him were more than mines of gold.
Light was my sleep; my days in transport roll'd:
With thoughtless joy I stretch'd along the shore
My father's nets, or watched, when from the fold
High o'er the cliffs I led my fleecy store,
A dizzy depth below! his boat and twinkling oar.

My father was a good and pious man,
An honest man by honest parents bred,
And I believe that, soon as I began
To lisp, he made me kneel beside my bed,
And in his hearing there my prayers I said:
And afterwards, by my good father taught,
I read, and loved the books in which I read;
For books in every neighbouring house I sought,
And nothing to my mind a sweeter pleasure brought.

Can I forget what charms did once adorn
My garden, stored with pease, and mint, and thyme,
And rose and lily for the sabbath morn?
The sabbath bells, and their delightful chime;
The gambols and wild freaks at shearing time;
My hen's rich nest through long grass scarce espied;
The cowslip-gathering at May's dewy prime;
The swans, that, when I sought the water-side,
From far to meet me came, spreading their snowy pride.

The staff I yet remember which upbore
The bending body of my active sire;
His seat beneath the honeyed sycamore
When the bees hummed, and chair by winter fire;
When market-morning came, the neat attire
With which, though bent on haste, myself I deck'd;
My watchful dog, whose starts of furious ire,

When stranger passed, so often I have check'd;
The red-breast known for years, which at my casement peck'd.

The suns of twenty summers danced along,—
Ah! little marked, how fast they rolled away:
Then rose a mansion proud our woods among,
And cottage after cottage owned its sway,
No joy to see a neighbouring house, or stray
Through pastures not his own, the master took;
My Father dared his greedy wish gainsay;
He loved his old hereditary nook,
And ill could I the thought of such sad parting brook.

But, when he had refused the proffered gold,
To cruel injuries he became a prey,
Sore traversed in whate'er he bought and sold:
His troubles grew upon him day by day,
Till all his substance fell into decay.
His little range of water was denied;
All but the bed where his old body lay,
All, all was seized, and weeping, side by side,
We sought a home where we uninjured might abide.

Can I forget that miserable hour,
When from the last hill-top, my sire surveyed,
Peering above the trees, the steeple tower,
That on his marriage-day sweet music made?
Till then he hoped his bones might there be laid,
Close by my mother in their native bowers:
Bidding me trust in God, he stood and prayed,—
I could not pray:—through tears that fell in showers,
Glimmer'd our dear-loved home, alas! no longer ours!

There was a youth whom I had loved so long,
That when I loved him not I cannot say.
'Mid the green mountains many and many a song
We two had sung, like little birds in May.
When we began to tire of childish play
We seemed still more and more to prize each other:
We talked of marriage and our marriage day;
And I in truth did love him like a brother,
For never could I hope to meet with such another.

His father said, that to a distant town
He must repair, to ply the artist's trade.
What tears of bitter grief till then unknown!
What tender vows our last sad kiss delayed!
To him we turned:—we had no other aid.
Like one revived, upon his neck I wept,
And her whom he had loved in joy, he said
He well could love in grief: his faith he kept;
And in a quiet home once more my father slept.

Four years each day with daily bread was blest,
By constant toil and constant prayer supplied.
Three lovely infants lay upon my breast;
And often, viewing their sweet smiles, I sighed,
And knew not why. My happy father died
When sad distress reduced the children's meal:
Thrice happy! that from him the grave did hide
The empty loom, cold hearth, and silent wheel,
And tears that flowed for ills which patience could not heal.

'Twas a hard change, an evil time was come;
We had no hope, and no relief could gain.
But soon, with proud parade, the noisy drum
Beat round, to sweep the streets of want and pain.
My husband's arms now only served to strain
Me and his children hungering in his view:
In such dismay my prayers and tears were vain:
To join those miserable men he flew;
And now to the sea-coast, with numbers more, we drew.

There foul neglect for months and months we bore,
Nor yet the crowded fleet its anchor stirred.
Green fields before us and our native shore,
By fever, from polluted air incurred,
Ravage was made, for which no knell was heard.
Fondly we wished, and wished away, nor knew,
'Mid that long sickness, and those hopes deferr'd,
That happier days we never more must view:
The parting signal streamed, at last the land withdrew,

But from delay the summer calms were past.
On as we drove, the equinoctial deep
Ran mountains-high before the howling blast.
We gazed with terror on the gloomy sleep
Of them that perished in the whirlwind's sweep,
Untaught that soon such anguish must ensue,
Our hopes such harvest of affliction reap,
That we the mercy of the waves should rue.
We reached the western world, a poor, devoted crew.

Oh! dreadful price of being to resign
All that is dear *in* being! better far
In Want's most lonely cave till death to pine,
Unseen, unheard, unwatched by any star;
Or in the streets and walks where proud men are,
Better our dying bodies to obtrude,
Than dog-like, wading at the heels of war,
Protract a curst existence, with the brood
That lap (their very nourishment!) their brother's blood.

The pains and plagues that on our heads came down,
Disease and famine, agony and fear,
In wood or wilderness, in camp or town,
It would thy brain unsettle even to hear.
All perished—all, in one remorseless year,
Husband and children! one by one, by sword
And ravenous plague, all perished: every tear
Dried up, despairing, desolate, on board
A British ship I waked, as from a trance restored.

Peaceful as some immeasurable plain
By the first beams of dawning light impress'd,
In the calm sunshine slept the glittering main.
The very ocean has its hour of rest,
That comes not to the human mourner's breast.
Remote from man, and storms of mortal care,
A heavenly silence did the waves invest;
I looked and looked along the silent air,
Until it seemed to bring a joy to my despair.

Ah! how unlike those late terrific sleeps!
And groans, that rage of racking famine spoke,
Where locks inhuman dwelt on festering heaps!
The breathing pestilence that rose like smoke!
The shriek that from the distant battle broke!
The mine's dire earthquake, and the pallid host
Driven by the bomb's incessant thunder-stroke
To loathsome vaults, where heart-sick anguish toss'd,
Hope died, and fear itself in agony was lost!

Yet does that burst of woe congeal my frame,
When the dark streets appeared to heave and gape,
While like a sea the storming army came,
And Fire from Hell reared his gigantic shape,
And Murder, by the ghastly gleam, and Rape
Seized their joint prey, the mother and the child!
But from these crazing thoughts my brain, escape!
—For weeks the balmy air breathed soft and mild,
And on the gliding vessel Heaven and Ocean smiled.

Some mighty gulph of separation past,
I seemed transported to another world:—
A thought resigned with pain, when from the mast
The impatient mariner the sail unfurl'd,
And whistling, called the wind that hardly curled
The silent sea. From the sweet thoughts of home,
And from all hope I was forever hurled.
For me—farthest from earthly port to roam
Was best, could I but shun the spot where man might come.

And oft, robb'd of my perfect mind, I thought
At last my feet a resting-place had found:
Here will I weep in peace, (so fancy wrought,)
Roaming the illimitable waters round;
Here watch, of every human friend disowned,
All day, my ready tomb the ocean-flood—
To break my dream the vessel reached its bound:
And homeless near a thousand homes I stood,
And near a thousand tables pined, and wanted food.

By grief enfeebled was I turned adrift,
Helpless as sailor cast on desart rock;
Nor morsel to my mouth that day did lift,
Nor dared my hand at any door to knock.
I lay, where with his drowsy mates, the cock
From the cross timber of an out-house hung;
How dismal tolled, that night, the city clock!
At morn my sick heart hunger scarcely stung,
Nor to the beggar's language could I frame my tongue.

So passed another day, and so the third:
Then did I try, in vain, the crowd's resort,
In deep despair by frightful wishes stirr'd,
Near the sea-side I reached a ruined fort:
There, pains which nature could no more support,
With blindness linked, did on my vitals fall;
Dizzy my brain, with interruption short
Of hideous sense; I sunk, nor step could crawl,
And thence was borne away to neighbouring hospital.

Recovery came with food: but still, my brain
Was weak, nor of the past had memory.
I heard my neighbours, in their beds, complain
Of many things which never troubled me;
Of feet still bustling round with busy glee,
Of looks where common kindness had no part,
Of service done with careless cruelty,
Fretting the fever round the languid heart,
And groans, which, as they said, would make a dead man start.

These things just served to stir the torpid sense,
Nor pain nor pity in my bosom raised.
Memory, though slow, returned with strength; and thence
Dismissed, again on open day I gazed,
At houses, men, and common light, amazed.
The lanes I sought, and as the sun retired,
Came, where beneath the trees a faggot blazed;
The wild brood saw me weep, my fate enquired,
And gave me food, and rest, more welcome, more desired.

My heart is touched to think that men like these,
The rude earth's tenants, were my first relief:
How kindly did they paint their vagrant ease!
And their long holiday that feared not grief,
For all belonged to all, and each was chief.
No plough their sinews strained; on grating road
No wain they drove, and yet, the yellow sheaf
In every vale for their delight was stowed:
For them, in nature's meads, the milky udder flowed.

Semblance, with straw and panniered ass, they made
Of potters wandering on from door to door:
But life of happier sort to me pourtrayed,
And other joys my fancy to allure;
The bag-pipe dinning on the midnight moor
In barn uplighted, and companions boon
Well met from far with revelry secure,
In depth of forest glade, when jocund June
Rolled fast along the sky his warm and genial moon.

But ill it suited me, in journey dark
O'er moor and mountain, midnight theft to hatch;
To charm the surly house-dog's faithful bark,
Or hang on tiptoe at the lifted latch;
The gloomy lantern, and the dim blue match,
The black disguise, the warning whistle shrill,
And ear still busy on its nightly watch,
Were not for me, brought up in nothing ill;
Besides, on griefs so fresh my thoughts were brooding still.

What could I do, unaided and unblest?
Poor Father! gone was every friend of thine:
And kindred of dead husband are at best
Small help, and, after marriage such as mine,
With little kindness would to me incline.
Ill was I then for toil or service fit:
With tears whose course no effort could confine,
By high-way side forgetful would I sit
Whole hours, my idle arms in moping sorrow knit.

I lived upon the mercy of the fields,
And oft of cruelty the sky accused;
On hazard, or what general bounty yields,
Now coldly given, now utterly refused.
The fields I for my bed have often used:
But, what afflicts my peace with keenest ruth
Is, that I have my inner self abused,
Foregone the home delight of constant truth,
And clear and open soul, so prized in fearless youth.

Three years a wanderer, often have I view'd,
In tears, the sun towards that country tend
Where my poor heart lost all its fortitude:
And now across this moor my steps I bend—
Oh! tell me whither——for no earthly friend
Have I.——She ceased, and weeping turned away,
As if because her tale was at an end
She wept;—because she had no more to say
Of that perpetual weight which on her spirit lay.

Goody Blake, and Harry Gill

A TRUE STORY

Oh! what's the matter? what's the matter?
What is't that ails young Harry Gill?
That evermore his teeth they chatter,
Chatter, chatter, chatter still.
Of waistcoats Harry has no lack,
Good duffle grey, and flannel fine;
He has a blanket on his back,
And coats enough to smother nine.

In March, December, and in July,
'Tis all the same with Harry Gill;
The neighbours tell, and tell you truly,
His teeth they chatter, chatter still.
At night, at morning, and at noon,
'Tis all the same with Harry Gill;
Beneath the sun, beneath the moon,
His teeth they chatter, chatter still.

Young Harry was a lusty drover,
And who so stout of limb as he?
His cheeks were red as ruddy clover,
His voice was like the voice of three.
Auld Goody Blake was old and poor,
Ill fed she was, and thinly clad;
And any man who pass'd her door,
Might see how poor a hut she had.

All day she spun in her poor dwelling,
And then her three hours' work at night!
Alas! 'twas hardly worth the telling,
It would not pay for candle-light.
—This woman dwelt in Dorsetshire,
Her hut was on a cold hill-side,
And in that country coals are dear,
For they come far by wind and tide.

By the same fire to boil their pottage,
Two poor old dames, as I have known,
Will often live in one small cottage,
But she, poor woman, dwelt alone.
'Twas well enough when summer came,
The long, warm, lightsome summer-day.
Then at her door the *canty* dame
Would sit, as any linnet gay.

But when the ice our streams did fetter,
Oh! then how her old bones would shake!
You would have said, if you had met her,
'Twas a hard time for Goody Blake.
Her evenings then were dull and dead;
Sad case it was, as you may think,
For very cold to go to bed,
And then for cold not sleep a wink.

Oh joy for her! when e'er in winter
The winds at night had made a rout,
And scatter'd many a lusty splinter,
And many a rotten bough about.

Yet never had she, well or sick,
As every man who knew her says,
A pile before-hand, wood or stick,
Enough to warm her for three days.

Now, when the frost was past enduring,
And made her poor old bones to ache,
Could any thing be more alluring,
Than an old hedge to Goody Blake?
And now and then, it must be said,
When her old bones were cold and chill,
She left her fire, or left her bed,
To seek the hedge of Harry Gill.

Now Harry he had long suspected
This trespass of old Goody Blake,
And vow'd that she should be detected,
And he on her would vengeance take.
And oft from his warm fire he'd go,
And to the fields his road would take,
And there, at night, in frost and snow,
He watch'd to seize old Goody Blake.

And once, behind a rick of barley,
Thus looking out did Harry stand;
The moon was full and shining clearly,
And crisp with frost the stubble-land.
—He hears a noise—he's all awake—
Again?—on tip-toe down the hill
He softly creeps—'Tis Goody Blake,
She's at the hedge of Harry Gill.

Right glad was he when he beheld her:
Stick after stick did Goody pull,
He stood behind a bush of elder,
Till she had filled her apron full.
When with her load she turned about,
The bye-road back again to take,
He started forward with a shout,
And sprang upon poor Goody Blake.

And fiercely by the arm he took her,
And by the arm he held her fast,
And fiercely by the arm he shook her,
And cried, 'I've caught you then at last!'
Then Goody, who had nothing said,
Her bundle from her lap let fall;
And kneeling on the sticks, she pray'd
To God that is the judge of all.

She pray'd, her wither'd hand uprearing,
While Harry held her by the arm—
'God! who art never out of hearing,
'O may he never more be warm!'
The cold, cold moon above her head,
Thus on her knees did Goody pray,
Young Harry heard what she had said,
And icy-cold he turned away.

He went complaining all the morrow
That he was cold and very chill:
His face was gloom, his heart was sorrow,
Alas! that day for Harry Gill!
That day he wore a riding-coat,
But not a whit the warmer he:
Another was on Thursday brought,
And ere the Sabbath he had three.

'Twas all in vain, a useless matter,
And blankets were about him pinn'd;
Yet still his jaws and teeth they clatter,
Like a loose casement in the wind.
And Harry's flesh it fell away;
And all who see him say 'tis plain,
That, live as long as live he may,
He never will be warm again.

No word to any man he utters,
A-bed or up, to young or old;
But ever to himself he mutters,
'Poor Harry Gill is very cold.'

A-bed or up, by night or day;
His teeth they chatter, chatter still.
Now think, ye farmers all, I pray,
Of Goody Blake and Harry Gill.

Lines

WRITTEN AT A SMALL DISTANCE FROM MY HOUSE, AND SENT BY MY LITTLE BOY TO THE PERSON TO WHOM THEY ARE ADDRESSED

It is the first mild day of March:
Each minute sweeter than before,
The red-breast sings from the tall larch
That stands beside our door.

There is a blessing in the air,
Which seems a sense of joy to yield
To the bare trees, and mountains bare,
And grass in the green field.

My Sister! ('tis a wish of mine)
Now that our morning meal is done,
Make haste, your morning task resign;
Come forth and feel the sun.

Edward will come with you, and pray,
Put on with speed your woodland dress,
And bring no book, for this one day
We'll give to idleness.

No joyless forms shall regulate
Our living Calendar:
We from to-day, my friend, will date
The opening of the year.

Love, now an universal birth,
From heart to heart is stealing,
From earth to man, from man to earth,
—It is the hour of feeling.

One moment now may give us more
Than fifty years of reason;
Our minds shall drink at every pore
The spirit of the season.

Some silent laws our hearts may make,
Which they shall long obey;
We for the year to come may take
Our temper from to-day.

And from the blessed power that rolls
About, below, above;
We'll frame the measure of our souls,
They shall be tuned to love.

Then come, my sister! come, I pray,
With speed put on your woodland dress,
And bring no book; for this one day
We'll give to idleness.

Simon Lee,
The Old Huntsman,
WITH AN INCIDENT IN WHICH HE WAS CONCERNED

In the sweet shire of Cardigan,
Not far from pleasant Ivor-hall,
An old man dwells, a little man,
I've heard he once was tall.
Of years he has upon his back,
No doubt, a burthen weighty;
He says he is three score and ten,
But others say he's eighty.

A long blue livery-coat has he,
That's fair behind, and fair before;
Yet, meet him where you will, you see
At once that he is poor.

Full five and twenty years he lived
A running huntsman merry;
And, though he has but one eye left,
His cheek is like a cherry.

No man like him the horn could sound,
And no man was so full of glee;
To say the least, four counties round
Had heard of Simon Lee;
His master's dead, and no one now
Dwells in the hall of Ivor;
Men, dogs, and horses, all are dead;
He is the sole survivor.

His hunting feats have him bereft
Of his right eye, as you may see:
And then, what limbs those feats have left
To poor old Simon Lee!
He has no son, he has no child,
His wife, an aged woman,
Lives with him, near the waterfall,
Upon the village common.

And he is lean and he is sick,
His little body's half awry
His ancles they are swoln and thick;
His legs are thin and dry.
When he was young he little knew
Of husbandry or tillage;
And now he's forced to work, though weak,
—The weakest in the village.

He all the country could outrun,
Could leave both man and horse behind;
And often, ere the race was done,
He reeled and was stone-blind.
And still there's something in the world
At which his heart rejoices;
For when the chiming hounds are out,
He dearly loves their voices!

Old Ruth works out of doors with him,
And does what Simon cannot do;
For she, not over stout of limb,
Is stouter of the two.
And though you with your utmost skill
From labour could not wean them,
Alas! 'tis very little, all
Which they can do between them.

Beside their moss-grown hut of clay,
Not twenty paces from the door,
A scrap of land they have, but they
Are poorest of the poor.
This scrap of land he from the heath
Enclosed when he was stronger;
But what avails the land to them,
Which they can till no longer?

Few months of life has he in store,
As he to you will tell,
For still, the more he works, the more
His poor old ancles swell.
My gentle reader, I perceive
How patiently you've waited,
And I'm afraid that you expect
Some tale will be related.

O reader! had you in your mind
Such stores as silent thought can bring,
O gentle reader! you would find
A tale in every thing.
What more I have to say is short,
I hope you'll kindly take it;
It is no tale; but should you think,
Perhaps a tale you'll make it.

One summer-day I chanced to see
This old man doing all he could
About the root of an old tree,
A stump of rotten wood.

Blois c.1829 by J.M.W. Turner (1775–1851). In 1792 Wordsworth met Annette Vallon and moved to Blois where she had her home. In December of that year Annette bore him a child, Caroline.
By courtesy of the Ashmolean Museum, Oxford

Brougham Castle, near Penrith, depicted by Peter de Wint (1784–1849). A ruined 12th-century castle situated where the Rivers Eamont and Lowther meet, it was visited by William and Dorothy in the summer of 1789, their first meeting for nine years. Wordsworth used it as the setting for his song, "At the feast of Brougham Castle". By courtesy of the Fitzwilliam Museum, Cambridge

The mattock totter'd in his hand;
So vain was his endeavour
That at the root of the old tree
He might have worked for ever.

'You're overtasked, good Simon Lee,
Give me your tool' to him I said;
And at the word right gladly he
Received my proffer'd aid.
I struck, and with a single blow
The tangled root I sever'd,
At which the poor old man so long
And vainly had endeavour'd.

The tears into his eyes were brought,
And thanks and praises seemed to run
So fast out of his heart, I thought
They never would have done.
—I've heard of hearts unkind, kind deeds
With coldness still returning.
Alas! the gratitude of men
Has oftner left me mourning.

Anecdote for Fathers,

SHEWING HOW THE ART OF LYING MAY BE TAUGHT

I HAVE a boy of five years old,
His face is fair and fresh to see;
His limbs are cast in beauty's mould,
And dearly he loves me.

One morn we stroll'd on our dry walk,
Our quiet house all full in view,
And held such intermitted talk
As we are wont to do.

My thoughts on former pleasures ran;
I thought of Kilve's delightful shore,
My pleasant home, when spring began,
A long, long year before.

A day it was when I could bear
To think, and think, and think again;
With so much happiness to spare,
I could not feel a pain.

My boy was by my side, so slim
And graceful in his rustic dress!
And oftentimes I talked to him,
In very idleness.

The young lambs ran a pretty race;
The morning sun shone bright and warm;
'Kilve,' said I, 'was a pleasant place,
'And so is Liswyn farm.

'My little boy, which like you more,'
I said and took him by the arm—
'Our home by Kilve's delightful shore,
'Or here at Liswyn farm?'

'And tell me, had you rather be,'
I said and held him by the arm,
'At Kilve's smooth shore by the green sea,
'Or here at Liswyn farm?'

In careless mood he looked at me,
While still I held him by the arm,
And said, 'At Kilve I'd rather be
'Than here at Liswyn farm.'

'Now, little Edward, say why so;
My little Edward, tell me why;'
'I cannot tell, I do not know.'
'Why this is strange,' said I.

'For, here are woods and green-hills warm;
'There surely must some reason be
'Why you would change sweet Liswyn farm
'For Kilve by the green sea.'

At this, my boy, so fair and slim,
Hung down his head, nor made reply;
And five times did I say to him,
'Why? Edward, tell me why?'

His head he raised—there was in sight,
It caught his eye, he saw it plain—
Upon the house-top, glittering bright,
A broad and gilded vane.

Then did the boy his tongue unlock,
And thus to me he made reply;
'At Kilve there was no weather-cock,
'And that's the reason why.'

Oh dearest, dearest boy! my heart
For better lore would seldom yearn,
Could I but teach the hundredth part
Of what from thee I learn.

We are Seven

A SIMPLE child, dear brother Jim,
That lightly draws its breath,
And feels its life in every limb,
What should it know of death?

I met a little cottage girl,
She was eight years old, she said;
Her hair was thick with many a curl
That cluster'd round her head.

She had a rustic, woodland air,
And she was wildly clad;
Her eyes were fair, and very fair,
—Her beauty made me glad.

'Sisters and brothers, little maid,
'How many may you be?'
'How many? seven in all,' she said,
And wondering looked at me.

'And where are they, I pray you tell?'
She answered, 'Seven are we,
'And two of us at Conway dwell,
'And two are gone to sea.

'Two of us in the church-yard lie,
'My sister and my brother,
'And in the church-yard cottage, I
'Dwell near them with my mother.'

'You say that two at Conway dwell,
'And two are gone to sea,
'Yet you are seven; I pray you tell
'Sweet Maid, how this may be?'

Then did the little Maid reply,
'Seven boys and girls are we;
'Two of us in the church-yard lie,
'Beneath the church-yard tree.'

'You run about, my little maid,
'Your limbs they are alive;
'If two are in the church-yard laid,
'Then ye are only five.'

'Their graves are green, they may be seen,'
The little Maid replied,
'Twelve steps or more from my mother's door,
'And they are side by side.

'My stockings there I often knit,
'My 'kerchief there I hem;
'And there upon the ground I sit—
'I sit and sing to them.

'And often after sunset, Sir,
'When it is light and fair,
'I take my little porringer,
'And eat my supper there.

'The first that died was little Jane;
'In bed she moaning lay,
'Till God released her of her pain,
'And then she went away.

'So in the church-yard she was laid,
'And all the summer dry,
'Together round her grave we played,
'My brother John and I.

'And when the ground was white with snow,
'And I could run and slide,
'My brother John was forced to go,
'And he lies by her side.'

'How many are you then,' said I,
'If they two are in Heaven?'
The little Maiden did reply,
'O Master! we are seven.'

'But they are dead; those two are dead!
'Their spirits are in heaven!'
'Twas throwing words away; for still
The little Maid would have her will,
And said, 'Nay, we are seven!'

Lines
WRITTEN IN EARLY SPRING

I HEARD a thousand blended notes,
While in a grove I sate reclined,
In that sweet mood when pleasant thoughts
Bring sad thoughts to the mind.

To her fair works did nature link
The human soul that through me ran;
And much it griev'd my heart to think
What man has made of man.

Through primrose-tufts, in that sweet bower,
The periwinkle trail'd its wreathes;
And 'tis my faith that every flower
Enjoys the air it breathes.

The birds around me hopp'd and play'd:
Their thoughts I cannot measure,
But the least motion which they made,
It seem'd a thrill of pleasure.

The budding twigs spread out their fan,
To catch the breezy air;
And I must think, do all I can,
That there was pleasure there.

If I these thoughts may not prevent,
If such be of my creed the plan,
Have I not reason to lament
What man has made of man?

The Thorn

I

There is a thorn; it looks so old,
In truth you'd find it hard to say,
How it could ever have been young,
It looks so old and grey.
Not higher than a two-years' child
It stands erect this aged thorn;
No leaves it has, no thorny points;
It is a mass of knotted joints,
A wretched thing forlorn.
It stands erect, and like a stone
With lichens it is overgrown.

2

Like rock or stone, it is o'ergrown
With lichens to the very top,
And hung with heavy tufts of moss,
A melancholy crop:

Up from the earth these mosses creep,
And this poor thorn they clasp it round
So close, you'd say that they were bent
With plain and manifest intent,
To drag it to the ground;
And all had joined in one endeavour
To bury this poor thorn for ever.

3

High on a mountain's highest ridge,
Where oft the stormy winter gale
Cuts like a scythe, while through the clouds
It sweeps from vale to vale;
Not five yards from the mountain-path,
This thorn you on your left espy;
And to the left, three yards beyond,
You see a little muddy pond
Of water, never dry;
I've measured it from side to side:
'Tis three feet long, and two feet wide.

4

And close beside this aged thorn,
There is a fresh and lovely sight,
A beauteous heap, a hill of moss,
Just half a foot in height.
All lovely colours there you see,
All colours that were ever seen,
And mossy network too is there,
As if by hand of lady fair
The work had woven been,
And cups, the darlings of the eye,
So deep is their vermilion dye.

5

Ah me! what lovely tints are there!
Of olive-green and scarlet bright,
In spikes, in branches, and in stars,
Green, red, and pearly white.

This heap of earth o'ergrown with moss
Which close beside the thorn you see,
So fresh in all its beauteous dyes,
Is like an infant's grave in size
As like as like can be:
But never, never any where,
An infant's grave was half so fair.

6

Now would you see this aged thorn,
This pond and beauteous hill of moss,
You must take care and chuse your time
The mountain when to cross.
For oft there sits, between the heap
That's like an infant's grave in size,
And that same pond of which I spoke,
A woman in a scarlet cloak,
And to herself she cries,
'Oh misery! oh misery!
'Oh woe is me! oh misery!'

7

At all times of the day and night
This wretched woman thither goes,
And she is known to every star,
And every wind that blows;
And there beside the thorn she sits
When the blue day-light's in the skies,
And when the whirlwind's on the hill,
Or frosty air is keen and still,
And to herself she cries,
'Oh misery! oh misery!
'Oh woe is me! oh misery!'

8

'Now wherefore thus, by day and night,
'In rain, in tempest, and in snow,
'Thus to the dreary mountain-top
'Does this poor woman go?

'And why sits she beside the thorn
'When the blue day-light's in the sky,
'Or when the whirlwind's on the hill,
'Or frosty air is keen and still,
'And wherefore does she cry?—
'Oh wherefore? wherefore? tell me why
'Does she repeat that doleful cry?'

9

I cannot tell; I wish I could;
For the true reason no one knows,
But if you'd gladly view the spot,
The spot to which she goes;
The heap that's like an infant's grave,
The pond—and thorn, so old and grey,
Pass by her door—'tis seldom shut—
And if you see her in her hut,
Then to the spot away!—
I never heard of such as dare
Approach the spot when she is there.

10

'But wherefore to the mountain-top
'Can this unhappy woman go,
'Whatever star is in the skies,
'Whatever wind may blow?'
Nay rack your brain—'tis all in vain,
I'll tell you every thing I know;
But to the thorn, and to the pond
Which is a little step beyond,
I wish that you would go:
Perhaps when you are at the place
You something of her tale may trace.

11

I'll give you the best help I can:
Before you up the mountain go,
Up to the dreary mountain-top,
I'll tell you all I know.

'Tis now some two and twenty years,
Since she (her name is Martha Ray)
Gave with a maiden's true good will
Her company to Stephen Hill;
And she was blithe and gay,
And she was happy, happy still
Whene'er she thought of Stephen Hill.

12

And they had fix'd the wedding-day,
The morning that must wed them both;
But Stephen to another maid
Had sworn another oath;
And with this other maid to church
Unthinking Stephen went—
Poor Martha! on that woeful day
A cruel, cruel fire, they say,
Into her bones was sent:
It dried her body like a cinder,
And almost turn'd her brain to tinder.

13

They say, full six months after this,
While yet the summer-leaves were green,
She to the mountain-top would go,
And there was often seen.
'Tis said, a child was in her womb,
As now to any eye was plain;
She was with child, and she was mad,
Yet often she was sober sad
From her exceeding pain.
Oh me! ten thousand times I'd rather
That he had died, that cruel father!

14

Sad case for such a brain to hold
Communion with a stirring child!
Sad case, as you may think, for one
Who had a brain so wild!

Last Christmas when we talked of this,
Old Farmer Simpson did maintain,
That in her womb the infant wrought
About its mother's heart, and brought
Her senses back again:
And when at last her time drew near,
Her looks were calm, her senses clear.

15

No more I know, I wish I did,
And I would tell it all to you;
For what became of this poor child
There's none that ever knew:
And if a child was born or no,
There's no one that could ever tell;
And if 'twas born alive or dead,
There's no one knows, as I have said,
But some remember well,
That Martha Ray about this time
Would up the mountain often climb.

16

And all that winter, when at night
The wind blew from the mountain-peak,
'Twas worth your while, though in the dark
The church-yard path to seek:
For many a time and oft were heard
Cries coming from the mountain-head,
Some plainly living voices were,
And others, I've heard many swear,
Were voices of the dead:
I cannot think, whate'er they say,
They had to do with Martha Ray.

17

But that she goes to this old thorn,
The thorn which I've described to you,
And there sits in a scarlet cloak,
I will be sworn is true.

For one day with my telescope,
To view the ocean wide and bright,
When to this country first I came,
Ere I had heard of Martha's name,
I climbed the mountain's height:
A storm came on, and I could see
No object higher than my knee.

18

'Twas mist and rain, and storm and rain,
No screen, no fence could I discover,
And then the wind! in faith, it was
A wind full ten times over.
I looked around, I thought I saw
A jutting crag, and off I ran,
Head-foremost, through the driving rain,
The shelter of the crag to gain,
And, as I am a man,
Instead of jutting crag, I found
A woman seated on the ground.

19

I did not speak—I saw her face,
Her face it was enough for me;
I turned about and heard her cry.
'Oh misery! O misery!'
And there she sits, until the moon
Through half the clear blue sky will go,
And when the little breezes make
The waters of the pond to shake,
As all the country know,
She shudders and you hear her cry,
'Oh misery! oh misery!'

20

'But what's the thorn? and what's the pond?
'And what's the hill of moss to her?
'And what's the creeping breeze that comes
'The little pond to stir?'

I cannot tell; but some will say
She hanged her baby on the tree,
Some say she drowned it in the pond,
Which is a little step beyond,
But all and each agree,
The little babe was buried there,
Beneath that hill of moss so fair.

21

I've heard the scarlet moss is red
With drops of that poor infant's blood;
But kill a new-born infant thus!
I do not think she could.
Some say, if to the pond you go,
And fix on it a steady view,
The shadow of a babe you trace,
A baby and a baby's face,
And that it looks at you;
Whene'er you look on it, 'tis plain
The baby looks at you again.

22

And some had sworn an oath that she
Should be to public justice brought;
And for the little infant's bones
With spades they would have sought.
But then the beauteous hill of moss
Before their eyes began to stir;
And for full fifty yards around,
The grass it shook upon the ground;
But all do still aver
The little babe is buried there,
Beneath that hill of moss so fair.

23

I cannot tell how this may be,
But plain it is, the thorn is bound
With heavy tufts of moss, that strive
To drag it to the ground.

And this I know, full many a time,
When she was on the mountain high,
By day, and in the silent night,
When all the stars shone clear and bright,
That I have heard her cry,
'Oh misery! oh misery!
'O woe is me! oh misery!'

The Last of the Flock

In distant countries I have been,
And yet I have not often seen
A healthy man, a man full grown,
Weep in the public roads alone.
But such a one, on English ground,
And in the broad high-way, I met;
Along the broad high-way he came,
His cheeks with tears were wet.
Sturdy he seemed, though he was sad;
And in his arms a lamb he had.

He saw me, and he turned aside,
As if he wished himself to hide:
Then with his coat he made essay
To wipe those briny tears away.
I follow'd him, and said, 'My friend
'What ails you? wherefore weep you so?'
—'Shame on me, Sir! this lusty lamb,
He makes my tears to flow.
To-day I fetched him from the rock;
He is the last of all my flock.

When I was young, a single man,
And after youthful follies ran,
Though little given to care and thought,
Yet, so it was, a ewe I bought;
And other sheep from her I raised,
As healthy sheep as you might see,
And then I married, and was rich
As I could wish to be;
Of sheep I number'd a full score,
And every year encreas'd my store.

Year after year my stock it grew,
And from this one, this single ewe,
Full fifty comely sheep I raised,
As sweet a flock as ever grazed!
Upon the mountain did they feed;
They throve, and we at home did thrive.
—This lusty lamb of all my store
Is all that is alive:
And now I care not if we die,
And perish all of poverty.

Ten children, Sir! had I to feed,
Hard labour in a time of need!
My pride was tamed, and in our grief,
I of the parish ask'd relief.
They said I was a wealthy man;
My sheep upon the mountain fed,
And it was fit that thence I took
Whereof to buy us bread:'
'Do this; how can we give to you,'
They cried, 'what to the poor is due?'

I sold a sheep as they had said,
And bought my little children bread,
And they were healthy with their food;
For me it never did me good.
A woeful time it was for me,
To see the end of all my gains,
The pretty flock which I have reared
With all my care and pains,
To see it melt like snow away!
For me it was a woeful day.

Another still! and still another!
A little lamb, and then its mother!
It was a vein that never stopp'd,
Like blood-drops from my heart they dropp'd.
Till thirty were not left alive
They dwindled, dwindled, one by one,
And I may say that many a time
I wished they all were gone:
They dwindled one by one away;
For me it was a woeful day.

To wicked deeds I was inclined,
And wicked fancies cross'd my mind,
And every man I chanc'd to see,
I thought he knew some ill of me.
No peace, no comfort could I find,
No ease, within doors or without,
And crazily, and wearily,
I went my work about.
Oft-times I thought to run away;
For me it was a woeful day.

Sir! 'twas a precious flock to me,
As dear as my own children be;
For daily with my growing store
I loved my children more and more
Alas! it was an evil time;
God cursed me in my sore distress,
I prayed, yet every day I thought
I loved my children less;
And every week, and every day,
My flock, it seemed to melt away.

They dwindled, Sir, sad sight to see!
From ten to five, from five to three,
A lamb, a wether, and a ewe;
And then at last, from three to two;
And of my fifty, yesterday
I had but only one,
And here it lies upon my arm,
Alas! and I have none;
To-day I fetched it from the rock;
It is the last of all my flock.'

The Mad Mother

HER eyes are wild, her head is bare,
The sun has burnt her coal-black hair,
Her eye-brows have a rusty stain,
And she came far from over the main.

She has a baby on her arm,
Or else she were alone;
And underneath the hay-stack warm,
And on the green-wood stone,
She talked and sung the woods among;
And it was in the English tongue.

'Sweet babe! they say that I am mad,
But nay, my heart is far too glad;
And I am happy when I sing
Full many a sad and doleful thing:
Then, lovely baby, do not fear!
I pray thee have no fear of me,
But, safe as in a cradle, here
My lovely baby! thou shalt be,
To thee I know too much I owe;
I cannot work thee any woe.

A fire was once within my brain;
And in my head a dull, dull pain;
And fiendish faces one, two, three,
Hung at my breasts, and pulled at me.
But then there came a sight of joy;
It came at once to do me good;
I waked, and saw my little boy,
My little boy of flesh and blood;
Oh joy for me that sight to see!
For he was here, and only he.

Suck, little babe, oh suck again!
It cools my blood; it cools my brain;
Thy lips I feel them, baby! they
Draw from my heart the pain away.
Oh! press me with thy little hand;
It loosens something at my chest;
About that tight and deadly band
I feel thy little fingers press'd.
The breeze I see is in the tree;
It comes to cool my babe and me.

Oh! love me, love me, little boy!
Thou art thy mother's only joy;

And do not dread the waves below,
When o'er the sea-rock's edge we go;
The high crag cannot work me harm,
Nor leaping torrents when they howl;
The babe I carry on my arm,
He saves for me my precious soul;
Then happy lie, for blest am I;
Without me my sweet babe would die.

Then do not fear, my boy! for thee
Bold as a lion I will be;
And I will always be thy guide,
Through hollow snows and rivers wide.
I'll build an Indian bower; I know
The leaves that make the softest bed:
And if from me thou wilt not go,
But still be true 'till I am dead,
My pretty thing! then thou shalt sing,
As merry as the birds in spring.

Thy father cares not for my breast,
'Tis thine, sweet baby, there to rest:
'Tis all thine own! and if its hue
Be changed, that was so fair to view,
'Tis fair enough for thee, my dove!
My beauty, little child, is flown;
But thou wilt live with me in love,
And what if my poor cheek be brown?
'Tis well for me; thou canst not see
How pale and wan it else would be.

Dread not their taunts, my little life!
I am thy father's wedded wife;
And underneath the spreading tree
We two will live in honesty.
If his sweet boy he could forsake,
With me he never would have stay'd:
From him no harm my babe can take,
But he, poor man! is wretched made,
And every day we two will pray
For him that's gone and far away.

I'll teach my boy the sweetest things;
I'll teach him how the owlet sings.
My little babe! thy lips are still,
And thou hast almost suck'd thy fill.
—Where art thou gone my own dear child?
What wicked looks are those I see?
Alas! alas! that look so wild,
It never, never came from me:
If thou art mad, my pretty lad,
Then I must be for ever sad.

Oh! smile on me, my little lamb!
For I thy own dear mother am.
My love for thee has well been tried:
I've sought thy father far and wide.
I know the poisons of the shade,
I know the earth-nuts fit for food;
Then, pretty dear, be not afraid;
We'll find thy father in the wood.
Now laugh and be gay, to the woods away!
And there, my babe; we'll live for aye.

The Idiot Boy

'Tis eight o'clock,—a clear March night,
The moon is up—the sky is blue,
The owlet in the moonlight air,
He shouts from nobody knows where:
He lengthens out his lonely shout,
Halloo! halloo! a long halloo!

—Why bustle thus about your door,
What means this bustle, Betty Foy?
Why are you in this mighty fret?
And why on horseback have you set
Him whom you love, your idiot boy?

Beneath the moon that shines so bright,
Till she is tired, let Betty Foy
With girt and stirrup fiddle-faddle;
But wherefore set upon a saddle
Him whom she loves, her idiot boy?

There's scarce a soul that's out of bed;
Good Betty! put him down again;
His lips with joy they burr at you,
But, Betty! what has he to do
With stirrup, saddle, or with rein?

The world will say 'tis very idle,
Bethink you of the time of night;
There's not a mother, no not one,
But when she hears what you have done,
Oh! Betty she'll be in a fright.

But Betty's bent on her intent,
For her good neighbour, Susan Gale,
Old Susan, she who dwells alone,
Is sick, and makes a piteous moan,
As if her very life would fail.

There's not a house within a mile,
No hand to help them in distress:
Old Susan lies a bed in pain,
And sorely puzzled are the twain,
For what she ails they cannot guess.

And Betty's husband's at the wood,
Where by the week he doth abide,
A woodman in the distant vale;
There's none to help poor Susan Gale,
What must be done? what will betide?

And Betty from the lane has fetched
Her pony, that is mild and good,
Whether he be in joy or pain,
Feeding at will along the lane,
Or bringing faggots from the wood.

And he is all in travelling trim,
And by the moonlight, Betty Foy
Has up upon the saddle set,
The like was never heard of yet,
Him whom she loves, her idiot boy.

And he must post without delay
Across the bridge that's in the dale,
And by the church, and o'er the down,
To bring a doctor from the town,
Or she will die, old Susan Gale.

There is no need of boot or spur,
There is no need of whip or wand,
For Johnny has his holly-bough,
And with a hurly-burly now
He shakes the green bough in his hand.

And Betty o'er and o'er has told
The boy who is her best delight,
Both what to follow, what to shun,
What do, and what to leave undone,
How turn to left, and how to right.

And Betty's most especial charge,
Was, 'Johnny! Johnny! mind that you
'Come home again, nor stop at all,
'Come home again, whate'er befal,
'My Johnny do, I pray you do.'

To this did Johnny answer make,
Both with his head, and with his hand,
And proudly shook the bridle too,
And then! his words were not a few,
Which Betty well could understand.

And now that Johnny is just going,
Though Betty's in a mighty flurry,
She gently pats the pony's side,
On which her idiot boy must ride,
And seems no longer in a hurry.

But when the pony moved his legs,
Oh! then for the poor idiot boy!
For joy he cannot hold the bridle,
For joy his head and heels are idle,
He's idle all for very joy.

And while the pony moves his legs,
In Johnny's left-hand you may see,
The green bough's motionless and dead;
The moon that shines above his head
Is not more still and mute than he.

His heart it was so full of glee,
That till full fifty yards were gone,
He quite forgot his holly whip,
And all his skill in horsemanship,
Oh! happy, happy, happy John.

And Betty's standing at the door,
And Betty's face with joy o'erflows,
Proud of herself, and proud of him,
She sees him in his travelling trim;
How quietly her Johnny goes.

The silence of her idiot boy.
What hopes it sends to Betty's heart!
He's at the guide-post—he turns right,
She watches till he's out of sight,
And Betty will not then depart.

Burr, burr—now Johnny's lips they burr,
As loud as any mill, or near it,
Meek as a lamb the pony moves,
And Johnny makes the noise he loves,
And Betty listens, glad to hear it.

Away she hies to Susan Gale:
And Johnny's in a merry tune,
The owlets hoot, the owlets curr,
And Johnny's lips they burr, burr, burr,
And on he goes beneath the moon.

His steed and he right well agree,
For of this pony there's a rumour,
That should he lose his eyes and ears,
And should he live a thousand years,
He never will be out of humour.

But then he is a horse that thinks!
And when he thinks his pace is slack;
Now, though he knows poor Johnny well,
Yet for his life he cannot tell
What he has got upon his back.

So through the moonlight lanes they go,
And far into the moonlight dale,
And by the church, and o'er the down,
To bring a doctor from the town,
To comfort poor old Susan Gale.

And Betty, now at Susan's side,
Is in the middle of her story,
What comfort Johnny soon will bring,
With many a most diverting thing,
Of Johnny's wit and Johnny's glory.

And Betty's still at Susan's side:
By this time she's not quite so flurried;
Demure with porringer and plate
She sits, as if in Susan's fate
Her life and soul were buried.

But Betty, poor good woman! she,
You plainly in her face may read it,
Could lend out of that moment's store
Five years of happiness or more,
To any that might need it.

But yet I guess that now and then
With Betty all was not so well,
And to the road she turns her ears,
And thence full many a sound she hears,
Which she to Susan will not tell.

Poor Susan moans, poor Susan groans,
'As sure as there's a moon in heaven,'
Cries Betty, 'he'll be back again;
'They'll both be here, 'tis almost ten,
'They'll both be here before eleven.'

Poor Susan moans, poor Susan groans,
The clock gives warning for eleven;
'Tis on the stroke—'If Johnny's near,'
Quoth Betty 'he will soon be here,
'As sure as there's a moon in heaven.'

The clock is on the stroke of twelve,
And Johnny is not yet in sight,
The moon's in heaven, as Betty sees,
But Betty is not quite at ease;
And Susan has a dreadful night.

And Betty, half an hour ago,
On Johnny vile reflections cast;
'A little idle sauntering thing!'
With other names, an endless string,
But now that time is gone and past.

And Betty's drooping at the heart,
That happy time all past and gone,
'How can it be he is so late?
'The doctor he has made him wait,
'Susan! they'll both be here anon.'

And Susan's growing worse and worse,
And Betty's in a sad quandary;
And then there's nobody to say
If she must go or she must stay:
—She's in a sad quandary.

The clock is on the stroke of one;
But neither Doctor nor his guide
Appear along the moonlight road,
There's neither horse nor man abroad,
And Betty's still at Susan's side.

And Susan she begins to fear
Of sad mischances not a few,
That Johnny may perhaps be drown'd,
Or lost perhaps, and never found;
Which they must both for ever rue.

She prefaced half a hint of this
With, 'God forbid it should be true!'
At the first word that Susan said
Cried Betty, rising from the bed,
'Susan, I'd gladly stay with you.

'I must be gone, I must away,
'Consider, Johnny's but half-wise;
'Susan, we must take care of him,
'If he is hurt in life or limb'—
'Oh God forbid!' poor Susan cries.

'What can I do?' says Betty, going,
'What can I do to ease your pain?
'Good Susan tell me, and I'll stay;
'I fear you're in a dreadful way,
'But I shall soon be back again.'

'Good Betty go, good Betty go,
'There's nothing that can ease my pain.'
Then off she hies, but with a prayer
That God poor Susan's life would spare,
Till she comes back again.

So, through the moonlight lane she goes,
And far into the moonlight dale;
And how she ran, and how she walked,
And all that to herself she talked,
Would surely be a tedious tale.

In high and low, above, below,
In great and small, in round and square,
In tree and tower was Johnny seen,
In bush and brake, in black and green,
'Twas Johnny, Johnny, every where.

She's past the bridge that's in the dale,
And now the thought torments her sore,
Johnny perhaps his horse forsook,
To hunt the moon that's in the brook,
And never will be heard of more.

And now she's high upon the down,
Alone amid a prospect wide;
There's neither Johnny nor his horse,
Among the fern or in the gorse;
There's neither doctor nor his guide.

'Oh saints! what is become of him?
'Perhaps he's climbed into an oak,
'Where he will stay till he is dead;
'Or sadly he has been misled,
'And joined the wandering gypsey-folk.

'Or him that wicked pony's carried
'To the dark cave, the goblins' hall,
'Or in the castle he's pursuing,
'Among the ghosts, his own undoing;
'Or playing with the waterfall.'

At poor old Susan then she railed,
While to the town she posts away;
'If Susan had not been so ill,
'Alas! I should have had him still,
'My Johnny, till my dying day.'

Poor Betty! in this sad distemper,
The doctor's self would hardly spare,
Unworthy things she talked and wild,
Even he, of cattle the most mild,
The pony had his share.

And now she's got into the town,
And to the doctor's door she hies;
'Tis silence all on every side;
The town so long, the town so wide,
Is silent as the skies.

And now she's at the doctor's door,
She lifts the knocker, rap, rap, rap,
The doctor at the casement shews,
His glimmering eyes that peep and doze;
And one hand rubs his old night-cap.

'Oh Doctor! Doctor! where's my Johnny?'
'I'm here, what is't you want with me?'
'Oh Sir! you know I'm Betty Foy,
'And I have lost my poor dear boy,
'You know him—him you often see;

'He's not so wise as some folks be,'
'The devil take his wisdom!' said
The Doctor, looking somewhat grim,
'What, woman! should I know of him?'
And, grumbling, he went back to bed.

'O woe is me! O woe is me!
'Here will I die; here will I die;
'I thought to find my Johnny here,
'But he is neither far nor near,
'Oh! what a wretched mother I!'

She stops, she stands, she looks about,
Which way to turn she cannot tell.
Poor Betty! it would ease her pain
If she had heart to knock again;
—The clock strikes three—a dismal knell!

Then up along the town she hies,
No wonder if her senses fail,
This piteous news so much it shock'd her,
She quite forgot to send the Doctor,
To comfort poor old Susan Gale.

And now she's high upon the down,
And she can see a mile of road,
'Oh cruel! I'm almost three-score;
'Such night as this was ne'er before,
'There's not a single soul abroad.'

She listens, but she cannot hear
The foot of horse, the voice of man;
The streams with softest sound are flowing,
The grass you almost hear it growing,
You hear it now if e'er you can.

The owlets through the long blue night
Are shouting to each other still:
Fond lovers, yet not quite hob nob,
They lengthen out the tremulous sob,
That echoes far from hill to hill.

Poor Betty now has lost all hope,
Her thoughts are bent on deadly sin;
A green-grown pond she just has pass'd,
And from the brink she hurries fast,
Lest she should drown herself therein.

And now she sits her down and weeps;
Such tears she never shed before;
'Oh dear, dear pony! my sweet joy!
'Oh carry back my idiot boy!
'And we will ne'er o'erload thee more.'

A thought is come into her head;
'The pony he is mild and good,
'And we have always used him well;
'Perhaps he's gone along the dell,
'And carried Johnny to the wood.'

Then up she springs as if on wings;
She thinks no more of deadly sin;
If Betty fifty ponds should see,
The last of all her thoughts would be,
To drown herself therein.

Oh reader! now that I might tell
What Johnny and his horse are doing!
What they've been doing all this time.
Oh could I put into rhyme,
A most delightful tale pursuing!

Perhaps, and no unlikely thought!
He with his pony now doth roam
The cliffs and peaks so high that are,
To lay his hands upon a star,
And in his pocket bring it home.

Perhaps he's turned himself about,
His face unto his horse's tail,
And still and mute, in wonder lost,
All like a silent horseman-ghost,
He travels on along the vale.

And now, perhaps, he's hunting sheep,
A fierce and dreadful hunter he!
Yon valley, that's so trim and green,
In five months' time, should he be seen,
A desart wilderness will be.

Perhaps, with head and heels on fire,
And like the very soul of evil,
He's galloping away, away,
And so he'll gallop on for aye,
The bane of all that dread the devil.

I to the muses have been bound,
These fourteen years, by strong indentures;
Oh gentle muses! let me tell
But half of what to him befel,
For sure he met with strange adventures.

Oh gentle muses! is this kind?
Why will ye thus my suit repel?
Why of your further aid bereave me?
And can ye thus unfriended leave me?
Ye muses! whom I love so well.

Who's yon, that, near the waterfall,
Which thunders down with headlong force,
Beneath the moon, yet shining fair,
As careless as if nothing were,
Sits upright on a feeding horse?

Unto his horse, that's feeding free,
He seems, I think, the rein to give;
Of moon or stars he takes no heed;
Of such we in romances read,
—'Tis Johnny! Johnny! as I live.

And that's the very pony too.
Where is she, where is Betty Foy?
She hardly can sustain her fears;
The roaring waterfall she hears,
And cannot find her idiot boy.

Your pony's worth his weight in gold,
Then calm your terrors, Betty Foy!
She's coming from among the trees,
And now, all full in view, she sees
Him whom she loves, her idiot boy.

And Betty sees the pony too:
Why stand you thus Good Betty Foy?
It is no goglin, 'tis no ghost,
'Tis he whom you so long have lost,
He whom you love, your idiot boy.

She looks again—her arms are up—
She screams—she cannot move for joy;
She darts as with a torrent's force,
She almost has o'erturned the horse,
And fast she hold her idiot boy.

And Johnny burrs and laughs aloud,
Whether in cunning or in joy,
I cannot tell; but while he laughs,
Betty a drunken pleasure quaffs,
To hear again her idiot boy.

And now she's at the pony's tail,
And now she's at the pony's head,
On that side now, and now on this,
And almost stifled with her bliss,
A few sad tears does Betty shed.

She kisses o'er and o'er again,
Him whom she loves, her idiot boy,
She's happy here, she's happy there,
She is uneasy every where;
Her limbs are all alive with joy.

She pats the pony, where or when
She knows not, happy Betty Foy!
The little pony glad may be,
But he is milder far than she,
You hardly can perceive his joy.

'Oh! Johnny, never mind the Doctor;
'You've done your best, and that is all.'
She took the reins, when this was said,
And gently turned the pony's head
From the loud waterfall.

By this the stars were almost gone,
The moon was setting on the hill,
So pale you scarcely looked at her:
The little birds began to stir,
Though yet their tongues were still.

The pony, Betty, and her boy,
Wind slowly through the woody dale:
And who is she, be-times abroad,
That hobbles up the steep rough road?
Who is it, but old Susan Gale?

Long Susan lay deep lost in thought,
And many dreadful fears beset her,
Both for her messenger and nurse;
And as her mind grew worse and worse,
Her body it grew better.

She turned, she toss'd herself in bed,
On all sides doubts and terrors met her;
Point after point did she discuss;
And while her mind was fighting thus,
Her body still grew better.

'Alas! what is become of them?
'These fears can never be endured,
'I'll to the wood.'—The word scarce said,
Did Susan rise up from her bed,
As if by magic cured.

Away she posts up hill and down,
And to the wood at length is come,
She spies her friends, she shouts a greeting;
Oh me! it is a merry meeting,
As ever was in Christendom.

The owls have hardly sung their last,
While our four travellers homeward wend;
The owls have hooted all night long,
And with the owls began my song,
And with the owls must end.

For while they all were travelling home,
Cried Betty, 'Tell us Johnny, do,
'Where all this long night you have been,
'What you have heard, what you have seen,
'And Johnny, mind you tell us true.'

Now Johnny all night long had heard
The owls in tuneful concert strive;
No doubt too he the moon had seen;
For in the moonlight he had been
From eight o'clock till five.

And thus to Betty's question, he
Made answer, like a traveller bold,
(His very words I give to you,)
'The cocks did crow to-whoo, to-whoo,
'And the sun did shine so cold.'
—Thus answered Johnny in his glory,
And that was all his travel's story.

Lines

WRITTEN NEAR RICHMOND, UPON THE THAMES, AT EVENING

How rich the wave, in front, imprest
With evening-twilight's summer hues,
While, facing thus the crimson west,
The boat her silent path pursues!

Looking South down the lake to Lodore Falls by J.M.W. Turner (1775—1851). The lake is Derwentwater which features frequently in Wordsworth's works, including "The Female Vagrant".
By courtesy of the British Museum, London

Derwentwater from Castle Crag by John Emes (*fl.* 1783–1810). Near here, in early 1794, Wordsworth and Dorothy spent some weeks at Windy Brow, a cottage which belonged to the family of their friend Raisley Calvert and which gave them an early realization of their dream of a cottage together.
By courtesy of Abbot Hall Art Gallery, Kendal

And see how dark the backward stream!
A little moment past, so smiling!
And still, perhaps, with faithless gleam,
Some other loiterer beguiling.

Such views the youthful bard allure,
But, heedless of the following gloom,
He deems their colours shall endure
'Till peace go with him to the tomb.
—And let him nurse his fond deceit,
And what if he must die in sorrow!
Who would not cherish dreams so sweet,
Though grief and pain may come to-morrow?

Glide gently, thus for ever glide,
O Thames! that other bards may see,
As lovely visions by thy side
As now, fair river! come to me.
Oh glide, fair stream! for ever so;
Thy quiet soul on all bestowing,
'Till all our minds for ever flow,
As thy deep waters now are flowing.

Vain thought! yet be as now thou art,
That in thy waters may be seen
The image of a poet's heart,
How bright, how solemn, how serene!
Such heart did once the poet bless,
Who, pouring here a *later* ditty,
Could find no refuge from distress,
But in the milder grief of pity.

Remembrance! as we glide along,
For him suspend the dashing oar,
And pray that never child of Song
May know his freezing sorrows more.
How calm! how still! the only sound,
The dripping of the oar suspended!
—The evening darkness gathers round
By virtue's holiest powers attended.

Expostulation and Reply

'Why William, on that old grey stone,
'Thus for the length of half a day,
'Why William, sit you thus alone,
'And dream your time away?

'Where are your books? that light bequeath'd
'To beings else forlorn and blind!
'Up! Up! and drink the spirit breath'd
'From dead men to their kind.

'You look round on your mother earth,
'As if she for no purpose bore you;
'As if you were her first-born birth,
'And none had lived before you!'

One morning thus, by Esthwaite lake,
When life was sweet I knew not why,
To me my good friend Matthew spake,
And thus I made reply.

'The eye it cannot chuse but see,
'We cannot bid the ear be still;
'Our bodies feel, where'er they be,
'Against, or with our will.

'Nor less I deem that there are powers,
'Which of themselves our minds impress,
'That we can feed this mind of ours,
'In a wise passiveness.

'Think you, mid all this mighty sum
'Of things for ever speaking,
'That nothing of itself will come,
'But we must still be seeking?

'—Then ask not wherefore, here, alone,
'Conversing as I may,
'I sit upon this old grey stone,
'And dream my time away.'

The Tables Turned;

AN EVENING SCENE, ON THE SAME SUBJECT

Up! up! my friend, and clear your looks,
Why all this toil and trouble?
Up! up! my friend, and quit your books,
Or surely you'll grow double.

The sun above the mountain's head,
A freshening lustre mellow,
Through all the long green fields has spread,
His first sweet evening yellow.

Books! 'tis a dull and endless strife,
Come, hear the woodland linnet,
How sweet his music; on my life
There's more of wisdom in it.

And hark! how blithe the throstle sings!
And he is no mean preacher;
Come forth into the light of things,
Let Nature be your teacher.

She has a world of ready wealth,
Our minds and hearts to bless—
Spontaneous wisdom breathed by health,
Truth breathed by cheerfulness.

One impulse from a vernal wood
May teach you more of man;
Of moral evil and of good,
Than all the sages can.

Sweet is the lore which nature brings;
Our meddling intellect
Misshapes the beauteous forms of things
—We murder to dissect.

Enough of science and of art;
Close up these barren leaves;
Come forth, and bring with you a heart
That watches and receives.

Old Man Travelling;
ANIMAL TRANQUILLITY AND DECAY,
A SKETCH

The little hedge-row birds,
That peck along the road, regard him not.
He travels on, and in his face, his step,
His gait, is one expression; every limb,
His look and bending figure, all bespeak
A man who does not move with pain, but moves
With thought—He is insensibly subdued
To settled quiet: he is one by whom
All effort seems forgotten, one to whom
Long patience has such mild composure given,
That patience now doth seem a thing, of which
He hath no need. He is by nature led
To peace so perfect, that the young behold
With envy, what the old man hardly feels.
—I asked him whither he was bound, and what
The object of his journey; he replied
'Sir! I am going many miles to take
'A last leave of my son, a mariner,
'Who from a sea-fight has been brought to Falmouth,
And there is dying in an hospital.'

The Complaint of a Forsaken Indian Woman

[When a Northern Indian, from sickness, is unable to continue hi journey with his companions, he is left behind, covered over with Dee skins, and is supplied with water, food, and fuel if the situation of th place will afford it. He is informed of the track which his companion intend to pursue, and if he is unable to follow, or overtake them, h perishes alone in the Desart; unless he should have the good fortune to fall in with some other Tribes of Indians. It is unnecessary to add that the females are equally, or still more, exposed to the same fate. See that very interesting work, 'Hearne's Journey from Hudson's Bay to the Northern Ocean'. When the Northern Lights, as the same writer informs us, vary their position in the air, they make a rustling and a crackling noise. This circumstance is alluded to in the first stanza of the following poem].

BEFORE I see another day,
Oh let my body die away!
In sleep I heard the northern gleams;
The stars they were among my dreams;
In sleep did I behold the skies,
I saw the crackling flashes drive;
And yet they are upon my eyes,
And yet I am alive.
Before I see another day,
Oh let my body die away!

My fire is dead: it knew no pain;
Yet is it dead, and I remain.
All stiff with ice the ashes lie;
And they are dead, and I will die.
When I was well, I wished to live,
For clothes, for warmth, for food, and fire;
But they to me no joy can give,
No pleasure now, and no desire.
Then here contented will I lie;
Alone I cannot fear to die.

Alas! you might have dragged me on
Another day, a single one!
Too soon despair o'er me prevailed;
Too soon my heartless spirit failed;
When you were gone my limbs were stronger,
And Oh how grievously I rue,
That, afterwards, a little longer,
My friends, I did not follow you!
For strong and without pain I lay,
My friends, when you were gone away.

My child! they gave thee to another,
A woman who was not thy mother.

When from my arms my babe they took,
On me how strangely did he look!
Through his whole body something ran,
A most strange something did I see;
—As if he strove to be a man,
That he might pull the sledge for me.
And then he stretched his arms, how wild!
Oh mercy! like a little child.

My little joy! my little pride!
In two days more I must have died.
Then do not weep and grieve for me;
I feel I must have died with thee.
Oh wind that o'er my head art flying,
The way my friends their course did bend,
I should not feel the pain of dying,
Could I with thee a message send.
Too soon, my friends, you went away;
For I had many things to say.

I'll follow you across the snow,
You travel heavily and slow:
In spite of all my weary pain,
I'll look upon your tents again.
My fire is dead, and snowy white
The water which beside it stood;
The wolf has come to me to-night,
And he has stolen away my food.
For ever left alone am I,
Then wherefore should I fear to die?

My journey will be shortly run,
I shall not see another sun,
I cannot lift my limbs to know
If they have any life or no.
My poor forsaken child! if I
For once could have thee close to me,
With happy heart I then would die,
And my last thoughts would happy be.
I feel my body die away,
I shall not see another day.

The Convict

The glory of evening was spread through the west;
 —On the slope of a mountain I stood,
While the joy that precedes the calm season of rest
 Rang loud through the meadow and wood.

'And must we then part from a dwelling so fair?'
 In the pain of my spirit I said,
And with a deep sadness I turned, to repair
 To the cell where the convict is laid.

The thick-ribbed walls that o'ershadow the gate
 Resound; and the dungeons unfold:
I pause; and at length, through the glimmering grate,
 That outcast of pity behold.

His black matted head on his shoulder is bent,
 And deep is the sigh of his breath,
And with stedfast dejection his eyes are intent
 On the fetters that link him to death.

'Tis sorrow enough on that visage to gaze,
 That body dismiss'd from his care;
Yet my fancy has pierced to his heart, and pourtrays
 More terrible images there.

His bones are consumed, and his life-blood is dried,
 With wishes the past to undo;
And his crime, through the pains that o'erwhelm him, descried,
 Still blackens and grows on his view.

When from the dark synod, or blood-reeking field,
 To his chamber the monarch is led,
All soothers of sense their soft virtue shall yield,
 And quietness pillow his head.

But if grief, self-consumed, in oblivion would doze,
 And conscience her tortures appease,
'Mid tumult and uproar this man must repose;
 In the comfortless vault of disease.

When his fetters at night have so press'd on his limbs,
  That the weight can no longer be borne,
If, while a half-slumber his memory bedims,
  The wretch on his pallet should turn,

While the jail-mastiff howls at the dull clanking chain,
  From the roots of his hair there shall start
A thousand sharp punctures of cold-sweating pain,
  And terror shall leap at his heart.

But now he half-raises his deep-sunken eye,
  And the motion unsettles a tear;
The silence of sorrow it seems to supply,
  And asks of me why I am here.

'Poor victim! no idle intruder has stood
  'With o'erweening complacence our state to compare,
'But one, whose first wish is the wish to be good,
  'Is come as a brother thy sorrows to share.

'At thy name though compassion her nature resign,
  'Though in virtue's proud mouth thy report be a stain,
'My care, if the arm of the mighty were mine,
  'Would plant thee where yet thou might'st blossom again.

Lines

WRITTEN A FEW MILES ABOVE TINTERN ABBEY, ON REVISITING THE BANKS OF THE WYE DURING A TOUR, JULY 13, 1798

Five years have passed; five summers, with the length
Of five long winters! and again I hear
These waters, rolling from their mountain-springs
With a sweet inland murmur.—Once again
Do I behold these steep and lofty cliffs,
Which on a wild secluded scene impress
Thoughts of more deep seclusion; and connect
The landscape with the quiet of the sky.
The day is come when I again repose
Here, under this dark sycamore, and view

These plots of cottage-ground, these orchard-tufts,
Which, at this season, with their unripe fruits,
Among the woods and copses lose themselves,
Nor, with their green and simple hue, disturb
The wild green landscape. Once again I see
These hedge-rows, hardly hedge-rows, little lines
Of sportive wood run wild; these pastoral farms
Green to the very door; and wreathes of smoke
Sent up, in silence, from among the trees,
With some uncertain notice, as might seem,
Of vagrant dwellers in the houseless woods,
Or of some hermit's cave, where by his fire
The hermit sits alone.

Though absent long,
These forms of beauty have not been to me,
As is a landscape to a blind man's eye:
But oft, in lonely rooms, and mid the din
Of towns and cities, I have owed to them,
In hours of weariness, sensations sweet,
Felt in the blood, and felt along the heart,
And passing even into my purer mind
With tranquil restoration:—feelings too
Of unremembered pleasure; such, perhaps,
As may have had no trivial influence
On that best portion of a good man's life;
His little, nameless, unremembered acts
Of kindness and of love. Nor less, I trust,
To them I may have owed another gift,
Of aspect more sublime; that blessed mood,
In which the burthen of the mystery,
In which the heavy and the weary weight
Of all this unintelligible world
Is lighten'd:—that serene and blessed mood,
In which the affections gently lead us on,
Until, the breath of this corporeal frame,
And even the motion of our human blood
Almost suspended, we are laid asleep
In body, and become a living soul:
While with an eye made quiet by the power
Of harmony, and the deep power of joy,
We see into the life of things.

If this
Be but a vain belief, yet, oh! how oft,
In darkness, and amid the many shapes
Of joyless day-light; when the fretful stir
Unprofitable, and the fever of the world,
Have hung upon the beatings of my heart,
How oft, in spirit, have I turned to thee
O sylvan Wye! Thou wanderer through the woods,
How often has my spirit turned to thee!
And now, with gleams of half-extinguish'd thought,
With many recognitions dim and faint,
And somewhat of a sad perplexity,
The picture of the mind revives again:
While here I stand, not only with the sense
Of present pleasure, but with pleasing thoughts
That in this moment there is life and food
For future years. And so I dare to hope
Though changed, no doubt, from what I was, when first
I came among these hills; when like a roe
I bounded o'er the mountains, by the sides
Of the deep rivers, and the lonely streams,
Wherever nature led; more like a man
Flying from something that he dreads, than one
Who sought the thing he loved. For nature then
(The coarser pleasures of my boyish days,
And their glad animal movements all gone by,)
To me was all in all.—I cannot paint
What then I was. The sounding cataract
Haunted me like a passion: the tall rock,
The mountain, and the deep and gloomy wood,
Their colours and their forms, were then to me
An appetite: a feeling and a love,
That had no need of a remoter charm,
By thought supplied, or any interest
Unborrowed from the eye.—That time is past,
And all its aching joys are now no more,
And all its dizzy raptures. Not for this
Faint I, nor mourn nor murmur: other gifts
Have followed, for such loss, I would believe,
Abundant recompence. For I have learned
To look on nature, not as in the hour
Of thoughtless youth, but hearing oftentimes

The still, sad music of humanity,
Not harsh nor grating, though of ample power
To chasten and subdue. And I have felt
A presence that disturbs me with the joy
Of elevated thoughts; a sense sublime
Of something far more deeply interfused,
Whose dwelling is the light of setting suns,
And the round ocean, and the living air,
And the blue sky, and in the mind of man,
A motion and a spirit, that impels
All thinking things, all objects of all thought,
And rolls through all things. Therefore am I still
A lover of the meadows and the woods,
And mountains; and of all that we behold
From this green earth; of all the mighty world
Of eye and ear, both what they half-create,
And what perceive; well pleased to recognize
In nature and the language of the sense,
The anchor of my purest thoughts, the nurse,
The guide, the guardian of my heart, and soul
Of all my moral being.

Nor, perchance,
If I were not thus taught, should I the more
Suffer my genial spirits to decay:
For thou art with me, here, upon the banks
Of this fair river; thou, my dearest Friend,
My dear, dear Friend, and in thy voice I catch
The language of my former heart, and read
My former pleasures in the shooting lights
Of thy wild eyes. Oh! yet a little while
May I behold in thee what I was once,
My dear, dear Sister! And this prayer I make,
Knowing that Nature never did betray
The heart that loved her; 'tis her privilege,
Through all the years of this our life, to lead
From joy to joy: for she can so inform
The mind that is within us, so impress
With quietness and beauty, and so feed
With lofty thoughts, that neither evil tongues,
Rash judgments, nor the sneers of selfish men,
Nor greetings where no kindness is, nor all

The dreary intercourse of daily life,
Shall e'er prevail against us, or disturb
Our chearful faith that all which we behold
Is full of blessings. Therefore let the moon
Shine on thee in thy solitary walk;
And let the misty mountain winds be free
To blow against thee: and in after years,
When these wild ecstasies shall be matured
Into a sober pleasure, when thy mind
Shall be a mansion for all lovely forms,
Thy memory be as a dwelling-place
For all sweet sounds and harmonies; Oh! then,
If solitude, or fear, or pain, or grief,
Should be thy portion, with what healing thoughts
Of tender joy wilt thou remember me,
And these my exhortations! Nor, perchance,
If I should be, where I no more can hear
Thy voice, nor catch from thy wild eyes these gleams
Of past existence, wilt thou then forget
That on the banks of this delightful stream
We stood together; and that I, so long
A worshipper of Nature, hither came,
Unwearied in that service: rather say
With warmer love, oh! with far deeper zeal
Of holier love. Nor wilt thou then forget,
That after many wanderings, many years
Of absence, these steep woods and lofty cliffs,
And this green pastoral landscape, were to me
More dear, both for themselves, and for thy sake.

THE RECLUSE

Part First

BOOK FIRST: HOME AT GRASMERE

EDITOR'S NOTE

MOST of this was written in the Spring of 1800 and describes the fir months of William's and Dorothy's Grasmere home. The final passag beginning

On Man, on Nature, and on Human Life

was probably written two years earlier at Alfoxden. It was publishe in 1814 as a 'Prospectus' to the *Excursion.*

Otherwise, except for some short passages, the poem remained i manuscript until published in 1888. For copyright reasons it was e cluded from pre-1939 collected editions.

The text here printed was from a transcript of about the year 181 which embodied some corrections of the original.

THE RECLUSE

HOME AT GRASMERE

ONCE to the verge of yon steep barrier came
A roving School-boy; what the Adventurer's age
Hath now escaped his memory—but the hour,
One of a golden summer holiday,
He well remembers, though the year be gone.
Alone and devious from afar he came;
And, with a sudden influx overpowered
At sight of this seclusion, he forgot
His haste, for hasty had his footsteps been
As boyish his pursuits; and, sighing said,
'What happy fortune were it here to live!
And, if a thought of dying, if a thought
Of mortal separation, could intrude
With paradise before him, here to die!'
No Prophet was he, had not even a hope,
Scarcely a wish, but one bright pleasing thought,
A fancy in the heart of what might be
The lot of Others, never could be his.
  The Station whence he look'd was soft and green,
Not giddy yet aerial, with a depth
Of Vale below, a height of hills above.
For rest of body, perfect was the Spot,
All that luxurious nature could desire,
But stirring to the Spirit; who could gaze
And not feel motions there? He thought of clouds
That sail on winds; of Breezes that delight
To play on water, or in endless chase
Pursue each other through the yielding plain
Of grass or corn, over and through and through,
In billow after billow, evermore
Disporting. Nor unmindful was the Boy
Of sunbeams, shadows, butterflies and birds,
Of fluttering Sylphs and softly-gliding Fays,

Genii, and winged Angels that are Lords
Without restraint of all which they behold.
The illusion strengthening as he gazed, he felt
That such unfettered liberty was his,
Such power and joy; but only for this end,
To flit from field to rock, from rock to field,
From shore to island, and from isle to shore,
From open ground to covert, from a bed
Of meadow-flowers into a tuft of wood;
From high to low, from low to high, yet still
Within the bound of this high Concave; here
Must be his Home, this Valley be his World.
  Since that day forth the place to him—*to me*
(For I who live to register the truth
Was that same young and happy Being) became
As beautiful to thought, as it had been,
When present, to the bodily sense; a haunt
Of pure affections, shedding upon joy
A brighter joy; and through such damp and gloom
Of the gay mind, as ofttimes splenetic Youth
Mistakes for sorrow, darting beams of light
That no self-cherished sadness could withstand:
And now 'tis mine, perchance for life, dear Vale,
Beloved Grasmere (let the Wandering Streams
Take up, the cloud-capt hills repeat, the Name),
One of thy lowly Dwellings is my Home.
  And was the cost so great? and could it seem
An act of courage, and the thing itself
A conquest? who must bear the blame? sage Man
Thy prudence, thy experience—thy desires,
Thy apprehensions—blush thou for them all.
  Yes, the realities of life so cold,
So cowardly, so ready to betray,
So stinted in the measure of their grace
As we pronounce them, doing them much wrong,
Have been to me more bountiful than hope,
Less timid than desire—but that is passed.
  On Nature's invitation do I come,
By Reason sanctioned—Can the choice mislead,
That made the calmest, fairest spot of earth,
With all its unappropriated good,
My own; and not mine only, for with me

Entrenched, say rather peacefully embowered,
Under yon Orchard, in yon humble Cot,
A younger Orphan of a Home extinct,
The only Daughter of my Parents, dwells.
Aye, think on that, my Heart, and cease to stir,
Pause upon that, and let the breathing frame
No longer breathe, but all be satisfied.
—Oh if such silence be not thanks to God
For what hath been bestowed, then where, where then
Shall gratitude find rest? Mine eyes did ne'er
Fix on a lovely object, nor my mind
Take pleasure in the midst of happy thoughts,
But either She whom now I have, who now
Divides with me this loved Abode, was there,
Or not far off. Where'er my footsteps turned,
Her Voice was like a hidden Bird that sang,
The thought of her was like a flash of light,
Or an *unseen* companionship, a breath
Of fragrance independent of the wind.
In all my goings, in the new and old
Of all my meditations, and in this
Favorite of all, in this the most of all.
—What Being, therefore, since the birth of Man
Had ever more abundant cause to speak
Thanks, and if favours of the Heavenly Muse
Make him more thankful, then to call on verse
To aid him, and in Song resound his joy.
The boon is absolute; surpassing grace
To me hath been vouchsafed; among the bowers
Of blissful Eden this was neither given,
Nor could be given, possession of the good
Which had been sighed for, ancient thought fulfilled
And dear Imaginations realized
Up to their highest measure, yea and more.
Embrace me then, ye Hills, and close me in,
Now in the clear and open day I feel
Your guardianship; I take it to my heart;
'Tis like the solemn shelter of the night.
But I would call thee beautiful, for mild
And soft, and gay, and beautiful thou art,
Dear Valley, having in thy face a smile
Though peaceful, full of gladness. Thou art pleased,

Pleased with thy crags, and woody steeps, thy Lake,
Its one green Island and its winding shores;
The multitude of little rocky hills,
Thy Church and Cottages of mountain stone
Clustered like stars some few, but single most,
And lurking dimly in their shy retreats,
Or glancing at each other chearful looks,
Like separated stars with clouds between.
What want we? have we not perpetual streams,
Warm woods, and sunny hills, and fresh green fields,
And mountains not less green, and flocks and herds,
And thickets full of songsters, and the voice
Of lordly birds, an unexpected sound
Heard now and then from morn to latest eve,
Admonishing the man who walks below
Of solitude, and silence in the sky?
These have we, and a thousand nooks of earth
Have also these, but nowhere else is found,
Nowhere (or is it fancy?) can be found
The one sensation that is here; 'tis here,
Here as it found its way into my heart
In childhood, here as it abides by day,
By night, here only; or in chosen minds
That take it with them hence, where'er they go.
'Tis, but I cannot name it, 'tis the sense
Of majesty, and beauty, and repose,
A blended holiness of earth and sky,
Something that makes this individual Spot,
This small Abiding-place of many Men,
A termination, and a last retreat,
A Centre, come from wheresoe'er you will,
A Whole without dependence or defect,
Made for itself; and happy in itself,
Perfect Contentment, Unity entire.
   Bleak season was it, turbulent and bleak,
When hitherward we journeyed, side by side,
Through bursts of sunshine and through flying showers,
Paced the long Vales, how long they were, and yet
How fast that length of way was left behind,
Wensley's rich Vale, and Sedbergh's naked heights.
The frosty wind, as if to make amends
For its keen breath, was aiding to our steps,

And drove us onward like two ships at sea,
Or like two Birds, companions in mid air,
Parted and reunited by the blast.
Stern was the face of Nature; we rejoiced
In that stern countenance, for our Souls thence drew
A feeling of their strength. The naked Trees,
The icy brooks, as on we passed, appeared
To question us. 'Whence come ye? to what end?'
They seemed to say; 'What would ye,' said the shower,
'Wild Wanderers, whither through my dark domain?'
The sunbeam said, 'be happy.' When this Vale
We entered, bright and solemn was the sky
That faced us with a passionate welcoming,
And led us to our threshold. Daylight failed
Insensibly, and round us gently fell
Composing darkness, with a quiet load
Of full contentment, in a little Shed
Disturbed, uneasy in itself as seemed,
And wondering at its new inhabitants.
It loves us now, this Vale so beautiful
Begins to love us! By a sullen storm,
Two months unwearied of severest storm,
It put the temper of our minds to proof,
And found us faithful through the gloom, and heard
The Poet mutter his prelusive songs
With chearful heart, an unknown voice of joy,
Among the silence of the woods and hills;
Silent to any gladsomeness of sound
With all their Shepherds.
But the gates of Spring
Are opened; churlish Winter hath given leave
That she should entertain for this one day,
Perhaps for many genial days to come,
His guests, and make them jocund. They are pleased,
But most of all the Birds that haunt the flood,
With the mild summons; inmates though they be
Of Winter's household, they keep festival
This day, who drooped, or seemed to droop, so long;
They show their pleasure, and shall I do less?
Happier of happy though I be, like them
I cannot take possession of the sky,
Mount with a thoughtless impulse, and wheel there,

One of a mighty multitude, whose way
Is a perpetual harmony and dance
Magnificent. Behold, how with a grace
Of ceaseless motion, that might scarcely seem
Inferior to angelical, they prolong
Their curious pastime, shaping in mid air,
And sometimes with ambitious wing that soars
High as the level of the mountain tops,
A circuit ampler than the lake beneath,
Their own domain;—but ever, while intent
On tracing and retracing that large round,
Their jubilant activity evolves
Hundreds of curves and circlets, to and fro,
Upwards and downwards, progress intricate
Yet unperplexed, as if one spirit swayed
Their indefatigable flight. 'Tis done—
Ten times and more, I fancied it had ceased;
But lo! the vanished company again
Ascending, they approach—I hear their wings
Faint, faint at first; and then an eager sound
Passed in a moment—and as faint again!
They tempt the sun to sport among their plumes;
Tempt the smooth water, or the gleaming ice,
To show them a fair image,—'tis themselves,
Their own fair forms upon the glimmering plain,
Painted more soft and fair as they descend,
Almost to touch;—then up again aloft,
Up with a sally, and a flash of speed,
As if they scorned both resting-place and rest!
This day is a thanksgiving, 'tis a day
Of glad emotion and deep quietness;
Not upon me alone hath been bestowed,
Me rich in many onward-looking thoughts,
The penetrating bliss; oh surely these
Have felt it, not the happy Quires of Spring,
Her own peculiar family of love
That sport among green leaves, a blither train.
  But two are missing—two, a lonely pair
Of milk-white Swans, wherefore are they not seen
Partaking this day's pleasure? From afar
They came, to sojourn here in solitude,
Chusing this Valley, they who had the choice

Of the whole world. We saw them day by day,
Through those two months of unrelenting storm,
Conspicuous at the centre of the Lake,
Their safe retreat; we knew them well, I guess
That the whole Valley knew them; but to us
They were more dear than may be well believed,
Not only for their beauty, and their still
And placid way of life, and constant love
Inseparable, not for these alone,
But that their state so much resembled ours,
They having also chosen this abode;
They strangers, and we strangers; they a pair,
And we a solitary pair like them.
They should not have departed; many days
Did I look forth in vain, nor on the wing
Could see them, nor in that small open space
Of blue unfrozen water, where they lodged,
And lived so long in quiet, side by side.
Shall we behold them, consecrated friends,
Faithful Companions, yet another year
Surviving, they for us, and we for them,
And neither pair be broken? Nay perchance
It is too late already for such hope,
The Dalesmen may have aimed the deadly tube,
And parted them; or haply both are gone
One death, and that were mercy given to both.
Recal, my song, the ungenerous thought; forgive,
Thrice favoured Region, the conjecture harsh
Of such inhospitable penalty,
Inflicted upon confidence so pure.
Ah, if I wished to follow where the sight
Of all that is before my eyes, the voice
Which speaks from a presiding Spirit here,
Would lead me, I should whisper to myself;
They who are dwellers in this holy place
Must needs themselves be hallowed, they require
No benediction from the Stranger's lips,
For they are blest already. None would give
The greeting 'peace be with you' unto them,
For peace they have, it cannot but be theirs,
And mercy, and forbearance. Nay—not these,
Their healing offices a pure good-will

Precludes, and charity beyond the bounds
Of charity—an overflowing love,
Not for the Creature only, but for all
That is around them, love for every thing
Which in their happy Region they behold!

Thus do we soothe ourselves, and when the thought
Is pass'd we blame it not for having come.
What if I floated down a pleasant Stream,
And now am landed, and the motion gone,
Shall I reprove myself? Ah no, the Stream
Is flowing, and will never cease to flow,
And I shall float upon that Stream again.
By such forgetfulness the Soul becomes,
Words cannot say, how beautiful; then hail,
Hail to the visible Presence, hail to thee,
Delightful Valley, habitation fair!
And to whatever else of outward form
Can give an inward help, can purify,
And elevate, and harmonize, and soothe,
And steal away, and for a while deceive
And lap in pleasing rest, and bear us on
Without desire in full complacency,
Contemplating perfection absolute
And entertained as in a placid sleep.

But not betrayed by tenderness of mind
That feared, or wholly overlook'd the truth,
Did we come hither, with romantic hope
To find in midst of so much loveliness
Love, perfect love; of so much majesty
A like majestic frame of mind in those
Who here abide, the persons like the place.
Not from such hope, or aught of such belief
Hath issued any portion of the joy
Which I have felt this day. An awful voice,
'Tis true, hath in my walks been often heard,
Sent from the mountains or the sheltered fields,
Shout after shout—reiterated whoop
In manner of a bird that takes delight
In answering to itself; or like a hound
Single at chase among the lonely woods,
His yell repeating; yet it was in truth
A human voice—a Spirit of coming night,

How solemn when the sky is dark, and earth
Not dark, nor yet enlightened, but by snow
Made visible, amid a noise of winds
And bleatings manifold of mountain sheep,
Which in that iteration recognize
Their summons, and are gathering round for food,
Devoured with keenness, ere to grove or bank
Or rocky *bield* with patience they retire.
That very voice, which, in some timid mood
Of superstitious fancy, might have seemed
Awful as ever stray Demoniac uttered,
His steps to govern in the Wilderness;
Or as the Norman Curfew's regular beat,
To hearths when first they darkened at the knell:
That Shepherd's voice, it may have reached mine ear
Debased and under profanation, made
The ready Organ of articulate sounds
From ribaldry, impiety, or wrath
Issuing when shame hath ceased to check the brawls
Of some abused Festivity—so be it.
I came not dreaming of unruffled life,
Untainted manners; born among the hills,
Bred also there, I wanted not a scale
To regulate my hopes. Pleased with the good,
I shrink not from the evil with disgust,
Or with immoderate pain. I look for Man,
The common Creature of the brotherhood,
Differing but little from the Man elsewhere,
For selfishness, and envy, and revenge,
Ill neighbourhood—pity that this should be—
Flattery and double-dealing, strife and wrong.
Yet is it something gained, it is in truth
A mighty gain, that Labour here preserves
His rosy face, a Servant only here
Of the fireside or of the open field,
A Freeman, therefore, sound and unimpaired;
That extreme penury is here unknown,
And cold and hunger's abject wretchedness,
Mortal to body, and the heaven-born mind;
That they who want, are not too great a weight
For those who can relieve. Here may the heart
Breathe in the air of fellow-suffering

Dreadless, as in a kind of fresher breeze
Of her own native element, the hand
Be ready and unwearied without plea
From tasks too frequent, or beyond its power
For languor, or indifference, or despair.
And as these lofty barriers break the force
Of winds, this deep Vale—as it doth in part
Conceal us from the Storm—so here abides
A Power and a protection for the mind,
Dispensed indeed to other solitudes,
Favored by noble privilege like this,
Where kindred independence of estate
Is prevalent, where he who tills the field,
He, happy Man! is Master of the field,
And treads the mountains which his Fathers trod.
Not less than half-way up yon Mountain's side
Behold a dusky spot, a grove of Firs,
That seems still smaller than it is; this grove
Is haunted—by what ghost? a gentle Spirit
Of memory faithful to the call of love;
For, as reports the Dame, whose fire sends up
Yon curling smoke from the grey cot below,
The trees (her first-born Child being then a babe)
Were planted by her husband and herself,
That ranging o'er the high and houseless ground
Their sheep might neither want (from perilous storms
Of winter, nor from summer's sultry heat)
A friendly covert. 'And they knew it well,'
Said she, 'for thither as the trees grew up,
We to the patient creatures carried food
In times of heavy snow.' She then began
In fond obedience to her private thoughts
To speak of her dead Husband: is there not
An art, a music, and a strain of words
That shall be life, the acknowledged voice of life,
Shall speak of what is done among the fields,
Done truly there, or felt, of solid good
And real evil, yet be sweet withal,
More grateful, more harmonious than the breath,
The idle breath of softest pipe attuned
To pastoral fancies? Is there such a stream,
Pure and unsullied, flowing from the heart

With motions of true dignity and grace?
Or must we seek that stream where Man is not?
Methinks I could repeat in tuneful verse,
Delicious as the gentlest breeze that sounds
Through that aerial fir-grove, could preserve
Some portion of its human history
As gathered from the Matron's lips, and tell
Of tears that have been shed at sight of it,
And moving dialogues between this Pair,
Who in their prime of wedlock, with joint hands
Did plant the grove, now flourishing, while they
No longer flourish, he entirely gone,
She withering in her loneliness. Be this
A task above my skill; the silent mind
Has her own treasures, and I think of these,
Love what I see, and honour humankind.
No, we are not alone, we do not stand,
My Sister, here misplaced and desolate,
Loving what no one cares for but ourselves;
We shall not scatter through the plains and rocks
Of this fair Vale, and o'er its spacious heights
Unprofitable kindliness, bestowed
On objects unaccustomed to the gifts
Of feeling, which were chearless and forlorn
But few weeks past, and would be so again
Were we not here; we do not tend a lamp
Whose lustre we alone participate,
Which shines dependent upon us alone,
Mortal though bright, a dying, dying flame.
Look where we will, some human hand has been
Before us with its offering; not a tree
Sprinkles these little pastures but the same
Hath furnished matter for a thought; perchance,
For some one serves as a familiar friend.
Joy spreads, and sorrow spreads; and this whole Vale,
Home of untutored Shepherds as it is,
Swarms with sensation, as with gleams of sunshine,
Shadows or breezes, scents or sounds. Nor deem
These feelings, though subservient more than ours
To every day's demand for daily bread,
And borrowing more their spirit, and their shape
From self-respecting interests, deem them not

Unworthy therefore, and unhallowed: no,
They lift the animal being, do themselves
By Nature's kind and ever-present aid
Refine the selfishness from which they spring,
Redeem by love the individual sense
Of anxiousness, with which they are combined.
And thus it is that fitly they become
Associates in the joy of purest minds,
They blend therewith congenially: meanwhile,
Calmly they breathe their own undying life
Through this their mountain sanctuary; long
Oh long may it remain inviolate,
Diffusing health and sober chearfulness,
And giving to the moments as they pass
Their little boons of animating thought
That sweeten labour, make it seen and felt
To be no arbitrary weight imposed,
But a glad function natural to Man.
Fair proof of this, Newcomer though I be,
Already have I gained. The inward frame
Though slowly opening, opens every day
With process not unlike to that which chears
A pensive Stranger, journeying at his leisure
Through some Helvetian dell, when low-hung mists
Break up, and are beginning to recede;
How pleased he is where thin and thinner grows
The veil, or where it parts at once, to spy
The dark pines thrusting forth their spiky heads;
To watch the spreading lawns with cattle grazed,
Then to be greeted by the scattered huts,
As they shine out; and *see* the streams whose murmur
Had soothed his ear while they were hidden: how pleased
To have about him, which way e'er he goes,
Something on every side concealed from view,
In every quarter something visible,
Half-seen or wholly, lost and found again,
Alternate progress and impediment,
And yet a growing prospect in the main.
Such pleasure now is mine, albeit forced,
Herein less happy than the Traveller
To cast from time to time a painful look
Upon unwelcome things, which unawares

Reveal themselves; not therefore is my heart
Depressed, nor does it fear what is to come,
But confident, enriched at every glance.
The more I see the more delight my mind
Receives, or by reflexion can create.
Truth justifies herself, and as she dwells
With Hope, who would not follow where she leads?
  Nor let me pass unheeded other loves
Where no fear is, and humbler sympathies.
Already hath sprung up within my heart
A liking for the small grey horse that bears
The paralytic Man, and for the brute—
In Scripture sanctified—the patient brute,
On which the cripple, in the Quarry maim'd,
Rides to and fro: I know them and their ways.
The famous Sheep-dog, first in all the Vale,
Though yet to me a Stranger, will not be
A Stranger long; nor will the blind man's guide,
Meek and neglected thing, of no renown!
Soon will peep forth the primrose; ere it fades
Friends shall I have at dawn, blackbird and thrush
To rouse me, and a hundred Warblers more;
And if those Eagles to their ancient Hold
Return, Helvellyn's Eagles! with the Pair
From my own door I shall be free to claim
Acquaintance—as they sweep from cloud to cloud.
The Owl that gives the name to Owlet-Crag
Have I heard whooping, and he soon will be
A chosen one of my regards. See there
The Heifer in yon little croft belongs
To one who holds it dear; with duteous care
She reared it, and in speaking of her charge
I heard her scatter some endearing words
Domestic, and in spirit motherly
She being herself a Mother, happy Beast
If the caresses of a human voice
Can make it so, and care of human hands.
  And ye as happy under Nature's care,
Strangers to me, and all men, or at least
Strangers to all particular amity,
All intercourse of knowledge or of love
That parts the individual from his kind,

Whether in large communities ye keep
From year to year, not shunning Man's abode,
A settled residence, or be from far,
Wild creatures, and of many homes, that come
The gift of winds, and whom the winds again
Take from us at your pleasure—yet shall ye
Not want, for this, your own subordinate place
In my affections. Witness the delight
With which erewhile I saw that multitude
Wheel through the sky, and see them now at rest,
Yet not at rest, upon the glassy lake.
They *cannot* rest, they gambol like young whelps;
Active as lambs, and overcome with joy,
They try all frolic motions; flutter, plunge,
And beat the passive water with their wings.
Too distant are they for plain view, but lo!
Those little fountains, sparkling in the sun,
Betray their occupation, rising up,
First one and then another silver spout,
As one or other takes the fit of glee,
Fountains and spouts, yet somewhat in the guise
Of play-thing fire-works, that on festal nights
Sparkle about the feet of wanton boys.
—How vast the compass of this theatre,
Yet nothing to be seen but lovely pomp
And silent majesty: the birch-tree woods
Are hung with thousand thousand diamond drops
Of melted hoar-frost, every tiny knot
In the bare twigs, each little budding-place
Cased with its several bead, what myriads there
Upon one tree, while all the distant grove
That rises to the summit of the steep
Shows like a mountain built of silver light.
See yonder the same pageant, and again
Behold the universal imagery
Inverted, all its sun-bright features touched
As with the varnish, and the gloss of dreams;
Dreamlike the blending also of the whole
Harmonious landscape; all along the shore
The boundary lost, the line invisible
That parts the image from reality;
And the clear hills, as high as they ascend

Heavenward, so deep piercing the lake below.
Admonished of the days of love to come
The raven croaks, and fills the upper air
With a strange sound of genial harmony;
And in and all about that playful band,
Incapable although they be of rest,
And in their fashion very rioters,
There is a stillness, and they seem to make
Calm revelry in that their calm abode.
Them leaving to their joyous hours I pass,
Pass with a thought the life of the whole year
That is to come, the throng of woodland flowers,
And lilies that will dance upon the waves.
  Say boldly then that solitude is not
Where these things are: he truly is alone,
He of the multitude whose eyes are doomed
To hold a vacant commerce day by day
With objects wanting life, repelling love;
He by the vast Metropolis immured,
Where pity shrinks from unremitting calls,
Where numbers overwhelm humanity,
And neighbourhood serves rather to divide
Than to unite. What sighs more deep than his,
Whose nobler will hath long been sacrificed;
Who must inhabit, under a black sky,
A City, where, if indifference to disgust
Yield not, to scorn, or sorrow, living Men
Are ofttimes to their fellow-men no more
Than to the Forest Hermit are the leaves
That hang aloft in myriads—nay, far less,
For they protect his walk from sun and shower,
Swell his devotion with their voice in storms,
And whisper while the stars twinkle among them
His lullaby. From crowded streets remote,
Far from the living and dead wilderness
Of the thronged World, Society is here
A true Community, a genuine frame
Of many into one incorporate.
That must be looked for here, paternal sway,
One household, under God, for high and low,
One family, and one mansion; to themselves
Appropriate, and divided from the world

As if it were a cave, a multitude
Human and brute, possessors undisturbed
Of this Recess, their legislative Hall,
Their Temple, and their glorious Dwelling-place.
  Dismissing therefore, all Arcadian dreams,
All golden fancies of the golden Age,
The bright array of shadowy thoughts from times
That were before all time, or are to be
Ere time expire, the pageantry that stirs
Or will be stirring when our eyes are fixed
On lovely objects, and we wish to part
With all remembrance of a jarring world,
—Take we at once this one sufficient hope,
What need of more? that we shall neither droop,
Nor pine for want of pleasure in the life
Scattered about us, nor through dearth of aught
That keeps in health the insatiable mind;
That we shall have for knowledge and for love
Abundance; and that, feeling as we do
How goodly, how exceeding fair, how pure
From all reproach is yon ethereal vault,
And this deep Vale its earthly counterpart,
By which, and under which, we are enclosed
To breathe in peace, we shall moreover find
(If sound, and what we ought to be ourselves,
If rightly we observe and justly weigh)
The Inmates not unworthy of their home
The Dwellers of their Dwelling.
                                        And if this
Were otherwise, we have within ourselves
Enough to fill the present day with joy,
And overspread the future years with hope,
Our beautiful and quiet home, enriched
Already with a Stranger whom we love
Deeply, a Stranger of our Father's House,
A never-resting Pilgrim of the Sea,
Who finds at last an hour to his content
Beneath our roof. And others whom we love
Will seek us also, Sisters of our hearts,
And One, like them, a Brother of our hearts,
Philosopher and Poet, in whose sight
These Mountains will rejoice with open joy.

—Such is our wealth; O Vale of Peace, we are
And must be, with God's will, a happy Band.
  Yet 'tis not to enjoy that we exist,
For that end only; something must be done.
I must not walk in unreproved delight
These narrow bounds, and think of nothing more,
No duty that looks further, and no care.
Each Being has his office, lowly some
And common, yet all worthy if fulfilled
With zeal, acknowledgment that with the gift
Keeps pace a harvest answering to the seed—
Of ill-advised Ambition and of Pride
I would stand clear, but yet to me I feel
That an internal brightness is vouchsafed
That must not die, that must not pass away.
Why does this inward lustre fondly seek,
And gladly blend with outward fellowship?
Why do *they* shine around me whom I love?
Why do they teach me whom I thus revere?
Strange question, yet it answers not itself.
That humble Roof embowered among the trees,
That calm fire-side, it is not even in them,
Blest as they are, to furnish a reply
That satisfies and ends in perfect rest.
Possessions have I that are solely mine,
Something within which yet is shared by none,
Not even the nearest to me and most dear,
Something which power and effort may impart,
I would impart it, I would spread it wide,
Immortal in the world which is to come.
Forgive me if I add another claim,
And would not wholly perish even in this,
Lie down and be forgotten in the dust,
I and the modest Partners of my days
Making a silent company in death;
Love, Knowledge, all my manifold delights,
All buried with me without monument
Or profit unto any but ourselves.
It must not be, if I, divinely taught,
Be privileged to speak as I have felt
Of what in man is human or divine.

While yet an innocent Little-one, with a heart
That doubtless wanted not its tender moods,
I breathed (for this I better recollect)
Among wild appetites and blind desires,
Motions of savage instinct my delight
And exaltation. Nothing at that time
So welcome, no temptation half so dear
As that which urged me to a daring feat.
Deep pools, tall trees, black chasms, and dizzy crags,
And tottering towers; I loved to stand and read
Their looks forbidding, read and disobey,
Sometimes in act, and evermore in thought.
With impulses, that scarcely were by these
Surpassed in strength, I heard of danger, met
Or sought with courage; enterprise forlorn
By one, sole keeper of his own intent,
Or by a resolute few who for the sake
Of glory, fronted multitudes in arms.
Yea to this hour I cannot read a tale
Of two brave Vessels matched in deadly fight,
And fighting to the death, but I am pleased,
More than a wise man ought to be. I wish,
Fret, burn, and struggle, and in soul am there;
But me hath Nature tamed, and bade to seek
For other agitations, or be calm;
Hath dealt with me as with a turbulent Stream,
Some nursling of the mountains, which she leads
Through quiet meadows, after he has learnt
His strength, and had his triumph and his joy,
His desperate course of tumult and of glee.
That which in stealth by Nature was performed
Hath Reason sanctioned. Her deliberate Voice
Hath said, 'Be mild and cleave to gentle things,
Thy glory and thy happiness be there.
Nor fear, though thou confide in me, a want
Of aspirations that *have* been, of foes
To wrestle with, and victory to complete,
Bounds to be leapt, darkness to be explored,
All that inflamed thy infant heart, the love,
The longing, the contempt, the undaunted quest,
All shall survive—though changed their office, all
Shall live—it is not in their power to die'.

Then farewell to the Warrior's schemes, farewell
The forwardness of Soul which looks that way
Upon a less incitement than the cause
Of Liberty endangered, and farewell
That other hope, long mine, the hope to fill
The heroic trumpet with the Muse's breath!
Yet in this peaceful Vale we will not spend
Unheard-of days, though loving peaceful thought.
A Voice shall speak, and what will be the theme?
On Man, on Nature, and on Human Life,
Musing in solitude, I oft perceive
Fair trains of imagery before me rise,
Accompanied by feelings of delight
Pure, or with no unpleasing sadness mixed;
And I am conscious of affecting thoughts
And dear remembrances, whose presence soothes
Or elevates the Mind, intent to weigh
The good and evil of our mortal state.
—To these emotions, whencesoe'er they come,
Whether from breath of outward circumstance,
Or from the Soul—an impulse to herself—
I would give utterance in numerous verse.
Of Truth, of Grandeur, Beauty, Love, and Hope,
And melancholy Fear subdued by Faith;
Of blessèd consolations in distress;
Of moral strength, and intellectual Power;
Of joy in widest commonalty spread;
Of the individual Mind that keeps her own
Inviolate retirement, subject there
To Conscience only, and the law supreme
Of that Intelligence which governs all—
I sing:—'fit audience let me find though few!'
So prayed, more gaining than he asked, the Bard—
In holiest mood. Urania, I shall need
Thy guidance, or a greater Muse, if such
Descend to earth or dwell in highest heaven!
For I must tread on shadowy ground, must sink
Deep—and, aloft ascending, breathe in worlds
To which the heaven of heavens is but a veil.
All strength—all terror, single or in bands,
That ever was put forth in personal form—
Jehovah—with his thunder, and the choir

Of shouting Angels, and the empyreal thrones—
I pass them unalarmed. Not Chaos, not
The darkest pit of lowest Erebus,
Nor aught of blinder vacancy, scooped out
By help of dreams—can breed such fear and awe
As fall upon us often when we look
Into our Minds, into the Mind of Man—
My haunt, and the main region of my song.
—Beauty—a living Presence of the earth,
Surpassing the most fair ideal Forms
Which craft of delicate Spirits hath composed
From earth's materials—waits upon my steps;
Pitches her tents before me as I move,
An hourly neighbour. Paradise, and groves
Elysian, Fortunate Fields—like those of old
Sought in the Atlantic Main—why should they be
A history only of departed things,
Or a mere fiction of what never was?
For the discerning intellect of Man,
When wedded to this goodly universe
In love and holy passion, shall find these
A simple produce of the common day.
—I, long before the blissful hour arrives,
Would chant, in lonely peace, the spousal verse
Of this great consummation:—and, by words
Which speak of nothing more than what we are,
Would I arouse the sensual from their sleep
Of Death, and win the vacant and the vain
To noble raptures; while my voice proclaims
How exquisitely the individual Mind
(And the progressive powers perhaps no less
Of the whole species) to the external World
Is fitted:—and how exquisitely, too—
Theme this but little heard of among men—
The external World is fitted to the Mind;
And the creation (by no lower name
Can it be called) which they with blended might
Accomplish:—this is our high argument.
—Such grateful haunts foregoing, if I oft
Must turn elsewhere—to travel near the tribes
And fellowships of men, and see ill sights
Of madding passions mutually inflamed;

Must hear Humanity in fields and groves
Pipe solitary anguish; or must hang
Brooding above the fierce confederate storm
Of sorrow, barricadoed evermore
Within the walls of cities—may these sounds
Have their authentic comment; that even these
Hearing, I be not downcast or forlorn!—
Descend, prophetic Spirit! that inspir'st
The human Soul of universal earth,
Dreaming on things to come; and dost possess
A metropolitan temple in the hearts
Of mighty Poets: upon me bestow
A gift of genuine insight; that my Song
With star-like virtue in its place may shine,
Shedding benignant influence, and secure,
Itself, from all malevolent effect
Of those mutations that extend their sway
Throughout the nether sphere!—And if with this
I mix more lowly matter; with the thing
Contemplated, describe the Mind and Man
Contemplating; and who, and what he was—
The transitory Being that beheld
This Vision; when and where, and how he lived,
Be not this labour useless. If such theme
May sort with highest objects, then—dread Power!
Whose gracious favour is the primal source
Of all illumination,—may my Life
Express the image of a better time,
More wise desires, and simpler manners;—nurse
My Heart in genuine freedom:—all pure thoughts
Be with me;—so shall thy unfailing love
Guide, and support, and cheer me to the end!

from

LYRICAL BALLADS, 1800

WITH

PASTORAL AND OTHER POEMS

EDITOR'S NOTE

THIS second volume of *Lyrical Ballads* was first published at the beginning of 1801 (dated 1800). Another edition appeared in 1802, and another in 1805. The text of 1805 is here followed. Wordsworth described the 1800 text as 'vilely printed'. In the 1802 and 1805 editions he corrected the misprints and made other minor changes, usually for the better. There were also considerable additions to *Ruth,* which in 1800 contained only 38 stanzas as against 45 in 1805. Other changes appear only in the intermediate 1802 version. *Poor Susan* had a final stanza in 1800 which was removed in consequence of a protest by Charles Lamb. It ran:—

Poor Outcast! return—to receive thee once more
The house of thy Father will open its door,
And thou once again, in thy plain russet gown,
May'st hear the thrush sing from a tree of its own.

The *Preface* as here given is that of 1802 and 1805, much enlarged from that of 1800. In particular the whole passage from 'language of such Poetry' (p. 239) to 'remind the Reader' (p. 245) was an addition. An *Appendix on Poetic Diction,* which first appeared in 1802, is not included here. That and the original 1800 version of the *Preface* will be found in *Lyrical Ballads, 1800–5* as published in Methuen's English Classics, pp. 344–50 and 369–92 respectively. It was prefixed to Volume I.

The footnotes here printed are Wordsworth's.

LYRICAL BALLADS, 1800

(1805 EDITION)

PREFACE

THE first Volume of these Poems has already been submitted to general perusal. It was published, as an experiment, which, I hoped, might be of some use to ascertain, how far, by fitting to metrical arrangement a selection of the real language of men in a state of vivid sensation, that sort of pleasure and that quantity of pleasure may be imparted, which a Poet may rationally endeavour to impart.

I had formed no very inaccurate estimate of the probable effect of those Poems: I flattered myself that they who should be pleased with them would read them with more than common pleasure: and, on the other hand, I was well aware, that by those who should dislike them they would be read with more than common dislike. The result has differed from my expectation in this only, that I have pleased a greater number, than I ventured to hope I should please.

For the sake of variety, and from a consciousness of my own weakness, I was induced to request the assistance of a Friend, who furnished me with the Poems of the ANCIENT MARINER, the FOSTER-MOTHER'S TALE, the NIGHTINGALE, and the Poem entitled LOVE. I should not, however, have requested this assistance, had I not believed that the Poems of my Friend would in a great measure have the same tendency as my own, and that, though there would be found a difference, there would be found no discordance in the colours of our style; as our opinions on the subject of poetry do almost entirely coincide.

Several of my Friends are anxious for the success of these Poems from a belief, that, if the views with which they were composed were indeed realized, a class of Poetry would be produced, well adapted to interest mankind permanently, and not unimportant in the multiplicity, and in the quality of its moral relations: and on this account they have advised me to prefix a systematic defence of the theory upon which the poems were written. But I was unwilling to undertake the task, because I knew that on this occasion the Reader would look coldly upon my arguments, since I might be suspected of having been principally influenced by the selfish and foolish hope of *reasoning* him into an approbation of these particular Poems: and I was still more unwilling to undertake the task, because, adequately to display my opinions, and fully to enforce my arguments, would require a space wholly disproportionate to the nature of a preface. For to treat the subject with the clearness and coherence, of which I believe it susceptible, it would be necessary to give a full account of the present state of the public taste in this country, and to determine how far this taste is healthy or depraved; which, again, could not be determined, without pointing out, in what manner language and the human mind act and re-act on each other, and without retracing the revolutions, not of literature alone, but likewise of society itself. I have therefore altogether declined to enter regularly upon this defence; yet I am sensible, that there would be some impropriety in abruptly obtruding upon the Public, without a few words of introduction, Poems so materially different from those, upon which general approbation is at present bestowed.

It is supposed, that by the act of writing in verse an Author makes a formal engagement that he will gratify certain known habits of association; that he not only thus apprizes the Reader that certain classes of ideas and expressions will be found in this book, but that the others will be carefully excluded. This exponent or symbol held forth by metrical language must in different æras of literature have excited very different expectations: for example, in the age of Catullus, Terence and Lucretius, and that of Statius or Claudian; and in our own country, in the age of Shakespeare and Beaumont and Fletcher, and that of Donne and Cowley, or Dryden, or Pope. I will not take upon me to determine the exact import of the promise which by the act of writing in verse an Author, in the present day, makes to his Reader; but I am certain, it will appear to many persons that I have not fulfilled the terms of an engagement thus voluntarily contracted. They who have been accustomed to the gaudiness and inane phraseology of many modern writers, if they persist in reading this book to its conclusion, will, no doubt, frequently have to struggle with feelings of strangeness and aukwardness: they will look round for poetry, and will be induced to inquire by what species of courtesy these attempts can be permitted to assume that title. I hope therefore the Reader will not censure me, if I attempt to state what I have proposed to myself to perform; and also, (as far as the limits of a preface will permit) to explain some of the chief reasons which have determined me in the choice of my purpose: that at least he may be spared any unpleasant feeling of disappointment, and that I myself may be protected from the most dishonourable accusation which can be brought against an Author, namely, that of an indolence which prevents him from endeavouring to ascertain what is his duty, or, when his duty is ascertained, prevents him from performing it.

The principal object, then, which I proposed to myself in these Poems was to choose incidents and situations from common life, and to relate or describe them, throughout, as far as was possible, in a selection of language really used by men; and, at the same time, to throw over them a certain colouring of imagination, whereby ordinary things should be presented to the mind in an unusual way; and, further, and above all, to make these incidents and situations interesting by tracing in them, truly though not ostentatiously, the primary laws of our nature: chiefly, as far as regards the manner in which we associate ideas in a state of excitement. Low and rustic life was generally chosen, because in that condition, the essential passions of the heart find a better soil in which they can attain their maturity, are less under restraint, and speak a plainer and more emphatic language; because in that condition of life our elementary feelings co-exist in a state of greater simplicity, and, consequently, may be more accurately contemplated, and more forcibly communicated; because the manners of rural life germinate from those elementary feelings; and, from the necessary character of rural occupations, are more easily comprehended; and are more durable; and lastly, because in that condition the passions of men are incorporated with the beautiful and permanent forms of nature. The language, too, of these men is adopted (purified indeed from what appear to be its real defects, from all lasting and rational causes of dislike or disgust) because such men hourly communicate with the best objects from which the best part of language is originally derived; and because, from their rank in society and the sameness and narrow circle of their intercourse, being less under the influence of social vanity they convey their feelings and notions in simple and unelaborated expressions. Accordingly, such a language, arising out of repeated experience and regular feelings, is a more permanent, and a far more philosophical language, than that which is frequently substituted for it by Poets, who think that they are conferring honour upon themselves and their art, in proportion as they separate themselves from the sympathies of men, and indulge in arbitrary and capricious habits of expression, in order to furnish food for fickle tastes, and fickle appetites, of their own creation.*

I cannot, however, be insensible of the present outcry against the triviality and meanness both of thought and language, which some of my contemporaries have occasionally introduced into their metrical compositions; and I acknowledge that this defect, where it exists, is more dishonourable to the Writer's own character than false refinement or arbitrary innovation, though I should contend at the same time that it is far less pernicious in the sum of its consequences. From such verses the Poems in these volumes will be found distinguished at least by one mark of difference, that each of them has a worthy *purpose*. Not that I mean to say, that I always began to write with a distinct purpose formally conceived; but I believe that my habits of meditation have so formed my feelings, as that my descriptions of such objects as strongly excite those feelings, will be found to carry along with them a *purpose*. If in this opinion I am mistaken, I can have little right to the name of a Poet. For all good poetry is the spontaneous overflow of powerful feelings: but though this be true, Poems to which any value can be attached, were never produced on any variety of subjects but by a man, who being possessed of more than usual organic sensibility, had also thought long and deeply. For our continued influxes of feeling are modified and directed by our thoughts, which are indeed the representatives of all our past feelings; and, as by contemplating the relation of these general representatives to each other we discover what is really important to men, so, by the repetition and continuance of this act, our feelings will be connected with important subjects, till at length, if we be originally possessed of much sensibility, such habits of mind will be produced, that, by obeying blindly and mechanically the impulses of those habits, we shall describe objects, and utter sentiments, of such a nature and in such connection with each other, that the understanding of the being to whom we address ourselves, if he be in a healthful state of association, must necessarily be in some degree enlightened, and his affections ameliorated.

I have said that each of these poems has a purpose. I have also informed my Reader what this purpose will be found principally to be: namely, to illustrate the manner in which our feelings and ideas are associated in a state of excitement. But, speaking in language somewhat more appropriate, it is to follow the fluxes and

* It is worth while here to observe that the affecting parts of Chaucer are almost always expressed in language pure and universally intelligible even to this day.

efluxes of the mind when agitated by the great and simple affections of our nature. This object I have endeavoured in these short essays to attain by various means; by tracing the maternal passion through many of its more subtile windings, as in the poems of the IDIOT BOY and the MAD MOTHER; by accompanying the last struggles of a human being, at the approach of death, cleaving in solitude to life and society, as in the Poem of the FORSAKEN INDIAN; by showing, as in the Stanzas entitled WE ARE SEVEN, the perplexity and obscurity which in childhood attend our notion of death, or rather our utter inability to admit that notion; or by displaying the strength of fraternal, or to speak more philosophically, of moral attachment when early associated with the great and beautiful objects of nature, as in THE BROTHERS; or, as in the incident of SIMON LEE, by placing my Reader in the way of receiving from ordinary moral sensations another and more salutary impression than we are accustomed to receive from them. It has also been part of my general purpose to attempt to sketch characters under the influence of less impassioned feelings, as in the TWO APRIL MORNINGS, THE FOUNTAIN, THE OLD MAN TRAVELLING, THE TWO THIEVES, &c. characters of which the elements are simple, belonging rather to nature than to manners, such as exist now, and will probably always exist, and which from their constitution may be distinctly and profitably contemplated. I will not abuse the indulgence of my Reader by dwelling longer upon this subject; but it is proper that I should mention one other circumstance which distinguishes these Poems from the popular Poetry of the day; it is this, that the feeling therein developed gives importance to the action and situation, and not the action and situation to the feeling. My meaning will be rendered perfectly intelligible by referring my Reader to the Poems entitled POOR SUSAN and the CHILDLESS FATHER, particularly to the last Stanza of the latter Poem.

I will not suffer a sense of false modesty to prevent me from asserting, that I point my Reader's attention to this mark of distinction, far less for the sake of these particular Poems than from the general importance of the subject. The subject is indeed important! For the human mind is capable of being excited without the application of gross and violent stimulants; and he must have a very faint perception of its beauty and dignity who does not know this, and who does not further know, that one being is elevated above another, in proportion as he possesses this capability. It has therefore appeared to me, that to endeavour to produce or enlarge this capability is one of the best services in which, at any period a Writer can be engaged; but this service, excellent at all times, is especially so at the present day. For a multitude of causes, unknown to former times, are now acting with a combined force to blunt the discriminating powers of the mind, and unfitting it for all voluntary exertion to reduce it to a state of almost savage torpor. The most effective of these causes are the great national events which are daily taking place, and the increasing accumulation of men in cities, where the uniformity of their occupations produces a craving for extraordinary incident, which the rapid communication of intelligence hourly gratifies. To this tendency of life and manners the literature and theatrical exhibitions of the country have conformed themselves. The invaluable works of our elder writers, I had almost said the works of Shakespeare and Milton, are driven into neglect by frantic novels, sickly and stupid German Tragedies, and deluges of idle and extravagant stories in verse.—When I think upon this degrading thirst after outrageous stimulation, I am almost ashamed to have spoken of the feeble effort with which I have endeavoured to counteract it; and, reflecting upon the magnitude of the general evil, I should be oppressed with no dishonourable melancholy, had I not a deep impression of certain inherent and indestructible qualities of the human mind, and likewise of certain powers in the great and permanent objects that act upon it, which are equally inherent and indestructible; and did I not further add to this impression a belief, that the time is approaching when the evil will be systematically opposed, by men of greater powers, and with far more distinguished success.

Having dwelt thus long on the subjects and aim of these Poems, I shall request the Reader's permission to apprize him of a few circumstances relating to their *style,* in order, among other reasons, that I may not be censured for not having performed what I never attempted. The Reader will find that personifications of abstract ideas rarely occur in these volumes; and, I hope, are utterl rejected as an ordinary device to elevate the style, and raise i above prose. I have proposed to myself to imitate, and, as far a is possible, to adopt the very language of men; and assuredly suc personifications do not make any natural or regular part of tha language. They are, indeed, a figure of speech occasionally promp ted by passion, and I have made use of them as such, but I hav endeavoured utterly to reject them as a mechanical device of style or as a family language which Writers in metre seem to lay clain to by prescription. I have wished to keep my Reader in the compan of flesh and blood, persuaded that by so doing I shall interest him. I am, however, well aware that others who pursue a different track may interest him likewise; I do not interfere with their claim, I only wish to prefer a different claim of my own. There will also be found in these volumes little of what is usually called poetic diction; I have taken as much pains to avoid it as others ordinarily take to produce it; this I have done for the reason already alleged, to bring my language near to the language of men, and further, because the pleasure which I have proposed to myself to impart is of a kind very different from that which is supposed by many persons to be the proper object of poetry. I do not know how, without being culpably particular, I can give my Reader a more exact notion of the style in which I wished these poems to be written, than by informing him that I have at all times endeavoured to look steadily at my subject, consequently, I hope that there is in these Poems little falsehood of description, and that my ideas are expressed in language fitted to their respective importance. Something I must have gained by this practice, as it is friendly to one property of all good poetry, namely, good sense; but it has necessarily cut me off from a large portion of phrases and figures of speech which from father to son have long been regarded as the common inheritance of Poets. I have also thought it expedient to restrict myself still further, having abstained from the use of many expressions, in themselves proper and beautiful, but which have been foolishly repeated by bad Poets, till such feelings of disgust are connected with them as it is scarcely possible by any art of association to overpower.

If in a poem there should be found a series of lines, or even a single line, in which the language, though naturally arranged, and according to the strict laws of metre, does not differ from that of prose, there is a numerous class of critics, who, when they stumble upon these prosaisms, as they call them, imagine that they have made a notable discovery, and exult over the Poet as over a man ignorant of his own profession. Now these men would establish a canon of criticism which the Reader will conclude he must utterly reject, if he wishes to be pleased with these volumes. And it would be a most easy task to prove to him, that not only the language of a large portion of every good poem, even of the most elevated character, must necessarily, except with reference to the metre, in no respect differ from that of good prose, but likewise that some of the most interesting parts of the best poems will be found to be strictly the language of prose, when prose is well writtten. The truth of this assertion might be demonstrated by innumerable passages from almost all the poetical writings, even of Milton himself. I have not space for much quotation; but, to illustrate the subject in a general manner, I will here adduce a short composition of Gray, who was at the head of those who, by their reasonings, have attempted to widen the space of separation betwixt Prose and Metrical composition, and was more than any other man curiously elaborate in the structure of his own poetic diction.

In vain to me the smiling mornings shine,
And reddening Phœbus lifts his golden fire:
The birds in vain their amorous descant join,
Or cheerful fields resume their green attire.
These ears, alas! for other notes repine;
A different object do these eyes require;
My lonely anguish melts no heart but mine;
And in my breast the imperfect joys expire;
Yet morning smiles the busy race to cheer,
And new-born pleasure brings to happier men;
The fields to all their wonted tribute bear;
To warm their little loves the birds complain.
I fruitless mourn to him that cannot hear,
And weep the more because I weep in vain.

It will easily be perceived that the only part of this Sonnet which is of any value is the lines printed in Italics: it is equally obvious, that, except in the rhyme, and in the use of the single word 'fruitless' for fruitlessly, which is so far a defect, the language of these lines does in no respect differ from that of prose.

By the foregoing quotation I have shown that the language of Prose may yet be well adapted to Poetry; and I have previously asserted that a large portion of the language of every good poem can in no respect differ from that of good Prose. I will go further. I do not doubt that it may be safely affirmed, that there neither is, nor can be, any essential difference between the language of prose and metrical composition. We are fond of tracing the resemblance between Poetry and Painting, and, accordingly, we call them Sisters: but where shall we find bonds of connection sufficiently strict to typify the affinity betwixt metrical and prose composition? They both speak by and to the same organs; the bodies in which both of them are clothed may be said to be of the same substance, their affections are kindred, and almost identical, not necessarily differing even in degree; Poetry* sheds no tears 'such as Angels weep.' but natural and human tears; she can boast of no celestial Ichor that distinguishes her vital juices from those of prose; the same human blood circulates through the veins of them both.

If it be affirmed that rhyme and metrical arrangement of themselves constitute a distinction which overturns what I have been saying on the strict affinity of metrical language with that of prose, and paves the way for other artificial distinctions which the mind voluntarily admits, I answer that the language of such Poetry as I am recommending is, as far as is possible, a selection of the language really spoken by men; that this selection, wherever it is made with true taste and feeling, will of itself form a distinction far greater than would at first be imagined, and will entirely separate the composition from the vulgarity and meanness of ordinary life; and, if metre be superadded thereto, I believe that a dissimilitude will be produced altogether sufficient for the gratification of a rational mind. What other distinction would he have? Whence is it to come? And where is it to exist? Not, surely, where the Poet speaks through the mouths of his characters: it cannot be necessary here, either for elevation of style, or any of its supposed ornaments: for, if the Poet's subject be judiciously chosen, it will naturally, and upon fit occasion, lead him to passions the language of which, if selected truly and judiciously, must necessarily be dignified and variegated, and alive with metaphors and figures. I forbear to speak of an incongruity which would shock the intelligent Reader, should the Poet interweave any foreign splendour of his own with that which the passion naturally suggests: it is sufficient to say that such addition is unnecessary. And, surely, it is more probable that those passages, which with propriety abound with metaphors and figures, will have their due effect, if, upon other occasions where the passions are of a milder character, the style also be subdued and temperate.

But, as the pleasure which I hope to give by the Poems I now present to the Reader must depend entirely on just notions upon this subject, and, as it is in itself of the highest importance to our taste and moral feelings, I cannot content myself with these detached remarks. And if, in what I am about to say, it shall appear

* I here use the word 'Poetry' (though against my own judgment) as opposed to the word Prose, and synonymous with metrical composition. But much confusion has been introduced into criticism by this contradistinction of Poetry and Prose, instead of the more philosophical one of Poetry and Matter of Fact, or Science. The only strict antithesis to Prose is Metre; nor is this, in truth, a *strict* antithesis; because lines and passages of metre so naturally occur in writing prose, that it would be scarcely possible to avoid them, even were it desirable.

to some that my labour is unnecessary, and that I am like a man fighting a battle without enemies, I would remind such persons, that, whatever may be the language outwardly holden by men, a practical faith in the opinions which I am wishing to establish is almost unknown. If my conclusions are admitted, and carried as far as they must be carried if admitted at all, our judgments concerning the works of the greatest Poets both ancient and modern will be far different from what they are at present, both when we praise, and when we censure: and our moral feelings influencing, and influenced by these judgments will, I believe, be corrected and purified.

Taking up the subject, then, upon general grounds, I ask what is meant by the word Poet? What is a Poet? To whom does he address himself? And what language is to be expected from him? He is a man speaking to men: a man, it is true, endued with more lively sensibility, more enthusiasm and tenderness, who has a greater knowledge of human nature, and a more comprehensive soul, than are supposed to be common among mankind; a man pleased with his own passions and volitions, and who rejoices more than other men in the spirit of life that is in him; delighting to contemplate similar volitions and passions as manifested in the goings-on of the Universe, and habitually impelled to create them where he does not find them. To these qualities he has added a disposition to be affected more than other men by absent things as if they were present; an ability of conjuring up in himself passions, which are indeed far from being the same as those produced by real events, yet (especially in those parts of the general sympathy which are pleasing and delightful) do more nearly resemble the passions produced by real events, than any thing which, from the motions of their own minds merely, other men are accustomed to feel in themselves; whence, and from practice, he has acquired a greater readiness and power in expressing what he thinks and feels, and especially those thoughts and feelings which by his own choice, or from the structure of his own mind, arise in him without immediate external excitement.

But, whatever portion of this faculty we may suppose even the greatest Poet to possess, there cannot be a doubt but that the language which it will suggest to him, must, in liveliness and truth fall far short of that which is uttered by men in real life, under the actual pressure of those passions, certain shadows of which the Poet thus produces, or feels to be produced, in himself. However exalted a notion we would wish to cherish of the character of a

Poet, it is obvious, that, while he describes and imitates passions, his situation is altogether slavish and mechanical, compared with the freedom and power of real and substantial action and suffering. So that it will be the wish of the Poet to bring his feelings near to those of the persons whose feelings he describes, nay, for short spaces of time perhaps, to let himself slip into an entire delusion, and even confound and identify his own feelings with theirs; modifying only the language which is thus suggested to him, by a consideration that he describes for a particular purpose, that of giving pleasure. Here, then, he will apply the principle of which I have so much insisted, namely, that of selection; on this he will depend for removing what would otherwise be painful or disgusting in the passion; he will feel that there is no necessity to trick out or to elevate nature: and, the more industriously he applies this principle, the deeper will be his faith that no words, which his fancy or imagination can suggest, will be to be compared with those which are the emanations of reality and truth.

But it may be said by those who do not object to the general spirit of these remarks, that, as it is impossible for the Poet to produce upon all occasions language as exquisitely fitted for the passion as that which the real passion itself suggests, it is proper that he should consider himself as in the situation of a translator, who deems himself justified when he substitutes excellences of another kind for those which are unattainable by him; and endeavours occasionally to surpass his original, in order to make some amends for the general inferiority to which he feels that he must submit. But this would be to encourage idleness and unmanly despair. Further, it is the language of men who speak of what they do not understand; who talk of Poetry as of a matter of amusement and idle pleasure; who will converse with us as gravely about a *taste* for Poetry, as they express it, as if it were a thing as indifferent as a taste for Rope-dancing, or Frontiniac or Sherry. Aristotle, I have been told, hath said, that Poetry is the most philosophic of all writing: it is so: its object is truth, not individual and local, but general, and operative; not standing upon external testimony, but carried alive into the heart by passion; truth which is its own testimony, which gives strength and divinity to the tribunal to which it appeals, and receives them from the same tribunal. Poetry is the image of man and nature. The obstacles which stand in the way of the fidelity of the Biographer and Historian, and of their consequent utility, are incalculably greater than those which are to be encountered by the Poet who has an adequate notion of the dignity of his art. The Poet writes under one restriction only, namely, that of the necessity of giving immediate pleasure to a human Being possessed of that information which may be expected from him, not as a lawyer, a physician, a mariner, an astronomer or a natural philosopher, but as a Man. Except this one restriction, there is no object standing between the Poet and the image of things; between this, and the Biographer and Historian there are a thousand.

Nor let this necessity of producing immediate pleasure be considered as a degradation of the Poet's art. It is far otherwise. It is an acknowledgment of the beauty of the universe, an acknowledgment the more sincere, because it is not formal, but indirect; it is a task light and easy to him who looks at the world in the spirit of love: further, it is a homage paid to the native and naked dignity of man, to the grand elementary principle of pleasure, by which he knows, and feels, and lives, and moves. We have no sympathy but what is propagated by pleasure: I would not be misunderstood; but wherever we sympathize with pain it will be found that the sympathy is produced and carried on by subtle combinations with pleasure. We have no knowledge, that is, no general principles drawn from the contemplation of particular facts, but what has been built up by pleasure, and exists in us by pleasure alone. The Man of Science, the Chemist and Mathematician, whatever difficulties and disgusts they may have had to struggle with, know and feel this. However painful may be the objects with which the Anatomist's knowledge is connected, he feels that his knowledge is pleasure; and where he has no pleasure he has no knowledge. What then does the Poet? He considers man and the objects that surround him as acting and re-acting upon each other, so as to produce an infinite complexity of pain and pleasure; he considers man in his own nature and in his ordinary life as contemplating this with a certain quantity of immediate knowledge, with certain convictions, intuitions, and deductions which by habit become of the nature of intuitions; he considers him as looking upon his complex scene of ideas and sensations, and finding every where objects that immediately excite in him sympathies which, from the necessities of his nature, are accompanied by an overbalance of enjoyment.

To this knowledge which all men carry about with them, and to these sympathies in which without any other discipline than that of our daily life we are fitted to take delight, the Poet principally directs his attention. He considers man and nature as essentially adapted to each other, and the mind of man as naturally the mirror of the fairest and most interesting qualities of nature. And thus the Poet, prompted by this feeling of pleasure which accompanies him through the whole course of his studies, converses with general nature with affections akin to those, which, through labour and length of time, the Man of Science has raised up in himself, by conversing with those particular parts of nature which are the object of his studies. The knowledge both of the Poet and the Man of Science is pleasure; but the knowledge of the one cleaves to us as a necessary part of our existence, our natural and unalienable inheritance; the other is a personal and individual acquisition, slow to come to us, and by no habitual and direct sympathy connecting us with our fellow-beings. The Man of Science seeks truth as a remote and unknown benefactor; he cherishes and loves it in his solitude: the Poet, singing a song in which all human beings join with him, rejoices in the presence of truth as our visible friend and hourly companion. Poetry is the breath and finer spirit of all knowledge: it is the impassioned expression which is in the countenance of all Science. Emphatically may it be said of the Poet, as Shakespeare hath said of man, 'that he looks before and after.' He is the rock of defence of human nature; an upholder and preserver, carrying every where with him relationship and love. In spite of difference of soil and climate, of language and manners, of laws and customs, in spite of things silently gone out of mind and things violently destroyed, the Poet binds together by passion and knowledge the vast empire of human society, as it is spread over the whole earth, and over all time. The objects of the Poet's thoughts are every where; though the eyes and senses of men are, it is true, his favourite guides, yet he will follow wheresoever he can find an atmosphere of sensation in which to move his wings. Poetry is the first and last of all knowledge—it is as immortal as the heart of man. If the labours of Men of Science should ever create any material revolution, direct or indirect, in our condition, and in the impressions which we habitually receive, the Poet will sleep then no more than at present, but he will be ready to follow the steps of the Man of Science, not only in those general indirect effects, but he will be at his side, carrying sensation into the midst of the objects of the Science itself. The remotest discoveries of the Chemist, the Botanist, or Mineralogist, will be as proper objects of the Poet's art as any upon which it can be employed, if the time should ever come when these things shall be familiar to us, and the relations under which they are contemplated by the followers of these respective Sciences shall be manifestly and palpably material to us as enjoying and suffering beings. If the time should ever come when what is now called Science, thus familiarized to men, shall be ready to put on, as it were, a form of flesh and blood, the Poet will lend his divine spirit to aid the transfiguration, and will welcome the Being thus produced, as a dear and genuine inmate of the household of man.—It is not, then, to be supposed that any one, who holds that sublime notion of Poetry which I have attempted to convey, will break in upon the sanctity and truth of his pictures by transitory and accidental ornaments, and endeavour to excite admiration of himself by arts, the necessity of which must manifestly depend upon the assumed meanness of his subject.

What I have thus far said applies to Poetry in general; but especially to those parts of composition where the Poet speaks through the mouths of his characters; and upon this point it appears to have such weight that I will conclude, there are few persons of good sense, who would not allow that the dramatic parts of composition are defective, in proportion as they deviate from the real language of nature, and are coloured by a diction of the Poet's own, either peculiar to him as an individual Poet, or belonging simply to Poets in general, to a body of men who, from the circumstance of their compositions being in metre, it is expected will employ a particular language.

It is not, then, in the dramatic parts of composition that we look for this distinction of language; but still it may be proper and necessary where the Poet speaks to us in his own person and character. To this I answer by referring my Reader to the description which I have before given of a Poet. Among the qualities which I have enumerated as principally conducing to form a Poet is implied nothing differing in kind from other men, but only in degree. The sum of what I have there said is, that the Poet is chiefly distinguished from other men by a greater promptness to think and feel without immediate external excitement, and a greater power in expressing such thoughts and feelings as are produced in him in that manner. But these passions and thoughts and feelings are the general passions and thoughts and feelings of men. And with what are they connected? Undoubtedly with our moral sentiments and animal sensations, and with the causes which excite these; with the operations of the elements and the appearances of the visible universe; with storm and sun-shine, with the revolutions of the seasons, with cold and heat, with loss of friends and kindred with injuries and resentments, gratitude and hope, with fear and sorrow. These, and the like, are the sensations and objects which the Poet describes, as they are the sensations of other men, and the objects which interest them. The Poet thinks and feels in the spirit of the passions of men. How, then, can his language differ in any material degree from that of all other men who feel vividly and see clearly? It might be *proved* that it is impossible. But supposing that this were not the case, the Poet might then be allowed to use a peculiar language when expressing his feelings for his own gratification, or that of men like himself. But Poets do not write for Poets alone, but for men. Unless therefore we are advocates for that admiration which depends upon ignorance, and that pleasure which arises from hearing what we do not understand, the Poet must descend from this supposed height, and, in order to excite rational sympathy, he must express himself as other men express themselves. To this it may be added, that while he is only selecting from the real language of men, or, which amounts to the same thing, composing accurately in the spirit of such selection, he is treading upon safe ground, and we know what we are to expect from him. Our feelings are the same with respect to metre; for, as it may be proper to remind the Reader, the distinction of metre is regular and uniform, and not like that which is produced by by what is usually called poetic diction. arbitrary, and subject to infinite caprices upon which no calculation whatever can be made. In the one case, the Reader is utterly at the mercy of the Poet respecting what imagery or diction he may choose to connect with the passion, whereas, in the other, the metre obeys certain laws, to which the Poet and Reader both willingly submit because they are certain, and because no interference is made by them with the passion but such as the concurring testimony of ages has shown to heighten and improve the pleasure which co-exists with it.

It will now be proper to answer an obvious question, namely, Why, professing these opinions, have I written in verse? To this, in addition to such answer as is included in what I have already said, I reply in the first place, Because, however I may have restricted myself, there is still left open to me what confessedly constitutes the most valuable object of all writing, whether in prose or verse, the great and universal passions of men, the most general and interesting of their occupations, and the entire world of nature, from which I am at liberty to supply myself with endless combinations of forms and imagery. Now, supposing for a moment that whatever is interesting in these objects may be as vividly described in prose, why am I to be condemned, if to such description I have endeavoured to superadd the charm which, by the consent of all nations, is acknowledged to exist in metrical language? To this, by such as are unconvinced by what I have already said, it may be answered, that a very small part of the pleasure given by Poetry depends upon the metre, and that it is injudicious to write in metre, unless it be accompanied with the other artificial distinctions of style with which metre is usually accompanied, and that by such deviation more will be lost from the shock which will be thereby given to the Reader's associations, than will be counterbalanced by any pleasure which he can derive from the general power of numbers. In answer to those who still contend for the necessity of accompanying metre with certain appropriate colours of style in order to the accomplishment of its appropriate end, and who also, in my opinion, greatly under-rate the power of metre in itself, it might perhaps, as far as relates to these Poems, have been almost sufficient to observe, that poems are extant, written upon more humble subjects, and in a more naked and simple style than I have aimed at, which poems have continued to give pleasure from generation to generation. Now, if nakedness and simplicity be a defect, the fact here mentioned affords a strong presumption that poems somewhat less naked and simple are capable of affording pleasure at the present day; and, what I wished *chiefly* to attempt, at present, was to justify myself for having written under the impression of this belief.

But I might point out various causes why, when the style is manly, and the subject of some importance, words metrically arranged will long continue to impart such a pleasure to mankind as he who is sensible of the extent of that pleasure will be desirous to impart. The end of Poetry is to produce excitement in co, existence with an overbalance of pleasure. Now, by the supposition-excitement is an unusual and irregular state of the mind; ideas and feelings do not in that state succeed each other in accustomed order. But, if the words by which this excitement is produced are in themselves powerful, or the images and feelings have an undue proportion of pain connected with them, there is some danger that the excitement may be carried beyond its proper bounds. Now the co-presence of something regular, something to which the mind has been accustomed in various moods and in a less excited state, cannot but have great efficacy in tempering and restraining the passion by an intertexture of ordinary feeling, and of feeling not rictly necessarily connected with the passion. This is unquestion-bly true, and hence, though the opinion will at first appear aradoxical, from the tendency of metre to divest language in a ertain degree of its reality, and thus to throw a sort of half onsciousness of unsubstantial existence over the whole compo-tion, there can be little doubt but that more pathetic situations nd sentiments, that is, those which have a greater proportion of ain connected with them, may be endured in metrical compo-tion, especially in rhyme, than in prose. The metre of the old allads is very artless; yet they contain many passages which would lustrate this opinion, and, I hope, if the following Poems be tentively perused, similar instances will be found in them. This pinion may be further illustrated by appealing to the Reader's wn experience of the reluctance with which he comes to the re-erusal of the distressful parts of Clarissa Harlowe, or the Gamester. Vhile Shakespeare's writings, in the most pathetic scenes, never ct upon us as pathetic beyond the bounds of pleasure—an effect hich, in a much greater degree than might at first be imagined, to be ascribed to small, but continual and regular impulses of leasurable surprise from the metrical arrangement.—On the other and (what it must be allowed will much more frequently happen) the Poet's words should be incommensurate with the passion, nd inadequate to raise the Reader to a height of desirable excite-ent, then, (unless the Poet's choice of his metre has been grossly ijudicious) in the feelings of pleasure which the Reader has been ccustomed to connect with metre in general, and in the feeling, hether cheerful or melancholy, which he has been accustomed connect with that particular movement of metre, there will be und something which will greatly contribute to impart passion the words, and to effect the complex end which the Poet roposes to himself.

If I had undertaken a systematic defence of the theory upon hich these poems are written, it would have been my duty to evelope the various causes upon which the pleasure received from etrical language depends. Among the chief of these causes is to e reckoned a principle which must be well known to those who ave made any of the Arts the object of accurate reflection; I ean the pleasure which the mind derives from the perception of milititude in dissimilitude. This principle is the great spring of the ctivity of our minds, and their chief feeder. From this principle e direction of the sexual appetite, and all the passions connected ith it, take their origin: it is the life of our ordinary conversation;

and upon the accuracy with which similitude in dissimilitude, and dissimilitude in similitude are perceived, depend our taste and our moral feelings. It would not have been a useless employment to have applied this principle to the consideration of metre, and to have shown that metre is hence enabled to afford much pleasure, and to have pointed out in what manner the pleasure is produced. But my limits will not permit me to enter upon this subject, and I must content myself with a general summary.

I have said that Poetry is the spontaneous overflow of powerful feelings: it takes its origin from emotion recollected in tranquillity: the emotion is contemplated till by a species of reaction the tranquillity gradually disappears, and an emotion, kindred to that which was before the subject of contemplation, is gradually produced, and does itself actually exist in the mind. In this mood successful composition generally begins, and in a mood similar to this it is carried on; but the emotion, of whatever kind and in whatever degree, from various causes is qualified by various pleasures, so that in describing any passions whatsoever, which are voluntarily described, the mind will upon the whole be in a state of enjoyment. Now, if Nature be thus cautious in preserving in a state of enjoyment a being thus employed, the Poet ought to profit by the lesson thus held forth to him, and ought especially to take care, that whatever passions he communicates to his Reader, those passions, if his Reader's mind be sound and vigorous, should always be accompanied with an overbalance of pleasure. Now the music of harmonious metrical language, the sense of difficulty overcome, and the blind association of pleasure which has been previously received from works of rhyme or metre of the same or similar construction, an indistinct perception perpetually renewed of language closely resembling that of real life, and yet, in the circumstance of metre, differing from it so widely, all these imperceptibly make up a complex feeling of delight, which is of the most important use in tempering the painful feeling which will always be found intermingled with powerful descriptions of the deeper passions. This effect is always produced in pathetic and impassioned poetry; while, in lighter compositions, the ease and gracefulness with which the Poet manages his numbers are themselves confessedly a principal source of the gratification of the Reader. I might perhaps include all which is *necessary* to say upon this subject by affirming, what few persons will deny, that, of two descriptions, either of passions, manners, or characters, each of them equally well executed, the one in prose and the other in verse, the verse will be read a hundred times where the prose is read once. We see that Pope, by the power of verse alone, has contrived to render the plainest common sense interesting, and even frequently to invest it with the appearance of passion. In consequence of these convictions I related in metre the Tale of Goody Blake and Harry Gill, which is one of the rudest of this collection. I wished to draw attention to the truth, that the power of the human imagination is sufficient to produce such changes even in our physical nature as might almost appear miraculous. The truth is an important one; the fact (for it is a *fact*) is a valuable illustration of it. And I have the satisfaction of knowing that it has been communicated to many hundreds of people who would never have heard of it, had it not been narrated as a Ballad, and in a more impressive metre than is usual in Ballads.

Having thus explained a few of the reasons why I have written in verse, and why I have chosen subjects from common life, and endeavoured to bring my language near to the real language of men, if I have been too minute in pleading my own cause, I have at the same time been treating a subject of general interest, and it is for this reason that I request the Reader's permission to add a few words with reference solely to these particular poems, and to some defects which will probably be found in them. I am sensible that my associations must have sometimes been particular instead of general, and that, consequently, giving to things a false importance, sometimes from diseased impulses I may have written upon unworthy subjects; but I am less apprehensive on this account, than that my language may frequently have suffered from those arbitrary connections of feelings and ideas with particular words and phrases, from which no man can altogether protect himself. Hence I have no doubt, that, in some instances, feelings even of the ludicrous may be given to my Readers by expressions which appeared to me tender and pathetic. Such faulty expressions, were I convinced they were faulty at present, and that they must necessarily continue to be so, I would willingly take all reasonable pains to correct. But it is dangerous to make these alterations on the simple authority of a few individuals, or even of certain classes of men; for where the understanding of an Author is not convinced, or his feelings altered, this cannot be done without great injury to himself: for his own feelings are his stay and support, and, if he sets them aside in one instance, he may be induced to repeat this act till his mind loses all confidence in itself, and becomes utterly debilitated. To this it may be added, that the Reader ought never to forget that he is himself exposed to the same errors as the Poet, and perhaps in a much greater degree: for there can be no presumption in saying, that it is not probable he will be so well acquainted with the various stages of meaning through which words have passed, or with the fickleness or stability of the relations of particular ideas to each other; and above all, since he is so much less interested in the subject, he may decide lightly and carelessly.

Long as I have detained my Reader, I hope he will permit me to caution him against a mode of false criticism which has been applied to Poetry in which the language closely resembles that of life and nature. Such verses have been triumphed over in parodies of which Doctor Johnson's stanza is a fair specimen.

I put my hat upon my head,
And walk'd into the Strand,
And there I met another man,
Whose hat was in his hand.

Immediately under these lines I will place one of the most justly admired stanzas of the '*Babes* in the Wood.'

These pretty Babes with hand in hand
Went wandering up and down;
But never more they saw the Man
Approaching from the Town.

In both these stanzas the words, and the order of the words, in no respect differ from the most unimpassioned conversation. There are words in both, for example, 'the Strand,' and 'the Town,' connected with none but the most familiar ideas; yet the one stanza we admit as admirable, and the other as a fair example of the superlatively contemptible. Whence arises this difference? Not from the metre, not from the language, not from the order of the words; but the *matter* expressed in Dr. Johnson's stanza is contemptible. The proper method of treating trivial and simple verses, to which Dr Johnson's stanza would be a fair parallelism, is not to say, This is a bad kind of poetry, or This is not poetry; but This wants sense; it is neither interesting in itself, nor can *lead* to anything interesting; the images neither originate in that sane state of feeling which arises out of thought, nor can excite thought or feeling in the Reader. This is the only sensible manner of dealing with such verses. Why trouble yourself about the species till you have previously decided upon the genus? Why take pains to prove that an ape is not a Newton, when it is self-evident that he is not a man?

I have one request to make of my Reader, which is, that in judging these Poems he would decide by his own feelings genuinely, and not by reflection upon what will probably be the judgment of others. How common is it to hear a person say, 'I myself do not object to this style of composition, or this or that expression, but to such and such classes of people it will appear mean or ludicrous.' This mode of criticism, so destructive of all sound unadulterated judgment, is almost universal: I have therefore to request, that the Reader would abide independently by his own feelings, and that if he finds himself affected he would not suffer such conjectures to interfere with his pleasure.

If an Author by any single composition has impressed us with respect for his talents, it is useful to consider this as affording a presumption, that, on other occasions where we have been displeased, he nevertheless may not have written ill or absurdly; and, further, to give him so much credit for this one composition as may induce us to review what has displeased us with more care than we should otherwise have bestowed upon it. This is not only an act of justice, but, in our decisions upon poetry especially, may conduce in a high degree to the improvement of our own taste: for an *accurate* taste in poetry, and in all the other arts, as Sir Joshua Reynolds has observed, is an *acquired* talent, which can only be produced by thought, and a long continued intercourse with the best models of composition. This is mentioned, not with so ridiculous a purpose as to prevent the most inexperienced Reader from judging for himself, (I have already said that I wish him to judge for himself;) but merely to temper the rashness of decision, and to suggest, that, if Poetry be a subject on which much time has not been bestowed, the judgment may be erroneous; and that in many cases it necessarily will be so.

I know that nothing would have so effectually contributed to further the end which I have in view, as to have shown of what kind the pleasure is, and how that pleasure is produced, which is confessedly produced by metrical composition essentially different from that which I have here endeavoured to recommend: for the Reader will say that he has been pleased by such composition; and what can I do more for him? The power of any art is limited; and he will suspect, that, if I propose to furnish him with new friends, it is only upon condition of his abandoning his old friends. Besides as I have said, the Reader is himself conscious of the pleasure which he has received from such composition, composition to which he has peculiarly attached the endearing name of Poetry; and all men feel an habitual gratitude, and something of an honourable bigotry for the objects which have long continued to please them; we not only wish to be pleased, but to be pleased in that particular way in which we have been accustomed to be pleased. There is a host of arguments in these feelings; and I should be the less able to combat them successfully, as I am willing to allow, that, in order entirely to enjoy the Poetry which I am recommending, it would be necessary to give up much of what is ordinarily enjoyed. But, would my limits have permitted me to point out how this pleasure is produced, I might have removed many obstacles, and assisted my Reader in perceiving that the powers of language are not so limited as he may suppose; and that it is possible that poetry may give other enjoyments, of a purer, more lasting, and more exquisite nature. This part of my subject I have not altogether neglected; but it has been less my present aim to prove, that the interest excited by some other kinds of poetry is less vivid, and less worthy of the nobler powers of the mind, than to offer reasons for presuming, that, if the object which I have proposed to myself were adequately attained, a species of poetry would be produced, which is genuine poetry; in its nature well adapted to interest mankind permanently, and likewise important in the multiplicity and quality of its moral relations.

From what has been said, and from a perusal of the Poems, the Reader will be able clearly to perceive the object which I have proposed to myself: he will determine how far I have attained this object; and, what is a much more important question, whether it be worth attaining: and upon the decision of these two questions will rest my claim to the approbation of the public.

Hart-Leap Well

HART-LEAP WELL is a small spring of water, about five miles from Richmond in Yorkshire, and near the side of the road which leads from Richmond to Askrigg. Its name is derived from a remarkable Chase, the memory of which is preserved by the monuments spoken of in the second Part of the following Poem, which monuments do now exist as I have there described them.

THE Knight had ridden down from Wensley moor
With the slow motion of a summer's cloud;
He turned aside towards a Vassal's door,
And, 'Bring another Horse!' he cried aloud.

'Another Horse!'—That shout the Vassal heard,
And saddled his best steed, a comely gray;
Sir Walter mounted him; he was the third
Which he had mounted on that glorious day.

Joy sparkled in the prancing Courser's eyes;
The Horse and Horseman are a happy pair;
But, though Sir Walter like a falcon flies,
There is a doleful silence in the air.

A rout this morning left Sir Walter's Hall,
That as they galloped made the echoes roar;
But Horse and Man are vanished, one and all;
Such race, I think, was never seen before.

Sir Walter, restless as a veering wind,
Calls to the few tired Dogs that yet remain:
Brach, Swift, and Music, noblest of their kind,
Follow, and up the weary mountain strain.

The Knight hallooed, he chid and cheered them on
With suppliant gestures and upbraidings stern;
But breath and eye-sight fail; and, one by one,
The Dogs are stretched among the mountain fern.

Where is the throng, the tumult of the race?
The bugles that so joyfully were blown?
—This Chase it looks not like an earthly Chase;
Sir Walter and the Hart are left alone.

The poor Hart toils along the mountain side;
I will not stop to tell how far he fled,
Nor will I mention by what death he died;
But now the Knight beholds him lying dead.

Dismounting then, he leaned against a thorn;
He had no follower, Dog, nor Man, nor Boy:
He neither smacked his whip, nor blew his horn,
But gazed upon the spoil with silent joy.

Close to the thorn on which Sir Walter leaned,
Stood his dumb partner in this glorious act;
Weak as a lamb the hour that it is yeaned,
And foaming like a mountain cataract.

Upon his side the Hart was lying stretched:
His nose half-touched a spring beneath a hill,
And with the last deep groan his breath had fetched
The waters of the spring were trembling still.

And now, too happy for repose or rest,
(Was never man in such a joyful case!)
Sir Walter walked all round, north, south, and west,
And gazed and gazed upon that darling place.

And climbing up the hill—(it was at least
Nine roods of sheer ascent) Sir Walter found
Three several hoof-marks which the hunted Beast
Had left imprinted on the verdant ground.

Sir Walter wiped his face and cried, 'Till now
Such sight was never seen by living eyes:
Three leaps have borne him from this lofty brow,
Down to the very fountain where he lies.

I'll build a Pleasure-house upon this spot,
And a small Arbour, made for rural joy;
'Twill be the Traveller's shed, the Pilgrim's cot,
A place of love for Damsels that are coy.

A cunning Artist will I have to frame
A bason for that Fountain in the dell;
And they who do make mention of the same
From this day forth, shall call it HART-LEAP WELL.

And, gallant brute! to make thy praises known,
Another monument shall here be raised;
Three several Pillars, each a rough hewn Stone,
And planted where thy hoofs the turf have grazed.

And in the summer-time when days are long,
I will come hither with my Paramour;
And with the Dancers, and the Minstrel's song,
We will make merry in that pleasant Bower.

Till the foundations of the mountains fail
My Mansion with its Arbour shall endure:—
The joy of them who till the fields of Swale,
And them who dwell among the woods of Ure!'

Then home he went, and left the Hart, stone-dead,
With breathless nostrils stretched above the spring.
And soon the Knight performed what he had said,
The fame whereof through many a land did ring.

Ere thrice the moon into her port had steered,
A Cup of Stone received the living Well;
Three Pillars of rude stone Sir Walter reared,
And built a House of Pleasure in the dell.

And near the fountain, flowers of stature tall
With trailing plants and trees were intertwined,
Which soon composed a little sylvan Hall,
A leafy shelter from the sun and wind.

And thither, when the summer-days were long,
Sir Walter journeyed with his Paramour;
And with the Dancers and the Minstrel's song
Made merriment within that pleasant Bower.

The Knight, Sir Walter, died in course of time,
And his bones lie in his paternal vale.—
But there is matter for a second rhyme,
And I to this would add another tale.

PART SECOND

The moving accident is not my trade:
To freeze the blood I have no ready arts;
'Tis my delight, alone in summer shade,
To pipe a simple song to thinking hearts.

As I from Hawes to Richmond did repair,
It chanced that I saw standing in a dell
Three Aspens at three corners of a square,
And one, not four yards distant, near a Well.

What this imported I could ill divine:
And, pulling now the rein my horse to stop,
I saw three Pillars standing in a line,
The last Stone Pillar on a dark hill-top.

The trees were gray, with neither arms nor head;
Half-wasted the square Mound of tawny green;
So that you just might say, as then I said,
'Here in old time the hand of man has been.'

I looked upon the hills both far and near,
More doleful place did never eye survey;
It seemed as if the spring-time came not here,
And Nature here were willing to decay.

I stood in various thoughts and fancies lost,
When one, who was in Shepherd's garb attired,
Came up the Hollow. Him did I accost,
And what this place might be I then inquired.

The Shepherd stopped, and that same story told
Which in my former rhyme I have rehearsed.
'A jolly place,' said he, 'in times of old!
But something ails it now; the spot is curst.

You see these lifeless Stumps of aspen wood—
Some say that they are beeches, others elms—
These were the Bower; and here a Mansion stood;
The finest palace of a hundred realms!

The Arbour does its own condition tell;
You see the Stones, the Fountain, and the Stream,
But as to the great Lodge! you might as well
Hunt half a day for a forgotten dream.

There's neither dog nor heifer, horse nor sheep,
Will wet his lips within that Cup of Stone;
And oftentimes, when all are fast asleep,
This water doth send forth a dolorous groan.

Some say that here a murder has been done,
And blood cries out for blood: but, for my part,
I've guessed, when I've been sitting in the sun,
That it was all for that unhappy Hart.

What thoughts must through the creature's brain
    have passed!
From the stone upon the summit of the steep
Are but three bounds—and look, Sir, at this last—
—O Master! it has been a cruel leap.

For thirteen hours he ran a desperate race;
And in my simple mind we cannot tell
What cause the Hart might have to love this place,
And come and make his death-bed near the Well.

Here on the grass perhaps asleep he sank,
Lulled by this Fountain in the summer-tide;
This water was perhaps the first he drank
When he had wandered from his mother's side.

In April here beneath the scented thorn
He heard the birds their morning carols sing;
And he, perhaps, for aught we know, was born
Not half a furlong from that self-same spring.

But now here's neither grass nor pleasant shade;
The sun on drearier Hollow never shone:
So will it be, as I have often said,
Till Trees, and Stones, and Fountain all are gone.'

'Gray-headed Shepherd, thou hast spoken well;
Small difference lies between thy creed and mine:
This Beast not unobserved by Nature fell;
His death was mourned by sympathy divine.

The Being, that is in the clouds and air,
That is in the green leaves among the groves,
Maintains a deep and reverential care
For them the quiet creatures whom he loves.

The Pleasure-house is dust:—behind, before,
This is no common waste, no common gloom;
But Nature, in due course of time, once more
Shall here put on her beauty and her bloom.

She leaves these objects to a slow decay,
That what we are, and have been, may be known;
But, at the coming of the milder day,
These monuments shall all be overgrown.

One lesson, Shepherd, let us two divide,
Taught both by what she shows, and what conceals,
Never to blend our pleasure or our pride
With sorrow of the meanest thing that feels.'

The Brothers†

A PASTORAL POEM

'These Tourists, Heaven preserve us! needs must live
A profitable life: some glance along
Rapid and gay, as if the earth were air,
And they were butterflies to wheel about
Long as their summer lasted: some, as wise,
Upon the forehead of a jutting crag
Sit perched, with book and pencil on their knee,
And look and scribble, and scribble on and look,
Until a man might travel twelve stout miles,
Or reap an acre of his neighbour's corn.
But, for that moping Son of Idleness,
Why can he tarry *yonder?*—In our church-yard
Is neither epitaph nor monument,
Tomb-stone nor name—only the turf we tread,
And a few natural graves.' To Jane, his wife,
Thus spake the homely Priest of Ennerdale.
It was a July evening; and he sate
Upon the long stone-seat beneath the eaves
Of his old cottage, as it chanced, that day,
Employed in winter's work. Upon the stone
His Wife sate near him, teasing matted wool,
While, from the twin cards toothed with glittering wire,
He fed the spindle of his youngest Child,
Who turned her large round wheel in the open air
With back and forward steps. Towards the field
In which the Parish Chapel stood alone,
Girt round with a bare ring of mossy wall,
While half an hour went by, the Priest had sent
Many a long look of wonder, and at last,
Risen from his seat, beside the snow-white ridge
Of carded wool which the old man had piled
He laid his implements with gentle care,

† This Poem was intended to be the concluding poem of a series of pastorals, the scene of which was laid among the mountains of Cumberland and Westmorland. I mention this to apologize for the abruptness with which the poem begins.

Each in the other locked; and, down the path
Which from his cottage to the church-yard led,
He took his way, impatient to accost
The Stranger, whom he saw still lingering there.

'Twas one well known to him in former days,
A Shepherd-lad: who ere his thirteenth year
Had changed his calling, with the mariners
A fellow-mariner, and so had fared
Through twenty seasons; but he had been reared
Among the mountains, and he in his heart
Was half a Shepherd on the stormy seas.
Oft in the piping shrouds had Leonard heard
The tones of waterfalls, and inland sounds
Of caves and trees:—and, when the regular wind
Between the tropics filled the steady sail,
And blew with the same breath through days and weeks,
Lengthening invisibly its weary line
Along the cloudless Main, he, in those hours
Of tiresome indolence, would often hang
Over the vessel's side, and gaze and gaze;
And, while the broad green wave and sparkling foam
Flashed round him images and hues, that wrought
In union with employment of his heart,
He, thus by feverish passion overcome,
Even with the organs of his bodily eye,
Below him, in the bosom of the deep,
Saw mountains, saw the forms of sheep that grazed
On verdant hills, with dwellings among trees,
And shepherds clad in the same country gray
Which he himself had worn.*
And now at length
From perils manifold, with some small wealth
Acquired by traffic in the Indian Isles,
To his paternal home he is returned,
With a determined purpose to resume
The life which he lived there; both for the sake
Of many darling pleasures, and the love
Which to an only brother he has borne
In all his hardships, since that happy time

* This description of the Calenture is sketched from an imperfect recollection of an admirable one in prose, by Mr. Gilbert, author of 'The Hurricane.'

When, whether it blew foul or fair, they two
Were brother Shepherds on their native hills.
—They were the last of all their race: and now
When Leonard had approached his home, his heart
Failed in him; and, not venturing to inquire
Tidings of one whom he so dearly loved,
Towards the church-yard he had turned aside,
That, as he knew in what particular spot
His family were laid, he thence might learn
If still his Brother lived, or to the file
Another grave was added.—He had found
Another grave, near which a full half-hour
He had remained; but, as he gazed, there grew
Such a confusion in his memory,
That he began to doubt, and he had hopes
That he had seen this heap of turf before,
That it was not another grave, but one
He had forgotten. He had lost his path,
As up the vale he came that afternoon,
Through fields which once had been well known to him.
And oh! what joy the recollection now
Sent to his heart! He lifted up his eyes,
And looking round he thought that he perceived
Strange alteration wrought on every side
Among the woods and fields, and that the rocks,
And the eternal hills, themselves were changed.

By this the Priest, who down the field had come
Unseen by Leonard, at the church-yard gate
Stopped short, and thence, at leisure, limb by limb
He scanned him with a gay complacency.
Aye, thought the Vicar, smiling to himself,
'Tis one of those who needs must leave the path
Of the world's business to go wild alone:
His arms have a perpetual holiday;
The happy Man will creep about the fields
Following his fancies by the hour, to bring
Tears down his cheeks, or solitary smiles
Into his face, until the setting sun
Write Fool upon his forehead. Planted thus
Beneath a shed that overarched the gate
Of this rude church-yard, till the stars appeared

The good man might have communed with himself,
But that the stranger, who had left the grave,
Approached; he recognized the Priest at once,
And, after greetings interchanged, and given
By Leonard to the Vicar as to one
Unknown to him, this dialogue ensued.

LEONARD

You live, Sir, in these dales, a quiet life:
Your years make up one peaceful family;
And who would grieve and fret, if, welcome come
And welcome gone, they are so like each other,
They cannot be remembered? Scarce a funeral
Comes to this church-yard once in eighteen months;
And yet, some changes must take place among you:
And you, who dwell here, even among these rocks
Can trace the finger of mortality,
And see, that with our threescore years and ten
We are not all that perish.—I remember,
For many years ago I passed this road,
There was a foot-way all along the fields
By the brook-side—'tis gone—and that dark cleft!
To me it does not seem to wear the face
Which then it had.

PRIEST

Why, Sir, for aught I know,
That chasm is much the same—

LEONARD

But, surely, yonder—

PRIEST

Aye, there, indeed, your memory is a friend
That does not play you false—On that tall pike
(It is the loneliest place of all these hills)
There were two Springs which bubbled side by side,
As if they had been made that they might be

Companions for each other: ten years back,
Close to those brother fountains, the huge crag
Was rent with lightning—one is dead and gone,
The other, left behind, is flowing still.——
For accidents and changes such as these,
Why, we have store of them! a water-spout
Will bring down half a mountain; what a feast
For folks that wander up and down like you
To see an acre's breadth of that wide cliff
One roaring cataract!—a sharp May storm
Will come with loads of January snow,
And in one night send twenty score of sheep
To feed the ravens; or a Shepherd dies
By some untoward death among the rocks:
The ice breaks up and sweeps away a bridge—
A wood is felled:—and then for our own homes!
A Child is born or christened, a Field ploughed,
A Daughter sent to service, a Web spun,
The old House-clock is decked with a new face;
And hence, so far from wanting facts or dates
To chronicle the time, we all have here
A pair of diaries, one serving, Sir,
For the whole dale, and one for each fire-side—
Yours was a stranger's judgment: for Historians,
Commend me to these valleys.

LEONARD

Yet your Church-yard
Seems, if such freedom may be used with you,
To say that you are heedless of the past.
An orphan could not find his mother's grave:
Here's neither head- nor foot-stone, plate of brass,
Cross-bones or skull, type of our earthly state
Or emblem of our hopes: the dead man's home
Is but a fellow to that pasture-field.

PRIEST

Why, there, Sir, is a thought that's new to me.
The Stone-cutters, 'tis true, might beg their bread
If every English Church-yard were like ours:
Yet your conclusion wanders from the truth.

We have no need of names and epitaphs;
We talk about the dead by our fire-sides,
And then, for our immortal part! *we* want
No symbols, Sir, to tell us that plain tale:
The thought of death sits easy on the man
Who has been born and dies among the mountains.

LEONARD

Your Dalesmen, then, do in each other's thoughts
Possess a kind of second life: no doubt
You, Sir, could help me to the history
Of half these Graves?

PRIEST

For eight-score winters past,
With what I've witnessed, and with what I've heard,
Perhaps I might; and, on a winter's evening,
If you were seated at my chimney's nook,
By turning o'er these hillocks one by one
We two could travel, Sir, through a strange round,
Yet all in the broad high-way of the world.
Now there's a grave—your foot is half upon it,
It looks just like the rest; and yet that Man
Died broken-hearted.

LEONARD

'Tis a common case.
We'll take another : who is he that lies
Beneath yon ridge, the last of those three graves ?
It touches on that piece of native rock
Left in the church-yard wall.

PRIEST

That's Walter Ewbank.
He had as white a head and fresh a cheek
As ever were produced by youth and age
Engendering in the blood of hale fourscore.
For five long generations had the heart

Of Walter's forefathers o'erflowed the bounds
Of their inheritance, that single cottage,—
You see it yonder!—and those few green fields.
They toiled and wrought, and still, from Sire to Son,
Each struggled, and each yielded as before
A little—yet a little—and old Walter,
They left to him the family heart, and land
With other burthens than the crop it bore.
Year after year the old man still kept up
A cheerful mind, and buffeted with bond,
Interest and mortgages; at last he sank,
And went into his grave before his time.
Poor Walter! whether it was care that spurred him
God only knows, but to the very last
He had the lightest foot in Ennerdale:
His pace was never that of an old man:
I almost see him tripping down the path
With his two Grandsons after him—but You,
Unless our Landlord be your host to-night,
Have far to travel, and in these rough paths
Even in the longest day of midsummer—

LEONARD

But these two Orphans!

PRIEST

Orphans! Such they were—
Yet not while Walter lived—for, though their parents
Lay buried side by side as now they lie,
The old Man was a father to the boys,
Two fathers in one father: and if tears,
Shed when he talked of them where they were not,
And hauntings from the infirmity of love,
Are aught of what makes up a mother's heart,
This old Man in the day of his old age
Was half a mother to them.—If you weep, Sir,
To hear a Stranger talking about Strangers,
Heaven bless you when you are among your kindred!

Aye. You may turn that way—it is a grave
Which will bear looking at.

LEONARD

These Boys—I hope
They loved this good old Man?—

PRIEST

They did—and truly:
But that was what we almost overlooked,
They were such darlings of each other. For
Though from their cradles they had lived with Walter,
The only Kinsman near them in the house,
Yet he being old, they had much love to spare,
And it all went into each other's hearts.
Leonard, the elder by just eighteen months,
Was two years taller: 'twas a joy to see,
To hear, to meet them! from their house the School
Was distant three short miles—and in the time
Of storm and thaw, when every water-course
And unbridged stream, such as you may have noticed
Crossing our roads at every hundred steps,
Was swoln into a noisy rivulet,
Would Leonard then, when elder boys perhaps
Remained at home, go staggering through the fords
Bearing his Brother on his back. I've seen him,
On windy days, in one of those stray brooks,
Aye, more than once I've seen him mid-leg deep,
Their two books lying both on a dry stone
Upon the hither side: and once I said,
As I remember, looking round these rocks
And hills on which we all of us were born,
That God who made the great book of the world
Would bless such piety—

LEONARD

It may be then—

PRIEST

Never did worthier lads break English bread!
The finest Sunday that the Autumn saw,
With all its mealy clusters of ripe nuts,
Could never keep these boys away from church,
Or tempt them to an hour of sabbath breach.
Leonard and James! I warrant, every corner
Among these rocks, and every hollow place
Where foot could come, to one or both of them
Was known as well as to the flowers that grow there.
Like Roe-bucks they went bounding o'er the hills:
They played like two young Ravens on the crags:
Then they could write, aye and speak too, as well
As many of their betters—and for Leonard!
The very night before he went away,
In my own house I put into his hand
A Bible, and I'd wager twenty pounds,
That, if he is alive, he has it yet.

LEONARD

It seems, these Brothers have not lived to be
A comfort to each other.—

PRIEST

That they might
Live to that end, is what both old and young
In this our valley all of us have wished,
And what, for my part, I have often prayed:
But Leonard—

LEONARD

Then James still is left among you?

PRIEST

'Tis of the elder Brother I am speaking:
They had an Uncle, he was at that time
A thriving man, and trafficked on the seas:

And, but for this same Uncle, to this hour
Leonard had never handled rope or shroud.
For the Boy loved the life which we lead here;
And, though a very Stripling, twelve years old,
His soul was knit to this his native soil.
But, as I said, old Walter was too weak
To strive with such a torrent; when he died,
The Estate and House were sold, and all their Sheep,
A pretty flock, and which, for aught I know,
Had clothed the Ewbanks for a thousand years.
Well—all was gone, and they were destitute.
And Leonard, chiefly for his Brother's sake,
Resolved to try his fortune on the seas.
'Tis now twelve years since we had tidings from him.
If there was one among us who had heard
That Leonard Ewbank was come home again,
From the great Gavel,* down by Leeza's Banks,
And down the Enna, far as Egremont,
The day would be a very festival,
And those two bells of ours, which there you see
Hanging in the open air—but, O good Sir!
This is sad talk—they'll never sound for him
Living or dead.—When last we heard of him
He was in slavery among the Moors
Upon the Barbary Coast.—'Twas not a little
That would bring down his spirit, and, no doubt,
Before it ended in his death, the Lad
Was sadly crossed—Poor Leonard! when we parted,
He took me by the hand and said to me,
If ever the day came when he was rich,
He would return, and on his Father's Land
He would grow old among us.

LEONARD

If that day
Should come, 'twould needs be a glad day for him;
He would himself, no doubt, be happy then
As any that should meet him—

* The Great Gavel, so called, I imagine, from its resemblance to the Gable end c a house, is one of the highest of the Cumberland mountains. It stands at the head c the several vales of Ennerdale, Wastdale, and Borrowdale. The Leeza is a river whic flows into the Lake of Ennerdale: on issuing from the Lake, it changes its name, an is called the End, Eyne, or Enna. It falls into the sea a little below Egremont.

PRIEST

Happy! Sir—

LEONARD

You said his kindred all were in their graves,
And that he had one Brother—

PRIEST

That is but
A fellow tale of sorrow. From his youth
James, though not sickly, yet was delicate;
And Leonard being always by his side
Had done so many offices about him,
That, though he was not of a timid nature,
Yet still the spirit of a Mountain Boy
In him was somewhat checked; and, when his Brother
Was gone to sea and he was left alone,
The little colour that he had was soon
Stolen from his cheek, he drooped, and pined and pined—

LEONARD

But these are all the graves of full-grown men!

PRIEST

Aye, Sir, that passed away: we took him to us.
He was the Child of all the dale—he lived
Three months with one, and six months with another;
And wanted neither food, nor clothes, nor love:
And many, many happy days were his.
But, whether blithe or sad, 'tis my belief
His absent Brother still was at his heart.
And, when he lived beneath our roof, we found
(A practice till this time unknown to him)
That often, rising from his bed at night,
He in his sleep would walk about, and sleeping
He sought his Brother Leonard.—You are moved!
Forgive me, Sir: before I spoke to you,
I judged you most unkindly.

LEONARD

But this Youth,
How did he die at last?

PRIEST

One sweet May morning,
It will be twelve years since, when Spring returns,
He had gone forth among the new-dropped lambs,
With two or three Companions whom it chanced
Some further business summoned to a house
Which stands at the Dale-head. James, tired perhaps,
Or from some other cause, remained behind.
You see yon Precipice—it almost looks
Like some vast building made of many crags;
And in the midst is one particular rock
That rises like a column from the vale,
Whence by our shepherds it is called the Pillar.
James pointed to its summit, over which
They all had purposed to return together,
And told them that he there would wait for them:
They parted, and his Comrades passed that way
Some two hours after, but they did not find him
Upon the Pillar—at the appointed place.
Of this they took no heed: but one of them,
Going by chance, at night, into the house
Which at that time was James's home, there learned
That nobody had seen him all that day:
The morning came, and still, he was unheard of:
The neighbours were alarmed, and to the Brook
Some went, and some towards the Lake: ere noon
They found him at the foot of that same Rock—
Dead, and with mangled limbs. The third day after
I buried him, poor Lad, and there he lies.

LEONARD

And that then *is* his grave?—Before his death
You said that he saw many happy years?

PRIEST

Aye, that he did—

LEONARD

And all went well with him—

PRIEST

If he had one, the Lad had twenty homes.

LEONARD

And you believe, then, that his mind was easy—

PRIEST

Yes, long before he died, he found that time
Is a true friend to sorrow; and unless
His thoughts were turned on Leonard's luckless fortune,
He talked about him with a cheerful love.

LEONARD

He could not come to an unhallowed end!

PRIEST

Nay, God forbid! You recollect I mentioned
A habit which disquietude and grief
Had brought upon him; and we all conjectured
That, as the day was warm, he had lain down
Upon the grass, and, waiting for his comrades,
He there had fallen asleep; that in his sleep
He to the margin of the precipice
Had walked, and from the summit had fallen headlong.
And so no doubt he perished: at the time,
We guess, that in his hands he must have had
His Shepherd's staff; for midway in the cliff
It had been caught; and there for many years
It hung—and mouldered there.
The Priest here ended—
The Stranger would have thanked him, but he felt
Tears rushing in. Both left the spot in silence;
And Leonard, when they reached the church-yard gate,

As the Priest lifted up the latch, turned round,
And, looking at the grave, he said, 'My Brother.'
The Vicar did not hear the words: and now,
Pointing towards the Cottage, he entreated
That Leonard would partake his homely fare:
The other thanked him with a fervent voice,
But added, that, the evening being calm,
He would pursue his journey. So they parted.

It was not long ere Leonard reached a grove
That overhung the road: he there stopped short,
And, sitting down beneath the trees, reviewed
All that the priest had said: his early years
Were with him in his heart: his cherished hopes,
And thoughts which had been his an hour before,
All pressed on him with such a weight, that now,
This vale, where he had been so happy, seemed
A place in which he could not bear to live:
So he relinquished all his purposes.
He travelled on to Egremont: and thence,
That night, he wrote a letter to the Priest
Reminding him of what had passed between them;
And adding, with a hope to be forgiven,
That it was from the weakness of his heart
He had not dared to tell him who he was.

This done, he went on shipboard, and is now
A Seaman, a gray-headed Mariner.

'Strange Fits of Passion I Have Known'

STRANGE fits of passion I have known:
And I will dare to tell,
But in the Lover's ear alone,
What once to me befel.

When she I loved, was strong and gay
And like a rose in June,
I to her cottage bent my way,
Beneath the evening Moon.

Upon the Moon I fixed my eye,
All over the wide lea:
My Horse trudged on—and we drew nigh
Those paths so dear to me.

And now we reached the orchard plot;
And, as we climbed the hill,
Towards the roof of Lucy's cot
The Moon descended still.

In one of those sweet dreams I slept,
Kind Nature's gentlest boon!
And, all the while, my eyes I kept
On the descending Moon.

My Horse moved on; hoof after hoof
He raised, and never stopped:
When down behind the cottage roof
At once the Planet dropped.

What fond and wayward thoughts will slide
Into a Lover's head—
'O mercy!' to myself I cried,
'If Lucy should be dead!'

'She Dwelt among th' Untrodden Ways'

She dwelt among th' untrodden ways
  Beside the springs of Dove,
A Maid whom there were none to praise,
  And very few to love.

A Violet by a mossy stone
  Half-hidden from the eye!
—Fair as a star, when only one
  Is shining in the sky.

She lived unknown, and few could know
  When Lucy ceased to be;
But she is in her Grave, and oh!
  The difference to me.

'A Slumber did my Spirit Seal'

A SLUMBER did my spirit seal;
I had no human fears:
She seemed a thing that could not feel
The touch of earthly years.

No motion has she now, no force;
She neither hears nor sees,
Rolled round in earth's diurnal course
With rocks and stones and trees!

Lucy Gray

OFT I had heard of Lucy Gray:
And, when I crossed the Wild,
I chanced to see at break of day
The solitary Child.

No Mate, no comrade Lucy knew;
She dwelt on a wide Moor,
—The sweetest thing that ever grew
Beside a human door!

You yet may spy the Fawn at play,
The Hare upon the Green;
But the sweet face of Lucy Gray
Will never more be seen.

'To-night will be a stormy night—
You to the Town must go;
And take a lantern, Child, to light
Your Mother through the snow.'

'That, Father! will I gladly do;
'Tis scarcely afternoon—
The Minster-clock has just struck two,
And yonder is the Moon.'

At this the Father raised his hook
And snapped a faggot-band;
He plied his work and Lucy took
The lantern in her hand.

Not blither is the mountain roe:
With many a wanton stroke
Her feet disperse the powdery snow,
That rises up like smoke.

The storm came on before its time:
She wandered up and down;
And many a hill did Lucy climb,
But never reached the Town.

The wretched Parents all that night
Went shouting far and wide;
But there was neither sound nor sight
To serve them for a guide.

At day-break on a hill they stood
That overlooked the Moor;
And thence they saw the Bridge of wood,
A furlong from their door.

And now they homeward turned, and cried
'In Heaven we all shall meet!'
—When in the snow the Mother spied
The print of Lucy's feet.

Then downward from the steep hill's edge
They tracked the footmarks small;
And through the broken hawthorn-hedge,
And by the long stone-wall:

And then an open field they crossed:
The marks were still the same;
They tracked them on, nor ever lost;
And to the Bridge they came.

They followed from the snowy bank
The footmarks, one by one,
Into the middle of the plank;
And further there was none.

—Yet some maintain that to this day
She is a living Child;
That you may see sweet Lucy Gray
Upon the lonesome Wild.

O'er rough and smooth she trips along,
And never looks behind;
And sings a solitary song
That whistles in the wind.

The Idle Shepherd-Boys, or, Dungeon-Gill Force†

A PASTORAL

I

THE valley rings with mirth and joy;
Among the hills the Echoes play
A never never ending song
To welcome in the May.
The Magpie chatters with delight;
The mountain Raven's youngling Brood
Have left the Mother and the Nest;
And they go rambling east and west
In search of their own food;
Or through the glittering Vapors dart
In very wantonness of heart.

† *Gill* in the dialect of Cumberland and Westmorland is a short, and, for the most part, a steep narrow valley, with a stream running through it. *Force* is the word universally employed in these dialects for Waterfall.

2

Beneath a rock, upon the grass,
Two Boys are sitting in the sun;
It seems they have no work to do,
Or that their work is done.
On pipes of sycamore they play
The fragments of a Christmas Hymn;
Or with that plant which in our dale
We call Stag-horn, or Fox's Tail,
Their rusty Hats they trim:
And thus, as happy as the Day,
Those Shepherds wear the time away.

3

Along the river's stony marge
The Sand-lark chants a joyous song;
The Thrush is busy in the wood,
And carols loud and strong.
A thousand Lambs are on the rocks,
All newly born! both earth and sky
Keep jubilee; and more than all,
Those Boys with their green Coronal;
They never hear the cry,
That plaintive cry! which up the hill
Comes from the depth of Dungeon-Gill

4

Said Walter, leaping from the ground,
'Down to the stump of yon old yew
We'll for our Whistles run a race.'
—Away the Shepherds flew.
They leapt—they ran—and when they came
Right opposite to Dungeon-Gill,
Seeing that he should lose the prize,
'Stop!' to his comrade Walter cries—
James stopped with no good will:
Said Walter then, 'Your task is here,
'Twill keep you working half a year.

5

'Now cross where I shall cross—come on,
And follow me where I shall lead'—
The other took him at his word,
But did not like the deed.
It was a spot, which you may see
If ever you to Langdale go:
Into a chasm a mighty Block
Hath fallen, and made a Bridge of rock:
The gulph is deep below;
And in a bason black and small
Receives a lofty Waterfall.

6

With staff in hand across the cleft
The Challenger began his march;
And now, all eyes and feet, hath gained
The middle of the arch.
When list! he hears a piteous moan—
Again!—his heart within him dies—
His pulse is stopped, his breath is lost,
He totters, pale as any ghost,
And, looking down, he spies
A Lamb, that in the pool is pent
Within that black and frightful Rent.

7

The Lamb had slipped into the stream,
And safe without a bruise or wound
The Cataract had borne him down
Into the gulph profound.
His Dam had seen him when he fell,
She saw him down the torrent borne;
And, while with all a mother's love
She from the lofty rocks above
Sent forth a cry forlorn,
The Lamb, still swimming round and round,
Made answer to that plaintive sound.

8

When he had learnt what thing it was,
That sent this rueful cry; I ween,
The Boy recovered heart, and told
The sight which he had seen.
Both gladly now deferred their task;
Nor was there wanting other aid—
A Poet, one who loves the brooks
Far better than the sages' books,
By chance had thither strayed;
And there the helpless Lamb he found
By those huge rocks encompassed round.

9

He drew it gently from the pool,
And brought it forth into the light:
The Shepherds met him with his Charge,
An unexpected sight!
Into their arms the Lamb they took,
Said they, 'He's neither maimed nor scarred.'
Then up the steep ascent they hied,
And placed him at his Mother's side;
And gently did the Bard
Those idle Shepherd-boys upbraid,
And bade them better mind their trade.

Poor Susan

At the corner of Wood-street, when day-light appears,
There's a Thrush that sings loud, it has sung for three years:
Poor Susan has passed by the spot, and has heard
In the silence of morning the song of the Bird.

'Tis a note of enchantment; what ails her? She sees
A mountain ascending, a vision of trees;
Bright volumes of vapour through Lothbury glide,
And a river flows on through the vale of Cheapside.

Green pastures she views in the midst of the dale,
Down which she so often has tripped with her pail;
And a single small cottage, a nest like a dove's,
The one only Dwelling on earth that she loves.

She looks, and her Heart is in heaven: but they fade,
The mist and the river, the hill and the shade;
The stream will not flow, and the hill will not rise,
And the colours have all passed away from her eyes.

Inscription

FOR THE SPOT WHERE THE HERMITAGE STOOD ON ST. HERBERT'S ISLAND, DERWENT-WATER

If Thou in the dear love of some one Friend
Hast been so happy, that thou know'st what thoughts
Will, sometimes, in the happiness of love
Make the heart sick, then wilt thou reverence
This quiet spot.——St. Herbert hither came,
And here, for many seasons, from the world
Removed, and the affections of the world,
He dwelt in solitude.—But he had left
A Fellow-labourer; whom the good Man loved
As his own soul. And, when within his cave
Alone he knelt before the crucifix
While o'er the Lake the cataract of Lodore
Pealed to his orisons, and when he paced
Along the beach of this small isle and thought
Of his Companions, he would pray that both
Might die in the same moment. Nor in vain
So prayed he:—as our Chronicles report,
Though here the Hermit numbered his last days,
Far from St. Cuthbert his beloved Friend,
Those holy Men both died in the same hour.

Lines

WRITTEN WITH A PENCIL UPON A STONE IN THE WALL OF THE HOUSE (AN OUT-HOUSE) ON THE ISLAND AT GRASMERE

Rude is this Edifice, and Thou hast seen
Buildings, albeit rude, that have maintained
Proportions more harmonious, and approached
To somewhat of a closer fellowship
With the ideal grace. Yet as it is
Do take it in good part; for he, the poor
Vitruvius of our village, had no help
From the great City; never on the leaves
Of red Morocco folio saw displayed
The skeletons and pre-existing ghosts
Of Beauties yet unborn, the rustic Box,
Snug Cot, with Coach-house, Shed and Hermitage.
It is a homely Pile, yet to these walls
The heifer comes in the snow-storm, and here
The new-dropped lamb finds shelter from the wind.
And hither does one Poet sometimes row
His Pinnace, a small vagrant Barge, up-piled
With plenteous store of heath and withered fern,
(A lading which he with his sickle cuts
Among the mountains,) and beneath this roof
He makes his summer couch, and here at noon
Spreads out his limbs, while, yet unshorn, the Sheep
Panting beneath the burthen of their wool
Lie round him, even as if they were a part
Of his own Household: nor, while from his bed
He through that door-place looks toward the lake
And to the stirring breezes, does he want
Creations lovely as the work of sleep,
Fair sights, and visions of romantic joy.

Andrew Jones

'I HATE that Andrew Jones: he'll breed
His children up to waste and pillage.
I wish the press-gang or the drum
With its tantara sound, would come
And sweep him from the village!'

I said not this, because he loves
Through the long day to swear and tipple;
But for the poor dear sake of one
To whom a foul deed he had done,
A friendless Man, a travelling Cripple.

For this poor crawling helpless wretch
Some Horseman who was passing by
A penny on the ground had thrown;
But the poor Cripple was alone,
And could not stoop—no help was nigh.

Inch-thick the dust lay on the ground,
For it had long been droughty weather:
So with his staff the Cripple wrought
Among the dust till he had brought
The halfpennies together.

It chanced that Andrew passed that way
Just at the time; and there he found
The Cripple in the mid-day heat
Standing alone, and at his feet
He saw the penny on the ground.

He stooped and took the penny up:
And when the Cripple nearer drew,
Quoth Andrew, 'Under half-a-crown,
What a man finds is all his own,
And so, my friend, good day to you.'

And *hence* I said, that Andrew's boys
Will all be trained to waste and pillage;
And wished the press-gang, or the drum
With its tantara sound, would come
And sweep him from the village!

Ruth

WHEN Ruth was left half desolate
Her Father took another Mate;
And Ruth, not seven years old,
A slighted Child, at her own will
Went wandering over dale and hill,
In thoughtless freedom bold.

And she had made a Pipe of Straw
And from that oaten Pipe could draw
All sounds of winds and floods;
Had built a Bower upon the green,
As if she from her birth had been
An infant of the woods.

Beneath her Father's roof, alone
She seemed to live; her thoughts her own;
Herself her own delight:
Pleased with herself, nor sad nor gay,
She passed her time; and in this way
Grew up to Woman's height.

There came a Youth from Georgia's shore—
A military Casque he wore
With splendid feathers drest;
He brought them from the Cherokees;
The feathers nodded in the breeze,
And made a gallant crest.

From Indian blood you deem him sprung:
Ah, no! he spake the English tongue,
And bore a Soldier's name;
And, when America was free
From battle and from jeopardy,
He 'cross the ocean came.

With hues of genius on his cheek
In finest tones the Youth could speak
—While he was yet a Boy
The moon, the glory of the sun,
And streams that murmur as they run,
Had been his dearest joy.

He was a lovely Youth! I guess
The panther in the wilderness
Was not so fair as he;
And when he chose to sport and play,
No dolphin ever was so gay
Upon the tropic sea.

Among the Indians he had fought;
And with him many tales he brought
Of pleasure and of fear;
Such tales as, told to any Maid
By such a Youth, in the green shade,
Were perilous to hear.

He told of Girls, a happy rout!
Who quit their fold with dance and shout,
Their pleasant Indian Town
To gather strawberries all day long,
Returning with a choral song
When day-light is gone down.

He spake of plants divine and strange
That every hour their blossoms change,
Ten thousand lovely hues!
With budding, fading, faded flowers
They stand the wonder of the bowers
From morn to evening dews.

Of march and ambush, siege and fight,
Then did he tell; and with delight
The heart of Ruth would ache;
Wild histories they were, and dear:
But 'twas a thing of heaven to hear
When of himself he spake!

Sometimes most earnestly he said;
'O Ruth! I have been worse than dead:
False thoughts, thoughts bold and vain,
Encompassed me on every side
When I, in confidence and pride,
Had crossed the Atlantic Main.

'It was a fresh and glorious world,
A banner bright that was unfurled
Before me suddenly:
I looked upon those hills and plains,
And seemed as if let loose from chains
To live at liberty.

'But wherefore speak of this? for now,
Sweet Ruth! with thee, I know not how,
I feel my spirit burn—
Even as the east when day comes forth;
And to the west, and south, and north,
The morning doth return.

'It is a purer, better mind:
O Maiden innocent and kind,
What sights I might have seen!
Even now upon my eyes they break!'
—And he again began to speak
Of Lands where he had been.

He told of the Magnolia,* spread
High as a cloud, high over head!
The Cypress and her spire,
—Of flowers† that with one scarlet gleam
Cover a hundred leagues, and seem
To set the hills on fire.

* Magnolia grandiflora.

† The splendid appearance of these scarlet flowers, which are scattered with such profusion over the Hills in the Southern parts of North America, is frequently mentioned by Bartram in his Travels.

The Youth of green savannahs spake,
And many an endless, endless lake,
With all its fairy crowds
Of islands, that together lie
As quietly as spots of sky
Among the evening clouds.

And then he said 'How sweet it were
A fisher or a hunter there,
A gardener in the shade,
Still wandering with an easy mind
To build a household fire, and find
A home in every glade!

'What days and what sweet years! Ah me!
Our life were life indeed, with thee
So passed in quiet bliss,
And all the while,' said he, 'to know
That we were in a world of woe,
On such an earth as this!'

And then he sometimes interwove
Dear thoughts about a Father's love.
'For there,' said he, 'are spun
Around the heart such tender ties,
That our own children to our eyes
Are dearer than the sun.

Sweet Ruth! and could you go with me
My helpmate in the woods to be,
Our shed at night to rear;
Or run, my own adopted Bride,
A sylvan Huntress at my side,
And drive the flying deer!

Beloved Ruth!'—No more he said.
Sweet Ruth alone at midnight shed
A solitary tear.
She thought again—and did agree
With him to sail across the sea,
And drive the flying deer.

'And now, as fitting is and right,
We in the Church our faith will plight,
A Husband and a Wife.'
Even so they did; and I may say
That to sweet Ruth that happy day
Was more than human life.

Through dream and vision did she sink,
Delighted all the while to think
That, on those lonesome floods,
And green savannahs, she should share
His board with lawful joy, and bear
His name in the wild woods.

But, as you have before been told,
This Stripling, sportive, gay, and bold,
And with his dancing crest
So beautiful, through savage lands
Had roamed about with vagrant bands
Of Indians in the West.

The winds, the tempest roaring high,
The tumult of a tropic sky,
Might well be dangerous food
For him, a Youth to whom was given
So much of earth so much of Heaven,
And such impetuous blood.

Whatever in those Climes he found
Irregular in sight or sound
Did to his mind impart
A kindred impulse, seemed allied
To his own powers, and justified
The workings of his heart.

Nor less to feed voluptuous thought
The beauteous forms of nature wrought,
Fair trees and lovely flowers;
The breezes their own languor lent;
The stars had feelings, which they sent
Into those magic bowers.

Yet, in his worst pursuits, I ween
That sometimes there did intervene
Pure hopes of high intent;
For passions linked to forms so fair
And stately needs must have their share
Of noble sentiment.

But ill he lived, much evil saw
With men to whom no better law
Nor better life was known;
Deliberately and undeceived
Those wild men's vices he received,
And gave them back his own.

His genius and his moral frame
Were thus impaired, and he became
The slave of low desires:
A Man who without self-controul
Would seek what the degraded soul
Unworthily admires.

And yet he with no feigned delight
Had wooed the maiden, day and night
Had loved her, night and morn:
What could he less than love a Maid
Whose heart with so much nature played?
So kind and so forlorn!

But now the pleasant dream was gone;
No hope, no wish remained, not one,
They stirred him now no more;
New objects did new pleasure give,
And once again he wished to live
As lawless as before.

Meanwhile, as thus with him it fared,
They for the voyage were prepared,
And went to the sea-shore;
But, when they thither came, the Youth
Deserted his poor Bride, and Ruth
Could never find him more.

Morning amongst the Coniston Fells c.1798 by J.M.W. Turner (1775–1851). The River Duddon which runs amongst the fells inspired Wordsworth to write a number of sonnets, including "To the River Duddon".
By courtesy of the Tate Gallery, London

Coniston Fells c.1798 by J.M.W. Turner (1775–1851).
By courtesy of The Whitworth Art Gallery, University of Manchester

'God help thee, Ruth!'—Such pains she had
That she in half a year was mad
And in a prison housed;
And there, exulting in her wrongs,
Among the music of her songs
She fearfully caroused.

Yet sometimes milder hours she knew,
Nor wanted sun, nor rain, nor dew,
Nor pastimes of the May,
—They all were with her in her cell;
And a wild brook with cheerful knell
Did o'er the pebbles play.

When Ruth three seasons thus had lain
There came a respite to her pain,
She from her prison fled;
But of the Vagrant none took thought;
And where it liked her best she sought
Her shelter and her bread.

Among the fields she breathed again:
The master-current of her brain
Ran permanent and free;
And, coming to the banks of Tone,*
There did she rest; and dwell alone
Under the greenwood tree.

The engines of her pain, the tools
That shaped her sorrow, rocks and pools,
And airs that gently stir
The vernal leaves, she loved them still,
Nor ever taxed them with the ill
Which had been done to her.

A Barn her *winter* bed supplies;
But till the warmth of summer skies
And summer days is gone,

* The Tone is a River of Somersetshire at no great distance from the Quantock Hills. These hills, which are alluded to a few Stanzas below, are extremely beautiful, and in most places richly covered with Coppice woods.

(And all do in this tale agree)
She sleeps beneath the greenwood tree,
And other home hath none.

An innocent life, yet far astray!
And Ruth will, long before her day,
Be broken down and old.
Sore aches she needs must have! but less
Of mind, than body's wretchedness,
From damp, and rain, and cold.

If she is pressed by want of food,
She from her dwelling in the wood
Repairs to a road-side;
And there she begs at one steep place,
Where up and down with easy pace
The horsemen-travellers ride.

That oaten Pipe of hers is mute,
Or thrown away; but with a flute
Her loneliness she cheers:
This flute, made of a hemlock stalk,
At evening in his homeward walk
The Quantock Woodman hears.

I, too, have passed her on the hills
Setting her little water-mills
By spouts and fountains wild—
Such small machinery as she turned
Ere she had wept, ere she had mourned,
A young and happy Child!

Farewell! and when thy days are told,
Ill-fated Ruth! in hallowed mould
Thy corpse shall buried be;
For thee a funeral bell shall ring,
And all the congregation sing
A Christian psalm for thee.

Lines

WRITTEN WITH A SLATE-PENCIL, UPON A STONE, THE LARGEST OF A HEAP LYING NEAR A DESERTED QUARRY, UPON ONE OF THE ISLANDS AT RYDALE

STRANGER! this hillock of misshapen stones
Is not a ruin of the antient time,
Nor, as perchance thou rashly deem'st, the Cairn
Of some old British Chief: 'tis nothing more
Than the rude embryo of a little Dome
Or Pleasure-house, once destined to be built
Among the birch-trees of this rocky isle.
But, as it chanced, Sir William having learned
That from the shore a full-grown man might wade,
And make himself a freeman of this spot
At any hour he chose, the Knight forthwith
Desisted, and the quarry and the mound
Are monuments of his unfinished task.——
The block on which these lines are traced, perhaps,
Was once selected as the corner-stone
Of the intended Pile, which would have been
Some quaint odd play-thing of elaborate skill,
So that, I guess, the linnet and the thrush,
And other little Builders who dwell here,
Had wondered at the work. But blame him not,
For old Sir William was a gentle Knight
Bred in this vale, to which he appertained
With all his ancestry. Then peace to him,
And for the outrage which he had devised
Entire forgiveness!——But if thou art one
On fire with thy impatience to become
An inmate of these mountains, if, disturbed
By beautiful conceptions, thou hast hewn
Out of the quiet rock the elements
Of thy trim mansion destined soon to blaze
In snow-white glory, think again, and, taught
By old Sir William and his quarry, leave
Thy fragments to the bramble and the rose;
There let the vernal Slow-worm sun himself,
And let the Redbreast hop from stone to stone.

'*If Nature, for a Favourite Child*'

In the School of —— is a Tablet, on which are inscribed, in gilt letters, the names of several persons who have been Schoolmasters there since the foundation of the School, with the time at which they entered upon and quitted their office. Opposite one of those names the Author wrote the following lines.

If Nature, for a favourite Child
In thee hath tempered so her clay,
That every hour thy heart runs wild,
Yet never once doth go astray,

Read o'er these lines; and then review
This tablet, that thus humbly rears
In such diversity of hue
Its history of two hundred years.

—When through this little wreck of fame,
Cypher and syllable! thine eye
Has travelled down to Matthew's name,
Pause with no common sympathy.

And, if a sleeping tear should wake,
Then be it neither checked nor stayed:
For Matthew a request I make
Which for himself he had not made.

Poor Matthew, all his frolics o'er,
Is silent as a standing pool;
Far from the chimney's merry roar,
And murmur of the village school.

The sighs which Matthew heaved were sighs
Of one tired out with fun and madness;
The tears which came to Matthew's eyes
Were tears of light, the oil of gladness.

Yet, sometimes, when the secret cup
Of still and serious thought went round,
It seemed as if he drank it up—
He felt with spirit so profound.

—Thou soul of God's best earthly mould!
Thou happy soul! and can it be
That these two words of glittering gold
Are all that must remain to thee?

The Two April Mornings

We walked along, while bright and red
Uprose the morning sun;
And Matthew stopped, he looked, and said,
'The will of God be done!'

A village Schoolmaster was he,
With hair of glittering gray;
As blithe a man as you could see
On a spring holiday.

And on that morning, through the grass,
And by the steaming rills,
We travelled merrily, to pass
A day among the hills.

'Our work,' said I, 'was well begun;
Then, from thy breast what thought,
Beneath so beautiful a sun,
So sad a sigh has brought?'

A second time did Matthew stop;
And fixing still his eye
Upon the eastern mountain-top,
To me he made reply:

'Yon cloud with that long purple cleft
Brings fresh into my mind
A day like this which I have left
Full thirty years behind.

'And just above yon slope of corn
Such colours, and no other
Were in the sky, that April morn,
Of this the very brother.

'With rod and line my silent sport
I plied by Derwent's wave;
And, coming to the church, stopp'd short
Beside my daughter's grave.

'Nine summers had she scarcely seen,
The pride of all the vale;
And then she sung;—she would have been
A very nightingale.

'Six feet in earth my Emma lay;
And yet I loved her more,
For so it seemed, than till that day
I e'er had loved before.

'And turning from her grave, I met
Beside the church-yard Yew
A blooming Girl, whose hair was wet
With points of morning dew.

'A basket on her head she bare;
Her brow was smooth and white:
To see a Child so very fair,
It was a pure delight!

'No fountain from its rocky cave
E'er tripped with foot so free;
She seemed as happy as a wave
That dances on the sea.

'There came from me a sigh of pain
Which I could ill confine;
I looked at her and looked again:
—And did not wish her mine.'

Matthew is in his grave, yet now
Methinks I see him stand,
As at that moment, with his bough
Of wilding in his hand.

The Fountain

A CONVERSATION

We talked with open heart, and tongue
Affectionate and true;
A pair of Friends, though I was young,
And Matthew seventy-two.

We lay beneath a spreading oak,
Beside a mossy seat;
And from the turf a fountain broke,
And gurgled at our feet.

'Now, Matthew! let us try to match
This water's pleasant tune
With some old Border-song, or Catch
That suits a summer's noon.

'Or of the Church-clock and the chimes
Sing here beneath the shade,
That half-mad thing of witty rhymes
Which you last April made!'

In silence Matthew lay, and eyed
The spring beneath the tree;
And thus the dear old man replied,
The gray-haired man of glee:

'Down to the vale this water steers,
How merrily it goes!
'Twill murmur on a thousand years,
And flow as now it flows.

'And here, on this delightful day,
I cannot choose but think
How oft, a vigorous man, I lay
Beside this Fountain's brink.

'My eyes are dim with childish tears,
My heart is idly stirred,
For the same sound is in my ears
Which in those days I heard.

'Thus fares it still in our decay:
And yet the wiser mind
Mourns less for what age takes away
Than what it leaves behind.

'The Blackbird in the summer trees,
The Lark upon the hill,
Let loose their carols when they please,
Are quiet when they will.

'With Nature never do *they* wage
A foolish strife; they see
A happy youth, and their old age
Is beautiful and free:

'But we are pressed by heavy laws;
And often, glad no more,
We wear a face of joy, because
We have been glad of yore.

'If there is one who need bemoan
His kindred laid in earth,
The household hearts that were his own,
It is the man of mirth.

'My days, my Friend, are almost gone,
My life has been approved,
And many love me; but by none
Am I enough beloved.'

'Now both himself and me he wrongs,
The man who thus complains!
I live and sing my idle songs
Upon these happy plains,

'And, Matthew, for thy Children dead
I'll be a son to thee!'
At this he grasped his hands, and said
'Alas! that cannot be.'

We rose up from the fountain-side;
And down the smooth descent
Of the green sheep-track did we glide;
And through the wood we went;

And, ere we came to Leonard's Rock,
He sang those witty rhymes
About the crazy old church clock
And the bewildered chimes.

'Three Years she grew in Sun and Shower'

THREE years she grew in sun and shower,
Then Nature said, 'A lovelier flower
On earth was never sown;
This Child I to myself will take;
She shall be mine, and I will make
A Lady of my own.

'Myself will to my darling be
Both law and impulse; and with me
The Girl, in rock and plain,
In earth and heaven, in glade and bower,
Shall feel an overseeing power
To kindle or restrain.

'She shall be sportive as the Fawn
That wild with glee across the lawn
Or up the mountain springs;
And hers shall be the breathing balm,
And hers the silence and the calm
Of mute insensate things.

'The floating Clouds their state shall lend
To her; for her the willow bend;
Nor shall she fail to see
Even in the motions of the Storm
Grace that shall mould the Maiden's form
By silent sympathy.

'The Stars of midnight shall be dear
To her; and she shall lean her ear
In many a secret place
Where Rivulets dance their wayward round,
And beauty born of murmuring sound
Shall pass into her face.

'And vital feelings of delight
Shall rear her form to stately height,
Her virgin bosom swell;
Such thoughts to Lucy I will give
While she and I together live
Here in this happy Dell.'

Thus Nature spake—The work was done—
How soon my Lucy's race was run!
She died, and left to me
This heath, this calm, and quiet scene;
The memory of what has been,
And never more will be.

The Pet-Lamb

A PASTORAL

THE dew was falling fast, the stars began to blink;
I heard a voice; it said, 'Drink, pretty Creature, drink!'
And, looking o'er the hedge, before me I espied
A snow-white mountain Lamb with a Maiden at its side.

No other sheep were near, the Lamb was all alone,
And by a slender cord was tethered to a stone;
With one knee on the grass did the little Maiden kneel
While to that Mountain Lamb she gave its evening meal.

The Lamb while from her hand he thus his supper took
Seemed to feast with head and ears; and his tail with pleasure shook,
'Drink, pretty Creature, drink,' she said in such a tone
That I almost received her heart into my own.

'Twas little Barbara Lewthwaite, a Child of beauty rare!
I watched them with delight, they were a lovely pair.
Now with her empty Can the Maiden turned away;
But ere ten yards were gone her footsteps did she stay.

Towards the Lamb she looked; and from that shady place
I unobserved could see the workings of her face:
If Nature to her tongue could measured numbers bring,
Thus, thought I, to her Lamb that little Maid might sing.

'What ails thee, Young One? What? Why pull so at thy cord?
Is it not well with thee? Well both for bed and board?
Thy plot of grass is soft, and green as grass can be;
Rest, little Young One, rest; what is't that aileth thee?

'What is it thou wouldst seek? What is wanting to thy heart?
Thy limbs are they not strong? And beautiful thou art:
This grass is tender grass; these flowers they have no peers;
And that green corn all day is rustling in thy ears!

'If the Sun be shining hot, do but stretch thy woollen chain,
This beech is standing by, its cover thou canst gain;
For rain and mountain storms! the like thou need'st not fear—
The rain and storm are things which scarcely can come here.

'Rest, little Young One, rest; thou hast forgot the day
When my Father found thee first in places far away;
Many flocks were on the hills, but thou wert owned by none;
And thy mother from thy side for evermore was gone.

'He took thee in his arms, and in pity brought thee home:
A blessed day for thee! then whither wouldst thou roam?
A faithful Nurse thou hast, the Dam that did thee yean
Upon the mountain tops no kinder could have been.

'Thou know'st that twice a day I have brought thee in this Can
Fresh water from the brook as clear as ever ran.

And twice in the day when the ground is wet with dew
I bring thee draughts of milk, warm milk it is and new.

'Thy limbs will shortly be twice as stout as they are now,
Then I'll yoke thee to my cart like a pony n the plough;
My Playmate thou shalt be; and when the wind is cold
Our hearth shall be thy bed, our house shall be thy fold.

'It will not, will not rest!—poor Creature, can it be
That 'tis thy mother's heart which is working so in thee?
Things that I know not of belike to thee are dear,
And dreams of things which thou canst neither see nor hear.

'Alas, the mountain tops that look so green and fair!
I've heard of fearful winds and darkness that come there;
The little Brooks that seem all pastime and all play,
When they are angry, roar like Lions for their prey.

'Here thou need'st not dread the raven in the sky;
Night and day thou art safe,—our cottage is hard by.
Why bleat so after me? Why pull so at thy chain?
Sleep—and at break of day I will come to thee again!'

—As homeward through the lane I went with lazy feet,
This song to myself did I oftentimes repeat;
And it seemed, as I retraced the ballad line by line,
That but half of it was hers, and one half of it was mine.

Again, and once again did I repeat the song;
'Nay,' said I, 'more than half to the Damsel must belong,
For she looked with such a look, and she spake with such a tone,
That I almost received her heart into my own.'

Written in Germany

ON ONE OF THE COLDEST DAYS OF THE CENTURY

I MUST apprise the Reader that the stoves in North Germany generally have the impression of a galloping Horse upon them, this being part of the Brunswick Arms.

A FIG for your languages, German and Norse!
Let me have the song of the Kettle;
And the tongs and the poker, instead of that Horse
That gallops away with such fury and force
On this dreary dull plate of black metal.

Our earth is no doubt made of excellent stuff;
But her pulses beat slower and slower:
The weather in Forty was cutting and rough,
And then, as Heaven knows, the Glass stood low enough;
And *now* it is four degrees lower.

Here's a Fly, a disconsolate creature, perhaps
A child of the field, or the grove;
And, sorrow for him! this dull treacherous heat
Has seduced the poor fool from his winter retreat,
And he creeps to the edge of my stove.

Alas! how he fumbles about the domains
Which this comfortless oven environ!
He cannot find out in what track he must crawl,
Now back to the tiles, and now back to the wall,
And now on the brink of the iron.

Stock-still there he stands like a traveller bemazed;
The best of his skill he has tried;
His feelers methinks I can see him put forth
To the East and the West, and the South and the North;
But he finds neither Guide-post nor Guide.

See! his spindles sink under him, foot, leg and thigh;
His eyesight and hearing are lost;
Between life and death his blood freezes and thaws,
And his two pretty pinions of blue dusky gauze
Are glued to his sides by the frost.

No Brother, no Friend has he near him—while I
Can draw warmth from the cheek of my Love;
As blest and as glad in this desolate gloom,
As if green summer grass were the floor of my room,
And woodbines were hanging above.

Yet, God is my witness, thou small helpless Thing!
Thy life I would gladly sustain
Till summer comes up from the South, and with crowds
Of thy brethren a march thou shouldst sound through the clouds,
And back to the forests again.

The Childless Father

'Up, Timothy, up with your Staff and away!
Not a soul in the village this morning will stay;
The Hare has just started from Hamilton's grounds,
And Skiddaw is glad with the cry of the hounds.'

—Of coats and of jackets gray, scarlet and green,
On the slopes of the pastures all colours were seen;
With their comely blue aprons, and caps white as snow,
The Girls on the hills made a holiday show.

The bason of box-wood,* just six months before,
Had stood on the table at Timothy's door;
A Coffin through Timothy's threshold had passed;
One Child did it bear, and that Child was his last.

Now fast up the dell came the noise and the fray,
The horse and the horn and the hark! hark away!

* In several parts of the North of England, when a funeral takes place, a bason full of Sprigs of Box-wood is placed at the door of the house from which the Coffin is taken up, and each person who attends the funeral ordinarily takes a Sprig of this Box-wood, and throws it into the grave of the deceased.

Old Timothy took up his staff, and he shut
With a leisurely motion the door of his hut.

Perhaps to himself at that moment he said,
'The key I must take, for my Ellen is dead.'
But of this in my ears not a word did he speak,
And he went to the chase with a tear on his cheek.

The Old Cumberland Beggar

A DESCRIPTION

The class of Beggars to which the Old Man here described belongs will probably soon be extinct. It consisted of poor, and mostly, old and infirm persons, who confined themselves to a stated round in their neighbourhood, and had certain fixed days, on which, at different houses, they regularly received alms, sometimes in money, but mostly in provisions.

I saw an aged beggar in my walk,
And he was seated by the highway side
On a low structure of rude masonry
Built at the foot of a huge hill, that they
Who lead their horses down the steep rough road
May thence remount at ease. The aged Man
Had placed his staff across the broad smooth stone
That overlays the pile, and from a bag
All white with flour, the dole of village dames,
He drew his scraps and fragments one by one,
And scanned them with a fixed and serious look
Of idle computation. In the sun,
Upon the second step of that small pile,
Surrounded by those wild unpeopled hills,
He sat, and ate his food in solitude:
And ever, scattered from his palsied hand,
That, still attempting to prevent the waste,
Was baffled still, the crumbs in little showers
Fell on the ground, and the small mountain birds,
Not venturing yet to peck their destined meal,
Approached within the length of half his staff.

Him from my childhood have I known; and then
He was so old, he seems not older now;
He travels on, a solitary Man,
So helpless in appearance, that for him
The sauntering Horseman-traveller does not throw
With careless hand his alms upon the ground,
But stops, that he may safely lodge the coin
Within the old Man's hat; nor quits him so,
But still when he has given his horse the rein
Towards the aged Beggar turns a look,
Sidelong and half-reverted. She who tends
The Toll-gate, when in summer at her door
She turns her wheel, if on the road she sees
The aged Beggar coming, quits her work,
And lifts the latch for him that he may pass.
The Post-boy, when his rattling wheels o'ertake
The aged Beggar in the woody lane,
Shouts to him from behind, and, if perchance
The old Man does not change his course, the Boy
Turns with less noisy wheels to the road-side,
And passes gently by, without a curse
Upon his lips, or anger at his heart.
He travels on, a solitary Man,
His age has no companion. On the ground
His eyes are turned, and, as he moves along,
They move along the ground; and, evermore,
Instead of common and habitual sight
Of fields with rural works, of hill and dale,
And the blue sky, one little span of earth
Is all his prospect. Thus, from day to day,
Bowbent, his eyes for ever on the ground,
He plies his weary journey; seeing still,
And never knowing that he sees, some straw,
Some scattered leaf, or marks which, in one track
The nails of cart or chariot wheel have left
Impressed on the white road, in the same line,
At distance still the same. Poor Traveller!
His staff trails with him; scarcely do his feet
Disturb the summer dust; he is so still
In looks and motion, that the cottage curs,
Ere he have passed the door, will turn away,
Weary of barking at him. Boys and Girls,

The vacant and the busy, Maids and Youths,
And Urchins newly breeched all pass him by:
Him even the slow-paced Waggon leaves behind.

But deem not this Man useless.—Statesmen! ye
Who are so restless in your wisdom, ye
Who have a broom still ready in your hands
To rid the world of nuisances; ye proud,
Heart-swoln, while in your pride ye contemplate
Your talents, power, and wisdom, deem him not
A burthen of the earth. 'Tis Nature's law
That none, the meanest of created things,
Of forms created the most vile and brute,
The dullest or most noxious, should exist
Divorced from good—a spirit and pulse of good,
A life and soul to every mode of being
Inseparably linked. While thus he creeps
From door to door, the Villagers in him
Behold a record which together binds
Past deeds and offices of charity,
Else unremembered, and so keeps alive
The kindly mood in hearts which lapse of years,
And that half-wisdom half-experience gives,
Make slow to feel, and by sure steps resign
To selfishness and cold oblivious cares.
Among the farms and solitary huts,
Hamlets and thinly-scattered villages,
Where'er the aged Beggar takes his rounds,
The mild necessity of use compels
To acts of love; and habit does the work
Of reason; yet prepares that after joy
Which reason cherishes. And thus the soul,
By that sweet taste of pleasure unpursued,
Doth find itself insensibly disposed
To virtue and true goodness. Some there are,
By their good works exalted, lofty minds
And meditative, authors of delight
And happiness, which to the end of time
Will live, and spread, and kindle; minds like these,
In childhood, from this solitary Being,
This helpless Wanderer, have perchance received
(A thing more precious far than all that books

Or the solicitudes of love can do!)
That first mild touch of sympathy and thought,
In which they found their kindred with a world
Where want and sorrow were. The easy Man
Who sits at his own door, and, like the pear
Which overhangs his head from the green wall,
Feeds in the sunshine; the robust and young,
The prosperous and unthinking, they who live
Sheltered, and flourish in a little grove
Of their own kindred, all behold in him
A silent monitor, which on their minds
Must needs impress a transitory thought
Of self-congratulation, to the heart
Of each recalling his peculiar boons,
His charters and exemptions; and, perchance,
Though he to no one give the fortitude
And circumspection needful to preserve
His present blessings, and to husband up
The respite of the season, he, at least,
And 'tis no vulgar service, makes them felt.

Yet further.——Many, I believe, there are
Who live a life of virtuous decency,
Men who can hear the Decalogue and feel
No self-reproach; who of the moral law
Established in the land where they abide
Are strict observers; and not negligent,
Meanwhile, in any tenderness of heart
Or act of love to those with whom they dwell,
Their kindred, and the children of their blood.
Praise be to such, and to their slumbers peace!
—But of the poor man ask, the abject poor,
Go and demand of him, if there be here
In this cold abstinence from evil deeds,
And these inevitable charities,
Wherewith to satisfy the human soul?
No—Man is dear to Man; the poorest poor
Long for some moments in a weary life
When they can know and feel that they have been
Themselves the fathers and the dealers out
Of some small blessings, have been kind to such

As needed kindness, for this single cause,
That we have all of us one human heart.
—Such pleasure is to one kind Being known;
My Neighbour, when with punctual care, each week
Duly as Friday comes, though prest herself
By her own wants, she from her chest of meal
Takes one unsparing handful for the scrip
Of this old Mendicant, and, from her door
Returning with exhilarated heart,
Sits by her fire and builds her hope in heaven.

Then let him pass, a blessing on his head!
And while in that vast solitude to which
The tide of things has led him, he appears
To breathe and live but for himself alone,
Unblamed, uninjured, let him bear about
The good which the benignant law of Heaven
Has hung around him; and, while life is his,
Still let him prompt the unlettered Villagers
To tender offices and pensive thoughts.
Then let him pass, a blessing on his head!
And, long as he can wander, let him breathe
The freshness of the valleys; let his blood
Struggle with frosty air and winter snows;
And let the chartered wind that sweeps the heath
Beat his gray locks against his withered face.
Reverence the hope whose vital anxiousness
Gives the last human interest to his heart.
May never House, misnamed of Industry!
Make him a captive! for that pent-up din,
Those life-consuming sounds that clog the air,
Be his the natural silence of old age!
Let him be free of mountain solitudes;
And have around him, whether heard or not,
The pleasant melody of woodland birds.
Few are his pleasures: if his eyes, which now
Have been so long familiar with the earth,
No more behold the horizontal sun
Rising or setting, let the light at least
Find a free entrance to their languid orbs.
And let him, *where* and *when* he will, sit down
Beneath the trees, or by the grassy bank

Of high-way side, and with the little birds
Share his chance-gathered meal; and, finally,
As in the eye of Nature he has lived,
So in the eye of Nature let him die.

Rural Architecture

THERE'S George Fisher, Charles Fleming, and Reginald Shore,
Three rosy-cheeked School-boys, the highest not more
Than the height of a Counsellor's bag;
To the top of GREAT HOW* did it please them to climb;
And there they had built up, without mortar or lime,
A Man on the peak of the crag.

They built him of stones gathered up as they lay;
They built him and christened him all in one day,
An Urchin both vigorous and hale;
And so without scruple they called him Ralph Jones.
Now Ralph is renowned for the length of his bones;
The Magog of Legberthwaite dale.

Just half a week after, the wind sallied forth,
And, in anger or merriment, out of the North
Coming on with a terrible pother,
From the peak of the crag blew the Giant away.
And what did these School-boys?—The very next day
They went and they built up another.

*Great How is a single and conspicuous hill, which rises towards the foot of Thirl-mere, on the western side of the beautiful dale of Legberthwaite, along the high road between Keswick and Ambleside.

A Poet's Epitaph

ART thou a Statesman, in the van
Of public business trained and bred?
—First learn to love one living man;
Then mayst thou think upon the dead.

A lawyer art thou?—draw not nigh;
Go, carry to some other place
The hardness of thy coward eye,
The falsehood of thy sallow face.

Art thou a Man of purple cheer?
A rosy Man, right plump to see?
Approach; yet, Doctor, not too near:
This grave no cushion is for thee.

Art thou a man of gallant pride,
A soldier, and no man of chaff?
Welcome!—but lay thy sword aside,
And lean upon a Peasant's staff.

Physician art thou? One, all eyes,
Philosopher! a fingering slave,
One that would peep and botanize
Upon his mother's grave?

Wrappt closely in thy sensual fleece
O turn aside, and take, I pray,
That he below may rest in peace,
Thy pin-point of a soul away!

—A Moralist perchance appears:
Led, Heaven knows how! to this poor sod
And he has neither eyes nor ears;
Himself his world, and his own God;

One to whose smoothed-rubbed soul can cling
Nor form, nor feeling, great nor small;
A reasoning, self-sufficient thing,
An intellectual All in All!

Shut close the door; press down the latch;
Sleep in thy intellectual crust;
Nor lose ten tickings of thy watch
Near this unprofitable dust.

But who is He, with modest looks,
And clad in homely russet brown?
He murmurs near the running brooks
A music sweeter than their own.

He is retired as noontide dew,
Or fountain in a noonday grove;
And you must love him, ere to you
He will seem worthy of your love.

The outward shows of sky and earth,
Of hill and valley, he has viewed;
And impulses of deeper birth
Have come to him in solitude.

In common things that round us lie
Some random truths he can impart,
—The harvest of a quiet eye
That broods and sleeps on his own heart.

But he is weak, both Man and Boy,
Hath been an idler in the land;
Contented if he might enjoy
The things which others understand.

—Come hither in thy hour of strength;
Come, weak as is a breaking wave!
Here stretch thy body at full length;
Or build thy house upon this grave.

POEMS ON THE NAMING OF PLACES

ADVERTISEMENT

By Persons resident in the country and attached to rural objects, many places will be found unnamed or of unknown names, where little Incidents will have occurred, or feelings been experienced, which will have given to such places a private and peculiar interest. From a wish to give some sort of record to such Incidents, or renew the gratification of such Feelings, Names have been given to Places by the Author and some of his Friends, and the following Poems written in consequence.

I

It was an April morning: fresh and clear
The Rivulet, delighting in its strength,
Ran with a young man's speed; and yet the voice
Of waters which the winter had supplied
Was softened down into a vernal tone.
The spirit of enjoyment and desire,
And hopes and wishes, from all living things
Went circling, like a multitude of sounds.
The budding groves appeared as if in haste
To spur the steps of June; as if their shades
Of *various* green were hindrances that stood
Between them and their object: yet, meanwhile,
There was such deep contentment in the air
That every naked ash, and tardy tree
Yet leafless, seemed as though the countenance
With which it looked on this delightful day
Were native to the summer.—Up the brook
I roamed in the confusion of my heart,
Alive to all things and forgetting all.
At length I to a sudden turning came
In this continuous glen, where down a rock
The stream, so ardent in its course before,
Sent forth such sallies of glad sound, that all
Which I till then had heard, appeared the voice

Of common pleasure: beast and bird, the Lamb,
The Shepherd's Dog, the Linnet and the Thrush
Vied with this Waterfall, and made a song
Which, while I listened, seemed like the wild growth
Or like some natural produce of the air
That could not cease to be. Green leaves were here,
But 'twas the foliage of the rocks, the birch,
The yew, the holly, and the bright green thorn,
With hanging islands of resplendent furze:
And on a summit, distant a short space,
By any who should look beyond the dell,
A single mountain Cottage might be seen.
I gazed and gazed, and to myself I said,
'Our thoughts at least are ours; and this wild nook,
My EMMA, I will dedicate to thee.'
——Soon did the spot become my other home,
My dwelling, and my out-of-doors abode.
And, of the Shepherds who have seen me there,
To whom I sometimes in our idle talk
Have told this fancy, two or three, perhaps,
Years after we are gone and in our graves,
When they have cause to speak of this wild place,
May call it by the name of EMMA'S DELL.

To Joanna

IN Cumberland and Westmoreland are several Inscriptions, upon the native rock, which, from the wasting of Time, and the rudeness of the Workmanship, had been mistaken for Runic. They are without doubt Roman.

The Rotha, mentioned in this poem, is the River which, flowing through the Lakes of Grasmere and Rydale, falls into Wyndermere. On Helm-Crag, that impressive single Mountain at the head of the Vale of Grasmere, is a Rock which from most points of view bears a striking resemblance to an Old Woman cowering. Close by this rock is one of those Fissures or Caverns which in the language of the Country are called Dungeons. Most of the Mountains here mentioned immediately surround the Vale of Grasmere; of the others, some are at a considerable distance, but they belong to the same cluster.

Amid the smoke of cities did you pass
Your time of early youth; and there you learned,
From years of quiet industry, to love
The living Beings by your own fire-side,
With such a strong devotion, that your heart
Is slow towards the sympathies of them
Who look upon the hills with tenderness,
And make dear friendships with the streams and groves.
Yet we, who are transgressors in this kind,
Dwelling retired in our simplicity
Among the woods and fields, we love you well,
Joanna! and I guess, since you have been
So distant from us now for two long years,
That you will gladly listen to discourse
However trivial, if you thence are taught
That they, with whom you once were happy, talk
Familiarly of you and of old times.

While I was seated, now some ten days past,
Beneath those lofty firs, that overtop
Their antient neighbour, the old Steeple tower,
The Vicar from his gloomy house hard by
Came forth to greet me; and when he had asked,
'How fares Joanna, that wild-hearted Maid!
And when will she return to us?' he paused;
And, after short exchange of village news,
He with grave looks demanded, for what cause,
Reviving obsolete Idolatry,
I, like a Runic Priest, in characters
Of formidable size had chiseled out
Some uncouth name upon the native rock,
Above the Rotha, by the forest side.
—Now, by those dear immunities of heart
Engendered betwixt malice and true love,
I was not loth to be so catechized,
And this was my reply:—'As it befel,
One summer morning we had walked abroad
At break of day, Joanna and myself.
—'Twas that delightful season, when the broom
Full-flowered, and visible on every steep,
Along the copses runs in veins of gold.
Our pathway led us on to Rotha's banks;

And when we came in front of that tall rock
Which looks towards the East, I there stopped short,
And traced the lofty barrier with my eye
From base to summit; such delight I found
To note in shrub and tree, in stone and flower,
That intermixture of delicious hues,
Along so vast a surface, all at once,
In one impression, by connecting force
Of their own beauty, imaged in the heart.
—When I had gazed perhaps two minutes' space
Joanna, looking in my eyes, beheld
That ravishment of mine, and laughed aloud.
The rock, like something starting from a sleep,
Took up the Lady's voice, and laughed again:
That antient Woman seated on Helm-crag
Was ready with her cavern; Hammar-Scar,
And the tall Steep of Silver-How sent forth
A noise of laughter; southern Loughrigg heard,
And Fairfield answered with a mountain tone:
Helvellyn far into the clear blue sky
Carried the Lady's voice,—old Skiddaw blew
His speaking-trumpet;—back out of the clouds
Of Glaramara southward came the voice;
And Kirkstone tossed it from his misty head.
Now whether, (said I to our cordial Friend
Who in the hey-day of astonishment
Smiled in my face) this were in simple truth
A work accomplished by the brotherhood
Of antient mountains, or my ear was touched
With dreams and visionary impulses,
Is not for me to tell; but sure I am
That there was a loud uproar in the hills.
And, while we both were listening, to my side
The fair Joanna drew, as if she wished
To shelter from some object of her fear.
—And hence, long afterwards, when eighteen moons
Were wasted, as I chanced to walk alone
Beneath this rock, at sunrise, on a calm
And silent morning, I sat down, and there,
In memory of affections old and true,
I chiseled out in those rude characters
Joanna's name upon the living stone.

And I, and all who dwell by my fire-side,
Have called the lovely rock, JOANNA'S ROCK.'

3

THERE is an Eminence,—of these our hills
The last that parleys with the setting sun.
We can behold it from our Orchard-seat;
And, when at evening we pursue our walk
Along the public way, this Cliff, so high
Above us, and so distant in its height,
Is visible, and often seems to send
Its own deep quiet to restore our hearts.
The meteors make of it a favourite haunt:
The star of Jove, so beautiful and large
In the mid heavens, is never half so fair
As when he shines above it. 'Tis in truth
The loneliest place we have among the clouds.
And She who dwells with me, whom I have loved
With such communion, that no place on earth
Can ever be a solitude to me,
Hath said, this lonesome Peak shall bear my name.

4

A NARROW girdle of rough stones and crags,
A rude and natural causeway, interpos'd
Between the water and a winding slope
Of copse and thicket, leaves the eastern shore
Of Grasmere safe in its own privacy.
And there, myself and two beloved Friends,
One calm September morning, ere the mist
Had altogether yielded to the sun,
Sauntered on this retired and difficult way.
——Ill suits the road with one in haste, but we
Played with our time; and, as we strolled along,
It was our occupation to observe
Such objects as the waves had tossed ashore,
Feather, or leaf, or weed, or withered bough,
Each on the other heaped along the line
Of the dry wreck. And, in our vacant mood,

Not seldom did we stop to watch some tuft
Of dandelion seed or thistle's beard,
Which, seeming lifeless half, and half impelled
By some internal feeling, skimmed along
Close to the surface of the lake that lay
Asleep in a dead calm—ran closely on
Along the dead calm lake, now here, now there,
In all its sportive wanderings all the while
Making report of an invisible breeze
That was its wings, its chariot, and its horse,
Its very playmate, and its moving soul.
——And often, trifling with a privilege
Alike indulged to all, we paused, one now,
And now the other, to point out, perchance
To pluck, some flower or water-weed, too fair
Either to be divided from the place
On which it grew, or to be left alone
To its own beauty. Many such there are,
Fair Ferns and Flowers, and chiefly that tall Fern
So stately, of the Queen Osmunda named;
Plant lovelier in its own retired abode
On Grasmere's beach, than Naiad by the side
Of Grecian brook, or Lady of the Mere
Sole-sitting by the shores of old Romance.
—So fared we that sweet morning: from the fields,
Meanwhile, a noise was heard, the busy mirth
Of Reapers, Men and Women, Boys and Girls.
Delighted much to listen to those sounds,
And, in the fashion which I have described,
Feeding unthinking fancies, we advanced
Along the indented shore; when suddenly,
Through a thin veil of glittering haze, we saw
Before us on a point of jutting land
The tall and upright figure of a Man
Attired in peasant's garb, who stood alone
Angling beside the margin of a lake.
That way we turned our steps; nor was it long
Ere, making ready comments on the sight
Which then we saw, with one and the same voice
We all cried out, that he must be indeed
An idle man, who thus could lose a day
Of the mid harvest, when the labourer's hire

Is ample, and some little might be stored
Wherewith to cheer him in the winter time.
Thus talking of that Peasant we approached
Close to the spot where with his rod and line
He stood alone; whereat he turned his head
To greet us—and we saw a man worn down
By sickness, gaunt and lean, with sunken cheeks
And wasted limbs, his legs so long and lean
That for my single self I looked at them,
Forgetful of the body they sustained.—
Too weak to labour in the harvest field,
The Man was using his best skill to gain
A pittance from the dead unfeeling lake
That knew not of his wants. I will not say
What thoughts immediately were ours, nor how
The happy idleness of that sweet morn,
With all its lovely images, was changed
To serious musing and to self-reproach.
Nor did we fail to see within ourselves
What need there is to be reserved in speech,
And temper all our thoughts with charity.
—Therefore, unwilling to forget that day,
My Friend, Myself, and She who then received
The same admonishment, have called the place
By a memorial name, uncouth indeed
As e'er by Mariner was given to Bay
Or Foreland on a new-discovered coast,
And POINT RASH-JUDGMENT is the Name it bears.

5

To M. H.

OUR walk was far among the antient trees;
There was no road, nor any wood-man's path;
But the thick umbrage, checking the wild growth
Of weed and sapling, on the soft green turf
Beneath the branches of itself had made
A track, which brought us to a slip of lawn,
And a small bed of water in the woods.

All round this pool both flocks and herds might drink
On its firm margin, even as from a Well,
Or some Stone-bason which the Herdsman's hand
Had shaped for their refreshment; nor did sun
Or wind from any quarter ever come,
But as a blessing, to this calm recess,
This glade of water and this one green field;
The spot was made by Nature for herself:
The travellers know it not, and 'twill remain
Unknown to them: but it is beautiful;
And if a man should plant his cottage near,
Should sleep beneath the shelter of its trees,
And blend its waters with his daily meal,
He would so love it that in his death hour
Its image would survive among his thoughts:
And therefore, my sweet MARY, this still nook
With all its beeches we have named for You.

The Two Thieves

OR THE LAST STAGE OF AVARICE

O NOW that the genius of Bewick were mine,
And the skill which he learned on the banks of the Tyne!
Then the Muses might deal with me just as they chose,
For I'd take my last leave both of verse and of prose.

What feats would I work with my magical hand!
Book learning and books should be banished the land:
And for hunger and thirst and such troublesome calls!
Every Ale-house should then have a feast on its walls.

The Traveller would hang his wet clothes on a chair;
Let them smoke, let them burn, not a straw would he care;
For the Prodigal Son, Joseph's Dream and his Sheaves,
Oh, what would they be to my tale of two Thieves?

Little Dan is unbreeched, he is three birth-days old;
His Grandsire that age more than thirty times told;
There are ninety good seasons of fair and foul weather
Between them, and both go a-stealing together.

With chips is the Carpenter strewing his floor?
Is a cart-load of peats at an old Woman's door?
Old Daniel his hand to the treasure will slide;
And his Grandson's as busy at work by his side.

Old Daniel begins, he stops short—and his eye
Through the last look of dotage is cunning and sly.
'Tis a look which at this time is hardly his own,
But tells a plain tale of the days that are flown.

Dan once had a heart which was moved by the wires
Of manifold pleasures and many desires:
And what if he cherished his purse? 'Twas no more
Than treading a path trod by thousands before.

'Twas a path trod by thousands; but Daniel is one
Who went something further than others have gone;
And now with old Daniel you see how it fares;
You see to what end he has brought his gray hairs.

The Pair sally forth hand in hand: ere the sun
Has peered o'er the beeches their work is begun:
And yet, into whatever sin they may fall,
This Child but half knows it, and that not at all.

They hunt through the streets with deliberate tread,
And each in his turn is both leader and led;
And, wherever they carry their plots and their wiles,
Every face in the village is dimpled with smiles.

Neither checked by the rich nor the needy they roam;
For gray-headed Dan has a daughter at home,
Who will gladly repair all the damage that's done;
And three, were it asked, would be rendered for one.

Old Man! whom so oft I with pity have eyed,
I love thee, and love the sweet Boy at thy side:
Long yet mayst thou live! for a teacher we see
That lifts up the veil of our nature in thee.

'A Whirl-Blast from behind the Hill'

A WHIRL-BLAST from behind the hill
Rushed o'er the wood with startling sound:
Then all at once the air was still,
And showers of hail-stones pattered round.
Where leafless Oaks towered high above,
I sat within an undergrove
Of tallest hollies, tall and green;
A fairer bower was never seen.
From year to year the spacious floor
With withered leaves is covered o'er,
You could not lay a hair between:
And all the year the bower is green.
But see! where'er the hailstones drop
The withered leaves all skip and hop,
There's not a breeze—no breath of air—
Yet here, and there, and every where
Along the floor, beneath the shade
By those embowering hollies made,
The leaves in myriads jump and spring,
As if with pipes and music rare
Some Robin Good-fellow were there,
And all those leaves, that jump and spring,
Were each a joyous, living thing.

Oh! grant me Heaven a heart at ease,
That I may never cease to find,
Even in appearances like these,
Enough to nourish and to stir my mind!

Michael

A PASTORAL POEM

IF from the public way you turn your steps
Up the tumultuous brook of Green-head Gill,
You will suppose that with an upright path
Your feet must struggle; in such bold ascent

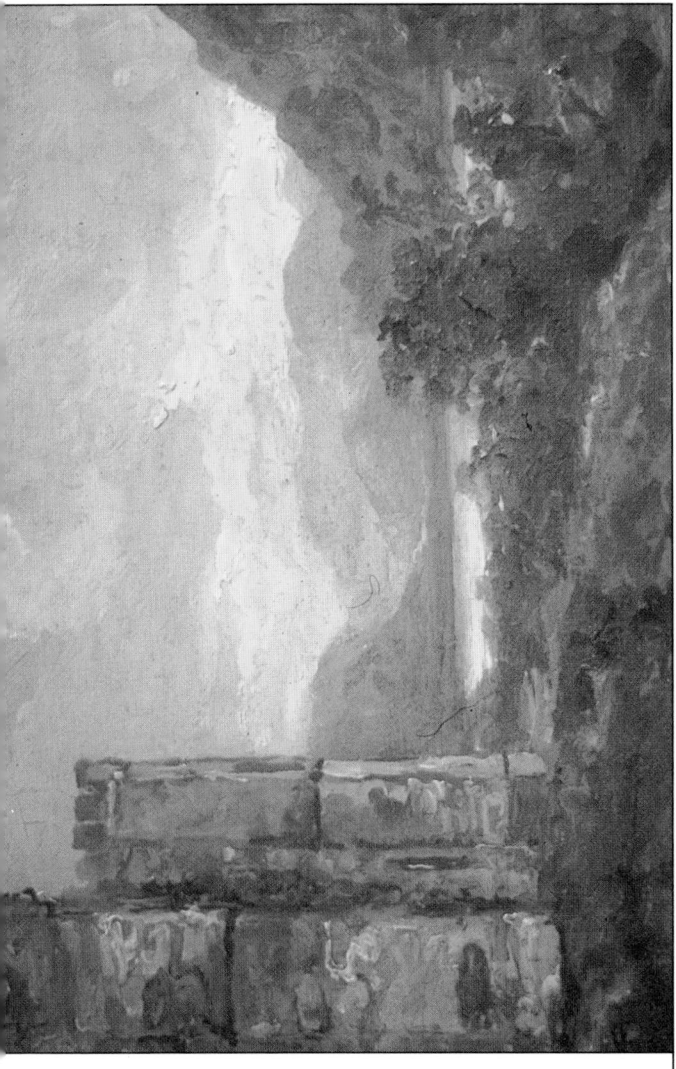

Lyulph's Tower, Gowbarrow Park, Ullswater by Thomas Churchyard (1798–1865). Built in 1780, the Tower was a summer home of the Duke of Norfolk. It was near here that Wordsworth and his sister Dorothy saw the flowers which inspired "Daffodils".
By courtesy of Abbot Hall Art Gallery, Kendal

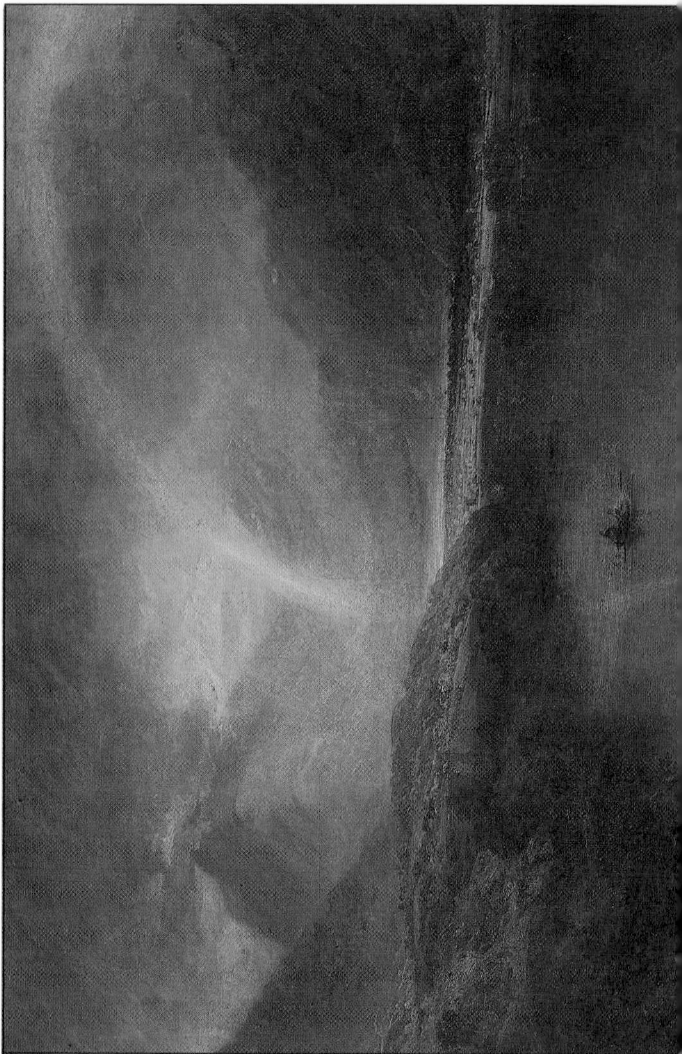

Lake Buttermere by J.M.W. Turner (1775–1851). Lake Buttermere was visited more than once by Wordsworth, and by the "Friend" of *The Prelude,* Samuel Taylor Coleridge.
By courtesy of the Trustees of the Tate Gallery, London.

The pastoral Mountains front you, face to face.
But, courage! for beside that boisterous Brook
The mountains have all opened out themselves,
And made a hidden valley of their own.
No habitation there is seen; but such
As journey thither find themselves alone
With a few sheep, with rocks and stones, and kites
That overhead are sailing in the sky.
It is in truth an utter solitude;
Nor should I have made mention of this Dell
But for one object which you might pass by,
Might see and notice not. Beside the brook
There is a straggling heap of unhewn stones!
And to that place a story appertains,
Which, though it be ungarnished with events,
Is not unfit, I deem, for the fire-side,
Or for the summer shade. It was the first,
The earliest of those tales that spake to me
Of Shepherds, dwellers in the valleys, men
Whom I already loved, not verily
For their own sakes, but for the fields and hills
Where was their occupation and abode.
And hence this Tale, while I was yet a Boy
Careless of books, yet having felt the power
Of Nature, by the gentle agency
Of natural objects led me on to feel
For passions that were not my own, and think
(At random and imperfectly indeed)
On man, the heart of man, and human life.
Therefore, although it be a history
Homely and rude, I will relate the same
For the delight of a few natural hearts,
And, with yet fonder feeling, for the sake
Of youthful Poets, who among these Hills
Will be my second self when I am gone.

UPON the Forest-side in Grasmere Vale
There dwelt a Shepherd, Michael was his name,
An old man, stout of heart, and strong of limb.
His bodily frame had been from youth to age
Of an unusual strength: his mind was keen,
Intense and frugal, apt for all affairs,

And in his Shepherd's calling he was prompt
And watchful more than ordinary men.
Hence he had learned the meanings of all winds,
Of blasts of every tone; and, oftentimes,
When others heeded not, He heard the South
Make subterraneous music, like the noise
Of Bagpipers on distant Highland hills;
The Shepherd, at such warning, of his flock
Bethought him, and he to himself would say,
'The winds are now devising work for me!'
And, truly, at all times the storm, that drives
The Traveller to a shelter, summoned him
Up to the mountains: he had been alone
Amid the heart of many thousand mists,
That came to him and left him on the heights.
So lived he till his eightieth year was past.

And grossly that man errs, who should suppose
That the green Valleys, and the Streams and Rocks
Were things indifferent to the Shepherd's thoughts.
Fields, where with cheerful spirits he had breathed
The common air; the hills, which he so oft
Had climbed with vigorous steps; which had impressed
So many incidents upon his mind
Of hardship, skill or courage, joy or fear;
Which like a book preserved the memory
Of the dumb animals, whom he had saved,
Had fed or sheltered, linking to such acts,
So grateful in themselves, the certainty
Of honourable gain; these fields, these hills,
Which were his living Being, even more
Than his own blood—what could they less? had laid
Strong hold on his affections, were to him
A pleasurable feeling of blind love,
The pleasure which there is in life itself.
He had not passed his days in singleness.
He had a Wife, a comely Matron, old—
Though younger than himself full twenty years.
She was a woman of a stirring life,
Whose heart was in her house: two wheels she had
Of antique form, this large for spinning wool,
That small for flax; and if one wheel had rest,

It was because the other was at work.
The Pair had but one Inmate in their house,
An only Child, who had been born to them
When Michael telling o'er his years began
To deem that he was old,—in Shepherd's phrase,
With one foot in the grave. This only Son,
With two brave Sheep-dogs tried in many a storm,
The one of an inestimable worth,
Made all their Household. I may truly say,
That they were as a proverb in the vale
For endless industry. When day was gone,
And from their occupations out of doors
The Son and Father were come home, even then
Their labour did not cease; unless when all
Turned to their cleanly supper-board, and there,
Each with a mess of pottage and skimmed milk,
Sat round their basket piled with oaten cakes,
And their plain home-made cheese. Yet when their meal
Was ended, Luke (for so the Son was named)
And his old Father both betook themselves
To such convenient work as might employ
Their hands by the fire-side; perhaps to card
Wool for the Housewife's spindle, or repair
Some injury done to sickle, flail, or scythe,
Or other implement of house or field.

Down from the ceiling by the chimney's edge,
Which in our antient uncouth country style
Did with a huge projection overbrow
Large space beneath, as duly as the light
Of day grew dim the Housewife hung a Lamp;
An aged utensil, which had performed
Service beyond all others of its kind.
Early at evening did it burn and late,
Surviving Comrade of uncounted Hours,
Which going by from year to year had found
And left the couple neither gay perhaps
Nor cheerful, yet with objects and with hopes,
Living a life of eager industry.
And now, when Luke was in his eighteenth year,
There by the light of this old Lamp they sat,
Father and Son, while late into the night

The Housewife plied her own peculiar work,
Making the cottage through the silent hours
Murmur as with the sound of summer flies.
The Light was famous in its neighbourhood,
And was a public Symbol of the life
The thrifty Pair had lived. For, as it chanced,
Their Cottage on a plot of rising ground
Stood single, with large prospect, North and South,
High into Easedale, up to Dumnal-Raise,
And Westward to the village near the Lake;
And from this constant light, so regular
And so far seen, the House itself, by all
Who dwelt within the limits of the vale,
Both old and young, was named The EVENING STAR.
Thus living on through such a length of years,
The Shepherd, if he loved himself, must needs
Have loved his Help-mate; but to Michael's heart
This son of his old age was yet more dear—
Effect which might perhaps have been produced
By that instinctive tenderness, the same
Blind Spirit, which is in the blood of all—
Or that a child, more than all other gifts,
Brings hope with it, and forward-looking thoughts,
And stirrings of inquietude, when they
By tendency of nature needs must fail.
From such, and other causes, to the thoughts
Of the old Man his only Son was now
The dearest object that he knew on earth.
Exceeding was the love he bare to him,
His Heart and his Heart's joy! For oftentimes
Old Michael, while he was a babe in arms,
Had done him female service, not alone
For dalliance and delight, as is the use
Of Fathers, but with patient mind enforced
To acts of tenderness; and he had rocked
His cradle with a woman's gentle hand.

And, in a later time, ere yet the Boy
Had put on Boy's attire, did Michael love,
Albeit of a stern unbending mind,
To have the young one in his sight, when he
Had worked by his own door, or when he sat

With sheep before him on his Shepherd's stool,
Beneath that large old Oak, which near their door
Stood, and, from its enormous breadth of shade
Chosen for the Shearer's covert from the sun,
Thence in our rustic dialect was called
The CLIPPING TREE*, a name which yet it bears.
There, while they two were sitting in the shade,
With others round them, earnest all and blithe,
Would Michael exercise his heart with looks
Of fond correction and reproof bestowed
Upon the Child, if he disturbed the sheep
By catching at their legs, or with his shouts
Scared them, while they lay still beneath the shears.

And when by Heaven's good grace the Boy grew up
A healthy Lad, and carried in his cheek
Two steady roses that were five years old,
Then Michael from a winter coppice cut
With his own hand a sapling, which he hooped
With iron, making it throughout in all
Due requisites a perfect Shepherd's Staff,
And gave it to the Boy; wherewith equipt
He as a Watchman oftentimes was placed
At gate or gap, to stem or turn the flock;
And to his office prematurely called
There stood the Urchin, as you will divine,
Something between a hindrance and a help;
And for this cause not always, I believe,
Receiving from his Father hire of praise.
Though nought was left undone which staff or voice,
Or looks, or threatening gestures could perform.
　But soon as Luke, full ten years old, could stand
Against the mountain blasts, and to the heights,
Not fearing toil, nor length of weary ways,
He with his Father daily went, and they
Were as companions, why should I relate
That objects which the Shepherd loved before
Were dearer now? that from the Boy there came
Feelings and emanations, things which were
Light to the sun and music to the wind;

* Clipping is the word used in the North of England for shearing.

And that the Old Man's heart seemed born again.
  Thus in his Father's sight the Boy grew up:
And now when he had reached his eighteenth year,
He was his comfort and his daily hope.

While in the fashion which I have described
This simple Household thus were living on
From day to day, to Michael's ear there came
Distressful tidings. Long before the time
Of which I speak, the Shepherd had been bound
In surety for his Brother's Son, a man
Of an industrious life, and ample means,—
But unforeseen misfortunes suddenly
Had pressed upon him,—and old Michael now
Was summoned to discharge the forfeiture,
A grievous penalty, but little less
Than half his substance. This unlooked-for claim,
At the first hearing, for a moment took
More hope out of his life than he supposed
That any old man ever could have lost.
As soon as he had gathered so much strength
That he could look his trouble in the face,
It seemed that his sole refuge was to sell
A portion of his patrimonial fields.
Such was his first resolve; he thought again,
And his heart failed him. 'Isabel,' said he,
Two evenings after he had heard the news,
'I have been toiling more than seventy years,
And in the open sun-shine of God's love
Have we all lived; yet if these fields of ours
Should pass into a Stranger's hand, I think
That I could not lie quiet in my grave.
Our lot is a hard lot; the Sun itself
Has scarcely been more diligent than I,
And I have lived to be a fool at last
To my own family. An evil Man
That was, and made an evil choice, if he
Were false to us; and if he were not false,
There are ten thousand to whom loss like this
Had been no sorrow. I forgive him—but
'Twere better to be dumb than to talk thus.
When I began, my purpose was to speak

Of remedies and of a cheerful hope.
Our Luke shall leave us, Isabel; the land
Shall not go from us, and it shall be free;
He shall possess it, free as is the wind
That passes over it. We have, thou knowest,
Another Kinsman—he will be our friend
In this distress. He is a prosperous man,
Thriving in trade—and Luke to him shall go,
And with his Kinsman's help and his own thrift
He quickly will repair this loss, and then
May come again to us. If here he stay,
What can be done? Where every one is poor
What can be gained?' At this the old man paused,
And Isabel sat silent, for her mind
Was busy, looking back into past times.
There's Richard Bateman, thought she to herself,
He was a Parish-boy—at the Church-door
They made a gathering for him, shillings, pence,
And halfpennies, wherewith the neighbours bought
A Basket, which they filled with Pedlar's wares;
And with this Basket on his arm the Lad
Went up to London, found a Master there,
Who out of many chose the trusty Boy
To go and overlook his merchandise
Beyond the seas; where he grew wondrous rich,
And left estates and moneys to the poor,
And at his birth-place built a Chapel floored
With Marble, which he sent from foreign lands.
These thoughts, and many others of like sort,
Passed quickly through the mind of Isabel,
And her face brightened. The Old Man was glad
And thus resumed:—'Well, Isabel! this scheme
These two days has been meat and drink to me.
Far more than we have lost is left us yet.
—We have enough—I wish indeed that I
Were younger,—but this hope is a good hope.
—Make ready Luke's best garments, of the best
Buy for him more, and let us send him forth
Tomorrow, or the next day, or tonight:
—If he could go, the Boy should go tonight.'
Here Michael ceased, and to the fields went forth
With a light heart. The Housewife for five days

Was restless morn and night, and all day long
Wrought on with her best fingers to prepare
Things needful for the journey of her Son.
But Isabel was glad when Sunday came
To stop her in her work: for, when she lay
By Michael's side, she for the two last nights
Heard him, how he was troubled in his sleep:
And when they rose at morning she could see
That all his hopes were gone. That day at noon
She said to Luke, while they two by themselves
Were sitting at the door, 'Thou must not go:
We have no other child but thee to lose,
None to remember—do not go away,
For if thou leave thy Father he will die.'
The Lad made answer with a jocund voice;
And Isabel, when she had told her fears,
Recovered heart. That evening her best fare
Did she bring forth, and all together sat
Like happy people round a Christmas fire.

Next morning Isabel resumed her work;
And all the ensuing week the house appeared
As cheerful as a grove in Spring: at length
The expected letter from their Kinsman came,
With kind assurances that he would do
His utmost for the welfare of the Boy;
To which requests were added that forthwith
He might be sent to him. Ten times or more
The letter was read over; Isabel
Went forth to show it to the neighbours round;
Nor was there at that time on English Land
A prouder heart than Luke's. When Isabel
Had to her house returned, the Old Man said,
'He shall depart tomorrow.' To this word
The Housewife answered, talking much of things
Which, if at such short notice he should go,
Would surely be forgotten. But at length
She gave consent, and Michael was at ease.

Near the tumultuous brook of Green-head Gill,
In that deep Valley, Michael had designed
To build a sheep-fold; and, before he heard

The tidings of his melancholy loss,
For this same purpose he had gathered up
A heap of stones, which close to the brook side
Lay thrown together, ready for the work.
With Luke that evening thitherward he walked;
And soon as they had reached the place he stopped,
And thus the Old Man spake to him:—'My Son,
Tomorrow thou wilt leave me: with full heart
I look upon thee, for thou art the same
That wert a promise to me ere thy birth,
And all thy life hast been my daily joy.
I will relate to thee some little part
Of our two histories; 'twill do thee good
When thou art from me, even if I should speak
Of things thou canst not know of.——After thou
First cam'st into the world, as it befalls
To new-born infants, thou didst sleep away
Two days, and blessings from thy Father's tongue
Then fell upon thee. Day by day passed on,
And still I loved thee with increasing love.
Never to living ear came sweeter sounds
Than when I heard thee by our own fire-side
First uttering, without words, a natural tune;
When thou, a feeding babe, didst in thy joy
Sing at thy Mother's breast. Month followed month,
And in the open fields my life was passed
And in the mountains, else I think that thou
Hadst been brought up upon thy Father's knees.
But we were playmates, Luke: among these hills,
As well thou know'st, in us the old and young
Have played together, nor with me didst thou
Lack any pleasure which a boy can know.'
Luke had a manly heart; but at these words
He sobbed aloud. The Old Man grasped his hand,
And said, 'Nay, do not take it so—I see
That these are things of which I need not speak.
—Even to the utmost I have been to thee
A kind and a good Father: and herein
I but repay a gift which I myself
Received at others' hands; for, though now old
Beyond the common life of man, I still
Remember them who loved me in my youth.

Both of them sleep together: here they lived,
As all their Forefathers had done; and when
At length their time was come, they were not loth
To give their bodies to the family mould.
I wished that thou shouldst live the life they lived.
But 'tis a long time to look back, my Son,
And see so little gain from sixty years.
These fields were burthened when they came to me;
Till I was forty years of age, not more
Than half of my inheritance was mine.
I toiled and toiled; God blessed me in my work,
And till these three weeks past the land was free.
—It looks as if it never could endure
Another Master. Heaven forgive me, Luke,
If I judge ill for thee, but it seems good
That thou shouldst go.' At this the Old Man paus'd;
Then, pointing to the Stones near which they stood,
Thus, after a short silence, he resumed:
'This was a work for us; and now, my Son,
It is a work for me. But, lay one Stone—
Here, lay it for me, Luke, with thine own hands.
Nay, Boy, be of good hope:—we both may live
To see a better day. At eighty-four
I still am strong and stout;—do thou thy part,
I will do mine.—I will begin again
With many tasks that were resigned to thee;
Up to the heights, and in among the storms,
Will I without thee go again, and do
All works which I was wont to do alone,
Before I knew thy face.—Heaven bless thee, Boy!
Thy heart these two weeks has been beating fast
With many hopes—It should be so—Yes—yes—
I knew that thou couldst never have a wish
To leave me, Luke: thou hast been bound to me
Only by links of love: when thou art gone,
What will be left to us!—But, I forget
My purposes. Lay now the corner-stone,
As I requested; and hereafter, Luke,
When thou art gone away, should evil men
Be thy companions, think of me, my Son,
And of this moment; hither turn thy thoughts,
And God will strengthen thee: amid all fear

And all temptation, Luke, I pray that thou
Mayst bear in mind the life thy Fathers lived,
Who, being innocent, did for that cause
Bestir them in good deeds. Now, fare thee well—
When thou return'st, thou in this place wilt see
A work which is not here; a covenant
'Twill be between us—But whatever fate
Befall thee, I shall love thee to the last,
And bear thy memory with me to the grave.'

The Shepherd ended here: and Luke stooped down,
And, as his Father had requested, laid
The first stone of the Sheep-fold. At the sight
The Old Man's grief broke from him, to his heart
He pressed his Son, he kissed him and wept;
And to the House together they returned.

Next morning, as had been resolved, the Boy
Began his journey, and when he had reached
The public Way, he put on a bold face;
And all the Neighbours as he passed their doors
Came forth with wishes and with farewell prayers,
That followed him till he was out of sight.

A good report did from their Kinsman come,
Of Luke and his well-doing: and the Boy
Wrote loving letters, full of wondrous news,
Which, as the Housewife phrased it, were throughout
The prettiest letters that were ever seen.
Both parents read them with rejoicing hearts.
So, many months passed on: and once again
The Shepherd went about his daily work
With confident and cheerful thoughts; and now
Sometimes when he could find a leisure hour
He to that valley took his way, and there
Wrought at the Sheep-fold. Meantime Luke began
To slacken in his duty; and at length
He in the dissolute city gave himself
To evil courses: ignominy and shame
Fell on him, so that he was driven at last
To seek a hiding-place beyond the seas.

There is a comfort in the strength of love;
'Twill make a thing endurable, which else
Would break the heart:—Old Michael found it so
I have conversed with more than one who well
Remember the Old Man, and what he was
Years after he had heard this heavy news.
His bodily frame had been from youth to age
Of an unusual strength. Among the rocks
He went, and still looked up upon the sun,
And listened to the wind; and as before
Performed all kinds of labour for his Sheep,
And for the land his small inheritance.
And to that hollow Dell from time to time
Did he repair, to build the Fold of which
His flock had need. 'Tis not forgotten yet
The pity which was then in every heart
For the Old Man—and 'tis believed by all
That many and many a day he thither went,
And never lifted up a single stone.

There, by the Sheep-fold, sometimes was he seen
Sitting alone, with that his faithful Dog,
Then old, beside him, lying at his feet.
The length of full seven years from time to time
He at the building of this Sheep-fold wrought,
And left the work unfinished when he died.

Three years, or little more, did Isabel
Survive her Husband: at her death the estate
Was sold, and went into a Stranger's hand.
The Cottage which was named The EVENING STAR
Is gone—the ploughshare has been through the ground
On which it stood; great changes have been wrought
In all the neighbourhood:—yet the Oak is left
That grew beside their Door; and the remains
Of the unfinished Sheep-fold may be seen
Beside the boisterous brook of Green-head Gill.

PETER BELL

A TALE

Peter Bell, first written in the spring of 1798, belongs essentially to the same class as *Lyrical Ballads.* It is an 'experiment' in the sense of the 1798 *Advertisement.* It is also a sort of counterpart of *The Ancient Mariner,* the conversion being effected without recourse to the supernatural.

Wordsworth worked on the poem for some years. In Germany he was 'employed in hewing down *Peter Bell*'. Copies, with changes, were made in 1800, 1802 and 1806. More changes were made before and after publication in 1819. Many of them are very interesting and can be studied easily in de Selincourt's Oxford edition of Wordsworth, Vol. 2. Here are two of the most striking:

(1) Between the fourth and third stanzas from the end of Part 1 came a stanza found in all the manuscripts and in the 1819 publication but thereafter omitted on the insistence of friends.

Is it a party in a parlour ?
Cramm'd just as they on earth were cramm'd—
Some sipping punch, some sipping tea,
But, as you by their faces see,
All silent and all damn'd !

(2) A little after the middle of Part 3 the two stanzas beginning ''Tis said, meek Beast !' are found in none of the six manuscript copies but were evidently added for the 1819 publication.

The text here given is the latest.

PETER BELL

A TALE

What's in a Name?
Brutus will start a spirit as soon as Caesar !

TO ROBERT SOUTHEY, ESQ., P.L., ETC. ETC.

MY DEAR FRIEND,—The Tale of Peter Bell, which I now introduce to your notice, and to that of the Public, has, in its Manuscript state, nearly survived its *minority:*—for it first saw the light in the summer of 1798. During this long interval, pains have been taken at different times to make the production less unworthy of a favourable reception; or, rather, to fit it for filling *permanently* a station, however humble, in the Literature of our Country. This has, indeed, been the aim of all my endeavours in Poetry, which, you know, have been sufficiently laborious to prove that I deem the Art not lightly to be approached; and that the attainment of excellence in it may laudably be made the principal object of intellectual pursuit by any man, who, with reasonable consideration of circumstances, has faith in his own impulses.

The Poem of Peter Bell, as the Prologue will show, was composed under a belief that the Imagination not only does not require for its exercise the intervention of supernatural agency, but that, though such agency be excluded, the faculty may be called forth as imperiously and for kindred results of pleasure, by incidents within the compass of poetic probability, in the humblest departments of daily life. Since that Prologue was written, *you* have exhibited most splendid effects of judicious daring, in the opposite and usual course. Let this acknowledgment make my peace with the lovers of the supernatural; and I am persuaded it will be admitted that to you, as a Master in that province of the art, the following Tale, whether from contrast or congruity, is not an unappropriate offering. Accept it, then, as a public testimony of affectionate admiration from one with whose name yours has been often coupled (to use your own words) for evil and for good; and believe me to be, with earnest wishes that life and health may be granted you to complete the many important works in which you are engaged, and with high respect,

Most faithfully yours,

WILLIAM WORDSWORTH

RYDAL MOUNT, *April* 7, 1819

PETER BELL

PROLOGUE

THERE'S something in a flying horse,
There's something in a huge balloon;
But through the clouds I'll never float
Until I have a little Boat,
Shaped like the crescent-moon.

And now I *have* a little Boat,
In shape a very crescent-moon:
Fast through the clouds my Boat can sail;
But if perchance your faith should fail,
Look up—and you shall see me soon!

The woods, my Friends, are round you roaring,
Rocking and roaring like a sea;
The noise of danger's in your ears,
And ye have all a thousand fears
Both for my little Boat and me!

Meanwhile untroubled I admire
The pointed horns of my canoe;
And, did not pity touch my breast
To see how ye are all distrest,
Till my ribs ached I'd laugh at you!

Away we go, my Boat and I—
Frail man ne'er sate in such another;
Whether among the winds we strive,
Or deep into the clouds we dive,
Each is contented with the other.

Away we go—and what care we
For treasons, tumults, and for wars?
We are as calm in our delight
As is the crescent-moon so bright
Among the scattered stars.

Up goes my Boat among the stars
Through many a breathless field of light,
Through many a long blue field of ether,
Leaving ten thousand stars beneath her:
Up goes my little Boat so bright!

The Crab, the Scorpion, and the Bull—
We pry among them all; have shot
High o'er the red-haired race of Mars,
Covered from top to toe with scars;
Such company I like it not!

The towns in Saturn are decayed,
And melancholy Spectres throng them;—
The Pleiads, that appear to kiss
Each other in the vast abyss,
With joy I sail among them.

Swift Mercury resounds with mirth,
Great Jove is full of stately bowers;
But these, and all that they contain,
What are they to that tiny grain,
That little Earth of ours?

Then back to Earth, the dear green Earth:—
Whole ages if I here should roam,
The world for my remarks and me
Would not a whit the better be;
I've left my heart at home.

See! there she is, the matchless Earth!
There spreads the famed Pacific Ocean!
Old Andes thrusts yon craggy spear
Through the grey clouds; the Alps are here,
Like waters in commotion!

Yon tawny slip is Libya's sands;
That silver thread the river Dnieper;
And look, where clothed in brightest green
Is a sweetest Isle, of isles the Queen;
Ye fairies, from all evil keep her!

And see the town where I was born!
Around those happy fields we span
In boyish gambols;—I was lost
Where I have been, but on this coast
I feel I am a man.

Never did fifty things at once
Appear so lovely, never, never;—
How tunefully the forests ring!
To hear the earth's soft murmuring
Thus could I hang for ever!

'Shame on you!' cried my little Boat,
'Was ever such a homesick Loon,
Within a living Boat to sit,
And make no better use of it;
A Boat twin-sister of the crescent-moon!

'Ne'er in the breast of full-grown Poet
Fluttered so faint a heart before;—
Was it the music of the spheres
That overpowered your mortal ears?
—Such din shall trouble them no more.

'These nether precincts do not lack
Charms of their own;—then come with me—
I want a comrade, and for you
There's nothing that I would not do;
Nought is there that you shall not see.

'Haste! and above Siberian snows
We'll sport amid the boreal morning;
Will mingle with her lustres gliding
Among the stars, the stars now hiding,
And now the stars adorning.

'I know the secrets of a land
Where human foot did never stray;
Fair is that land as evening skies,
And cool, though in the depth it lies
Of burning Africa.

'Or we'll into the realm of Faery,
Among the lovely shades of things;
The shadowy forms of mountains bare,
And streams, and bowers, and ladies fair,
The shades of palaces and kings!

'Or, if you thirst with hardy zeal
Less quiet regions to explore,
Prompt voyage shall to you reveal
How earth and heaven are taught to feel
The might of magic lore!'

'My little vagrant Form of light,
My gay and beautiful Canoe,
Well have you played your friendly part;
As kindly take what from my heart
Experience forces—then adieu!

'Temptation lurks among your words;
But, while these pleasures you're pursuing
Without impediment or let,
No wonder if you quite forget
What on the earth is doing.

'There was a time when all mankind
Did listen with a faith sincere
To tuneful tongues in mystery versed;
Then Poets fearlessly rehearsed
The wonders of a wild career.

'Go—(but the world's a sleepy world,
And 'tis, I fear, an age too late)
Take with you some ambitious Youth!
For, restless Wanderer! I, in truth,
Am all unfit to be your mate.

'Long have I loved what I behold,
The night that calms, the day that cheers;
The common growth of mother-earth
Suffices me—her tears, her mirth,
Her humblest mirth and tears.

'The dragon's wing, the magic ring,
I shall not covet for my dower,
If I along that lowly way
With sympathetic heart may stray,
And with a soul of power.

'These given, what more need I desire
To stir, to soothe, or elevate?
What nobler marvels than the mind
May in life's daily prospect find,
May find or there create?

'A potent wand doth Sorrow wield;
What spell so strong as guilty Fear!
Repentance is a tender Sprite;
If aught on earth have heavenly might,
'Tis lodged within her silent tear.

'But grant my wishes,—let us now
Descend from this ethereal height;
Then take thy way, adventurous Skiff,
More daring far than Hippogriff,
And be thy own delight!

'To the stone-table in my garden,
Loved haunt of many a summer hour,
The Squire is come: his daughter Bess
Beside him in the cool recess
Sits blooming like a flower.

'With these are many more convened;
They know not I have been so far;—
I see them there, in number nine,
Beneath the spreading Weymouth-pine!
I see them—there they are!

'There sits the Vicar and his Dame;
And there my good friend, Stephen Otter;
And, ere the light of evening fail,
To them I must relate the Tale
Of Peter Bell the Potter.'

Off flew the Boat—away she flees,
Spurning her freight with indignation!
And I, as well as I was able,
On two poor legs, toward my stone-table
Limped on with sore vexation.

'O, here he is!' cried little Bess—
She saw me at the garden-door;
'We've waited anxiously and long,'
They cried, and all around me throng,
Full nine of them or more!

'Reproach me not—your fears be still—
Be thankful we again have met;—
Resume, my Friends! within the shade
Your seats, and quickly shall be paid
The well-remembered debt.'

I spake with faltering voice, like one
Not wholly rescued from the pale
Of a wild dream, or worse illusion;
But straight, to cover my confusion,
Began the promised Tale.

PART FIRST

All by the moonlight river-side
Groaned the poor Beast—alas! in vain;
The staff was raised to loftier height,
And the blows fell with heavier weight
As Peter struck—and struck again.

'Hold!' cried the Squire, 'against the rules
Of common sense you're surely sinning;
This leap is for us all too bold;
Who Peter was, let that be told,
And start from the beginning.'

——'A Potter,* Sir, he was by trade,'
Said I, becoming quite collected;
'And wheresoever he appeared,
Full twenty times was Peter feared
For once that Peter was respected.

He, two-and-thirty years or more,
Had been a wild and woodland rover;
Had heard the Atlantic surges roar
On farthest Cornwall's rocky shore,
And trod the cliffs of Dover.

And he had seen Caernarvon's towers,
And well he knew the spire of Sarum;
And he had been where Lincoln bell
Flings o'er the fen that ponderous knell—
A far-renowned alarum!

At Doncaster, at York, and Leeds,
And merry Carlisle had he been;
And all along the Lowlands fair,
All through the bonny shire of Ayr;
And far as Aberdeen.

And he had been at Inverness;
And Peter, by the mountain-rills,
Had danced his round with Highland lasses;
And he had lain beside his asses
On lofty Cheviot Hills:

And he had trudged through Yorkshire dales,
Among the rocks and winding *scars;*
Where deep and low the hamlets lie
Beneath their little patch of sky
And little lot of stars:

And all along the indented coast,
Bespattered with the salt-sea foam;
Where'er a knot of houses lay
On headland, or in hollow bay;—
Sure never man like him did roam!

* In the dialect of the North, a hawker of earthenware is thus designated.

As well might Peter in the Fleet
Have been fast bound, a begging debtor;—
He travelled here, he travelled there;—
But not the value of a hair
Was heart or head the better.

He roved among the vales and streams,
In the green wood and hollow dell;
They were his dwellings night and day,—
But nature ne'er could find the way
Into the heart of Peter Bell.

In vain, through every changeful year,
Did Nature lead him as before;
A primrose by a river's brim
A yellow primrose was to him,
And it was nothing more.

Small change it made in Peter's heart
To see his gentle panniered train
With more than vernal pleasure feeding,
Where'er the tender grass was leading
Its earliest green along the lane.

In vain, through water, earth, and air,
The soul of happy sound was spread,
When Peter on some April morn,
Beneath the broom or budding thorn,
Made the warm earth his lazy bed.

At noon, when, by the forest's edge
He lay beneath the branches high,
The soft blue sky did never melt
Into his heart; he never felt
The witchery of the soft blue sky!

On a fair prospect some have looked
And felt, as I have heard them say,
As if the moving time had been
A thing as steadfast as the scene
On which they gazed themselves away.

Within the breast of Peter Bell
These silent raptures found no place;
He was a Carl as wild and rude
As ever hue-and-cry pursued,
As ever ran a felon's race.

Of all that lead a lawless life,
Of all that love their lawless lives,
In city or in village small,
He was the wildest far of all;—
He had a dozen wedded wives.

Nay, start not!—wedded wives—and twelve!
But how one wife could e'er come near him,
In simple truth I cannot tell;
For, be it said of Peter Bell,
To see him was to fear him.

Though Nature could not touch his heart
By lovely forms, and silent weather,
And tender sounds, yet you might see
At once that Peter Bell and she
Had often been together.

A savage wildness round him hung
As of a dweller out of doors;
In his whole figure and his mien
A savage character was seen
Of mountains and of dreary moors.

To all the unshaped half-human thoughts
Which solitary Nature feeds
'Mid summer storms or winter's ice,
Had Peter joined whatever vice
The cruel city breeds.

His face was keen as is the wind
That cuts along the hawthorn-fence;
Of courage you saw little there,
But, in its stead, a medley air
Of cunning and of impudence.

He had a dark and sidelong walk;
And long and slouching was his gait;
Beneath his looks so bare and bold,
You might perceive, his spirit cold
Was playing with some inward bait.

His forehead wrinkled was and furred;
A work, one half of which was done
By thinking of his '*whens*' and '*hows*';
And half, by knitting of his brows
Beneath the glaring sun.

There was a hardness in his cheek,
There was a hardness in his eye,
As if a man had fixed his face,
In many a solitary place,
Against the wind and open sky!'

ONE night, (and now, my little Bess!
We've reached at last the promised Tale;)
One beautiful November night,
When the full moon was shining bright
Upon the rapid river Swale,

Along the river's winding banks
Peter was travelling all alone;—
Whether to buy or sell, or led
By pleasure running in his head,
To me was never known.

He trudged along through copse and brake,
He trudged along o'er hill and dale;
Nor for the moon cared he a tittle,
And for the stars he cared as little,
And for the murmuring river Swale.

But, chancing to espy a path
That promised to cut short the way;
As many a wiser man hath done,
He left a trusty guide for one
That might his steps betray.

To a thick wood he soon is brought
Where cheerily his course he weaves,
And whistling loud may yet be heard,
Though often buried, like a bird
Darkling, among the boughs and leaves.

But quickly Peter's mood is changed,
And on he drives with cheeks that burn
In downright fury and in wrath;—
There's little sign the treacherous path
Will to the road return!

The path grows dim, and dimmer still;
Now up, now down, the Rover wends,
With all the sail that he can carry,
Till brought to a deserted quarry—
And there the pathway ends.

He paused—for shadows of strange shape,
Massy and black, before him lay;
But through the dark, and through the cold,
And through the yawning fissures old,
Did Peter boldly press his way

Right through the quarry;—and behold
A scene of soft and lovely hue!
Where blue and grey, and tender green,
Together make as sweet a scene
As ever human eye did view.

Beneath the clear blue sky he saw
A little field of meadow ground;
But field or meadow name it not;
Call it of earth a small green plot,
With rocks encompassed round.

The Swale flowed under the grey rocks,
But he flowed quiet and unseen:—
You need a strong and stormy gale
To bring the noises of the Swale
To that green spot, so calm and green!

And is there no one dwelling here,
No hermit with his beads and glass?
And does no little cottage look
Upon this soft and fertile nook?
Does no one live near this green grass?

Across the deep and quiet spot
Is Peter driving through the grass—
And now has reached the skirting trees;
When, turning round his head, he sees
A solitary Ass.

'A prize!' cries Peter—but he first
Must spy about him far and near:
There's not a single house in sight,
No woodman's hut, nor cottage light—
Peter, you need not fear!

There's nothing to be seen but woods,
And rocks that spread a hoary gleam,
And this one Beast, that from the bed
Of the green meadow hangs his head
Over the silent stream.

His head is with a halter bound;
The halter seizing, Peter leapt
Upon the Creature's back, and plied
With ready heels his shaggy side;
But still the Ass his station kept.

Then Peter gave a sudden jerk,
A jerk that from a dungeon-floor
Would have pulled up an iron ring;
But still the heavy-headed Thing
Stood just as he had stood before!

Quoth Peter, leaping from his seat,
'There is some plot against me laid';
Once more the little meadow-ground
And all the hoary cliffs around
He cautiously surveyed.

All, all is silent—rocks and woods,
All still and silent—far and near!
Only the Ass, with motion dull,
Upon the pivot of his skull
Turns round his long left ear.

Thought Peter, What can mean all this?
Some ugly witchcraft must be here!
—Once more the Ass, with motion dull,
Upon the pivot of his skull
Turned round his long left ear.

Suspicion ripened into dread;
Yet, with deliberate action slow,
His staff high-raising, in the pride
Of skill, upon the sounding hide
He dealt a sturdy blow.

The poor Ass staggered with the shock;
And then, as if to take his ease,
In quiet uncomplaining mood,
Upon the spot where he had stood,
Dropped gently down upon his knees;

As gently on his side he fell;
And by the river's brink did lie;
And, while he lay like one that mourned,
The patient Beast on Peter turned
His shining hazel eye.

'Twas but one mild, reproachful look,
A look more tender than severe;
And straight in sorrow, not in dread,
He turned the eye-ball in his head
Towards the smooth river deep and clear.

Upon the Beast the sapling rings;
His lank sides heaved, his limbs they stirred;
He gave a groan, and then another,
Of that which went before the brother,
And then he gave a third.

All by the moonlight river side
He gave three miserable groans;
And not till now hath Peter seen
How gaunt the Creature is,—how lean
And sharp his staring bones!

With legs stretched out and stiff he lay:—
No word of kind commiseration
Fell at the sight from Peter's tongue;
With hard contempt his heart was wrung,
With hatred and vexation.

The meagre beast lay still as death;
And Peter's lips with fury quiver;
Quoth he, 'You little mulish dog,
I'll fling your carcass like a log
Head-foremost down the river!'

An impious oath confirmed the threat—
Whereat from the earth on which he lay
To all the echoes, south and north,
And east and west, the Ass sent forth
A long and clamorous bray!

This outcry, on the heart of Peter,
Seems like a note of joy to strike,—
Joy at the heart of Peter knocks;
But in the echo of the rocks
Was something Peter did not like.

Whether to cheer his coward breast,
Or that he could not break the chain,
In this serene and solemn hour,
Twined round him by demoniac power,
To the blind work he turned again.

Among the rocks and winding crags;
Among the mountains far away;
Once more the Ass did lengthen out
More ruefully a deep-drawn shout,
The hard dry see-saw of his horrible bray!

What is there now in Peter's heart?
Or whence the might of this strange sound?
The moon uneasy looked and dimmer,
The broad blue heavens appeared to glimmer,
And the rocks staggered all around—

From Peter's hand the sapling dropped!
Threat has he none to execute;
'If any one should come and see
That I am here, they'll think,' quoth he,
'I'm helping this poor dying brute.'

He scans the Ass from limb to limb,
And ventures now to uplift his eyes;
More steady looks the moon, and clear
More like themselves the rocks appear
And touch more quiet skies.

His scorn returns—his hate revives;
He stoops the Ass's neck to seize
With malice—that again takes flight;
For in the pool a startling sight
Meets him, among the inverted trees.

Is it the moon's distorted face?
The ghost-like image of a cloud?
Is it a gallows there portrayed?
Is Peter of himself afraid?
Is it a coffin,—or a shroud?

A grisly idol hewn in stone?
Or imp from witch's lap let fall?
Perhaps a ring of shining fairies?
Such as pursue their feared vagaries
In sylvan bower, or haunted hall?

Is it a fiend that to a stake
Of fire his desperate self is tethering?
Or stubborn spirit doomed to yell
In solitary ward or cell,
Ten thousand miles from all his brethren?

Never did pulse so quickly throb,
And never heart so loudly panted;
He looks, he cannot choose but look ;
Like some one reading in a book—
A book that is enchanted.

Ah, well-a-day for Peter Bell!
He will be turned to iron soon,
Meet Statue for the court of Fear!
His hat is up—and every hair
Bristles, and whitens in the moon!

He looks, he ponders, looks again;
He sees a motion—hears a groan;
His eyes will burst—his heart will break—
He gives a loud and frightful shriek,
And back he falls, as if his life were flown!

PART SECOND

We left our Hero in a trance,
Beneath the alders, near the river;
The Ass is by the river-side,
And, where the feeble breezes glide,
Upon the stream the moonbeams quiver.

A happy respite! but at length
He feels the glimmering of the moon;
Wakes with glazed eye, and feebly sighing—
To sink, perhaps, where he is lying,
Into a second swoon!

He lifts his head, he sees his staff;
He touches—'tis to him a treasure!
Faint recollection seems to tell
That he is yet where mortals dwell—
A thought received with languid pleasure!

His head upon his elbow propped,
Becoming less and less perplexed,
Sky-ward he looks—to rock and wood—
And then—upon the glassy flood
His wandering eye is fixed.

Thought he, that is the face of one
In his last sleep securely bound!
So toward the stream his head he bent,
And downward thrust his staff, intent
The river's depth to sound.

Now—like a tempest-shattered bark,
That overwhelmed and prostrate lies,
And in a moment to the verge
Is lifted of a foaming surge—
Full suddenly the Ass doth rise!

His staring bones all shake with joy,
And close by Peter's side he stands:
While Peter o'er the river bends,
The little Ass his neck extends,
And fondly licks his hands.

Such life is in the Ass's eyes,
Such life is in his limbs and ears;
That Peter Bell, if he had been
The veriest coward ever seen,
Must now have thrown aside his fears.

The Ass looks on—and to his work
Is Peter quietly resigned;
He touches here—he touches there—
And now among the dead man's hair
His sapling Peter has entwined.

He pulls—and looks—and pulls again;
And he whom the poor Ass had lost,
The man who had been four days dead,
Head-foremost from the river's bed
Uprises like a ghost!

And Peter draws him to dry land;
And through the brain of Peter pass
Some poignant twitches, fast and faster;
'No doubt,' quoth he, 'he is the Master
Of this poor miserable Ass!'

The meagre shadow that looks on—
What would he now? what is he doing?
His sudden fit of joy is flown,—
He on his knees hath laid him down,
As if he were his grief renewing;

But no—that Peter on his back
Must mount, he shows well as he can:
Thought Peter then, come weal or woe,
I'll do what he would have me do,
In pity to this poor drowned man.

With that resolve he boldly mounts
Upon the pleased and thankful Ass;
And then, without a moment's stay,
That earnest Creature turned away,
Leaving the body on the grass.

Intent upon his faithful watch,
The Beast four days and nights had past;
A sweeter meadow ne'er was seen,
And there the Ass four days had been,
Nor ever once did break his fast:

Yet firm his step, and stout his heart;
The mead is crossed—the quarry's mouth
Is reached; but there the trusty guide
Into a thicket turns aside,
And deftly ambles towards the south.

When hark a burst of doleful sound!
And Peter honestly might say,
The like came never to his ears,
Though he has been, full thirty years,
A rover—night and day!

'Tis not a plover of the moors,
'Tis not a bittern of the fen;
Nor can it be a barking fox,
Nor night-bird chambered in the rocks,
Nor wild-cat in a woody glen!

The Ass is startled—and stops short
Right in the middle of the thicket;
And Peter, wont to whistle loud
Whether alone or in a crowd,
Is silent as a silent cricket.

What ails you now, my little Bess?
Well may you tremble and look grave!
This cry—that rings along the wood,
This cry—that floats adown the flood,
Comes from the entrance of a cave:

I see a blooming Wood-boy there,
And if I had the power to say
How sorrowful the wanderer is,
Your heart would be as sad as his
Till you had kissed his tears away!

Grasping a hawthorn branch in hand,
All bright with berries ripe and red,
Into the cavern's mouth he peeps;
Thence back into the moonlight creeps;
Whom seeks he—whom?—the silent dead:

His father!—Him doth he require—
Him hath he sought with fruitless pains,
Among the rocks, behind the trees;
Now creeping on his hands and knees,
Now running o'er the open plains.

And hither is he come at last,
When he through such a day has gone,
By this dark cave to be distrest
Like a poor bird—her plundered nest
Hovering around with dolorous moan!

Of that intense and piercing cry
The listening Ass conjectures well;
Wild as it is, he there can read
Some intermingled notes that plead
With touches irresistible.

But Peter—when he saw the Ass
Not only stop but turn, and change
The cherished tenor of his pace
The lamentable cry to chase—
It wrought in him conviction strange;

A faith that, for the dead man's sake
And this poor slave who loved him well,
Vengeance upon his head will fall,
Some visitation worse than all
Which ever till this night befell.

Meanwhile the Ass to reach his home
Is striving stoutly as he may;
But, while he climbs the woody hill,
The cry grows weak—and weaker still;
And now at last it dies away.

So with his freight the Creature turns
Into a gloomy grove of beech,
Along the shade with footsteps true
Descending slowly, till the two
The open moonlight reach.

And there, along the narrow dell,
A fair smooth pathway you discern,
A length of green and open road—
As if it from a fountain flowed—
Winding away between the fern.

The rocks that tower on either side
Build up a wild fantastic scene;
Temples like those among the Hindoos,
And mosques, and spires, and abbey-windows,
And castles all with ivy green!

And while the Ass pursues his way
Along this solitary dell,
As pensively his steps advance,
The mosques and spires change countenance,
And look at Peter Bell!

That unintelligible cry
Hath left him high in preparation,—
Convinced that he, or soon or late,
This very night will meet his fate—
And so he sits in expectation!

The strenuous Animal hath clomb
With the green path; and now he wends
Where, shining like the smoothest sea,
In undisturbed immensity
A level plain extends.

But whence this faintly-rustling sound
By which the journeying pair are chased?
—A withered leaf is close behind,
Light plaything for the sportive wind
Upon that solitary waste.

When Peter spied the moving thing,
It only doubled his distress;
'Where there is not a bush or tree,
The very leaves they follow me—
So huge hath been my wickedness!'

To a close lane they now are come,
Where, as before, the enduring Ass
Moves on without a moment's stop,
Nor once turns round his head to crop
A bramble-leaf or blade of grass.

Between the hedges as they go,
The white dust sleeps upon the lane;
And Peter, ever and anon
Back-looking, sees, upon a stone,
Or in the dust, a crimson stain.

A stain—as of a drop of blood
By moonlight made more faint and wan;
Ha! why these sinkings of despair?
He knows not how the blood comes there—
And Peter is a wicked man.

At length he spies a bleeding wound,
Where he had struck the Ass's head;
He sees the blood, knows what it is,—
A glimpse of sudden joy was his,
But then it quickly fled;

Of him whom sudden death had seized
He thought,—of thee, O faithful Ass!
And once again those ghastly pains
Shoot to and fro through heart and reins,
And through his brain like lightning pass.

PART THIRD

I'VE heard of one, a gentle Soul,
Though given to sadne
And for the fact will v
It chanced that by a t
This man was reading

Bending, as you or I m
At night o'er any pious
When sudden blackness
The snow-white page o
And made the good ma

The chamber walls wer
And to his book he turned a
—The light had left the lonely taper,
And formed itself upon the paper
Into large letters—bright and plain!

The godly book was in his hand—
And on the page, more black than coal,
Appeared, set forth in strange array,
A *word*—which to his dying day
Perplexed the good man's gentle soul.

The ghostly word, thus plainly seen,
Did never from his lips depart;
But he hath said, poor gentle wight!
It brought full many a sin to light
Out of the bottom of his heart.

Dread Spirits! to confound the meek
Why wander from your course so far,
Disordering colour, form, and stature!
—Let good men feel the soul of nature,
And see things as they are.

Yet, potent Spirits! well I know,
How ye, that play with soul and sense,
Are not unused to trouble friends
Of goodness, for most gracious ends—
And this I speak in reverence!

But might I give advice to you,
Whom in my fear I love so well;
F[illegible] virtue go,
[illegible]ss and to gloom,
[illegible]uch,—one night
[illegible]per's light
[illegible]n his room;

[illegible]ight bend
[illegible] book,
[illegible] overspread
[illegible]n which he read,
[illegible]n round him look.

[illegible] dark all round,—
[illegible] of the M[illegible];
To-night, beneath the moonlight sky,
What may be done with Peter Bell!

—O, would that some more skilful voice
My further labour might prevent!
Kind Listeners, that around me sit,
I feel that I am all unfit
For such high argument.

I've played, I've danced, with my narration;
I loitered long ere I began:
Ye waited then on my good pleasure;
Pour out indulgence still, in measure
As liberal as ye can!

Our Travellers, ye remember well,
Are thridding a sequestered lane;
And Peter many tricks is trying,
And many anodynes applying,
To ease his conscience of its pain.

By this his heart is lighter far;
And, finding that he can account
So snugly for that crimson stain,
His evil spirit up again
Does like an empty bucket mount.

And Peter is a deep logician
Who hath no lack of wit mercurial;
'Blood drops—leaves rustle—yet,' quoth he,
'This poor man never but for me
Could have had Christian burial.

'And, say the best you can, 'tis plain,
That here has been some wicked dealing;
No doubt the devil in me wrought;
I'm not the man who could have thought
An Ass like this was worth the stealing!'

So from his pocket Peter takes
His shining horn tobacco-box;
And in a light and careless way,
As men who with their purpose play,
Upon the lid he knocks.

Let them whose voice can stop the clouds,
Whose cunning eye can see the wind,
Tell a curious world the cause
Why, making here a sudden pause,
The Ass turned round his head, and *grinned.*

Appalling process! I have marked
The like on heath, in lonely wood;
And, verily, have seldom met
A spectacle more hideous—yet
It suited Peter's present mood.

And, grinning in his turn, his teeth
He in jocose defiance showed—
When, to upset his spiteful mirth,
A murmur, pent within the earth,
In the dead earth beneath the road,

Rolled audibly!—it swept along,
A muffled noise—a rumbling sound!—
'Twas by a troop of miners made,
Plying with gunpowder their trade,
Some twenty fathoms under ground.

Small cause of dire effect! for, surely,
If ever mortal, King or Cotter,
Believed that earth was charged to quake
And yawn for his unworthy sake,
'Twas Peter Bell the Potter.

But as an oak in breathless air
Will stand though to the centre hewn;
Or as the weakest things, if frost
Have stiffened them, maintain their post;
So he, beneath the gazing moon!—

The Beast bestriding thus, he reached
A spot where, in a sheltering cove,
A little chapel stands alone,
With greenest ivy overgrown,
And tufted with an ivy grove;

Dying insensibly away
From human thoughts and purposes,
It seemed—wall, window, roof and tower—
To bow to some transforming power,
And blend with the surrounding trees.

As ruinous a place it was,
Thought Peter, in the shire of Fife
That served my turn, when following still
From land to land a reckless will
I married my sixth wife!

The unheeding Ass moves slowly on,
And now is passing by an inn
Brim-full of a carousing crew,
That make, with curses not a few,
An uproar and a drunken din.

I cannot well express the thoughts
Which Peter in those noises found;—
A stifling power compressed his frame,
While-as a swimming darkness came
Over that dull and dreary sound.

For well did Peter know the sound;
The language of those drunken joys
To him, a jovial soul, I ween,
But a few hours ago, had been
A gladsome and a welcome noise.

Now, turned adrift into the past,
He finds no solace in his course;
Like planet-stricken men of yore,
He trembles, smitten to the core
By strong compunction and remorse.

But, more than all, his heart is stung
To think of one, almost a child;
A sweet and playful Highland girl,
As light and beauteous as a squirrel,
As beauteous and as wild!

Her dwelling was a lonely house,
A cottage in a heathy dell;
And she put on her gown of green,
And left her mother at sixteen,
And followed Peter Bell.

But many good and pious thoughts
Had she; and, in the kirk to pray,
Two long Scotch miles, through rain or snow,
To kirk she had been used to go,
Twice every Sabbath-day.

And, when she followed Peter Bell,
It was to lead an honest life;
For he, with tongue not used to falter,
Had pledged his troth before the altar
To love her as his wedded wife.

A mother's hope is hers:—but soon
She drooped and pined like one forlorn;
From Scripture she a name did borrow;
Benoni, or the child of sorrow,
She called her babe unborn.

For she had learned how Peter lived,
And took it in most grievous part;
She to the very bone was worn,
And, ere that little child was born,
Died of a broken heart.

And now the Spirits of the Mind
Are busy with poor Peter Bell;
Upon the rights of visual sense
Usurping, with a prevalence
More terrible than magic spell.

Close by a brake of flowering furze
(Above it shivering aspens play)
He sees an unsubstantial creature,
His very self in form and feature,
Not four yards from the broad highway:

And stretched beneath the furze he sees
The Highland girl—it is no other;
And hears her crying as she cried,
The very moment that she died,
'My mother! oh my mother!'

The sweat pours down from Peter's face,
So grievous is his heart's contrition;
With agony his eye-balls ache
While he beholds by the furze-brake
This miserable vision!

Calm is the well-deserving brute,
His peace hath no offence betrayed;
But now, while down that slope he wends,
A voice to Peter's ear ascends,
Resounding from the woody glade:

The voice, though clamorous as a horn
Re-echoed by a naked rock,
Comes from that tabernacle—List!
Within, a fervent Methodist
Is preaching to no heedless flock!

'Repent! repent!' he cries aloud,
'While yet ye may find mercy;—strive
To love the Lord with all your might;
Turn to him, seek him day and night,
And save your souls alive!

'Repent! repent! though ye have gone,
Through paths of wickedness and woe,
After the Babylonian harlot;
And though your sins be red as scarlet,
They shall be white as snow!'

Even as he passed the door, these words
Did plainly come to Peter's ears;
And they such joyful tidings were,
The joy was more than he could bear!—
He melted into tears.

Sweet tears of hope and tenderness!
And fast they fell, a plenteous shower!
His nerves, his sinews seemed to melt;
Through all his iron frame was felt
A gentle, a relaxing, power!

Each fibre of his frame was weak;
Weak all the animal within;
But, in its helplessness, grew mild
And gentle as an infant child,
An infant that has known no sin.

'Tis said, meek Beast! that, through Heaven's grace,
He not unmoved did notice now
The cross upon thy shoulder scored,
For lasting impress, by the Lord
To whom all human-kind shall bow;

Memorial of his touch—that day
When Jesus humbly deigned to ride,
Entering the proud Jerusalem,
By an immeasurable stream
Of shouting people deified!

Meanwhile the persevering Ass
Turned towards a gate that hung in view
Across a shady lane; his chest
Against the yielding gate he pressed
And quietly passed through.

And up the stony lane he goes;
No ghost more softly ever trod;
Among the stones and pebbles he
Sets down his hoofs inaudibly,
As if with felt his hoofs were shod.

Along the lane the trusty Ass
Went twice two hundred yards or more,
And no one could have guessed his aim,—
Till to a lonely house he came,
And stopped beside the door.

Thought Peter, 'tis the poor man's home!
He listens—not a sound is heard
Save from the trickling household rill;
But, stepping o'er the cottage-sill,
Forthwith a little Girl appeared.

She to the Meeting-house was bound
In hopes some tidings there to gather:
No glimpse it is, no doubtful gleam;
She saw—and uttered with a scream,
'My father! here's my father!'

The very word was plainly heard,
Heard plainly by the wretched Mother—
Her joy was like a deep affright:
And forth she rushed into the light,
And saw it was another!

And instantly upon the earth,
Beneath the full moon shining bright,
Close to the Ass's feet she fell;
At the same moment Peter Bell
Dismounts in most unhappy plight.

As he beheld the Woman lie
Breathless and motionless, the mind
Of Peter sadly was confused;
But, though to such demands unused,
And helpless almost as the blind,

He raised her up; and while he held
Her body propped against his knee,
The Woman waked—and when she spied
The poor Ass standing by her side,
She moaned bitterly.

'Oh! God be praised—my heart's at ease—
For he is dead—I know it well!'
—At this she wept a bitter flood;
And, in the best way that he could,
His tale did Peter tell.

He trembles—he is pale as death;
His voice is weak with perturbation;
He turns aside his head, he pauses;
Poor Peter from a thousand causes
Is crippled sore in his narration.

At length she learned how he espied
The Ass in that small meadow-ground;
And that her Husband now lay dead,
Beside that luckless river's bed
In which he had been drowned.

A piercing look the Widow cast
Upon the Beast that near her stands;
She sees 'tis he, that 'tis the same;
She calls the poor Ass by his name,
And wrings, and wrings her hands.

'O wretched loss—untimely stroke!
If he had died upon his bed!
He knew not one forewarning pain;
He never will come home again—
Is dead, for ever dead!'

Beside the Woman Peter stands;
His heart is opening more and more;
A holy sense pervades his mind;
He feels what he for human-kind
Has never felt before.

At length, by Peter's arm sustained,
The Woman rises from the ground—
'Oh, mercy! something must be done,
My little Rachel, you must run,—
Some willing neighbour must be found.

'Make haste—my little Rachel—do,
The first you meet with—bid him come,
Ask him to lend his horse to-night,
And this good Man, whom Heaven requite,
Will help to bring the body home.'

Away goes Rachel weeping loud;—
An Infant, waked by her distress,
Makes in the house a piteous cry;
And Peter hears the Mother sigh,
'Seven are they, and all fatherless!'

And now is Peter taught to feel
That man's heart is a holy thing;
And Nature, through a world of death,
Breathes into him a second breath,
More searching than the breath of spring.

Upon a stone the Woman sits
In agony of silent grief—
From his own thoughts did Peter start;
He longs to press her to his heart,
From love that cannot find relief.

But roused, as if through every limb
Had past a sudden shock of dread
The Mother o'er the threshold flies,
And up the cottage stairs she hies,
And on the pillow lays her burning head.

And Peter turns his steps aside
Into a shade of darksome trees,
Where he sits down, he knows not how,
With his hands pressed against his brow,
His elbows on his tremulous knees.

There, self-involved, does Peter sit
Until no sign of life he makes,
As if his mind were sinking deep
Through years that have been long asleep!
The trance is passed away—he wakes;

He lifts his head—and sees the Ass
Yet standing in the clear moonshine;
'When shall I be as good as thou?
Oh! would, poor beast, that I had now
A heart but half as good as thine!'

But *He*—who deviously hath sought
His Father through the lonesome woods,
Hath sought, proclaiming to the ear
Of night his grief and sorrowful fear—
He comes, escaped from fields and floods;—

With weary pace is drawing nigh;
He sees the Ass—and nothing living
Had ever such a fit of joy
As hath this little orphan Boy,
For he has no misgiving!

Forth to the gentle Ass he springs,
And up about his neck he climbs;
In loving words he talks to him,
He kisses, kisses face and limb,—
He kisses him a thousand times!

This Peter sees, while in the shade
He stood beside the cottage-door;
And Peter Bell, the ruffian wild,
Sobs loud, he sobs even like a child,
'Oh! God, I can endure no more!'

—Here ends my Tale: for in a trice
Arrived a neighbour with his horse;
Peter went forth with him straightway;
And, with due care, ere break of day,
Together they brought back the Corse.

And many years did this poor Ass,
Whom once it was my luck to see
Cropping the shrubs of Leming-Lane,
Help by his labour to maintain
The Widow and her family.

And Peter Bell, who, till that night,
Had been the wildest of his clan,
Forsook his crimes, renounced his folly,
And, after ten months' melancholy,
Became a good and honest man.

STANZAS

WRITTEN IN MY POCKET-COPY OF THOMSON'S 'CASTLE OF INDOLENCE'

[Composed May 9–11, 1802.—Published 1815.]

WITHIN our happy Castle there dwelt One
Whom without blame I may not overlook;
For never sun on living creature shone
Who more devout enjoyment with us took:
Here on his hours he hung as on a book,
On his own time here would he float away,
As doth a fly upon a summer brook;
But go to-morrow, or belike to-day,
Seek for him,—he is fled; and whither none can say.

Thus often would he leave our peaceful home,
And find elsewhere his business or delight;
Out of our Valley's limits did he roam:
Full many a time, upon a stormy night,
His voice came to us from the neighbouring height:
Oft could we see him driving full in view
At mid-day when the sun was shining bright;
What ill was on him, what he had to do,
A mighty wonder bred among our quiet crew.

Ah! piteous sight it was to see this Man
When he came back to us, a withered flower,—
Or like a sinful creature, pale and wan.
Down would he sit; and without strength or power
Look at the common grass from hour to hour:
And oftentimes, how long I fear to say,
Where apple-trees in blossom made a bower,
Retired in that sunshiny shade he lay;
And, like a naked Indian, slept himself away.

Great wonder to our gentle tribe it was
Whenever from our Valley he withdrew;
For happier soul no living creature has
Than he had, being here the long day through.
Some thought he was a lover, and did woo:
Some thought far worse of him, and judged him wrong;
But verse was what he had been wedded to;
And his own mind did like a tempest strong
Come to him thus, and drove the weary Wight along.

With him there often walked in friendly guise,
Or lay upon the moss by brook or tree,
A noticeable Man with large grey eyes,
And a pale face that seemed undoubtedly
As if a blooming face it ought to be;
Heavy his low-hung lip did oft appear,
Deprest by weight of musing Phantasy;
Profound his forehead was, though not severe;
Yet some did think that he had little business here:

Sweet heaven forefend! his was a lawful right;
Noisy he was, and gamesome as a boy;
His limbs would toss about him with delight,
Like branches when strong winds the trees annoy.
Nor lacked his calmer hours device or toy
To banish listlessness and irksome care;
He would have taught you how you might employ
Yourself; and many did to him repair,—
And certes not in vain; he had inventions rare.

Expedients, too, of simplest sort he tried:
Long blades of grass, plucked round him as he lay,
Made, to his ear attentively applied,
A pipe on which the wind would deftly play;
Glasses he had, that little things display,
The beetle panoplied in gems and gold,
A mailèd angel on a battle-day;
The mysteries that cups of flowers enfold,
And all the gorgeous sights which fairies do behold.

He would entice that other Man to hear
His music, and to view his imagery:
And, sooth, these two were each to the other dear:
No livelier love in such a place could be:
There did they dwell—from earthly labour free,
As happy spirits as were ever seen;
If but a bird, to keep them company,
Or butterfly sate down, they were, I ween,
As pleased as if the same had been a Maiden-queen.

THE WAGGONER

THE WAGGONER

'In Cairo's crowded streets
The impatient Merchant, wondering, waits in vain,
And Mecca saddens at the long delay.'
THOMSON.

TO CHARLES LAMB, ESQ

MY DEAR FRIEND,

When I sent you, a few weeks ago, the Tale of Peter Bell, you asked 'why THE WAGGONER was not added?'—To say the truth,—from the higher tone of imagination, and the deeper touches of passion aimed at in the former, I apprehended this little Piece could not accompany it without disadvantage. In the year 1806, if I am not mistaken, THE WAGGONER was read to you in manuscript, and, as you have remembered it for so long a time, I am the more encouraged to hope that, since the localities on which the Poem partly depends did not prevent its being interesting to you, it may prove acceptable to others. Being therefore in some measure the cause of its present appearance, you must allow me the gratification of inscribing it to you; in acknowledgment of the pleasure I have derived from your Writings, and of the high esteem with which

I am very truly yours,

WILLIAM WORDSWORTH

RYDAL MOUNT, *May* 20, 1819.

CANTO FIRST

'TIS spent—this burning day of June!
Soft darkness o'er its latest gleams is stealing;
The buzzing dor-hawk, round and round, is
wheeling,—
That solitary bird
Is all that can be heard
In silence deeper far than that of deepest noon!

Confiding Glow-worms, 'tis a night
Propitious to your earth-born light!
But where the scattered stars are seen
In hazy straits the clouds between,

Each, in his station twinkling not,
Seems changed into a pallid spot.
The mountains against heaven's grave weight
Rise up, and grow to wondrous height.
The air, as in a lion's den,
Is close and hot;—and now and then
Comes a tired and sultry breeze
With a haunting and a panting,
Like the stifling of disease;
But the dews allay the heat,
And the silence makes it sweet.

Hush, there is some one on the stir!
'Tis Benjamin the Waggoner;
Who long hath trod this toilsome way,
Companion of the night and day.
That far-off tinkling's drowsy cheer,
Mixed with a faint yet grating sound
In a moment lost and found,
The Wain announces—by whose side
Along the banks of Rydal Mere
He paces on, a trusty Guide,—
Listen! you can scarcely hear!
Hither he his course is bending;—
Now he leaves the lower ground,
And up the craggy hill ascending
Many a stop and stay he makes,
Many a breathing-fit he takes;
Steep the way and wearisome,
Yet all the while his whip is dumb!

The Horses have worked with right good-will,
And so have gained the top of the hill;
He was patient, they were strong,
And now they smoothly glide along,
Recovering breath, and pleased to win
The praises of mild Benjamin.
Heaven shield him from mishap and snare!
But why so early with this prayer?—
Is it for threatenings in the sky?
Or for some other danger nigh?

No; none is near him yet, though he
Be one of much infirmity;
For at the bottom of the brow,
Where once the Dove and Olive-bough
Offered a greeting of good ale
To all who entered Grasmere Vale;
And called on him who must depart
To leave it with a jovial heart;
There, where the Dove and Olive-bough
Once hung, a Poet harbours now,
A simple water-drinking Bard;
Why need our Hero then (though frail
His best resolves) be on his guard?
He marches by, secure and bold;
Yet, while he thinks on times of old,
It seems that all looks wondrous cold;
He shrugs his shoulders, shakes his head,
And, for the honest folk within,
It is a doubt with Benjamin
Whether they be alive or dead!

Here is no danger,—none at all!
Beyond his wish he walks secure;
But pass a mile—and *then* for trial,—
Then for the pride of self-denial;
If he resist that tempting door,
Which with such friendly voice will call;
If he resist those casement panes,
And that bright gleam which thence will fall
Upon his Leaders' bells and manes,
Inviting him with cheerful lure:
For still, though all be dark elsewhere,
Some shining notice will be *there,*
Of open house and ready fare.

The place to Benjamin right well
Is known, and by as strong a spell
As used to be that sign of love
And hope—the Olive-bough and Dove;
He knows it to his cost, good Man!
Who does not know the famous Swan?

Object uncouth! and yet our boast,
For it was painted by the Host;
His own conceit the figure planned,
'Twas coloured all by his own hand;
And that frail Child of thirsty clay,
Of whom I sing this rustic lay,
Could tell with self-dissatisfaction
Quaint stories of the bird's attraction!*

Well! that is past—and in despite
Of open door and shining light.
And now the conqueror essays
The long ascent of Dunmail-raise;
And with his team is gentle here
As when he clomb from Rydal Mere;
His whip they do not dread—his voice
They only hear it to rejoice.
To stand or go is at *their* pleasure;
Their efforts and their time they measure
By generous pride within the breast;
And while they strain, and while they rest,
He thus pursues his thoughts at leisure.

Now am I fairly safe to-night—
And with proud cause my heart is light:
I trespassed lately worse than ever—
But Heaven has blest a good endeavour;
And, to my soul's content, I find
The evil One is left behind.
Yes, let my master fume and fret,
Here am I—with my horses yet!
My jolly team, he finds that ye
Will work for nobody but me!
Full proof of this the Country gained;
It knows how ye were vexed and strained,
And forced unworthy stripes to bear,
When trusted to another's care.
Here was it—on this rugged slope,
Which now ye climb with heart and hope,

* This rude piece of self-taught art (such is the progress of refinement) has been supplanted by a professional production.

I saw you, between rage and fear,
Plunge, and fling back a spiteful ear,
And ever more and more confused,
As ye were more and more abused:
As chance would have it, passing by
I saw you in that jeopardy:
A word from me was like a charm;
Ye pulled together with one mind;
And your huge burthen, safe from harm,
Moved like a vessel in the wind!
—Yes, without me, up hills so high
'Tis vain to strive for mastery.
Then grieve not, jolly team! though tough
The road we travel, steep, and rough;
Though Rydal-heights and Dunmail-raise,
And all their fellow banks and braes,
Full often make you stretch and strain,
And halt for breath and halt again,
Yet to their sturdiness 'tis owing
That side by side we still are going!

While Benjamin in earnest mood
His meditations thus pursued,
A storm, which had been smothered long,
Was growing inwardly more strong;
And, in its struggles to get free,
Was busily employed as he.
The thunder had begun to growl—
He heard not, too intent of soul;
The air was now without a breath—
He marked not that 'twas still as death.
But soon large rain-drops on his head
Fell with the weight of drops of lead;—
He starts—and takes, at the admonition,
A sage survey of his condition.
The road is black before his eyes,
Glimmering faintly where it lies;
Black is the sky—and every hill,
Up to the sky, is blacker still—
Sky, hill, and dale, one dismal room,
Hung round and overhung with gloom:

Save that above a single height
Is to be seen a lurid light,
Above Helm-crag*—a streak half dead,
A burning of portentous red;
And near that lurid light, full well
The Astrologer, sage Sidrophel,
Where at his desk and book he sits,
Puzzling aloft his curious wits;
He whose domain is held in common
With no one but the ANCIENT WOMAN,
Cowering beside her rifted cell,
As if intent on magic spell;—
Dread pair that, spite of wind and weather,
Still sit upon Helm-crag together!

The Astrologer was not unseen
By solitary Benjamin;
But total darkness came anon,
And he and every thing was gone:
And suddenly a ruffling breeze,
(That would have rocked the sounding trees,
Had aught of sylvan growth been there),
Swept through the Hollow long and bare:
The rain rushed down—the road was battered,
As with the force of billows shattered;
The horses are dismayed, nor know
Whether they should stand or go;
And Benjamin is groping near them,
Sees nothing, and can scarcely hear them.
He is astounded,—wonder not,—
With such a charge in such a spot;
Astounded in the mountain gap
With thunder-peals, clap after clap,
Close-treading on the silent flashes—
And somewhere, as he thinks, by crashes
Among the rocks; with weight of rain,
And sullen motions long and slow,
That to a dreary distance go—
Till, breaking in upon the dying strain,
A rending o'er his head begins the fray again.

* A mountain of Grasmere, the broken summit of which presents two figures, full as distinctly shaped as that of the famous Cobbler near Arroquhar in Scotland.

Meanwhile, uncertain what to do,
And oftentimes compelled to halt,
The horses cautiously pursue
Their way, without mishap or fault;
And now have reached that pile of stones,
Heaped over brave King Dunmail's bones,
He who had once supreme command,
Last king of rocky Cumberland;
His bones, and those of all his Power,
Slain here in a disastrous hour!

When, passing through this narrow strait,
Stony, and dark, and desolate,
Benjamin can faintly hear
A voice that comes from some one near,
A female voice:—'Whoe'er you be,
Stop,' it exclaimed, 'and pity me!'
And less in pity than in wonder,
Amid the darkness and the thunder,
The Waggoner, with prompt command,
Summons his horses to a stand.

While, with increasing agitation,
The Woman urged her supplication,
In rueful words, with sobs between—
The voice of tears that fell unseen;
There came a flash—a startling glare,
And all Seat-Sandal was laid bare!
'Tis not a time for nice suggestion,
And Benjamin, without a question,
Taking her for some way-worn rover,
Said, 'Mount, and get you under cover!'

Another voice, in tone as hoarse
As a swoln brook with rugged course,
Cried out, 'Good brother, why so fast?
I've had a glimpse of you—*avast!*
Or, since it suits you to be civil,
Take her at once—for good and evil!'

'It is my Husband,' softly said
The Woman, as if half afraid:
By this time she was snug within,
Through help of honest Benjamin;
She and her Babe, which to her breast
With thankfulness the Mother pressed;
And now the same strong voice more near
Said cordially, 'My Friend, what cheer?
Rough doings these! as God's my judge,
The sky owes somebody a grudge!
We've had in half an hour or less
A twelvemonth's terror and distress!'

Then Benjamin entreats the Man
Would Mount, too, quickly as he can:
The Sailor—Sailor now no more,
But such he had been heretofore—
To courteous Benjamin replied,
'Go you your way, and mind not me;
For I must have, whate'er betide,
My Ass and fifty things beside,—
Go, and I'll follow speedily!'

The Waggon moves—and with its load
Descends along the sloping road;
And the rough Sailor instantly
Turns to a little tent hard by:
For when, at closing-in of day,
The family had come that way,
Green pasture and the soft warm air
Tempted them to settle there.—
Green is the grass for beast to graze,
Around the stones of Dunmail-raise!

The Sailor gathers up his bed,
Takes down the canvas overhead;
And after farewell to the place,
A parting word—though not of grace,
Pursues, with Ass and all his store,
The way the Waggon went before.

CANTO SECOND

If Wytheburne's modest House of prayer,
As lowly as the lowliest dwelling,
Had, with its belfry's humble stock,
A little pair that hang in air,
Been mistress also of a clock,
(And one, too, not in crazy plight),
Twelve strokes that clock would have been telling
Under the brow of old Helvellyn—
Its bead-roll of midnight,
Then, when the Hero of my tale
Was passing by, and, down the vale
(The vale now silent, hushed, I ween,
As if a storm had never been)
Proceeding with a mind at ease;
While the old Familiar of the seas,
Intent to use his utmost haste,
Gained ground upon the Waggon fast,
And gives another lusty cheer;
For, spite of rumbling of the wheels,
A welcome greeting he can hear;—
It is a fiddle in its glee
Dinning from the Cherry Tree!

Thence the sound—the light is there—
As Benjamin is now aware,
Who, to his inward thoughts confined,
Had almost reached the festive door,
When, startled by the Sailor's roar,
He hears a sound and sees the light,
And in a moment calls to mind
That 'tis the village Merry-night!*

Although before in no dejection,
At this insidious recollection
His heart with sudden joy is filled,—
His ears are by the music thrilled,
His eyes take pleasure in the road
Glittering before him bright and broad;

* A term well known in the North of England, and applied to rural Festivals where young persons meet in the evening for the purpose of dancing.

And Benjamin is wet and cold,
And there are reasons manifold
That makes the good, tow'rds which he's yearning,
Look fairly like a lawful earning.

Nor has thought time to come and go,
To vibrate between yes and no;
For, cries the Sailor, 'Glorious chance
That blew us hither!—let him dance,
Who can or will!—my honest soul,
Our treat shall be a friendly bowl!'
He draws him to the door—'Come in,
Come, come,' cries he to Benjamin!
And Benjamin—ah, woe is me!
Gave the word—the horses heard
And halted, though reluctantly.

'Blithe souls and lightsome hearts have we
Feasting at the CHERRY TREE!'
This was the outside proclamation,
This was the inside salutation;
What bustling—jostling—high and low!
A universal overflow!
What tankards foaming from the tap!
What store of cakes in every lap!
What thumping—stumping—overhead!
The thunder had not been more busy:
With such a stir you would have said,
This little place may well be dizzy!
'Tis who can dance with greatest vigour—
'Tis what can be most prompt and eager;
As if it heard the fiddle's call,
The pewter clatters on the wall;
The very bacon shows its feeling,
Swinging from the smoky ceiling!

A steaming bowl, a blazing fire,
What greater good can heart desire?
'Twere worth a wise man's while to try
The utmost anger of the sky:
To *seek* for thoughts of a gloomy cast,
If such the bright amends at last.

Now should you say I judge amiss,
The CHERRY TREE shows proof of this;
For soon, of all the happy there,
Our Travellers are the happiest pair;
All care with Benjamin is gone—
A Caesar past the Rubicon!

He thinks not of his long, long strife;—
The Sailor, Man by nature gay,
Hath no resolves to throw away;
And he hath now forgot his Wife,
Hath quite forgotten her—or may be
Thinks her the luckiest soul on earth,
Within that warm and peaceful berth,
        Under cover,
        Terror over,
Sleeping by her sleeping Baby.

With bowl that sped from hand to hand,
The gladdest of the gladsome band,
Amid their own delight and fun,
They hear—when every dance is done,
When every whirling bout is o'er—
The fiddle's *squeak**—that call to bliss,
Ever followed by a kiss;
They envy not the happy lot,
But enjoy their own the more!

While thus our jocund Travellers fare,
Up springs the Sailor from his chair—
Limps (for I might have told before
That he was lame) across the floor—
Is gone—returns—and with a prize;
With what?—a Ship of lusty size;
A gallant stately Man-of-war,
Fixed on a smoothly-sliding car.
Surprise to all, but most surprise
To Benjamin, who rubs his eyes,
Not knowing that he had befriended
A Man so gloriously attended!

* At the close of each strathspey, or jig, a particular note from the fiddle summons the Rustic to the agreeable duty of saluting his partner.

'This,' cries the Sailor, 'a Third-rate is—
Stand back, and you shall see her gratis!
This was the Flag-ship at the Nile,
The VANGUARD—you may smirk and smile,
But, pretty Maid, if you look near,
You'll find you've much in little here!
A nobler ship did never swim,
And you shall see her in full trim:
I'll set, my friends, to do you honour,
Set every inch of sail upon her.'
So said, so done; and masts, sails, yards,
He names them all; and interlards
His speech with uncouth terms of art,
Accomplished in the showman's part;
And then, as from a sudden check,
Cries out—''Tis there, the quarter-deck
On which brave Admiral Nelson stood—
A sight that would have roused your blood!
One eye he had, which, bright as ten,
Burned like a fire among his men;
Let this be land, and that be sea,
Here lay the French—and *thus* came we!'

Hushed was by this the fiddle's sound,
The dancers all were gathered round,
And such the stillness of the house,
You might have heard a nibbling mouse;
While, borrowing helps where'er he may,
The Sailor through the story runs
Of ships to ships and guns to guns;
And does his utmost to display
The dismal conflict, and the might
And terror of that marvellous night!
'A bowl, a bowl of double measure,'
Cries Benjamin, 'a draught of length!
To Nelson, England's pride and treasure,
Her bulwark and her tower of strength!'
When Benjamin had seized the bowl,
The mastiff, from beneath the waggon,
Where he lay, watchful as a dragon,
Rattled his chain;—'twas all in vain,

For Benjamin, triumphant soul!
He heard the monitory growl;
Heard—and in opposition quaffed
A deep, determined, desperate draught!
Nor did the battered Tar forget,
Or flinch from what he deemed his debt:
Then, like a hero crowned with laurel,
Back to her place the ship he led;
Wheeled her back in full apparel;
And so, flag flying at mast head,
Re-yoked her to the Ass:—anon
Cries Benjamin, 'We must be gone.'
Thus, after two hours' hearty stay,
Again behold them on their way!

CANTO THIRD

Right gladly had the horses stirred,
When they the wished-for greeting heard,
The whip's loud notice from the door,
That they were free to move once more.
You think, those doings must have bred
In them disheartening doubts and dread;
No, not a horse of all the eight,
Although it be a moonless night,
Fears either for himself or freight;
For this they know (and let it hide,
In part, the offences of their guide)
That Benjamin, with clouded brains,
Is worth the best with all their pains;
And, if they had a prayer to make,
The prayer would be that they make take
With him whatever comes in course,
The better fortune or the worse;
That no one else may have business near them,
And, drunk or sober, he may steer them.

So forth in dauntless mood they fare,
And with them goes the guardian pair.

Now, heroes, for the true commotion,
The triumph of your late devotion!

Can aught on earth impede delight,
Still mounting to a higher height;
And higher still—a greedy flight!
Can any low-born care pursue her,
Can any mortal clog come to her?
No notion have they—not a thought,
That is from joyless regions brought!
And, while they coast the silent lake,
Their inspiration I partake;
Share their empyreal spirits—yea,
With their enraptured vision see—
O fancy—what a jubilee!
What shifting pictures—clad in gleams
Of colour bright as feverish dreams!
Earth, spangled sky, and lake serene,
Involved and restless all—a scene
Pregnant with mutual exaltation,
Rich change, and multiplied creation!
This sight to me the Muse imparts;—
And then, what kindness in their hearts!
What tears of rapture, what vow-making,
Profound entreaties, and hand-shaking!
What solemn, vacant, interlacing,
As if they'd fall asleep embracing!
Then, in the turbulence of glee,
And in the excess of amity,
Says Benjamin, 'That Ass of thine,
He spoils thy sport, and hinders mine:
If he were tethered to the waggon,
He'd drag as well what he is dragging;
And we, as brother should with brother,
Might trudge it alongside each other!'

Forthwith, obedient to command,
The horses made a quiet stand;
And to the wagon's skirts was tied
The Creature, by the Mastiff's side,
The Mastiff wondering, and perplext
With dread of what will happen next;
And thinking it but sorry cheer
To have such company so near!

This new arrangement made, the Wain
Through the still night proceeds again;
No moon hath risen her light to lend;
But indistinctly, may be kenned
The VANGUARD, following close behind,
Sails spread, as if to catch the wind!

'Thy wife and child are snug and warm,
Thy ship will travel without harm;
I like,' said Benjamin, 'her shape and stature:
And this of mine—this bulky creature
Of which I have the steering—this,
Seen fairly, is not much amiss!
We want your streamers, friend, you know;
But, altogether as we go,
We make a kind of handsome show!
Among these hills, from first to last,
We've weathered many a furious blast;
Hard passage forcing on, with head
Against the storm, and canvas spread.
I hate a boaster; but to thee
Will say't, who know'st both land and sea,
The unluckiest hulk that stems the brine
Is hardly worse beset than mine,
When cross-winds on her quarter beat;
And, fairly lifted from my feet,
I stagger onward—heaven knows how;
But not so pleasantly as now;
Poor pilot I, by snows confounded,
And many a foundrous pit surrounded!
Yet here we are, by night and day
Grinding through rough and smooth our way;
Through foul and fair our task fulfilling;
And long shall be so yet—God willing!'

'Ay,' said the Tar, 'through fair and foul—
But save us from yon screeching owl!'
That instant was begun a fray
Which called their thoughts another way:
The Mastiff, ill-conditioned carl!
What must he do but growl and snarl,

Still more and more dissatisfied
With the meek comrade at his side!
Till, not incensed though put to proof,
The Ass, uplifting a hind hoof,
Salutes the Mastiff on the head;
And so were better manners bred,
And all was calmed and quieted.

'Yon screech-owl,' says the Sailor, turning
Back to his former cause of mourning,
'Yon owl!—pray God that all be well!
'Tis worse than any funeral bell;
As sure as I've the gift of sight,
We shall be meeting ghosts to-night!'
—Said Benjamin, 'This whip shall lay
A thousand, if they cross our way.
I know that Wanton's noisy station,
I know him and his occupation;
The jolly bird hath learned his cheer
Upon the banks of Windermere;
Where a tribe of them make merry,
Mocking the Man that keeps the ferry;
Hallooing from an open throat,
Like travellers shouting for a boat.
—The tricks he learned at Windermere
This vagrant owl is playing here—
That is the worst of his employment:
He's at the top of his enjoyment!'

This explanation stilled the alarm,
Cured the foreboder like a charm;
This, and the manner, and the voice,
Summoned the Sailor to rejoice;
His heart is up—he fears no evil
From life or death, from man or devil;
He wheels—and, making many stops,
Brandished his crutch against the mountain tops;
And, while he talked of blows and scars,
Benjamin, among the stars,
Beheld a dancing—and a glancing;
Such retreating and advancing
As I ween, was never seen
In bloodiest battle since the days of Mars!

CANTO FOURTH

Thus they, with freaks of proud delight,
Beguile the remnant of the night;
And many a snatch of jovial song
Regales them as they wind along;
While to the music, from on high,
The echoes make a glad reply.—
But the sage Muse the revel heeds
No farther than her story needs;
Nor will she servilely attend
The loitering journey to its end.
—Blithe spirits of her own impel
The Muse, who scents the morning air,
To take of this transported pair
A brief and unreproved farewell;
To quit the slow-paced waggon's side,
And wander down yon hawthorn dell,
With murmuring Greta for her guide.
—There doth she ken the awful form
Of Raven-crag—black as a storm—
Glimmering through the twilight pale;
And Ghimmer-crag,* his tall twin brother,
Each peering forth to meet the other:—
And, while she roves through St. John's Vale,
Along the smooth unpathwayed plain,
By sheep-track or through cottage lane,
Where no disturbance comes to intrude
Upon the pensive solitude,
Her unsuspecting eye, perchance,
With the rude shepherd's favoured glance,
Beholds the faeries in array,
Whose party-coloured garments gay
The silent company betray:
Red, green, and blue; a moment's sight!
For Skiddaw-top with rosy light
Is touched—and all the band take flight.
—Fly also, Muse! and from the dell
Mount to the ridge of Nathdale Fell;

* The crag of the ewe lamb.

Thence look thou forth o'er wood and lawn
Hoar with the frost-like dews of dawn;
Across yon meadowy bottom look,
Where close fogs hide their parent brook;
And see, beyond that hamlet small
The ruined towers of Threlkeld-hall,
Lurking in a double shade,
By trees and lingering twilight made!
There, at Blencathara's rugged feet,
Sir Lancelot gave a safe retreat
To noble Clifford; from annoy
Concealed the persecuted boy,
Well pleased in rustic garb to feed
His flock, and pipe on shepherd's reed
Among this multitude of hills,
Crags, woodlands, waterfalls, and rills;
Which soon the morning shall enfold,
From east to west, in ample vest
Of massy gloom and radiance bold.

The mists, that o'er the streamlet's bed
Hung low, begin to rise and spread;
Even while I speak, their skirts of grey
Are smitten by a silver ray;
And, lo!—up Castrigg's naked steep
(Where, smoothly urged, the vapours sweep
Along—and scatter and divide,
Like fleecy clouds self-multiplied)
The stately waggon is ascending,
With faithful Benjamin attending,
Apparent now beside his team—
Now lost amid a glittering steam:
And with him goes his Sailor-friend,
By this time near their journey's end;
And, after their high-minded riot,
Sickening into thoughtful quiet;
As if the morning's pleasant hour
Had for their joys a killing power.
And sooth for Benjamin a vein
Is opened of still deeper pain,
As if his heart by notes were stung
From out the lowly hedge-rows flung;

As if the warbler lost in light
Reproved his soarings of the night,
In strains of rapture pure and holy
Upbraided his distempered folly.

Drooping is he, his step is dull;
But the horses stretch and pull;
With increasing vigour climb,
Eager to repair lost time;
Whether, by their own desert,
Knowing what cause there is for shame,
They are labouring to avert
As much as may be of the blame,
Which, they foresee, must soon alight
Upon *his* head, whom, in despite
Of all his failings, they love best;
Whether for him they are distrest;
Or, by length of fasting roused,
Are impatient to be housed:
Up against the hill they strain
Tugging at the iron chain,
Tugging all with might and main,
Last and foremost, every horse
To the utmost of his force!
And the smoke and respiration,
Rising like an exhalation,
Blend with the mist—a moving shroud
To form, an undissolving cloud;
Which, with slant ray, the merry sun
Takes delight to play upon.
Never golden-haired Apollo,
Pleased some favourite chief to follow
Through accidents of peace or war,
In a perilous moment threw
Around the object of his care
Veil of such celestial hue;
Interposed so bright a screen—
Him and his enemies between!

Alas! what boots it?—who can hide,
When the malicious Fates are bent
On working out an ill intent?
Can destiny be turned aside?

No—sad progress of my story!
Benjamin, this outward glory
Cannot shield thee from thy Master,
Who from Keswick has pricked forth,
Sour and surly as the north;
And, in fear of some disaster,
Comes to give what help he may,
And to hear what thou canst say;
If, as needs he must forbode,
Thou hast been loitering on the road!
His fears, his doubts, may now take flight—
The wished-for object is in sight;
Yet, trust the Muse, it rather hath
Stirred him up to livelier wrath;
Which he stifles, moody man!
With all the patience that he can;
To the end that, at your meeting,
He may give thee decent greeting.

There he is—resolved to stop,
Till the waggon gains the top;
But stop he cannot—must advance:
Him Benjamin, with lucky glance,
Espies—and instantly is ready,
Self-collected, poised and steady:
And, to be the better seen,
Issues from his radiant shroud,
From his close-attending cloud,
With careless air and open mien.
Erect his port, and firm his going;
So struts yon cock that now is crowing;
And the morning light in grace
Strikes upon his lifted face,
Hurrying the pallid hue away
That might his trespasses betray.
But what can all avail to clear him,
Or what need of explanation,
Parley or interrogation?
For the Master sees, alas!
The unhappy Figure near him,
Limping o'er the dewy grass,

Where the road it fringes, sweet,
Soft and cool to way-worn feet;
And, O indignity! an Ass,
By his noble Mastiff's side,
Tethered to the waggon's tail:
And the ship, in all her pride,
Following after in full sail!
Not to speak of babe and mother;
Who, contented with each other,
And snug as birds in leafy arbour,
Find, within, a blessed harbour!

With eager eyes the Master pries;
Looks in and out, and through and through;
Says nothing—till at last he spies
A wound upon the Mastiff's head,
A wound where plainly might be read
What feats an Ass's hoof can do!
But drop the rest:—this aggravation,
This complicated provocation,
A hoard of grievances unsealed;
All past forgiveness it repealed;
And thus, and through distempered blood
On both sides, Benjamin the good,
The patient, and the tender-hearted,
Was from his team and waggon parted;
When duty of that day was o'er,
Laid down his whip—and served no more.–
Nor could the waggon long survive,
Which Benjamin had ceased to drive:
It lingered on;—guide after guide
Ambitiously the office tried;
But each unmanageable hill
Called for *his* patience and *his* skill;—
And sure it is that through this night,
And what the morning brought to light,
Two losses had we to sustain,
We lost both WAGGONER and WAIN!

Accept, O Friend, for praise or blame,
The gift of this adventurous song;
A record which I dared to frame,
Though timid scruples checked me long;
They checked me—and I left the theme
Untouched;—in spite of many a gleam
Of fancy which thereon was shed,
Like pleasant sunbeams shifting still
Upon the side of a distant hill:
But Nature might not be gainsaid;
For what I have and what I miss
I sing of these;—it makes my bliss!
Nor is it I who play the part,
But a shy spirit in my heart,
That comes and goes—will sometimes leap
From hiding-places ten years deep;
Or haunts me with familiar face,
Returning, like a ghost unlaid,
Until the debt I owe be paid.
Forgive me then; for I had been
On friendly terms with this Machine:
In him, while he was wont to trace
Our roads, through many a long year's space,
A living almanack had we;
We had a speaking diary,
That in this uneventful place,
Gave to the days a mark and name
By which we knew them when they came.
—Yes, I, and all about me here,
Through all the changes of the year,
Had seen him through the mountains go,
In pomp of mist or pomp of snow,
Majestically huge and slow:
Or with a milder grace adorning
The landscape of a summer's morning;
While Grasmere smoothed her liquid plain
The moving image to detain;
And mighty Fairfield, with a chime
Of echoes, to his march kept time;
When little other business stirred,
And little other sound was heard;

In that delicious hour of balm,
Stillness, solitude, and calm,
While yet the valley is arrayed,
On this side with a sober shade;
On that is prodigally bright—
Crag, lawn, and wood—with rosy light.
—But most of all, thou lordly Wain!
I wish to have thee here again,
When windows flap and chimney roars,
And all is dismal out of doors;
And, sitting by my fire, I see
Eight sorry carts, no less a train!
Unworthy successors of thee,
Come straggling through the wind and rain:
And oft, as they pass slowly on,
Beneath my windows, one by one,
See, perched upon the naked height
The summit of a cumbrous freight,
A single traveller—and there
Another; then perhaps a pair—
The lame, the sickly, and the old;
Men, women, heartless with the cold;
And babes in wet and starveling plight;
Which once, be weather as it might,
Had still a nest within a nest,
Thy shelter—and their mother's breast!
Then most of all, then far the most,
Do I regret what we have lost;
Am grieved for the unhappy sin
Which robbed us of good Benjamin;—
And of his stately Charge, which none
Could keep alive when He was gone!

from

POEMS IN TWO VOLUMES, 1807

EDITOR'S NOTE

THE footnotes here printed are Wordsworth's. The notes he appended to each volume will be found in *Wordsworth: Poems Published in 1807*, ed. H. Darbishire (Oxford).

The date of the Westminster Bridge sonnet has here been corrected from 1803 to 1802 (see Introduction p. 50).

POEMS IN TWO VOLUMES, 1807

VOLUME ONE

To the Daisy

In youth from rock to rock I went,
From hill to hill, in discontent
Of pleasure high and turbulent,
Most pleas'd when most uneasy;
But now my own delights I make,
My thirst at every rill can slake,
And gladly Nature's love partake
Of thee, sweet Daisy!

When soothed a while by milder airs,
Thee Winter in the garland wears
That thinly shades his few grey hairs;
Spring cannot shun thee;
Whole summer fields are thine by right;
And Autumn, melancholy Wight!
Doth in thy crimson head delight
When rains are on thee.

In shoals and bands, a morrice train,
Thou greet'st the Traveller in the lane;
If welcome once thou count'st it gain;
Thou art not daunted,
Nor car'st if thou be set at naught;
And oft alone in nooks remote
We meet thee, like a pleasant thought,
When such are wanted.

Be Violets in their secret mews
The flowers the wanton Zephyrs chuse;
Proud be the Rose, with rains and dews
Her head impearling;

Thou liv'st with less ambitious aim,
Yet hast not gone without thy fame;
Thou art indeed by many a claim
The Poet's darling.

If to a rock from rains he fly,
Or, some bright day of April sky,
Imprison'd by hot sunshine lie
Near the green holly,
And wearily at length should fare;
He need but look about, and there
Thou art! a Friend at hand, to scare
His melancholy.

A hundred times, by rock or bower,
Ere thus I have lain couch'd an hour,
Have I derived from thy sweet power
Some apprehension;
Some steady love; some brief delight;
Some memory that had taken flight;
Some chime of fancy wrong or right;
Or stray invention.

If stately passions in me burn,
And one chance look to Thee should turn,
I drink out of an humbler urn
A lowlier pleasure;
The homely sympathy that heeds
The common life, our nature breeds;
A wisdom fitted to the needs
Of hearts at leisure.

When, smitten by the morning ray,
I see thee rise alert and gay,
Then, chearful Flower! my spirits play
With kindred motion:
At dusk, I've seldom mark'd thee press
The ground, as if in thankfulness,
Without some feeling, more or less,
Of true devotion.

And all day long I number yet,
All seasons through, another debt,
Which I wherever thou art met,
 To thee am owing;
An instinct call it, a blind sense;
A happy, genial influence,
Coming one knows not how nor whence,
 Nor whither going.

Child of the Year! that round dost run
Thy course, bold lover of the sun,
And chearful when the day's begun
 As morning Leveret,
Thou long the Poet's praise shalt gain;
Thou wilt be more belov'd by men
In times to come; thou not in vain
 Art Nature's Favorite.

Louisa

I MET Louisa in the shade;
And, having seen that lovely Maid,
Why should I fear to say
That she is ruddy, fleet, and strong;
And down the rocks can leap along,
Like rivulets in May?

And she hath smiles to earth unknown;
Smiles, that with motion of their own
Do spread, and sink, and rise;
That come and go with endless play,
And ever, as they pass away,
Are hidden in her eyes.

She loves her fire, her Cottage-home;
Yet o'er the moorland will she roam
In weather rough and bleak;
And when against the wind she strains,
Oh! might I kiss the mountain rains
That sparkle on her cheek.

Take all that's mine 'beneath the moon,'
If I with her but half a noon
May sit beneath the walls
Of some old cave, or mossy nook,
When up she winds along the brook,
To hunt the waterfalls.

Fidelity

A BARKING sound the Shepherd hears,
A cry as oı a Dog or Fox;
He halts, and searches with his eyes
Among the scatter'd rocks:
And now at distance can discern
A stirring in a brake of fern;
From which immediately leaps out
A Dog, and yelping runs about.

The Dog is not of mountain breed;
It's motions, too, are wild and shy;
With something, as the Shepherd thinks,
Unusual in it's cry:
Nor is there any one in sight
All round, in Hollow or on Height;
Nor shout, nor whistle strikes his ear;
What is the Creature doing here?

It was a Cove, a huge Recess,
That keeps till June December's snow;
A lofty Precipice in front,
A silent Tarn* below!
Far in the bosom of Helvellyn,
Remote from public Road or Dwelling,
Pathway, or cultivated land;
From trace of human foot or hand.

There, sometimes does a leaping Fish
Send through the Tarn a lonely chear;
The Crags repeat the Raven's croak,
In symphony austere;

* Tarn is a *small* Mere or Lake mostly high up in the mountains.

Thither the Rainbow comes, the Cloud;
And Mists that spread the flying shroud;
And Sun-beams; and the sounding blast,
That, if it could, would hurry past,
But that enormous Barrier binds it fast.

Not knowing what to think, a while
The Shepherd stood: then makes his way
Towards the Dog, o'er rocks and stones,
As quickly as he may;
Nor far had gone before he found
A human skeleton on the ground,
Sad sight! the Shepherd with a sigh
Looks round, to learn the history.

From those abrupt and perilous rocks,
The Man had fallen, that place of fear!
At length upon the Shepherd's mind
It breaks, and all is clear:
He instantly recall'd the Name,
And who he was, and whence he came;
Remember'd, too, the very day
On which the Traveller pass'd this way.

But hear a wonder now, for sake
Of which this mournful Tale I tell!
A lasting monument of words
This wonder merits well.
The Dog, which still was hovering nigh,
Repeating the same timid cry,
This Dog had been through three months' space
A Dweller in that savage place.

Yes, proof was plain that since the day
On which the Traveller thus had died
The Dog had watch'd about the spot,
Or by his Master's side:
How nourish'd here through such long time
He knows, who gave that love sublime,
And gave that strength of feeling, great
Above all human estimate.

'She was a Phantom of Delight'

She was a Phantom of delight
When first she gleam'd upon my sight;
A lovely Apparition, sent
To be a moment's ornament;
Her eyes as stars of Twilight fair;
Like Twilight's, too, her dusky hair;
But all things else about her drawn
From May-time and the chearful Dawn;
A dancing Shape, an Image gay,
To haunt, to startle, and way-lay.

I saw her upon nearer view,
A Spirit, yet a Woman too!
Her household motions light and free,
And steps of virgin liberty;
A countenance in which did meet
Sweet records, promises as sweet;
A Creature not too bright or good
For human nature's daily food;
For transient sorrows, simple wiles,
Praise, blame, love, kisses, tears, and smiles.

And now I see with eye serene
The very pulse of the machine;
A Being breathing thoughtful breath;
A Traveller betwixt life and death;
The reason firm, the temperate will,
Endurance, foresight, strength and skill;
A perfect Woman; nobly plann'd,
To warn, to comfort, and command;
And yet a Spirit still, and bright
With something of an angel light.

The Redbreast and the Butterfly

Art thou the Bird whom Man loves best,
The pious Bird with the scarlet breast,
        Our little English Robin;
The Bird that comes about our doors
When Autumn winds are sobbing?
Art thou the Peter of Norway Boors?
        Their Thomas in Finland,
        And Russia far inland?
The Bird, whom by some name or other
All men who know thee call their Brother,
The Darling of Children and men?
Could Father Adam open his eyes,
And see this sight beneath the skies,
He'd wish to close them again.

If the Butterfly knew but his friend
Hither his flight he would bend,
And find his way to me
Under the branches of the tree:
In and out, he darts about;
His little heart is throbbing:
Can this be the Bird, to man so good,
        Our consecrated Robin!
That, after their bewildering,
Did cover with leaves the little children,
        So painfully in the wood?

What ail'd thee Robin that thou could'st pursue
        A beautiful Creature,
That is gentle by nature?
Beneath the summer sky
From flower to flower let him fly;
'Tis all that he wishes to do.
The Chearer Thou of our in-door sadness,
He is the Friend of our summer gladness:
What hinders, then, that ye should be
Playmates in the sunny weather,
And fly about in the air together?

Like the hues of thy breast
His beautiful wings in crimson are drest,
A brother he seems of thine own:
If thou would'st be happy in thy nest,
O pious Bird! whom Man loves best,
Love him, or leave him alone!

The Sailor's Mother

One morning (raw it was and wet,
A foggy day in winter time)
A Woman in the road I met,
Not old, though something past her prime:
Majestic in her person, tall and straight;
And like a Roman matron's was her mien and gait.

The ancient Spirit is not dead;
Old times, thought I, are breathing there;
Proud was I that my country bred
Such strength, a dignity so fair:
She begg'd an alms, like one in poor estate;
I look'd at her again, nor did my pride abate.

When from these lofty thoughts I woke,
With the first word I had to spare
I said to her, 'Beneath your Cloak
What's that which on your arm you bear?'
She answer'd soon as she the question heard,
'A simple burthen, Sir, a little Singing-bird.'

And, thus continuing, she said,
'I had a Son, who many a day
Sail'd on the seas; but he is dead;
In Denmark he was cast away;
And I have been as far as Hull, to see
What clothes he might have left, or other property.

The Bird and Cage they both were his;
'Twas my Son's Bird; and neat and trim
He kept it: many voyages
This Singing-bird hath gone with him;

When last he sail'd he left the Bird behind;
As it might be, perhaps, from bodings of his mind.

He to a Fellow-lodger's care
Had left it, to be watch'd and fed,
Till he came back again; and there
I found it when my Son was dead;
And now, God help me for my little wit!
I trail it with me, Sir! he took so much delight in it.'

To the Small Celandine †

PANSIES, Lilies, Kingcups, Daisies,
Let them live upon their praises;
Long as there's a sun that sets
Primroses will have their glory;
Long as there are Violets,
They will have a place in story:
There's a flower that shall be mine,
'Tis the little Celandine.

Eyes of some men travel far
For the finding of a star;
Up and down the heavens they go,
Men that keep a mighty rout!
I'm as great as they, I trow,
Since the day I found thee out,
Little flower!—I'll make a stir
Like a great Astronomer.

Modest, yet withal an Elf
Bold, and lavish of thyself,
Since we needs must first have met
I have seen thee, high and low,
Thirty years or more, and yet
'Twas a face I did not know;
Thou hast now, go where I may,
Fifty greetings in a day.

† Common Pilewort.

Ere a leaf is on a bush,
In the time before the Thrush
Has a thought about it's nest,
Thou wilt come with half a call,
Spreading out thy glossy breast
Like a careless Prodigal;
Telling tales about the sun,
When we've little warmth, or none.

Poets, vain men in their mood!
Travel with the multitude;
Never heed them; I aver
That they all are wanton Wooers;
But the thrifty Cottager,
Who stirs little out of doors,
Joys to spy thee near her home,
Spring is coming, Thou art come!

Comfort have thou of thy merit.
Kindly, unassuming Spirit!
Careless of thy neighbourhood,
Thou dost shew thy pleasant face
On the moor, and in the wood,
In the lane—there's not a place,
Howsoever mean it be,
But 'tis good enough for thee.

Ill befal the yellow Flowers,
Children of the flaring hours!
Buttercups, that will be seen,
Whether we will see or no;
Others, too, of lofty mien;
They have done as worldlings do,
Taken praise that should be thine,
Little, humble Celandine!

Prophet of delight and mirth,
Scorn'd and slighted upon earth!
Herald of a mighty band,
Of a joyous train ensuing,
Singing at my heart's command,
In the lanes my thoughts pursuing,
I will sing, as doth behove,
Hymns in praise of what I love!

To the Same Flower

Pleasures newly found are sweet
When they lie about our feet:
February last my heart
First at sight of thee was glad;
All unheard of as thou art,
Thou must needs, I think, have had,
Celandine! and long ago,
Praise of which I nothing know.

I have not a doubt but he,
Whosoe'er the man might be,
Who the first with pointed rays,
(Workman worthy to be sainted)
Set the Sign-board in a blaze,
When the risen sun he painted,
Took the fancy from a glance
At thy glittering countenance.

Soon as gentle breezes bring
News of winter's vanishing,
And the children build their bowers,
Sticking 'kerchief-plots of mold
All about with full-blown flowers,
Thick as sheep in shepherd's fold
With the proudest Thou art there,
Mantling in the tiny square.

Often have I sigh'd to measure
By myself a lonely pleasure,
Sigh'd to think, I read a book
Only read perhaps by me;
Yet I long could overlook
Thy bright coronet and Thee,
And thy arch and wily ways,
And thy store of other praise.

Blithe of heart, from week to week
Thou dost play at hide-and-seek;
While the patient Primrose sits
Like a Beggar in the cold,
Thou, a Flower of wiser wits,
Slipp'st into thy shelter'd hold;
Bright as any of the train
When ye all are out again.

Thou art not beyond the moon,
But a thing 'beneath our shoon;'
Let, as old Magellen did,
Others roam about the sea;
Build who will a pyramid;
Praise it is enough for me,
If there be but three or four
Who will love my little Flower.

Character of the Happy Warrior

Who is the happy Warrior? Who is he
Whom every Man in arms should wish to be?
——It is the generous Spirit, when brought
Among the tasks of real life, hath wrought
Upon the plan that pleased his childish thought:
Whose high endeavours are an inward light
That make the path before him always bright:
Who, with a natural instinct to discern
What knowledge can perform, is diligent to learn;
Abides by this resolve, and stops not there,
But makes his moral being his prime care;
Who, doom'd to go in company with Pain,
And Fear, and Bloodshed, miserable train!
Turns his necessity to glorious gain;
In face of these doth exercise a power
Which is our human-nature's highest dower;
Controls them and subdues, transmutes, bereaves
Of their bad influence, and their good receives;
By objects, which might force the soul to abate
Her feeling, render'd more compassionate;

Is placable because occasions rise
So often that demand such sacrifice;
More skilful in self-knowledge, even more pure,
As tempted more; more able to endure,
As more expos'd to suffering and distress;
Thence, also, more alive to tenderness.
'Tis he whose law is reason; who depends
Upon that law as on the best of friends;
Whence, in a state where men are tempted still
To evil for a guard against worse ill,
And what in quality or act is best
Doth seldom on a right foundation rest,
He fixes good on good alone, and owes
To virtue every triumph that he knows:
—Who, if he rise to station of command,
Rises by open means; and there will stand
On honourable terms, or else retire,
And in himself possess his own desire;
Who comprehends his trust, and to the same
Keeps faithful with a singleness of aim;
And therefore does not stoop, nor lie in wait
For wealth, or honors, or for worldly state;
Whom they must follow; on whose head must fall,
Like showers of manna, if they come at all:
Whose powers shed round him in the common strife,
Or mild concerns of ordinary life,
A constant influence, a peculiar grace;
But who, if he be called upon to face
Some awful moment to which heaven has join'd
Great issues, good or bad for human-kind,
Is happy as a Lover; and attired
With sudden brightness like a Man inspired;
And through the heat of conflict keeps the law
In calmness made, and sees what he foresaw;
Or if an unexpected call succeed,
Come when it will, is equal to the need:
—He who, though thus endued as with a sense
And faculty for storm and turbulence,
Is yet a Soul whose master bias leans
To home-felt pleasures and to gentle scenes;
Sweet images! which, wheresoe'er he be,
Are at his heart; and such fidelity

It is his darling passion to approve;
More brave for this, that he hath much to love:
'Tis, finally, the Man, who, lifted high,
Conspicuous object in a Nation's eye,
Or left unthought-of in obscurity,
Who, with a toward or untoward lot,
Prosperous or adverse, to his wish or not,
Plays, in the many games of life, that one
Where what he most doth value must be won;
Whom neither shape of danger can dismay,
Nor thought of tender happiness betray;
Who, not content that former worth stand fast,
Looks forward, persevering to the last,
From well to better, daily self-surpast:
Who, whether praise of him must walk the earth
For ever, and to noble deeds give birth,
Or He must go to dust without his fame,
And leave a dead unprofitable name,
Finds comfort in himself and in his cause;
And, while the mortal mist is gathering, draws
His breath in confidence of Heaven's applause;
This is the happy Warrior; this is He
Whom every Man in arms should wish to be.

The above Verses were written soon after tidings had been received of the Death of Lord Nelson which event directed the Author's thoughts to the subject. His respect for the memory of this grea fellow-countryman induces him to mention this; though he is well aware that the Verses must suffe from any connection in the Reader's mind with a Name so illustrious.

The Affliction of Margaret——of——

WHERE art thou, my beloved Son,
Where art thou, worse to me than dead?
Oh find me prosperous or undone!
Or, if the grave be now thy bed,
Why am I ignorant of the same
That I may rest; and neither blame,
Nor sorrow may attend thy name?

Seven years, alas, to have received
No tidings of an only child;
To have despair'd, and have believ'd,
And be for evermore beguil'd;
Sometimes with thoughts of very bliss!
I catch at them, and then I miss;
Was ever darkness like to this?

He was among the prime in worth,
An object beauteous to behold;
Well born, well bred; I sent him forth
Ingenuous, innocent, and bold:
If things ensued that wanted grace,
As hath been said, they were not base;
And never blush was on my face.

Ah! little doth the Young One dream,
When full of play and childish cares,
What power hath even his wildest scream,
Heard by his Mother unawares!
He knows it not, he cannot guess:
Years to a Mother bring distress;
But do not make her love the less.

Neglect me! no, I suffer'd long
From that ill thought; and being blind,
Said, 'Pride shall help me in my wrong;
Kind mother have I been, as kind
As ever breathed:' and that is true;
I've wet my path with tears like dew,
Weeping for him when no one knew.

My Son, if thou be humbled, poor,
Hopeless of honour and of gain,
Oh! do not dread thy mother's door;
Think not of me with grief and pain:
I now can see with better eyes;
And worldly grandeur I despise,
And fortune with her gifts and lies.

Alas! the fowls of Heaven have wings,
And blasts of Heaven will aid their flight;
They mount, how short a voyage brings
The Wanderers back to their delight!
Chains tie us down by land and sea;
And wishes, vain as mine, may be
All that is left to comfort thee.

Perhaps some dungeon hears thee groan,
Maim'd, mangled by inhuman men;
Or thou upon a Desart thrown
Inheritest the Lion's Den;
Or hast been summoned to the Deep,
Thou, Thou and all thy mates, to keep
An incommunicable sleep.

I look for Ghosts; but none will force
Their way to me; 'tis falsely said
That there was ever intercourse
Betwixt the living and the dead;
For, surely, then I should have sight
Of Him I wait for day and night,
With love and longings infinite.

My apprehensions come in crowds;
I dread the rustling of the grass;
The very shadows of the clouds
Have power to shake me as they pass:
I question things, and do not find
One that will answer to my mind;
And all the world appears unkind.

Beyond participation lie
My troubles, and beyond relief:
If any chance to heave a sigh
They pity me, and not my grief.
Then come to me, my Son, or send
Some tidings that my woes may end;
I have no other earthly friend.

To H. C., Six Years Old

O Thou! whose fancies from afar are brought;
Who of thy words dost make a mock apparel,
And fittest to unutterable thought
The breeze-like motion and the self-born carol;
Thou Faery Voyager! that dost float
In such clear water, that thy Boat
May rather seem
To brood on air than on an earthly stream;
Suspended in a stream as clear as sky,
Where earth and heaven do make one imagery;
O blessed Vision! happy Child!
That art so exquisitely wild,
I think of thee with many fears
For what may be thy lot in future years.

I thought of times when Pain might be thy guest,
Lord of thy house and hospitality;
And grief, uneasy Lover! never rest
But when she sate within the touch of thee.
Oh! too industrious folly!
Oh! vain and causeless melancholy!
Nature will either end thee quite;
Or, lengthening out thy season of delight,
Preserve for thee, by individual right,
A young Lamb's heart among the full-grown flocks.
What hast Thou to do with sorrow,
Or the injuries of tomorrow?
Thou art a Dew-drop, which the morn brings forth,
Not doom'd to jostle with unkindly shocks;
Or to be trail'd along the soiling earth;
A Gem that glitters while it lives,
And no forewarning gives;
But, at the touch of wrong, without a strife
Slips in a moment out of life.

'Among all lovely things my Love had been'

Among all lovely things my Love had been;
Had noted well the stars, all flowers that grew
About her home; but she had never seen
A Glow-worm, never one, and this I knew.

While riding near her home one stormy night
A single Glow-worm did I chance to espy;
I gave a fervent welcome to the sight,
And from my Horse I leapt; great joy had I.

Upon a leaf the Glow-worm did I lay,
To bear it with me through the stormy night:
And, as before, it shone without dismay;
Albeit putting forth a fainter light.

When to the Dwelling of my Love I came,
I went into the Orchard quietly;
And left the Glow-worm, blessing it by name,
Laid safely by itself, beneath a Tree.

The whole next day, I hoped, and hoped with fear;
At night the Glow-worm shone beneath the Tree:
I led my Lucy to the spot, 'Look here!'
Oh! joy it was for her, and joy for me!

'I travell'd among unknown Men'

I travell'd among unknown Men,
In Lands beyond the Sea;
Nor England! did I know till then
What love I bore to thee.

'Tis past, that melancholy dream!
  Nor will I quit thy shore
A second time; for still I seem
  To love thee more and more.

Among thy mountains did I feel
  The joy of my desire;
And She I cherish'd turn'd her wheel
  Beside an English fire.

Thy mornings shew'd—thy nights conceal'd
  The bowers where Lucy play'd;
And thine is, too, the last green field
  Which Lucy's eyes survey'd!

Ode to Duty

STERN Daughter of the Voice of God!
O Duty! if that name thou love
Who art a Light to guide, a Rod
To check the erring, and reprove;
Thou who art victory and law
When empty terrors overawe;
From vain temptations dost set free;
From strife and from despair; a glorious ministry.

There are who ask not if thine eye
Be on them; who, in love and truth,
Where no misgiving is, rely
Upon the genial sense of youth:
Glad Hearts! without reproach or blot;
Who do thy work, and know it not:
May joy be theirs while life shall last!
And Thou, if they should totter, teach them to stand fast!

Serene will be our days and bright,
And happy will our nature be,
When love is an unerring light,
And joy its own security.

And bless'd are they who in the main
This faith, even now, do entertain:
Live in the spirit of this creed;
Yet find that other strength, according to their need.

I, loving freedom, and untried;
No sport of every random gust,
Yet being to myself a guide,
Too blindly have reposed my trust:
Resolved that nothing e'er should press
Upon my present happiness,
I shoved unwelcome tasks away;
But thee I now would serve more strictly, if I may.

Through no disturbance of my soul,
Or strong compunction in me wrought,
I supplicate for thy controul;
But in the quietness of thought:
Me this uncharter'd freedom tires;
I feel the weight of chance desires:
My hopes no more must change their name,
I long for a repose which ever is the same.

Yet not the less would I throughout
Still act according to the voice
Of my own wish; and feel past doubt
That my submissiveness was choice:
Not seeking in the school of pride
For 'precepts over dignified,'
Denial and restraint I prize
No farther than they breed a second Will more wise.

Stern Lawgiver! yet thou dost wear
The Godhead's most benignant grace;
Nor know we any thing so fair
As is the smile upon thy face;
Flowers laugh before thee on their beds;
And Fragrance in thy footing treads;
Thou dost preserve the Stars from wrong;
And the most ancient Heavens through Thee are fresh and strong.

To humbler functions, awful Power!
I call thee: I myself commend
Unto thy guidance from this hour;
Oh! let my weakness have an end!
Give unto me, made lowly wise,
The spirit of self-sacrifice;
The confidence of reason give;
And in the light of truth thy Bondman let me live!

POEMS
COMPOSED DURING A TOUR, CHIEFLY ON FOOT

I

Beggars

She had a tall Man's height, or more;
No bonnet screen'd her from the heat;
A long drab-colour'd Cloak she wore,
A Mantle reaching to her feet:
What other dress she had I could not know;
Only she wore a Cap that was as white as snow.

In all my walks, through field or town,
Such Figure had I never seen:
Her face was of Egyptian brown:
Fit person was she for a Queen,
To head those ancient Amazonian files:
Or ruling Bandit's Wife, among the Grecian Isles.

Before me begging did she stand,
Pouring out sorrows like a sea;
Grief after grief:—on English Land
Such woes I knew could never be;
And yet a boon I gave her; for the Creature
Was beautiful to see; a Weed of glorious feature!

I left her, and pursued my way;
And soon before me did espy
A pair of little Boys at play,
Chasing a crimson butterfly;
The Taller follow'd with his hat in hand,
Wreath'd round with yellow flow'rs, the gayest of the lan

The Other wore a rimless crown,
With leaves of laurel stuck about:
And they both follow'd up and down,
Each whooping with a merry shout;
Two Brothers seem'd they, eight and ten years old;
And like that Woman's face as gold is like to gold.

They bolted on me thus, and lo!
Each ready with a plaintive whine;
Said I, 'Not half an hour ago
Your Mother has had alms of mine.'
'That cannot be,' one answer'd, 'She is dead.'
'Nay but I gave her pence, and she will buy you bread.'

'She has been dead, Sir, many a day,'
'Sweet Boys, you're telling me a lie;
'It was your Mother, as I say—'
And in the twinkling of an eye,
'Come, come!' cried one; and, without more ado,
Off to some other play they both together flew.

3

' With how sad steps, O Moon '

'With how sad steps, O Moon thou climb'st the sky,
How silently, and with how wan a face!'*
Where art thou? Thou whom I have seen on high
Running among the clouds a Wood-nymph's race?
Unhappy Nuns, whose common breath's a sigh
Which they would stifle, move at such a pace!
The Northern Wind, to call thee to the chace,
Must blow tonight his bugle horn. Had I

* From a sonnet of Sir Philip Sydney.

The power of Merlin, Goddess! this should be:
And all the Stars, now shrouded up in heaven,
Should sally forth to keep thee company.
What strife would then be yours, fair Creatures, driv'n
Now up, now down, and sparkling in your glee!
But, Cynthia, should to Thee the palm be giv'n,
Queen both for beauty and for majesty.

4

Alice Fell

The Post-boy drove with fierce career,
For threat'ning clouds the moon had drown'd;
When suddenly I seem'd to hear
A moan, a lamentable sound.

As if the wind blew many ways
I heard the sound, and more and more:
It seem'd to follow with the Chaise,
And still I heard it as before.

At length I to the Boy call'd out,
He stopp'd his horses at the word;
But neither cry, nor voice, nor shout,
Nor aught else like it could be heard.

The Boy then smack'd his whip, and fast
The horses scamper'd through the rain;
And soon I heard upon the blast
The voice, and bade him halt again.

Said I, alighting on the ground,
'What can it be, this piteous moan?'
And there a little Girl I found,
Sitting behind the Chaise, alone.

'My Cloak!' the word was last and first,
And loud and bitterly she wept,
As if her very heart would burst;
And down from off the Chaise she leapt.

'What ails you, Child?' she sobb'd, 'Look here!'
I saw it in the wheel entangled,
A weather beaten Rag as e'er
From any garden scare-crow dangled.

'Twas twisted betwixt nave and spoke;
Her help she lent, and with good heed
Together we released the Cloak;
A wretched, wretched rag indeed!

'And whither are you going, Child,
To night along these lonesome ways?'
'To Durham' answer'd she half wild—
'Then come with me into the chaise.'

She sate like one past all relief;
Sob after sob she forth did send
In wretchedness, as if her grief
Could never, never, have an end.

'My Child, in Durham do you dwell?'
She check'd herself in her distress,
And said, 'My name is Alice Fell;
I'm fatherless and motherless.

And I to Durham, Sir, belong.'
And then, as if the thought would choke
Her very heart, her grief grew strong;
And all was for her tatter'd Cloak.

The chaise drove on; our journey's end
Was nigh; and, sitting by my side,
As if she'd lost her only friend
She wept, nor would be pacified.

Up to the Tavern-door we post;
Of Alice and her grief I told;
And I gave money to the Host,
To buy a new Cloak for the old.

'And let it be of duffil grey,
As warm a cloak as man can sell!'
Proud Creature was she the next day,
The little Orphan, Alice Fell!

5

Resolution and Independence

THERE was a roaring in the wind all night;
The rain came heavily and fell in floods;
But now the sun is rising calm and bright;
The birds are singing in the distant woods;
Over his own sweet voice the Stock-dove broods;
The Jay makes answer as the Magpie chatters;
And all the air is fill'd with pleasant noise of waters.

All things that love the sun are out of doors;
The sky rejoices in the morning's birth;
The grass is bright with rain-drops; on the moors
The Hare is running races in her mirth;
And with her feet she from the plashy earth
Raises a mist; which, glittering in the sun,
Runs with her all the way, wherever she doth run.

I was a Traveller then upon the moor;
I saw the Hare that rac'd about with joy;
I heard the woods, and distant waters, roar;
Or heard them not, as happy as a Boy:
The pleasant season did my heart employ:
My old remembrances went from me wholly;
And all the ways of men, so vain and melancholy.

But, as it sometimes chanceth, from the might
Of joy in minds that can no farther go,
As high as we have mounted in delight
In our dejection do we sink as low,
To me that morning did it happen so;
And fears, and fancies, thick upon me came;
Dim sadness, and blind thoughts I knew not nor could name.

I heard the Sky-lark singing in the sky;
And I bethought me of the playful Hare:
Even such a happy Child of earth am I;
Even as these blissful Creatures do I fare;
Far from the world I walk, and from all care;
But there may come another day to me,
Solitude, pain of heart, distress, and poverty.

My whole life I have liv'd in pleasant thought,
As if life's business were a summer mood;
As if all needful things would come unsought
To genial faith, still rich in genial good;
But how can He expect that others should
Build for him, sow for him, and at his call
Love him, who for himself will take no heed at all?

I thought of Chatterton, the marvellous Boy,
The sleepless Soul that perish'd in its pride;
Of Him who walk'd in glory and in joy
Behind his plough, upon the mountain-side:
By our own spirits are we deified;
We Poets in our youth begin in gladness;
But thereof comes in the end despondency and madness.

Now, whether it were by peculiar grace,
A leading from above, a something given,
Yet it befel, that, in this lonely place,
When up and down my fancy thus was driven,
And I with these untoward thoughts had striven,
I saw a Man before me unawares:
The oldest Man he seem'd that ever wore grey hairs.

My course I stopped as soon as I espied
The Old Man in that naked wilderness:
Close by a Pond, upon the further side,
He stood alone: a minute's space I guess
I watch'd him, he continuing motionless:
To the Pool's further margin then I drew;
He being all the while before me full in view.

As a huge Stone is sometimes seen to lie
Couch'd on the bald top of an eminence;
Wonder to all who do the same espy
By what means it could thither come, and whence;
So that it seems a thing endued with sense:
Like a Sea-beast crawl'd forth, which on a shelf
Of rock or sand reposeth, there to sun itself.

Such seem'd this Man, not all alive nor dead,
Nor all asleep; in his extreme old age:
His body was bent double, feet and head
Coming together in their pilgrimage;
As if some dire constraint of pain, or rage
Of sickness felt by him in times long past,
A more than human weight upon his frame had cast.

Himself he propp'd, his body, limbs, and face,
Upon a long grey Staff of shaven wood:
And, still as I drew near with gentle pace,
Beside the little pond or moorish flood
Motionless as a Cloud the Old Man stood;
That heareth not the loud winds when they call;
And moveth altogether, if it move at all.

At length, himself unsettling, he the Pond
Stirred with his Staff, and fixedly did look
Upon the muddy water, which he conn'd,
As if he had been reading in a book:
And now such freedom as I could I took;
And, drawing to his side, to him did say,
'This morning gives us promise of a glorious day.'

A gentle answer did the Old Man make,
In courteous speech which forth he slowly drew:
And him with further words I thus bespake,
'What kind of work is that which you pursue?
This is a lonesome place for one like you.'
He answer'd me with pleasure and surprize;
And there was, while he spake, a fire about his eyes.

His words came feebly, from a feeble chest,
Yet each in solemn order follow'd each,
With something of a lofty utterance drest;
Choice word, and measured phrase; above the reach
Of ordinary men; a stately speech!
Such as grave Livers do in Scotland use,
Religious men, who give to God and Man their dues.

He told me that he to this pond had come
To gather Leeches, being old and poor:
Employment hazardous and wearisome!
And he had many hardships to endure:
From Pond to Pond he roam'd, from moor to moor,
Housing, with God's good help, by choice or chance:
And in this way he gain'd an honest maintenance.

The Old Man still stood talking by my side;
But now his voice to me was like a stream
Scarce heard; nor word from word could I divide;
And the whole Body of the man did seem
Like one whom I had met with in a dream;
Or like a Man from some far region sent;
To give me human strength, and strong admonishment.

My former thoughts return'd: the fear that kills;
The hope that is unwilling to be fed;
Cold, pain, and labour, and all fleshly ills;
And mighty Poets in their misery dead.
And now, not knowing what the Old Man had said,
My question eagerly did I renew,
'How is it that you live, and what is it you do?'

He with a smile did then his words repeat;
And said, that, gathering Leeches, far and wide
He travelled; stirring thus about his feet
The waters of the Ponds where they abide.
'Once I could meet with them on every side;
But they have dwindled long by slow decay;
Yet still I persevere, and find them where I may.'

While he was talking thus, the lonely place,
The Old Man's shape, and speech, all troubled me:
In my mind's eye I seem'd to see him pace
About the weary moors continually,
Wandering about alone and silently.
While I these thoughts within myself pursued,
He, having made a pause, the same discourse renewed.

And soon with this he other matter blended,
Chearfully uttered, with demeanour kind,
But stately in the main; and, when he ended,
I could have laugh'd myself to scorn, to find
In that decrepit Man so firm a mind.
'God,' said I, 'be my help and stay secure;
I'll think of the Leech-gatherer on the lonely moor.'

SONNETS

Prefatory Sonnet

Nuns fret not at their Convent's narrow room;
And Hermits are contented with their Cells;
And Students with their pensive Citadels:
Maids at the Wheel, the Weaver at his Loom,
Sit blithe and happy; Bees that soar for bloom,
High as the highest Peak of Furness Fells,
Will murmur by the hour in Foxglove bells:
In truth, the prison, unto which we doom
Ourselves, no prison is: and hence to me,
In sundry moods, 'twas pastime to be bound
Within the Sonnet's scanty plot of ground:
Pleas'd if some Souls (for such there needs must be)
Who have felt the weight of too much liberty,
Should find short solace there, as I have found.

PART THE FIRST

MISCELLANEOUS SONNETS

I

How sweet it is, when mother Fancy rocks
The wayward brain, to saunter through a wood!
An old place, full of many a lovely brood,
Tall trees, green arbours, and ground flowers in flocks;
And Wild rose tip-toe upon hawthorn stocks,
Like to a bonny Lass, who plays her pranks
At Wakes and Fairs with wandering Mountebanks,
When she stands cresting the Clown's head, and mocks
The crowd beneath her. Verily I think,
Such place to me is sometimes like a dream
Or map of the whole world: thoughts, link by link,
Enter through ears and eyesight, with such gleam
Of all things, that at last in fear I shrink,
And leap at once from the delicious stream.

2

WHERE lies the Land to which yon Ship must go?
Festively she puts forth in trim array;
As vigorous as a Lark at break of day:
Is she for tropic suns, or polar snow?
What boots the enquiry? Neither friend nor foe
She cares for; let her travel where she may,
She finds familiar names, a beaten way
Ever before her, and a wind to blow.
Yet still I ask, what Haven is her mark?
And, almost as it was when ships were rare,
From time to time, like Pilgrims, here and there
Crossing the waters; doubt, and something dark,
Of the old Sea some reverential fear,
Is with me at thy farewell, joyous Bark!

3

Composed after a journey across the Hamilton Hills, Yorkshire

Ere we had reach'd the wish'd-for place, night fell:
We were too late at least by one dark hour,
And nothing could we see of all that power
Of prospect, whereof many thousands tell.
The western sky did recompence us well
With Grecian Temple, Minaret, and Bower;
And, in one part, a Minster with its Tower
Substantially distinct, a place for Bell
Or Clock to toll from. Many a glorious pile
Did we behold, sights that might well repay
All disappointment! and, as such, the eye
Delighted in them; but we felt, the while,
We should forget them: they are of the sky,
And from our earthly memory fade away.

4

. . . they are of the sky,
And from our earthly memory fade away

These words were utter'd in a pensive mood,
Even while mine eyes were on that solemn sight:
A contrast and reproach to gross delight,
And life's unspiritual pleasures daily woo'd!
But now upon this thought I cannot brood:
It is unstable, and deserts me quite;
Nor will I praise a Cloud, however bright,
Disparaging Man's gifts, and proper food.
The Grove, the sky-built Temple, and the Dome,
Though clad in colours beautiful and pure,
Find in the heart of man no natural home:
The immortal Mind craves objects that endure:
These cleave to it: from these it cannot roam,
Nor they from it: their fellowship is secure.

6

To Sleep

A FLOCK of sheep that leisurely pass by,
One after one; the sound of rain, and bees
Murmuring; the fall of rivers, winds and seas,
Smooth fields, white sheets of water, and pure sky;
I've thought of all by turns; and still I lie
Sleepless; and soon the small birds' melodies
Must hear, first utter'd from my orchard trees;
And the first Cuckoo's melancholy cry.
Even thus last night, and two nights more, I lay,
And could not win thee, Sleep! by any stealth:
So do not let me wear to-night away:
Without Thee what is all the morning's wealth?
Come, blessed barrier betwixt day and day,
Dear mother of fresh thoughts and joyous health!

8

WITH Ships the sea was sprinkled far and nigh,
Like stars in heaven, and joyously it showed;
Some lying fast at anchor in the road,
Some veering up and down, one knew not why.
A goodly Vessel did I then espy
Come like a Giant from a haven broad;
And lustily along the Bay she strode,
Her tackling rich, and of apparel high.
This Ship was nought to me, nor I to her,
Yet I pursued her with a Lover's look;
This Ship to all the rest did I prefer:
When will she turn, and whither? She will brook
No tarrying; where she comes the winds must stir:
On went She, and due north her journey took.

9

To the River Duddon

O MOUNTAIN Stream! the Shepherd and his Cot
Are privileg'd Inmates of deep solitude:
Nor would the nicest Anchorite exclude
A Field or two of brighter green, or Plot
Of tillage-ground, that seemeth like a spot
Of stationary sunshine: thou hast view'd
These only, Duddon! with their paths renew'd
By fits and starts, yet this contents thee not.
Thee hath some awful Spirit impell'd to leave,
Utterly to desert, the haunts of men,
Though simple thy Companions were and few;
And through this wilderness a passage cleave
Attended but by thy own Voice, save when
The Clouds and Fowls of the air thy way pursue.

13

Written in very early Youth

CALM is all nature as a resting wheel.
The Kine are couch'd upon the dewy grass;
The Horse alone, seen dimly as I pass,
Is up, and cropping yet his later meal:
Dark is the ground; a slumber seems to steal
O'er vale, and mountain, and the starless sky.
Now, in this blank of things, a harmony
Home-felt, and home-created seems to heal
That grief for which the senses still supply
Fresh food; for only then, when memory
Is hush'd, am I at rest. My Friends, restrain
Those busy cares that would allay my pain:
Oh! leave me to myself; nor let me feel
The officious touch that makes me droop again.

14

Composed upon Westminster Bridge

EARTH has not any thing to shew more fair:
Dull would he be of soul who could pass by
A sight so touching in it's majesty:
This City now doth like a garment wear
The beauty of the morning; silent, bare,
Ships, towers, domes, theatres, and temples lie
Open unto the fields, and to the sky;
All bright and glittering in the smokeless air.
Never did sun more beautifully steep
In his first splendor valley, rock, or hill;
Ne'er saw I, never felt, a calm so deep!
The river glideth at his own sweet will:
Dear God! the very houses seem asleep;
And all that mighty heart is lying still!

September 3, 1802

15

'BELOVED Vale!' I said, 'when I shall con
Those many records of my childish years,
Remembrance of myself and of my peers
Will press me down: to think of what is gone
Will be an awful thought, if life have one.'
But, when into the Vale I came, no fears
Distress'd me; I look'd round, I shed no tears;
Deep thought, or awful vision, I had none.
By thousand petty fancies I was cross'd,
To see the Trees, which I had thought so tall,
Mere dwarfs; the Brooks so narrow, Fields so small.
A Juggler's Balls old Time about him toss'd;
I looked, I stared, I smiled, I laughed; and all
The weight of sadness was in wonder lost.

16

METHOUGHT I saw the footsteps of a throne
Which mists and vapours from mine eyes did shroud,
Nor view of him who sate thereon allow'd;
But all the steps and ground about were strown
With sights the ruefullest that flesh and bone
Ever put on; a miserable crowd,
Sick, hale, old, young, who cried before that cloud,
'Thou art our king, O Death! to thee we groan.'
I seem'd to mount those steps; the vapours gave
Smooth way; and I beheld the face of one
Sleeping alone within a mossy cave,
With her face up to heaven; that seem'd to have
Pleasing remembrance of a thought foregone;
A lovely Beauty in a summer grave!

18

THE world is too much with us; late and soon,
Getting and spending, we lay waste our powers:
Little we see in nature that is ours;
We have given our hearts away, a sordid boon!
This Sea that bares her bosom to the moon;
The Winds that will be howling at all hours
And are up-gathered now like sleeping flowers;
For this, for every thing, we are out of tune;
It moves us not—Great God! I'd rather be
A Pagan suckled in a creed outworn;
So might I, standing on this pleasant lea,
Have glimpses that would make me less forlorn;
Have sight of Proteus coming from the sea;
Or hear old Triton blow his wreathed horn.

19

IT is a beauteous Evening, calm and free;
The holy time is quiet as a Nun
Breathless with adoration; the broad sun
Is sinking down in its tranquillity;
The gentleness of heaven is on the Sea:

Listen! the mighty Being is awake
And doth with his eternal motion make
A sound like thunder—everlastingly.
Dear Child! dear Girl! that walkest with me here,
If thou appear'st untouch'd by solemn thought,
Thy nature is not therefore less divine:
Thou liest in Abraham's bosom all the year;
And worshipp'st at the Temple's inner shrine,
God being with thee when we know it not.

20

To the Memory of Raisley Calvert

Calvert! it must not be unheard by them
Who may respect my name that I to thee
Ow'd many years of early liberty.
This care was thine when sickness did condemn
Thy youth to hopeless wasting, root and stem:
That I, if frugal and severe, might stray
Where'er I liked; and finally array
My temples with the Muse's diadem.
Hence, if in freedom I have lov'd the truth,
If there be aught of pure, or good, or great,
In my past verse; or shall be, in the lays
Of higher mood, which now I meditate,
It gladdens me, O worthy, short-lived Youth!
To think how much of this will be thy praise.

PART THE SECOND
SONNETS DEDICATED TO LIBERTY

I

Composed by the Sea-Side, near Calais

Fair Star of Evening, Splendor of the West,
Star of my Country! on the horizon's brink
Thou hangest, stooping, as might seem, to sink
On England's bosom; yet well pleas'd to rest,
Meanwhile, and be to her a glorious crest
Conspicuous to the Nations. Thou, I think,
Should'st be my Country's emblem; and should'st wink,
Bright Star! with laughter on her banners, drest
In thy fresh beauty. There! that dusky spot
Beneath thee, it is England; there it lies.
Blessings be on you both! one hope, one lot,
One life, one glory! I, with many a fear
For my dear Country, many heartfelt sighs,
Among Men who do not love her linger here.

2

Calais

Is it a Reed that's shaken by the wind,
Or what is it that ye go forth to see?
Lords, Lawyers, Statesmen, Squires of low degree,
Men known, and men unknown, Sick, Lame, and Blind,
Post forward all, like Creatures of one kind,
With first-fruit offerings crowd to bend the knee
In France, before the new-born Majesty.
'Tis ever thus. Ye Men of prostrate mind!
A seemly reverence may be paid to power;
But that's a loyal virtue, never sown
In haste, nor springing with a transient shower:
When truth, when sense, when liberty were flown
What hardship had it been to wait an hour?
Shame on you, feeble Heads, to slavery prone!

August 1802

3

To a Friend,

COMPOSED NEAR CALAIS, ON THE ROAD LEADING TO ARDRES

JONES! when from Calais southward you and I
Travell'd on foot together; then this Way,
Which I am pacing now, was like the May
With festivals of new-born Liberty:
A homeless sound of joy was in the Sky;
The antiquated Earth, as one might say,
Beat like the heart of Man: songs, garlands, play,
Banners, and happy faces, far and nigh!
And now, sole register that these things were,
Two solitary greetings have I heard,
'*Good morrow, Citizen!*' a hollow word,
As if a dead Man spake it! Yet despair
I feel not: happy am I as a Bird:
Fair seasons yet will come, and hopes as fair.

August 7, 1802

4

I GRIEV'D for Buonaparte, with a vain
And an unthinking grief! the vital blood
Of that Man's mind what can it be? What food
Fed his first hopes? What knowledge could He gain?
'Tis not in battles that from youth we train
The Governor who must be wise and good,
And temper with the sternness of the brain
Thoughts motherly, and meek as womanhood.
Wisdom doth live with children round her knees:
Books, leisure, perfect freedom, and the talk
Man holds with week-day man in the hourly walk
Of the mind's business: these are the degrees
By which true Sway doth mount; this is the stalk
True Power doth grow on; and her rights are these.

5

Calais

Festivals have I seen that were not names:
This is young Buonaparte's natal day;
And his is henceforth an established sway,
Consul for life. With worship France proclaims
Her approbation, and with pomps and games.
Heaven grant that other Cities may be gay!
Calais is not: and I have bent my way
To the Sea-coast, noting that each man frames
His business as he likes. Another time
That was, when I was here long years ago:
The senselessness of joy was then sublime!
Happy is he, who, caring not for Pope,
Consul, or King, can sound himself to know
The destiny of Man, and live in hope.

August 15, 1802

6

On the Extinction of the Venetian Republic

Once did She hold the gorgeous East in fee;
And was the safeguard of the West: the worth
Of Venice did not fall below her birth,
Venice, the eldest Child of Liberty.
She was a Maiden City, bright and free;
No guile seduced, no force could violate;
And when She took unto herself a Mate
She must espouse the everlasting Sea.
And what if she had seen those glories fade,
Those titles vanish, and that strength decay,
Yet shall some tribute of regret be paid
When her long life hath reach'd its final day:
Men are we, and must grieve when even the Shade
Of that which once was great is pass'd away.

8

To Toussaint L'Ouverture

Toussaint, the most unhappy Man of Men!
Whether the rural Milk-maid by her Cow
Sing in thy hearing, or thou liest now
Alone in some deep dungeon's earless den,
O miserable chieftain! where and when
Wilt thou find patience? Yet die not; do thou
Wear rather in thy bonds a chearful brow:
Though fallen Thyself, never to rise again,
Live, and take comfort. Thou hast left behind
Powers that will work for thee; air, earth, and skies;
There's not a breathing of the common wind
That will forget thee; thou hast great allies;
Thy friends are exultations, agonies,
And love, and Man's unconquerable mind.

9

We had a fellow-Passenger who came
From Calais with us, gaudy in array,
A Negro Woman like a Lady gay,
Yet silent as a woman fearing blame;
Dejected, meek, yea pitiably tame,
She sate, from notice turning not away,
But on our proffer'd kindness still did lay
A weight of languid speech, or at the same
Was silent, motionless in eyes and face.
She was a Negro Woman driv'n from France,
Rejected like all others of that race,
Not one of whom may now find footing there;
This the poor Out-cast did to us declare,
Nor murmur'd at the unfeeling Ordinance.

September 1, 1802

10

Composed in the Valley, near Dover on the Day of landing

DEAR fellow Traveller! here we are once more.
The Cock that crows, the Smoke that curls, that sound
Of Bells, those Boys that in yon meadow-ground
In white sleev'd shirts are playing by the score,
And even this little River's gentle roar,
All, all are English. Oft have I look'd round
With joy in Kent's green vales; but never found
Myself so satisfied in heart before.
Europe is yet in Bonds; but let that pass,
Thought for another moment. Thou art free
My Country! and 'tis joy enough and pride
For one hour's perfect bliss, to tread the grass
Of England once again, and hear and see,
With such a dear Companion at my side.

11

INLAND, within a hollow Vale, I stood,
And saw, while sea was calm and air was clear,
The Coast of France, the Coast of France how near!
Drawn almost into frightful neighbourhood.
I shrunk, for verily the barrier flood
Was like a Lake, or River bright and fair,
A span of waters; yet what power is there!
What mightiness for evil and for good!
Even so doth God protect us if we be
Virtuous and wise: Winds blow, and Waters roll,
Strength to the brave, and Power, and Deity,
Yet in themselves are nothing! One decree
Spake laws to *them*, and said that by the Soul
Only the Nations shall be great and free.

September, 1802

12

Thought of a Briton on the Subjugation of Switzerland

Two Voices are there; one is of the Sea,
One of the Mountains; each a mighty Voice:
In both from age to age Thou didst rejoice,
They were thy chosen Music, Liberty!
There came a Tyrant, and with holy glee
Thou fought'st against Him; but hast vainly striven;
Thou from thy Alpine Holds at length art driven,
Where not a torrent murmurs heard by thee.
Of one deep bliss thine ear hath been bereft:
Then cleave, O cleave to that which still is left!
For, high-soul'd Maid, what sorrow would it be
That mountain Floods should thunder as before,
And Ocean bellow from his rocky shore,
And neither awful Voice be heard by thee!

13

Written in London

O FRIEND! I know not which way I must look
For comfort, being, as I am, opprest,
To think that now our Life is only drest
For shew; mean handywork of craftsman, cook,
Or groom! We must run glittering like a Brook
In the open sunshine, or we are unblest:
The wealthiest man among us is the best:
No grandeur now in nature or in book
Delights us. Rapine, avarice, expence,
This is idolatry; and these we adore:
Plain living and high thinking are no more:
The homely beauty of 'the good old cause'
Is gone; our peace, our fearful innocence,
And pure religion breathing household laws.

September, 1802

14

London

Milton! thou should'st be living at this hour:
England hath need of thee: she is a fen
Of stagnant waters: altar, sword and pen,
Fireside, the heroic wealth of hall and bower,
Have forfeited their ancient English dower
Of inward happiness. We are selfish men;
Oh! raise us up, return to us again;
And give us manners, virtue, freedom, power.
Thy soul was like a Star and dwelt apart:
Thou hadst a voice whose sound was like the sea;
Pure as the naked heavens, majestic, free,
So didst thou travel on life's common way,
In chearful godliness; and yet thy heart
The lowliest duties on itself did lay.

1802

15

Great Men have been among us; hands that penn'd
And tongues that utter'd wisdom, better none:
The later Sydney, Marvel, Harrington,
Young Vane, and others who call'd Milton Friend.
These Moralists could act and comprehend:
They knew how genuine glory was put on;
Taught us how rightfully a nation shone
In splendor: what strength was, that would not bend
But in magnanimous meekness. France, 'tis strange,
Hath brought forth no such souls as we had then.
Perpetual emptiness! unceasing change!
No single Volume paramount, no code,
No master spirit, no determined road;
But equally a want of Books and Men!

16

It is not to be thought of that the Flood
Of British freedom, which to the open Sea
Of the world's praise from dark antiquity

Hath flowed, 'with pomp of waters, unwithstood,'
Road by which all might come and go that would,
And bear out freights of worth to foreign lands;
That this most famous Stream in Bogs and Sands
Should perish; and to evil and to good
Be lost for ever. In our Halls is hung
Armoury of the invincible Knights of old:
We must be free or die, who speak the tongue
That Shakespeare spake; the faith and morals hold
Which Milton held. In every thing we are sprung
Of Earth's first blood, have titles manifold.

17

When I have borne in memory what has tamed
Great Nations, how ennobling thoughts depart
When Men change Swords for Ledgers, and desert
The Student's bower for gold, some fears unnamed
I had, my Country! am I to be blamed?
But, when I think of Thee, and what Thou art,
Verily, in the bottom of my heart,
Of those unfilial fears I am ashamed.
But dearly must we prize thee; we who find
In thee a bulwark of the cause of men;
And I by my affection was beguiled.
What wonder, if a Poet, now and then,
Among the many movements of his mind,
Felt for thee as a Lover or a Child.

20

These times touch money'd Worldlings with dismay:
Even rich men, brave by nature, taint the air
With words of apprehension and despair:
While tens of thousands, thinking on the affray,
Men unto whom sufficient for the day
And minds not stinted or untill'd are given,
Sound, healthy Children of the God of Heaven,
Are cheerful as the rising Sun in May.
What do we gather hence but firmer faith
That every gift of noble origin
Is breathed upon by Hope's perpetual breath;

That virtue and the faculties within
Are vital, and that riches are akin
To fear, to change, to cowardice, and death!

October, 1803

21

ENGLAND! the time is come when thou shouldst wean
Thy heart from its emasculating food;
The truth should now be better understood;
Old things have been unsettled; we have seen
Fair seed-time, better harvest might have been
But for thy trespasses; and, at this day,
If for Greece, Egypt, India, Africa,
Aught good were destined, Thou wouldst step between.
England! all nations in this charge agree:
But worse, more ignorant in love and hate,
Far, far more abject is thine Enemy:
Therefore the wise pray for thee, though the freight
Of thy offences be a heavy weight:
Oh grief! that Earth's best hopes rest all with Thee!

23

To the Men of Kent

VANGUARD of Liberty, ye Men of Kent,
Now is the time to prove your hardiment!
To France be words of invitation sent!
They from their Fields can see the countenance
Of your fierce war, may ken the glittering lance,
And hear you shouting forth your brave intent.
Left single, in bold parley, Ye, of yore,
Did from the Norman win a gallant wreath;
Confirm'd the charters that were yours before;—
No parleying now! In Britain is one breath;
We all are with you now from Shore to Shore:—
Ye Men of Kent, 'tis Victory or Death!

October, 1803

24

Six thousand Veterans practis'd in War's game,
Tried Men, at Killicranky were array'd
Against an equal Host that wore the Plaid,
Shepherds and Herdsmen.—Like a whirlwind came
The Highlanders, the slaughter spread like flame;
And Garry thundering down his mountain-road
Was stopp'd, and could not breathe beneath the load
Of the dead bodies. 'Twas a day of shame
For them whom precept and the pedantry
Of cold mechanic battle do enslave.
Oh! for a single hour of that Dundee
Who on that day the word of onset gave!
Like conquest would the Men of England see;
And her Foes find a like inglorious Grave.

October, 1803

26

Another year!—another deadly blow!
Another mighty Empire overthrown!
And we are left, or shall be left, alone;
The last that dares to struggle with the Foe.
'Tis well! from this day forward we shall know
That in ourselves our safety must be sought;
That by our own right hands it must be wrought,
That we must stand unpropp'd, or be laid low.
O Dastard whom such foretaste doth not chear!
We shall exult, if They who rule the land
Be Men who hold its many blessings dear,
Wise, upright, valiant; not a venal Band,
Who are to judge of danger which they fear,
And honour which they do not understand.

November, 1806

POEMS IN TWO VOLUMES, 1807

VOLUME TWO

POEMS WRITTEN DURING A TOUR IN SCOTLAND

Rob Roy's Grave

THE History of Rob Roy is sufficiently known; his Grave is near the head of Loch Ketterine, in one of those small Pinfold-like Burial-grounds, of neglected and desolate appearance, which the Traveller meets with in the Highlands of Scotland.

A FAMOUS Man is Robin Hood,
The English Ballad-singer's joy!
And Scotland has a Thief as good,
An Outlaw of as daring mood,
She has her brave ROB ROY!
Then clear the weeds from off his Grave,
And let us chaunt a passing Stave
In honour of that Hero brave!

HEAVEN gave Rob Roy a dauntless heart,
And wondrous length and strength of arm.
Nor craved he more to quell his Foes,
  Or keep his Friends from harm.

Yet was Rob Roy as *wise* as brave;
Forgive me if the phrase be strong;—
A Poet worthy of Rob Roy
  Must scorn a timid song.

Say, then, that he was wise as brave;
As wise in thought as bold in deed:
For in the principles of things
  He sought his moral creed.

Said generous Rob, 'What need of Books?
'Burn all the Statutes and their shelves:
'They stir us up against our Kind;
'And worse, against Ourselves.

'We have a passion, make a law,
'Too false to guide us or controul!
'And for the law itself we fight
'In bitterness of soul.

'And, puzzled, blinded thus, we lose
'Distinctions that are plain and few:
'These find I graven on my heart:
'*That* tells me what to do.

'The Creatures see of flood and field,
'And those that travel on the wind!
'With them no strife can last; they live
'In peace, and peace of mind.

'For why?—because the good old Rule
'Sufficeth them, the simple Plan,
'That they should take who have the power,
'And they should keep who can.

'A lesson which is quickly learn'd,
'A signal this which all can see!
'Thus nothing here provokes the Strong
'To wanton cruelty.

'All freakishness of mind is check'd;
'He tam'd, who foolishly aspires;
'While to the measure of his might
'Each fashions his desires.

'All Kinds, and Creatures, stand and fall
'By strength of prowess or of wit:
''Tis God's appointment who must sway,
'And who is to submit.

Borrowdale, Cumberland by Joshua Cristall (1767–1847). "But worthier still of note / Are those fraternal Four of Borrowdale, / Joined in one solemn and capacious grove": the "Yew-Trees" of Borrowdale which stand to this day.
By courtesy of Abbot Hall Art Gallery, Kendal

Castle Crag, Borrowdale by Julius Caesar Ibbetson (1759–1817). A lofty wooded eminence from which, according to Wordsworth, springs "out . . . the antiquated circle of a Roman encampment". By courtesy of Abbot Hall Art Gallery, Kendal

'Since then,' said Robin, 'right is plain,
'And longest life is but a day;
'To have my ends, maintain my rights,
'I'll take the shortest way.'

And thus among these rocks he liv'd,
Through summer's heat and winter's snow:
The Eagle, he was Lord above,
And Rob was Lord below.

So was it—*would,* at least, have been
But through untowardness of fate:
For Polity was then too strong;
He came an age too late,

Or shall we say an age too soon?
For, were the bold Man living *now,*
How might he flourish in his pride,
With buds on every bough!

Then rents and Factors, rights of chace,
Sheriffs, and Lairds and their domains
Would all have seem'd but paltry things,
Not worth a moment's pains.

Rob Roy had never linger'd here,
To these few meagre Vales confin'd;
But thought how wide the world, the times
How fairly to his mind!

And to his Sword he would have said,
'Do Thou my sovereign will enact
'From land to land through half the earth!
'Judge thou of law and fact!

''Tis fit that we should do our part;
'Becoming, that mankind should learn
'That we are not to be surpass'd
'In fatherly concern.

'Of old things all are over old,
'Of good things none are good enough:—
'We'll shew that we can help to frame
'A world of other stuff.

'I, too, will have my Kings that take
'From me the sign of life and death:
'Kingdoms shall shift about, like clouds,
'Obedient to my breath.'

And, if the word had been fulfill'd,
As *might* have been, then, thought of joy!
France would have had her present Boast;
And we our brave Rob Roy!

Oh! say not so; compare them not;
I would not wrong thee, Champion brave!
Would wrong thee no where; least of all
Here standing by thy Grave.

For Thou, although with some wild thoughts,
Wild Chieftain of a Savage Clan!
Hadst this to boast of; thou didst love
The *liberty* of Man.

And, had it been thy lot to live
With us who now behold the light,
Thou would'st have nobly stirr'd thyself,
And battled for the Right.

For Robin was the poor Man's stay
The poor man's heart, the poor man's hand;
And all the oppress'd, who wanted strength,
Had Robin's to command.

Bear witness many a pensive sigh
Of thoughtful Herdsman when he strays
Alone upon Loch Veol's Heights,
And by Loch Lomond's Braes!

And, far and near, through vale and hill,
Are faces that attest the same;
And kindle, like a fire new stirr'd,
At sound of Rob Roy's name.

2

The Solitary Reaper

Behold her, single in the field,
Yon solitary Highland Lass!
Reaping and singing by herself;
Stop here, or gently pass!
Alone she cuts, and binds the grain,
And sings a melancholy strain;
O listen! for the Vale profound
Is overflowing with the sound.

No Nightingale did ever chaunt
So sweetly to reposing bands
Of Travellers in some shady haunt,
Among Arabian Sands:
No sweeter voice was ever heard
In spring-time from the Cuckoo-bird,
Breaking the silence of the seas
Among the farthest Hebrides.

Will no one tell me what she sings?
Perhaps the plaintive numbers flow
For old, unhappy, far-off things,
And battles long ago:
Or is it some more humble lay,
Familiar matter of today?
Some natural sorrow, loss, or pain,
That has been, and may be again!

Whate'er the theme, the Maiden sung
As if her song could have no ending;
I saw her singing at her work,
And o'er the sickle bending;

I listen'd till I had my fill:
And, as I mounted up the hill,
The music in my heart I bore,
Long after it was heard no more.

3

Stepping Westward

While my Fellow-traveller and I were walking by the side of Loch Ketterine, one fine evening after sun-set, in our road to a Hut where in the course of our Tour we had been hospitably entertained some weeks before, we met, in one of the loneliest parts of that solitary region, two well dressed Women, one of whom said to us, by way of greeting, 'What you are stepping westward?'

'*What, you are stepping westward?*'—'*Yea.*'
—'Twould be a wildish destiny,
If we, who thus together roam
In a strange Land, and far from home,
Were in this place the guests of Chance:
Yet who would stop, or fear to advance,
Though home or shelter he had none,
With such a Sky to lead him on?

The dewy ground was dark and cold;
Behind, all gloomy to behold;
And stepping westward seem'd to be
A kind of *heavenly* destiny;
I liked the greeting; 'twas a sound
Of something without place or bound;
And seem'd to give me spiritual right
To travel through that region bright.

The voice was soft, and she who spake
Was walking by her native Lake:
The salutation had to me
The very sound of courtesy:
It's power was felt; and while my eye
Was fixed upon the glowing sky,
The echo of the voice enwrought
A human sweetness with the thought
Of travelling through the world that lay
Before me in my endless way.

6

To a Highland Girl

(At Inversneyde, upon Loch Lomond)

Sweet Highland Girl, a very shower
Of beauty is thy earthly dower!
Twice seven consenting years have shed
Their utmost bounty on thy head:
And these gray Rocks; this household Lawn;
These Trees, a veil just half withdrawn;
This fall of water, that doth make
A murmur near the silent Lake;
This little Bay, a quiet Road
That holds in shelter thy Abode;
In truth together ye do seem
Like something fashion'd in a dream;
Such Forms as from their covert peep
When earthly cares are laid asleep!
Yet, dream and vision as thou art,
I bless thee with a human heart:
God shield thee to thy latest years!
I neither know thee nor thy peers;
And yet my eyes are fill'd with tears.

With earnest feeling I shall pray
For thee when I am far away:
For never saw I mien, or face,
In which more plainly I could trace
Benignity and home-bred sense
Ripening in perfect innocence.
Here, scatter'd like a random seed,
Remote from men, Thou dost not need
The embarrass'd look of shy distress,
And maidenly shamefacedness:
Thou wear'st upon thy forehead clear
The freedom of a Mountaineer.
A face with gladness overspread!
Sweet looks, by human kindness bred!

And seemliness complete, that sways
Thy courtesies, about thee plays;
With no restraint, but such as springs
From quick and eager visitings
Of thoughts, that lie beyond the reach
Of thy few words of English speech:
A bondage sweetly brook'd, a strife
That gives thy gestures grace and life!
So have I, not unmov'd in mind,
Seen birds of tempest-loving kind,
Thus beating up against the wind.

What hand but would a garland cull
For thee who art so beautiful?
O happy pleasure! here to dwell
Beside thee in some heathy dell;
Adopt your homely ways and dress,
A Shepherd, thou a Shepherdess!
But I could frame a wish for thee
More like a grave reality:
Thou art to me but as a wave
Of the wild sea; and I would have
Some claim upon thee, if I could,
Though but of common neighbourhood.
What joy to hear thee, and to see!
Thy elder Brother I would be,
Thy Father, any thing to thee!

Now thanks to Heaven! that of its grace
Hath led me to this lonely place.
Joy have I had; and going hence
I bear away my recompence.
In spots like these it is we prize
Our Memory, feel that she hath eyes:
Then, why should I be loth to stir?
I feel this place was made for her;
To give new pleasure like the past,
Continued long as life shall last.
Nor am I loth, though pleased at heart,
Sweet Highland Girl! from Thee to part;
For I, methinks, till I grow old,
As fair before me shall behold,

As I do now, the Cabin small,
The Lake, the Bay, the Waterfall;
And Thee, the Spirit of them all!

7

Sonnet

(COMPOSED AT —— CASTLE)

DEGENERATE Douglas! oh, the unworthy Lord!
Whom mere despite of heart could so far please,
And love of havoc (for with such disease
Fame taxes him) that he could send forth word
To level with the dust a noble horde,
A brotherhood of venerable Trees,
Leaving an ancient Dome, and Towers like these,
Beggared and outraged!—Many hearts deplor'd
The fate of those old Trees; and oft with pain
The Traveller, at this day, will stop and gaze
On wrongs, which Nature scarcely seems to heed:
For shelter'd places, bosoms, nooks and bays,
And the pure mountains, and the gentle Tweed,
And the green silent pastures, yet remain.

8

To the Sons of Burns

AFTER VISITING THEIR FATHER'S GRAVE
14 *August*, 1803

YE now are panting up life's hill!
'Tis twilight time of good and ill,
And more than common strength and skill
Must ye display
If ye would give the better will
Its lawful sway.

Strong bodied if ye be to bear
Intemperance with less harm, beware!
But if your Father's wit ye share,
Then, then indeed,
Ye Sons of Burns! for watchful care
There will be need.

For honest men delight will take
To shew you favor for his sake,
Will flatter you; and Fool and Rake
Your steps pursue:
And of your Father's name will make
A snare for you.

Let no mean hope your souls enslave;
Be independent, generous, brave!
Your Father such example gave,
And such revere!
But be admonish'd by this Grave,
And think, and fear!

9

Yarrow Unvisited

See the various Poems the scene of which is laid upon the Banks of the Yarrow; in particular, the exquisite Ballad of Hamilton, beginning

Busk ye, busk ye my bonny, bonny Bride,
Busk ye, busk ye my winsome Marrow!—

From Stirling Castle we had seen
The mazy Forth unravell'd;
Had trod the banks of Clyde, and Tay,
And with the Tweed had travell'd;
And, when we came to Clovenford,
Then said my '*winsome Marrow*',
'Whate'er betide, we'll turn aside,
'And see the Braes of Yarrow.'

'Let Yarrow Folk, *frae* Selkirk Town,
'Who have been buying, selling,
'Go back to Yarrow, 'tis their own,
'Each Maiden to her Dwelling!
'On Yarrow's Banks let herons feed,
'Hares couch, and rabbits burrow!
'But we will downwards with the Tweed,
'Nor turn aside to Yarrow.

'There's Galla Water, Leader Haughs,
'Both lying right before us;
'And Dryborough, where with chiming Tweed
'The Lintwhites sing in chorus;
'There's pleasant Tiviot Dale, a land
'Made blithe with plough and harrow;
'Why throw away a needful day
'To go in search of Yarrow?

'What's Yarrow but a River bare
'That glides the dark hills under?
'There are a thousand such elsewhere
'As worthy of your wonder.'
—Strange words they seem'd of slight and scorn;
My True-Love sigh'd for sorrow;
And look'd me in the face, to think
I thus could speak of Yarrow!

'Oh! green,' said I, 'are Yarrow's Holms,
'And sweet is Yarrow flowing!
'Fair hangs the apple frae the rock*,
'But we will leave it growing.
'O'er hilly path, and open Strath,
'We'll wander Scotland thorough;
'But, though so near, we will not turn
'Into the Dale of Yarrow.

'Let Beeves and home-bred Kine partake
'The sweets of Burn-mill meadow;
'The Swan on still St. Mary's Lake
'Float double, Swan and Shadow!

* See Hamilton's Ballad as above.

'We will not see them; will not go,
'Today, nor yet tomorrow;
'Enough if in our hearts we know,
'There's such a place as Yarrow.

'Be Yarrow Stream unseen, unknown!
'It must, or we shall rue it:
'We have a vision of our own;
'Ah! why should we undo it?
'The treasured dreams of times long past
'We'll keep them, winsome Marrow!
'For when we're there although 'tis fair
''Twill be another Yarrow!

'If Care with freezing years should come,
'And wandering seem but folly
'Should we be loth to stir from home,
'And yet be melancholy;
'Should life be dull, and spirits low,
''Twill soothe us in our sorrow
'That earth has something yet to show,
'The bonny Holms of Yarrow!'

MOODS OF MY OWN MIND

I

To a Butterfly

STAY near me—do not take thy flight!
A little longer stay in sight!
Much converse do I find in Thee,
Historian of my Infancy!
Float near me; do not yet depart!
Dead times revive in thee:
Thou bring'st, gay Creature as thou art!
A solemn image to my heart,
My Father's Family!

Oh! pleasant, pleasant were the days,
The time, when in our childish plays
My sister Emmeline and I
Together chaced the Butterfly!
A very hunter did I rush
Upon the prey:—with leaps and springs
I follow'd on from brake to bush;
But She, God love her! feared to brush
The dust from off its wings.

2

'The Sun has long been set'

The Sun has long been set:
The Stars are out by twos and threes;
The little Birds are piping yet
Among the bushes and trees;
There's a Cuckoo, and one or two thrushes;
And a noise of wind that rushes,
With a noise of water that gushes;
And the Cuckoo's sovereign cry
Fills all the hollow of the sky!

Who would go 'parading'
In London, and 'masquerading,'
On such a night of June?
With that beautiful soft half-moon,
And all these innocent blisses,
On such a night as this is!

3

'O Nightingale! thou surely art'

O Nightingale! thou surely art
A Creature of a fiery heart—
These notes of thine they pierce, and pierce;
Tumultuous harmony and fierce!

Thou sing'st as if the God of wine
Had help'd thee to a Valentine;
A song in mockery and despite
Of shades, and dews, and silent Night,
And steady bliss, and all the Loves
Now sleeping in these peaceful groves!

I heard a Stockdove sing or say
His homely tale, this very day.
His voice was buried among trees,
Yet to be come at by the breeze:
He did not cease; but coo'd—and coo'd;
And somewhat pensively he woo'd:
He sang of love with quiet blending,
Slow to begin, and never ending;
Of serious faith, and inward glee;
That was the Song, the Song for me!

4

'My heart leaps up when I behold'

(This poem is now generally known as *The Rainbow*)

My heart leaps up when I behold
A Rainbow in the sky:
So was it when my life began;
So is it now I am a Man;
So be it when I shall grow old,
Or let me die!
The Child is Father of the Man;
And I could wish my days to be
Bound each to each by natural piety.

6

The Small Celandine *

THERE is a Flower, the Lesser Celandine,
That shrinks, like many more, from cold and rain;
And, the first moment that the sun may shine,
Bright as the sun itself, 'tis out again!

When hailstones have been falling swarm on swarm,
Or blasts the green field and the trees distress'd,
Oft have I seen it muffled up from harm,
In close self-shelter, like a Thing at rest.

But lately, one rough day, this Flower I pass'd,
And recognized it, though an alter'd Form,
Now standing forth an offering to the Blast,
And buffeted at will by Rain and Storm.

I stopp'd, and said with inly muttered voice,
'It doth not love the shower, nor seek the cold:
This neither is it's courage nor it's choice,
But it's necessity in being old.

The sunshine may not bless it, nor the dew;
It cannot help itself in it's decay;
Stiff in it's members, wither'd, changed of hue.'
And, in my spleen, I smiled that it was grey.

To be a Prodigal's Favorite—then, worse truth,
A Miser's Pensioner—behold our lot!
O Man! that from thy fair and shining youth
Age might but take the things Youth needed not!

* Common Pilewort

7

'I wandered lonely as a Cloud'

(This poem is now generally known as *Daffodils*)

I WANDERED lonely as a Cloud
That floats on high o'er Vales and Hills,
When all at once I saw a crowd
A host of dancing Daffodils;
Along the Lake, beneath the trees,
Ten thousand dancing in the breeze.

The waves beside them danced, but they
Outdid the sparkling waves in glee:—
A Poet could not but be gay
In such a laughing company:
I gaz'd—and gaz'd—but little thought
What wealth the shew to me had brought:

For oft when on my couch I lie
In vacant or in pensive mood,
They flash upon that inward eye
Which is the bliss of solitude,
And then my heart with pleasure fills,
And dances with the Daffodils.

9

The Sparrow's Nest

LOOK, five blue eggs are gleaming there!
Few visions have I seen more fair,
Nor many prospects of delight
More pleasing than that simple sight!
I started seeming to espy
The home and shelter'd bed,

The Sparrow's dwelling, which, hard by
My Father's House, in wet or dry,
My Sister Emmeline and I
Together visited.

She look'd at it as if she fear'd it;
Still wishing, dreading to be near it:
Such heart was in her, being then
A little Prattler among men.
The Blessing of my later years
Was with me when a Boy;
She gave me eyes, she gave me ears;
And humble cares, and delicate fears;
A heart, the fountain of sweet tears;
And love, and thought, and joy.

10

Gipsies

YET are they here?—the same unbroken knot
Of human Beings, in the self-same spot!
Men, Women, Children, yea the frame
Of the whole Spectacle the same!
Only their fire seems bolder, yielding light:
Now deep and red, the colouring of night;
That on their Gipsy-faces falls,
Their bed of straw and blanket-walls.
—Twelve hours, twelve bounteous hours, are gone while I
Have been a Traveller under open sky,
Much witnessing of change and chear,
Yet as I left I find them here!

The weary Sun betook himself to rest.
—Then issued Vesper from the fulgent West,
Outshining like a visible God
The glorious path in which he trod.
And now, ascending, after one dark hour,
And one night's diminution of her power,

Behold the mighty Moon! this way
She looks as if at them—but they
Regard not her:—oh better wrong and strife,
Better vain deeds or evil than such life!
The silent Heavens have goings on;
The stars have tasks—but these have none.

II

To the Cuckoo

O BLITHE New-comer! I have heard,
I hear thee and rejoice:
O Cuckoo! shall I call thee Bird,
Or but a wandering Voice?

While I am lying on the grass,
I hear thy restless shout:
From hill to hill it seems to pass,
About, and all about!

To me, no Babbler with a tale
Of sunshine and of flowers,
Thou tellest, Cuckoo, in the vale
Of visionary hours.

Thrice welcome, Darling of the Spring!
Even yet thou art to me
No Bird; but an invisible Thing,
A voice, a mystery.

The same whom in my School-boy days
I listen'd to; that Cry
Which made me look a thousand ways;
In bush, and tree, and sky.

To seek thee did I often rove
Through woods and on the green;
And thou wert still a hope, a love;
Still long'd for, never seen!

And I can listen to thee yet;
Can lie upon the plain
And listen, till I do beget
That golden time again.

O Blessed Bird! the earth we pace
Again appears to be
An unsubstantial, faery place;
That is fit home for Thee!

12

To a Butterfly

I'VE watch'd you now a full half hour,
Self-pois'd upon that yellow flower;
And, little Butterfly! indeed
I know not if you sleep, or feed.
How motionless! not frozen seas
More motionless! and then
What joys awaits you, when the breeze
Hath found you out among the trees,
And calls you forth again!

This plot of Orchard-ground is ours;
My trees they are, my Sister's flowers;
Stop here whenever you are weary,
And rest as in a sanctuary!
Come often to us, fear no wrong;
Sit near us on the bough!
We'll talk of sunshine and of song;
And summer days, when we were young,
Sweet childish days, that were as long
As twenty days are now!

13

'It is no Spirit who from Heaven hath flown'

It is no Spirit who from Heaven hath flown,
And is descending on his embassy;
Nor Traveller gone from Earth the Heavens to espy!
'Tis Hesperus—there he stands with glittering crown,
First admonition that the sun is down!
For yet it is broad day-light: clouds pass by;
A few are near him still—and now the sky,
He hath it to himself—'tis all his own.
O most ambitious Star! an inquest wrought
Within me when I recognized thy light;
A moment I was startled at the sight:
And, while I gazed, there came to me a thought
That I might step beyond my natural race
As thou seem'st now to do; might one day trace
Some ground not mine; and, strong her strength above,
My Soul, an Apparition in the place,
Tread there, with steps that no one shall reprove!

The Green Linnet

The May is come again:—how sweet
To sit upon my Orchard-seat!
And Birds and Flowers once more to greet,
    My last year's Friends together:
My thoughts they all by turns employ;
A whispering Leaf is now my joy,
And then a Bird will be the toy
    That doth my fancy tether.

One have I mark'd, the happiest Guest
In all this covert of the blest:
Hail to Thee, far above the rest
    In joy of voice and pinion,

Thou, Linnet, in thy green array,
Presiding Spirit here to-day,
Dost lead the revels of the May,
And this is thy dominion.

While Birds, and Butterflies, and Flowers
Make all one Band of Paramours,
Thou, ranging up and down the bowers,
Art sole in thy employment;
A Life, a Presence like the Air,
Scattering thy gladness without care,
Too bless'd with any one to pair,
Thyself thy own enjoyment.

Upon yon tuft of hazel trees,
That twinkle to the gusty breeze,
Behold him perch'd in ecstasies,
Yet seeming still to hover;
There! where the flutter of his wings
Upon his back and body flings
Shadows and sunny glimmerings,
That cover him all over.

While thus before my eyes he gleams,
A Brother of the Leaves he seems;
When in a moment forth he teems
His little song in gushes:
As if it pleas'd him to disdain
And mock the Form which he did feign,
While he was dancing with the train
Of Leaves among the bushes.

To a Young Lady

WHO HAD BEEN REPROACHED FOR TAKING LONG WALKS IN THE COUNTRY

Dear Child of Nature, let them rail!
—There is a nest in a green dale,
A harbour and a hold,

Where thou a Wife and Friend, shalt see
Thy own delightful days, and be
A light to young and old.

There, healthy as a Shepherd-boy,
As if thy heritage were joy,
And pleasure were thy trade,
Thou, while thy Babes around thee cling,
Shalt shew us how divine a thing
A Woman may be made.

Thy thoughts and feelings shall not die,
Nor leave thee, when grey hairs are nigh,
A melancholy slave;
But an old age, alive and bright,
And lovely as a Lapland night,
Shall lead thee to thy grave.

'By their floating Mill'

'—Pleasure is spread through the earth
In stray gifts to be claim'd by whoever shall find.'

By their floating Mill,
Which lies dead and still,
Behold yon Prisoners three!
The Miller with two Dames, on the breast of the Thames;
The Platform is small, but there's room for them all;
And they're dancing merrily.

From the shore come the notes
To their Mill where it floats,
To their House and their Mill tether'd fast!
To the small wooden isle where their work to beguile
They from morning to even take whatever is given;—
And many a blithe day they have past.

In sight of the Spires
All alive with the fires
Of the Sun going down to his rest,
In the broad open eye of the solitary sky,
They dance—there are three, as jocund as free,
While they dance on the calm river's breast.

Man and Maidens wheel,
They themselves make the Reel,
And their Music's a prey which they seize;
It plays not for them,—what matter! 'tis their's;
And if they had care it has scattered their cares,
While they dance, crying, 'Long as ye please!'

They dance not for me,
Yet mine is their glee!
Thus pleasure is spread through the earth
In stray gifts to be claim'd by whoever shall find;
Thus a rich loving-kindness, redundantly kind,
Moves all nature to gladness and mirth.

The Showers of the Spring
Rouze the Birds and they sing;
If the Wind do but stir for his proper delight,
Each Leaf, that and this, his neighbour will kiss,
Each Wave, one and t'other, speeds after his Brother;
They are happy, for that is their right!

Star Gazers

WHAT crowd is this? what have we here? we must not pass it by;
A Telescope upon its frame, and pointed to the sky:
Long is it as a Barber's Poll, or Mast of little Boat,
Some little Pleasure-Skiff, that doth on Thames's waters float.

The Show-man chuses well his place, 'tis Leicester's busy Square;
And he's as happy in his night, for the heavens are blue and fair;
Calm, though impatient is the Crowd; Each is ready with the fee,
And envies him that's looking—what an insight must it be!

Yet, Show-man, where can lie the cause? Shall thy Implement have blame,
A Boaster, that when he is tried, fails, and is put to shame?
Or is it good as others are, and be their eyes in fault?
Their eyes, or minds? or, finally, is this resplendent Vault?

Is nothing of that radiant pomp so good as we have here?
Or gives a thing but small delight that never can be dear?
The silver Moon with all her Vales, and Hills of mightiest fame,
Do they betray us when they're seen? and are they but a name?

Or is it rather that Conceit rapacious is and strong,
And bounty never yields so much but it seems to do her wrong?
Or is it, that when human Souls a journey long have had,
And are returned into themselves, they cannot but be sad?

Or must we be constrain'd to think that these Spectators rude,
Poor in estate, of manners base, men of the multitude,
Have souls which never yet have ris'n, and therefore prostrate lie?
No, no, this cannot be—Men thirst for power and majesty!

Does, then, a deep and earnest thought the blissful mind employ
Of him who gazes, or has gazed? a grave and steady joy,
That doth reject all shew of pride, admits no outward sign,
Because not of this noisy world, but silent and divine!

Whatever be the cause, 'tis sure that they who pry and pore
Seem to meet with little gain, seem less happy than before:
One after One they take their turns, nor have I one espied
That doth not slackly go away, as if dissatisfied.

Power of Music

An Orpheus! An Orpheus!—yes, Faith may grow bold,
And take to herself all the wonders of old;—
Near the stately Pantheon you'll meet with the same,
In the street that from Oxford hath borrowed its name.

His station is there;—and he works on the crowd.
He sways them with harmony merry and loud;
He fills with his power all their hearts to the brim—
Was aught ever heard like his fiddle and him!

What an eager assembly! what an empire is this!
The weary have life and the hungry have bliss;
The mourner is cheared, and the anxious have rest;
And the guilt-burthened Soul is no longer opprest.

As the Moon brightens round her the clouds of the night,
So he where he stands is a center of light;
It gleams on the face, there, of dusky-faced Jack,
And the pale-visaged Baker's, with basket on back.

That errand-bound 'Prentice was passing in haste—
What matter! he's caught—and his time runs to waste–
The News-man is stopped, though he stops on the fret,
And the half-breathless Lamp-lighter he's in the net!

The Porter sits down on the weight which he bore;
The Lass with her barrow wheels hither her store;—
If a Thief could be here he might pilfer at ease;
She sees the Musician, 'tis all that she sees!

He stands, back'd by the Wall;—he abates not his din;
His hat gives him vigour, with boons dropping in,
From the Old and the Young, from the Poorest; and there!
The one-pennied Boy has his penny to spare.

O blest are the Hearers and proud be the Hand
Of the pleasure it spreads through so thankful a Band;
I am glad for him, blind as he is!—all the while
If they speak 'tis to praise, and they praise with a smile.

That tall Man, a Giant in bulk and in height,
Not an inch of his body is free from delight;
Can he keep himself still, if he would? oh, not he!
The music stirs in him like wind through a tree.

There's a Cripple who leans on his Crutch; like a Tower
That long has lean'd forward, leans hour after hour!—
A Mother, whose Spirit in fetters is bound,
While she dandles the babe in her arms to the sound.

Now, Coaches and Chariots, roar on like a stream;
Here are twenty souls happy as Souls in a dream:
They are deaf to your murmurs—they care not for you,
Nor what ye are flying, or what ye pursue!

Incident

CHARACTERISTIC OF A FAVOURITE DOG, WHICH BELONGED TO A FRIEND OF THE AUTHOR

ON his morning rounds the Master
Goes to learn how all things fare;
Searches pasture after pasture,
Sheep and Cattle eyes with care;
And, for silence or for talk,
He hath Comrades in his walk;
Four Dogs, each pair of different breed,
Distinguished two for scent, and two for speed.

See, a Hare before him started!
—Off they fly in earnest chace;
Every Dog is eager-hearted,
All the four are in the race!
And the Hare whom they pursue
Hath an instinct what to do;
Her hope is near: no turn she makes;
But, like an arrow, to the River takes.

Deep the River was, and crusted
Thinly by a one night's frost;
But the nimble Hare hath trusted
To the ice, and safely crost;
She hath crost, and without heed
All are following at full speed,
When, lo! the ice, so thinly spread,
Breaks—and the Greyhound, DART, is over head!

Better fate have PRINCE and SWALLOW—
See them cleaving to the sport!
MUSIC has no heart to follow,
Little MUSIC, she stops short.
She hath neither wish nor heart,
Her's is now another part:
A loving Creature she, and brave!
And doth her best her struggling Friend to save.

From the brink her paws she stretches,
Very hands as you would say!
And afflicting moans she fetches,
As he breaks the ice away.
For herself she hath no fears,
Him alone she sees and hears,
Makes efforts and complainings; nor gives o'er
Until her Fellow sunk, and reappear'd no more.

Sonnet

ADMONITION
INTENDED MORE PARTICULARLY FOR THE PERUSAL OF THOSE WHO MAY HAVE HAPPENED TO BE ENAMOURED OF SOME BEAUTIFUL PLACE OF RETREAT, IN THE COUNTRY OF THE LAKES

Yes, there is holy pleasure in thine eye!
—The lovely Cottage in the guardian nook
Hath stirr'd thee deeply; with its own dear brook,
Its own small pasture, almost its own sky!
But covet not th' Abode—oh! do not sigh,
As many do, repining while they look,
Sighing a wish to tear from Nature's Book
This blissful leaf, with worst impiety.
Think what the home would be if it were thine,
Even thine, though few thy wants!—Roof, window, door,
The very flowers are sacred to the Poor,
The roses to the porch which they entwine:
Yea, all, that now enchants thee, from the day
On which it should be touch'd, would melt, and melt away

Sonnet
To Thomas Clarkson

ON THE FINAL PASSING OF THE BILL FOR THE ABOLITION OF THE SLAVE TRADE

Clarkson! it was an obstinate Hill to climb;
How toilsome, nay how dire it was, by Thee
Is known,—by none, perhaps, so feelingly;
But Thou, who, starting in thy fervent prime,

Didst first lead forth this pilgrimage sublime,
Hast heard the constant Voice its charge repeat,
Which, out of thy young heart's oracular seat,
First roused thee.—O true yoke-fellow of Time
With unabating effort, see, the palm
Is won, and by all Nations shall be worn!
The bloody Writing is for ever torn,
And Thou henceforth shalt have a good Man's calm,
A great Man's happiness; thy zeal shall find
Repose at length, firm Friend of human kind!

March, 1807

'Once in a lonely Hamlet I sojourn'd'

(This poem was later entitled *The Emigrant Mother*)

ONCE in a lonely Hamlet I sojourn'd
In which a Lady driv'n from France did dwell;
The big and lesser griefs, with which she mourn'd,
In friendship she to me would often tell.

This Lady, dwelling upon English ground,
Where she was childless, daily did repair
To a poor neighbouring Cottage; as I found,
For sake of a young Child whose home was there.

Once did I see her clasp the Child about,
And take it to herself; and I, next day,
Wish'd in my native tongue to fashion out
Such things as she unto this Child might say:
And thus, from what I knew, had heard, and guess'd,
My song the workings of her heart express'd.

'Dear Babe, thou Daughter of another,
One moment let me be thy Mother!
An Infant's face and looks are thine;
And sure a Mother's heart is mine:
Thy own dear Mother's far away,
At labour in the harvest-field:
Thy little Sister is at play;—
What warmth, what comfort would it yield

To my poor heart, if Thou wouldst be
One little hour a child to me!

Across the waters I am come,
And I have left a Babe at home:
A long, long way of land and sea!
Come to me—I'm no enemy:
I am the same who at thy side
Sate yesterday, and made a nest
For thee, sweet Baby!—thou hast tried,
Thou know'st, the pillow of my breast:
Good, good art thou; alas! to me
Far more than I can be to thee.

Here little Darling dost thou lie;
An Infant Thou, a Mother I!
Mine wilt thou be, thou hast no fears;
Mine art thou—spite of these my tears.
Alas! before I left the spot,
My Baby and its dwelling-place;
The Nurse said to me, 'Tears should not
Be shed upon an Infant's face,
It was unlucky'—no, no, no;
No truth is in them who say so!

My own dear Little-one will sigh,
Sweet Babe! and they will let him die.
'He pines,' they'll say, 'it is his doom,
And you may see his hour is come.'
Oh! had he but thy chearful smiles,
Limbs stout as thine, and lips as gay,
Thy looks, thy cunning, and thy wiles,
And countenance like a summer's day,
They would have hopes of him—and then
I should behold his face again!

'Tis gone—forgotten—let me do
My best—there was a smile or two,
I can remember them, I see
The smiles, worth all the world to me.

Dear Baby! I must lay thee down;
Thou troublest me with strange alarms;
Smiles hast Thou, sweet ones of thy own;
I cannot keep thee in my arms,
For they confound me: as it is,
I have forgot those smiles of his.

Oh! how I love thee! we will stay
Together here this one half day.
My Sister's Child, who bears my name,
From France across the Ocean came;
She with her Mother cross'd the sea;
The Babe and Mother near me dwell:
My Darling, she is not to me
What thou art! though I love her well:
Rest, little Stranger, rest thee here;
Never was any Child more dear!

—I cannot help it—ill intent
I've none, my pretty Innocent!
I weep—I know they do thee wrong,
These tears—and my poor idle tongue.
Oh what a kiss was that! my cheek
How cold it is! but thou art good;
Thine eyes are on me—they would speak,
I think, to help me if they could.
Blessings upon that quiet face,
My heart again is in its place!

While thou art mine, my little Love,
This cannot be a sorrowful grove;
Contentment, hope, and Mother's glee,
I seem to find them all in thee:
Here's grass to play with, here are flowers;
I'll call thee by my Darling's name;
Thou hast, I think, a look of ours,
Thy features seem to me the same;
His little Sister thou shalt be;
And, when once more my home I see,
I'll tell him many tales of Thee.'

A Complaint

THERE is a change—and I am poor;
Your Love hath been, nor long ago,
A Fountain at my fond Heart's door,
Whose only business was to flow;
And flow it did; not taking heed
Of its own bounty, or my need.

What happy moments did I count!
Bless'd was I then all bliss above!
Now, for this consecrated Fount
Of murmuring, sparkling, living love,
What have I? shall I dare to tell?
A comfortless, and hidden WELL.

A Well of love—it may be deep—
I trust it is, and never dry:
What matter? if the Waters sleep
In silence and obscurity.
—Such change, and at the very door
Of my fond Heart, hath made me poor.

'I am not One who much or oft delight'

(These four sonnets were later entitled *Personal Talk*)

I AM not One who much or oft delight
To season my fireside with personal talk,
About Friends, who live within an easy walk,
Or Neighbours, daily, weekly, in my sight:
And, for my chance-acquaintance, Ladies bright,
Sons, Mothers, Maidens withering on the stalk,
These all wear out of me, like Forms, with chalk
Painted on rich men's floors, for one feast-night.

Better than such discourse doth silence long,
Long, barren silence, square with my desire;
To sit without emotion, hope, or aim,
By my half-kitchen my half-parlour fire,
And listen to the flapping of the flame,
Or kettle, whispering it's faint undersong.

'Yet life,' you say, 'is life; we have seen and see,
And with a living pleasure we describe;
And fits of sprightly malice do but bribe
The languid mind into activity.
Sound sense, and love itself, and mirth and glee,
Are foster'd by the comment and the gibe.'
Even be it so: yet still among your tribe,
Our daily world's true Worldlings, rank not me!
Children are blest, and powerful; their world lies
More justly balanced; partly at their feet,
And part far from them:—sweetest melodies
Are those that are by distance made more sweet;
Whose mind is but the mind of his own eyes,
He is a Slave; the meanest we can meet!

Wings have we, and as far as we can go
We may find pleasure: wilderness and wood,
Blank ocean and mere sky, support that mood
Which with the lofty sanctifies the low:
Dreams, books, are each a world; and books, we know,
Are a substantial world, both pure and good:
Round these, with tendrils strong as flesh and blood,
Our pastime and our happiness will grow.
There do I find a never-failing store
Of personal themes, and such as I love best;
Matter wherein right voluble I am:
Two will I mention, dearer than the rest;
The gentle Lady, married to the Moor;
And heavenly Una with her milk-white Lamb.

Nor can I not believe but that hereby
Great gains are mine: for thus I live remote
From evil-speaking; rancour, never sought,
Comes to me not; malignant truth, or lie.

Hence have I genial seasons, hence have I
Smooth passions, smooth discourse, and joyous thought:
And thus from day to day my little Boat
Rocks in its harbour, lodging peaceably.
Blessings be with them, and eternal praise,
Who gave us nobler loves, and nobler cares,
The Poets, who on earth have made us Heirs
Of truth and pure delight by heavenly lays!
Oh! might my name be numbered among theirs,
Then gladly would I end my mortal days.

'Yes! full surely 'twas the Echo'

Yes! full surely 'twas the Echo,
Solitary, clear, profound,
Answering to Thee, shouting Cuckoo!
Giving to thee Sound for Sound.

Whence the Voice? from air or earth?
This the Cuckoo cannot tell;
But a startling sound had birth,
As the Bird must know full well;

Like the voice through earth and sky
By the restless Cuckoo sent;
Like her ordinary cry,
Like—but oh how different!

Hears not also mortal Life?
Hear not we, unthinking Creatures!
Slaves of Folly, Love, or Strife,
Voices of two different Natures?

Have not We too? Yes we have
Answers, and we know not whence;
Echoes from beyond the grave,
Recogniz'd intelligence!

Such within ourselves we hear
Oft-times, ours though sent from far;
Listen, ponder, hold them dear;
For of God, of God they are!

To the Spade of a Friend

(AN AGRICULTURIST)

COMPOSED WHILE WE WERE LABOURING TOGETHER IN HIS PLEASURE-GROUND

SPADE! with which Wilkinson hath till'd his Lands,
And shap'd these pleasant walks by Emont's side,
Thou art a tool of honour in my hands;
I press thee through the yielding soil with pride.

Rare Master has it been thy lot to know;
Long hast Thou serv'd a Man to reason true;
Whose life combines the best of high and low,
The toiling many and the resting few;

Health, quiet, meekness, ardour, hope secure,
And industry of body and of mind;
And elegant enjoyments, that are pure
As Nature is; too pure to be refined.

Here often hast Thou heard the Poet sing
In concord with his River murmuring by;
Or in some silent field, while timid Spring
Is yet uncheer'd by other minstrelsy.

Who shall inherit Thee when Death hath laid
Low in the darksome Cell thine own dear Lord?
That Man will have a trophy, humble Spade!
More noble than the noblest Warrior's sword.

If he be One that feels, with skill to part
False praise from true, or greater from the less,
Thee will he welcome to his hand and heart,
Thou monument of peaceful happiness!

With Thee he will not dread a toilsome day,
His powerful Servant, his inspiring Mate!
And, when thou art past service, worn away,
Thee a surviving soul shall consecrate.

Dorothy Wordsworth (1771–1855), Wordsworth's sister, portrayed by S. Crosthwaite. Dorothy and William had many common interests, and she devoted her life to looking after him.
By courtesy of Dove Cottage Trust, Grasmere, Ambleside

Rydal Mount, Grasmere, Ambleside, Wordsworth's home for the last 33 years of his life and where he died in 1850. It is now a museum. By courtesy of the English Tourist Board, London

His thrift thy uselessness will never scorn;
An *Heir-loom* in his cottage wilt thou be:—
High will he hang thee up, and will adorn
His rustic chimney with the last of Thee!

Song

AT THE FEAST OF BROUGHAM CASTLE, UPON THE RESTORATION OF LORD CLIFFORD, THE SHEPHERD, TO THE ESTATES AND HONOURS OF HIS ANCESTORS

HIGH in the breathless Hall the Minstrel sate,
And Emont's murmur mingled with the Song.—
The words of ancient time I thus translate,
A festal Strain that hath been silent long.

'From Town to Town, from Tower to Tower,
The Red Rose is a gladsome Flower.
Her thirty years of Winter past,
The Red Rose is revived at last;

She lifts her head for endless spring,
For everlasting blossoming!
Both Roses flourish, Red and White.
In love and sisterly delight
The two that were at strife are blended,
And all old sorrows now are ended.—
Joy! joy to both! but most to her
Who is the Flower of Lancaster!
Behold her how She smiles to day
On this great throng, this bright array!
Fair greeting doth she send to all
From every corner of the Hall;
But, chiefly, from above the Board
Where sits in state our rightful Lord,
A Clifford to his own restored.

They came with banner, spear, and shield;
And it was proved in Bosworth-field.
Not long the Avenger was withstood,
Earth help'd him with the cry of blood:
St. George was for us, and the might
Of blessed Angles crown'd the right.

Loud voice the Land hath utter'd forth,
We loudest in the faithful North:
Our Fields rejoice, our Mountains ring,
Our Streams proclaim a welcoming;
Our Strong-abodes and Castles see
The glory of their loyalty.
How glad is Skipton at this hour
Though she is but a lonely Tower!
Silent, deserted of her best,
Without an Inmate or a Guest,
Knight, Squire, or Yeoman, Page, or Groom;
We have them at the Feast of Brough'm.
How glad Pendragon though the sleep
Of years be on her!—She shall reap
A taste of this great pleasure, viewing
As in a dream her own renewing.
Rejoiced is Brough, right glad I deem
Beside her little humble Stream;
And she that keepeth watch and ward
Her statelier Eden's course to guard;
They both are happy at this hour,
Though each is but a lonely Tower:—
But here is perfect joy and pride
For one fair House by Emont's side,
This day distinguished without peer
To see her Master and to cheer;
Him, and his Lady Mother dear.

Oh! it was a time forlorn
When the Fatherless was born—
Give her wings that she may fly,
Or she sees her Infant die!
Swords that are with slaughter wild
Hunt the Mother and the Child.
Who will take them from the light?
—Yonder is a Man in sight—
Yonder is a House—but where?
No, they must not enter there.
To the Caves, and to the Brooks,
To the Clouds of Heaven she looks;
She is speechless, but her eyes
Pray in ghostly agonies.

Blissful Mary, Mother mild,
Maid and Mother undefiled,
Save a Mother and her Child!

Now Who is he that bounds with joy
On Carrock's side, a Shepherd Boy?
No thoughts hath he but thoughts that pass
Light as the wind along the grass.
Can this be He who hither came
In secret, like a smothered flame?
O'er whom such thankful tears were shed
For shelter, and a poor Man's bread?
God loves the Child; and God hath will'd
That those dear words should be fulfill'd,
The Lady's words, when forc'd away,
The last she to her Babe did say,
'My own, my own, thy Fellow-guest
I may not be; but rest thee, rest,
For lowly Shepherd's life is best!'

Alas! when evil men are strong
No life is good, no pleasure long.
The Boy must part from Mosedale's Groves,
And leave Blencathara's rugged Coves,
And quit the Flowers that Summer brings
To Glenderamakin's lofty springs;
Must vanish, and his careless cheer
Be turned to heaviness and fear.
—Give Sir Lancelot Threlkeld praise!
Hear it, good Man, old in days!
Thou Tree of covert and of rest
For this young Bird that is distrest,
Among thy branches safe he lay,
And he was free to sport and play,
When Falcons were abroad for prey.

A recreant Harp, that sings of fear
And heaviness in Clifford's ear!
I said, when evil Men are strong,
No life is good, no pleasure long,
A weak and cowardly untruth!
Our Clifford was a happy Youth,

And thankful through a weary time,
That brought him up to manhood's prime.

—Again he wanders forth at will,
And tends a Flock from hill to hill:
His garb is humble; ne'er was seen
Such garb with such a noble mien;
Among the Shepherd-grooms no Mate
Hath he, a Child of strength and state!
Yet acks not friends for solemn glee,
And a chearful company,
That learn'd of him submissive ways;
And comforted his private days.
To his side the Fallow-deer
Came, and rested without fear;
The Eagle, Lord of land and sea,
Stoop'd down to pay him fealty;
And both the undying Fish that swim
Through Bowscale-Tarn did wait on him,
The pair were Servants of his eye
In their immortality,
They moved about in open sight,
To and fro, for his delight.
He knew the Rocks which Angels haunt
On the Mountains visitant;
He hath kenn'd them taking wing:
And the Caves where Faeries sing
He hath entered; and been told
By Voices how Men liv'd of old.
Among the Heavens his eye can see
Face of thing that is to be;
And, if Men report him right,
He can whisper words of might.
—Now another day is come,
Fitter hope, and nobler doom:
He hath thrown aside his Crook,
And hath buried deep his Book;
Armour rusting in his Halls
On the blood of Clifford calls;—
'Quell the Scot,' exclaims the Lance,
Bear me to the heart of France,
Is the longing of the Shield—

Tell thy name, thou trembling Field;
Field of death, where'er thou be,
Groan thou with our victory!
Happy day, and mighty hour,
When our Shepherd, in his power,
Mail'd and hors'd, with lance and sword,
To his Ancestors restored,
Like a reappearing Star,
Like a glory from afar,
First shall head the Flock of War!'

Alas! the fervent Harper did not know
That for a tranquil Soul the Lay was framed,
Who, long compell'd in humble walks to go,
Was softened into feeling, sooth'd, and tamed.

Love had he found in huts where poor Men lie,
His daily Teachers had been Woods and Rills,
The silence that is in the starry sky,
The sleep that is among the lonely hills.

In him the savage Virtue of the Race,
Revenge, and all ferocious thoughts were dead:
Nor did he change; but kept in lofty place
The wisdom which adversity had bred.

Glad were the Vales, and every cottage hearth;
The Shepherd Lord was honour'd more and more:
And, ages after he was laid in earth,
'The Good Lord Clifford' was the name he bore.

Lines

COMPOSED AT GRASMERE, DURING A WALK, ONE EVENING, AFTER A STORMY DAY, THE AUTHOR HAVING JUST READ IN A NEWSPAPER THAT THE DISSOLUTION OF MR. FOX WAS HOURLY EXPECTED.

LOUD is the Vale! the Voice is up
With which she speaks when storms are gone,
A mighty Unison of streams!
Of all her Voices, One!

Loud is the Vale;—this inland Depth
In peace is roaring like the Sea;
Yon Star upon the mountain-top
Is listening quietly.

Sad was I, ev'n to pain depress'd,
Importunate and heavy load!
The Comforter hath found me here,
Upon this lonely road;

And many thousands now are sad,
Wait the fulfilment of their fear;
For He must die who is their Stay,
Their Glory disappear.

A Power is passing from the earth
To breathless Nature's dark abyss;
But when the Mighty pass away
What is it more than this,

That Man, who is from God sent forth,
Doth yet again to God return?—
Such ebb and flow must ever be,
Then wherefore should we mourn?

Elegiac Stanzas

SUGGESTED BY A PICTURE OF PEELE CASTLE, IN A STORM, PAINTED BY SIR GEORGE BEAUMONT

I WAS thy Neighbour once, thou rugged Pile!
Four summer weeks I dwelt in sight of thee:
I saw thee every day; and all the while
Thy Form was sleeping on a glassy sea.

So pure the sky, so quiet was the air!
So like, so very like, was day to day!
Whene'er I look'd, thy Image still was there;
It trembled, but it never pass'd away.

How perfect was the calm! it seem'd no sleep;
No mood, which season takes away, or brings:
I could have fancied that the mighty Deep
Was even the gentlest of all gentle Things.

Ah! THEN, if mine had been the Painter's hand,
To express what then I saw; and add the gleam,
The light that never was, on sea or land,
The consecration, and the Poet's dream;

I would have planted thee, thou hoary Pile!
Amid a world how different from this!
Beside a sea that could not cease to smile;
On tranquil land, beneath a sky of bliss:

Thou shouldst have seem'd a treasure-house, a mine
Of peaceful years; a chronicle of heaven:—
Of all the sunbeams that did ever shine
The very sweetest had to thee been given.

A Picture had it been of lasting ease,
Elysian quiet, without toil or strife;
No motion but the moving tide, a breeze,
Or merely silent Nature's breathing life.

Such, in the fond delusion of my heart,
Such Picture would I at that time have made:
And seen the soul of truth in every part;
A faith, a trust, that could not be betray'd.

So once it would have been,—'tis so no more;
I have submitted to a new controul:
A power is gone, which nothing can restore;
A deep distress hath humaniz'd my Soul.

Not for a moment could I now behold
A smiling sea and be what I have been:
The feeling of my loss will ne'er be old;
This, which I know, I speak with mind serene.

Then, Beaumont, Friend! who would have been the
 Friend,
If he had lived, of Him whom I deplore,
This Work of thine I blame not, but commend;
This sea in anger, and that dismal shore.

Oh 'tis a passionate Work!—yet wise and well;
Well chosen is the spirit that is here;
That Hulk which labours in the deadly swell,
This rueful sky, this pageantry of fear!

And this huge Castle, standing here sublime,
I love to see the look with which it braves,
Cased in the unfeeling armour of old time,
The light'ning, the fierce wind, and trampling waves.

Farewell, farewell the Heart that lives alone,
Hous'd in a dream, at distance from the Kind!
Such happiness, wherever it be known,
Is to be pitied; for 'tis surely blind.

But welcome fortitude, and patient chear,
And frequent sights of what is to be born!
Such sights, or worse, as are before me here.—
Not without hope we suffer and we mourn.

Ode

Paulo Majora Canamus

There was a time when meadow, grove, and stream,
The earth, and every common sight,
 To me did seem
 Apparell'd in celestial light,
The glory and the freshness of a dream.
It is not now as it has been of yore;—
 Turn wheresoe'er I may,
 By night or day,
The things which I have seen I now can see no more.

The Rainbow comes and goes,
And lovely is the Rose,
The Moon doth with delight
Look round her when the heavens are bare;
Waters on a starry night
Are beautiful and fair;
The sunshine is a glorious birth;
But yet I know, where'er I go,
That there hath pass'd away a glory from the earth.

Now, while the Birds thus sing a joyous song,
And while the young Lambs bound
As to the tabor's sound,
To me alone there came a thought of grief:
A timely utterance gave that thought relief,
And I again am strong.
The Cataracts blow their trumpets from the steep,
No more shall grief of mine the season wrong;
I hear the Echoes through the mountains throng,
The Winds come to me from the fields of sleep,
And all the earth is gay,
Land and sea
Give themselves up to jollity,
And with the heart of May
Doth every Beast keep holiday,
Thou Child of Joy
Shout round me, let me hear thy shouts, thou happy
Shepherd Boy!

Ye blessed Creatures, I have heard the call
Ye to each other make; I see
The heavens laugh with you in your jubilee;
My heart is at your festival,
My head hath it's coronal,
The fullness of your bliss, I feel—I feel it all.
Oh evil day! if I were sullen
While the Earth herself is adorning,
This sweet May-morning,
And the Children are pulling,
On every side,
In a thousand vallies far and wide,

Fresh flowers; while the sun shines warm,
And the Babe leaps up on his mother's arm:—
I hear, I hear, with joy I hear!
—But there's a Tree, of many one,
A single Field which I have look'd upon,
Both of them speak of something that is gone:
The Pansy at my feet
Doth the same tale repeat:
Whither is fled the visionary gleam?
Where is it now, the glory and the dream?

Our birth is but a sleep and a forgetting:
The Soul that rises with us, our life's Star,
Hath had elsewhere it's setting,
And cometh from afar:
Not in entire forgetfulness,
And not in utter nakedness,
But trailing clouds of glory do we come
From God, who is our home:
Heaven lies about us in our infancy!
Shades of the prison-house begin to close
Upon the growing Boy,
But He beholds the light, and whence it flows,
He sees it in his joy;
The Youth, who daily farther from the East
Must travel, still is Nature's Priest,
And by the vision splendid
Is on his way attended;
At length the Man perceives it die away,
And fade into the light of common day.

Earth fills her lap with pleasures of her own;
Yearnings she hath in her own natural kind,
And, even with something of a Mother's mind,
And no unworthy aim,
The homely Nurse doth all she can
To make her Foster-child, her Inmate Man,
Forget the glories he hath known,
And that imperial palace whence he came.

Behold the Child among his new-born blisses,
A four year's Darling of a pigmy size!
See, where mid work of his own hand he lies,
Fretted by sallies of his Mother's kisses,
With light upon him from his Father's eyes!
See, at his feet, some little plan or chart,
Some fragment from his dream of human life,
Shap'd by himself with newly-learned art;
    A wedding or a festival,
    A mourning or a funeral;
        And this hath now his heart,
    And unto this he frames his song:
        Then will he fit his tongue
To dialogues of business, love, or strife;
    But it will not be long
    Ere this be thrown aside,
    And with new joy and pride
The little Actor cons another part,
Filling from time to time his 'humourous stage'
With all the Persons, down to palsied Age,
That Life brings with her in her Equipage;
    As if his whole vocation
    Were endless imitation.

Thou, whose exterior semblance doth belie
    Thy Soul's immensity;
Thou best Philosopher, who yet dost keep
Thy heritage, thou Eye among the blind,
That, deaf and silent, read'st the eternal deep,
Haunted for ever by the eternal mind,—
    Mighty Prophet! Seer blest!
    On whom those truths do rest,
Which we are toiling all our lives to find;
Thou, over whom thy Immortality
Broods like the Day, a Master o'er a Slave,
A Presence which is not to be put by;
        To whom the grave
Is but a lonely bed without the sense or sight
    Of day or the warm light,
A place of thought where we in waiting lie;
Thou little Child, yet glorious in the might
Of untam'd pleasures, on thy Being's height,

Why with such earnest pains dost thou provoke
The Years to bring the inevitable yoke,
Thus blindly with thy blessedness at strife?
Full soon thy Soul shall have her earthly freight,
And custom lie upon thee with a weight,
Heavy as frost, and deep almost as life!

O joy! that in our embers
Is something that doth live,
That nature yet remembers
What was so fugitive!
The thought of our past years in me doth breed
Perpetual benedictions: not indeed
For that which is most worthy to be blest;
Delight and liberty, the simple creed
Of Childhood, whether fluttering or at rest,
With new-born hope for ever in his breast:—
Not for these I raise
The song of thanks and praise;
But for those obstinate questionings
Of sense and outward things,
Fallings from us, vanishings;
Blank misgivings of a Creature
Moving about in worlds not realiz'd,
High instincts, before which our mortal Nature
Did tremble like a guilty Thing surpriz'd:
But for those first affections,
Those shadowy recollections,
Which, be they what they may,
Are yet the fountain light of all our day,
Are yet a master light of all our seeing;
Uphold us, cherish us, and make
Our noisy years seem moments in the being
Of the eternal Silence: truths that wake,
To perish never;
Which neither listlessness, nor mad endeavour,
Nor Man nor Boy,
Nor all that is at enmity with joy,
Can utterly abolish or destroy!
Hence, in a season of calm weather,
Though inland far we be,
Our Souls have sight of that immortal sea

Which brought us hither,
Can in a moment travel thither,
And see the Children sport upon the shore,
And hear the mighty waters rolling evermore.

Then, sing ye Birds, sing, sing a joyous song!
And let the young Lambs bound
As to the tabor's sound!
We in thought will join your throng,
Ye that pipe and ye that play,
Ye that through your hearts to day
Feel the gladness of the May!
What though the radiance which was once so bright
Be now for ever taken from my sight,
Though nothing can bring back the hour
Of splendour in the grass, of glory in the flower;
We will grieve not, rather find
Strength in what remains behind,
In the primal sympathy
Which having been must ever be,
In the soothing thoughts that spring
Out of human suffering,
In the faith that looks through death,
In years that bring the philosophic mind.

And oh ye Fountains, Meadows, Hills, and Groves,
Think not of any severing of our loves!
Yet in my heart of hearts I feel your might;
I only have relinquish'd one delight
To live beneath your more habitual sway.
I love the Brooks which down their channels fret,
Even more than when I tripp'd lightly as they;
The innocent brightness of a new-born Day
Is lovely yet;
The Clouds that gather round the setting sun
Do take a sober colouring from an eye
That hath kept watch o'er man's mortality;
Another race hath been, and other palms are won.
Thanks to the human heart by which we live,
Thanks to its tenderness, its joys, and fears,
To me the meanest flower that blows can give
Thoughts that do often lie too deep for tears.

from

THE EXCURSION, 1814

THE EXCURSION, 1814

The Wanderer

ARGUMENT

A SUMMER forenoon.—The Author reaches a ruined Cottage upon a Common, and there meets with a revered Friend, the Wanderer, of whose education and course of life he gives an account.—The Wanderer, while resting under the shade of the Trees that surround the Cottage, relates the History of its last Inhabitant.

'TWAS summer, and the sun had mounted high:
Southward the landscape indistinctly glared
Through a pale steam; but all the northern downs,
In clearest air ascending, showed far off
A surface dappled o'er with shadows flung
From brooding clouds; shadows that lay in spots
Determined and unmoved, with steady beams
Of bright and pleasant sunshine interposed;
To him most pleasant who on soft cool moss
Extends his careless limbs along the front
Of some huge cave, whose rocky ceiling casts
A twilight of its own, an ample shade,
Where the wren warbles, while the dreaming man,
Half conscious of the soothing melody,
With side-long eye looks out upon the scene,
By power of that impending covert thrown
To finer distance. Mine was at that hour
Far other lot, yet with good hope that soon
Under a shade as grateful I should find
Rest, and be welcomed there to livelier joy.
Across a bare wide Common I was toiling
With languid steps that by the slippery turn
Were baffled; nor could my weak arm disperse
The host of insects gathering round my face,
And ever with me as I paced along.

Upon that open moorland stood a grove,
The wished-for port to which my course was bound.
Thither I came, and there, amid the gloom
Spread by a brotherhood of lofty elms,

Appeared a roofless Hut; four naked walls
That stared upon each other!—I looked round,
And to my wish and to my hope espied
The Friend I sought; a Man of reverend age,
But stout and hale, for travel unimpaired.
There was he seen upon the cottage-bench,
Recumbent in the shade, as if asleep;
An iron-pointed staff lay at his side.

Him had I marked the day before—alone
And stationed in the public way, with face
Turned toward the sun then setting, while that staff
Afforded, to the figure of the man
Detained for contemplation or repose,
Graceful support; his countenance as he stood
Was hidden from my view, and he remained
Unrecognised; but, stricken by the sight,
With slackened footsteps I advanced, and soon
A glad congratulation we exchanged
At such unthought-of meeting.—For the night
We parted, nothing willingly; and now
He by appointment waited for me here,
Under the covert of these clustering elms.

We were tried Friends: amid a pleasant vale,
In the antique market-village where was passed
My school-time, an apartment he had owned,
To which at intervals the Wanderer drew,
And found a kind of home or harbour there.
He loved me; from a swarm of rosy boys
Singled out me, as he in sport would say,
For my grave looks, too thoughtful for my years.
As I grew up, it was my best delight
To be his chosen comrade. Many a time,
On holidays, we rambled through the woods:
We sate—we walked; he pleased me with report
Of things which he had seen; and often touched
Abstrusest matter, reasonings of the mind
Turned inward; or at my request would sing
Old songs, the product of his native hills;
A skilful distribution of sweet sounds,
Feeding the soul, and eagerly imbibed

As cool refreshing water, by the care
Of the industrious husbandman, diffused
Through a parched meadow-ground, in time of drought.
Still deeper welcome found his pure discourse:
How precious when in riper days I learned
To weigh with care his words, and to rejoice
In the plain presence of his dignity!

Oh! many are the Poets that are sown
By Nature; men endowed with highest gifts,
The vision and the faculty divine;
Yet wanting the accomplishments of verse,
(Which, in the docile season of their youth,
It was denied them to acquire, through lack
Of culture and the inspiring aid of books,
Or haply by a temper too severe,
Or a nice backwardness afraid of shame)
Nor having e'er, as life advanced, been led
By circumstance to take unto the height
The measure of themselves, these favoured Beings,
All but a scattered few, live out their time,
Husbanding that which they possess within,
And go to the grave, unthought of. Strongest minds
Are often those of whom the noisy world
Hears least; else surely this Man had not left
His graces unrevealed and unproclaimed.
But, as the mind was filled with inward light,
So not without distinction had he lived,
Beloved and honoured—far as he was known.
And some small portion of his eloquent speech,
And something that may serve to set in view
The feeling pleasures of his loneliness,
His observations, and the thoughts his mind
Had dealt with—I will here record in verse;
Which, if with truth it correspond, and sink
Or rise as venerable Nature leads
The high and tender Muses shall accept
With gracious smile, deliberately pleased,
And listening Time reward with sacred praise.

Among the hills of Athol he was born;
Where, on a small hereditary farm,

An unproductive slip of rugged ground,
His Parents, with their numerous offspring, dwelt;
A virtuous household, though exceeding poor!
Pure livers were they all, austere and grave,
And fearing God; the very children taught
Stern self-respect, a reverence for God's word,
And an habitual piety, maintained
With strictness scarcely known on English ground.

From his sixth year, the Boy of whom I speak,
In summer, tended cattle on the hills;
But, through the inclement and the perilous days
Of long-continuing winter, he repaired,
Equipped with satchel, to a school, that stood
Sole building on a mountain's dreary edge,
Remote from view of city spire, or sound
Of minster clock! From that bleak tenement
He, many an evening, to his distant home
In solitude returning, saw the hills
Grow larger in the darkness; all alone
Beheld the stars come out above his head,
And travelled through the wood, with no one near
To whom he might confess the things he saw.

So the foundations of his mind were laid.
In such communion, not from terror free,
While yet a child, and long before his time,
Had he perceived the presence and the power
Of greatness; and deep feelings had impressed
So vividly great objects that they lay
Upon his mind like substances, whose presence
Perplexed the bodily sense. He had received
A precious gift; for, as he grew in years,
With these impressions would he still compare
All his remembrances, thoughts, shapes, and forms;
And, being still unsatisfied with aught
Of dimmer character, he thence attained
An active power to fasten images
Upon his brain; and on their pictured lines
Intensely brooded, even till they acquired
The liveliness of dreams. Nor did he fail,
While yet a child, with a child's eagerness

Incessantly to turn his ear and eye
On all things which the moving seasons brought
To feed such appetite—nor this alone
Appeased his yearning:—in the after-day
Of boyhood, many an hour in caves forlorn,
And 'mid the hollow depths of naked crags
He sate, and even in their fixed lineaments,
Or from the power of a peculiar eye,
Or by creative feeling overborne,
Or by predominance of thought oppressed,
Even in their fixed and steady lineaments
He traced an ebbing and a flowing mind,
Expression ever varying!
Thus informed,
He had small need of books; for many a tale
Traditionary round the mountains hung,
And many a legend, peopling the dark woods,
Nourished Imagination in her growth,
And gave the Mind that apprehensive power
By which she is made quick to recognise
The moral properties and scope of things.
But eagerly he read, and read again
Whate'er the minister's old shelf supplied;
The life and death of martyrs, who sustained,
With will inflexible, those fearful pangs
Triumphantly displayed in records left
Of persecution, and the Covenant—times
Whose echo rings through Scotland to this hour!
And there, by lucky hap, had been preserved
A straggling volume, torn and incomplete,
That left half-told the preternatural tale,
Romance of giants, chronicle of fiends,
Profuse in garniture of wooden cuts
Strange and uncouth; dire faces, figures dire,
Sharp-kneed, sharp-elbowed, and lean-ankled too,
With long and ghostly shanks—forms which once seen
Could never be forgotten!
In his heart,
Where Fear sate thus, a cherished visitant,
Was wanting yet the pure delight of love
By sound diffused, or by the breathing air,
Or by the silent looks of happy things

Or flowing from the universal face
Of earth and sky. But he had felt the power
Of Nature, and already was prepared,
By his intense conceptions, to receive
Deeply the lesson deep of love which he,
Whom Nature, by whatever means, has taught
To feel intensely, cannot but receive.

Such was the Boy—but for the growing Youth
What soul was his, when, from the naked top
Of some bold headland, he beheld the sun
Rise up, and bathe the world in light! He looked—
Ocean and earth, the solid frame of earth
And ocean's liquid mass, in gladness lay
Beneath him:—Far and wide the clouds were touched,
And in their silent faces could he read
Unutterable love. Sound needed none,
Nor any voice of joy; his spirit drank
The spectacle: sensation, soul, and form,
All melted into him; they swallowed up
His animal being; in them did he live,
And by them did he live; they were his life.
In such access of mind, in such high hour
Of visitation from the living God,
Thought was not; in enjoyment it expired.
No thanks he breathed, he proffered no request;
Rapt into still communion that transcends
The imperfect offices of prayer and praise,
His mind was a thanksgiving to the power
That made him; it was blessedness and love!

A Herdsman on the lonely mountain-tops,
Such intercourse was his, and in this sort
Was his existence oftentimes *possessed.*
O then how beautiful, how bright, appeared
The written promise! Early had he learned
To reverence the volume that displays
The mystery, the life which cannot die;
But in the mountains did he *feel* his faith.
All things, responsive to the writing, there
Breathed immortality, revolving life,
And greatness still revolving; infinite:

There littleness was not; the least of things
Seemed infinite; and there his spirit shaped
Her prospects, nor did he believe,—he *saw*.
What wonder if his being thus became
Sublime and comprehensive! Low desires,
Low thoughts had there no place; yet was his heart
Lowly; for he was meek in gratitude,
Oft as he called those ecstasies to mind,
And whence they flowed; and from them he acquired
Wisdom, which works thro' patience; thence he learned
In oft-recurring hours of sober thought
To look on Nature with a humble heart,
Self-questioned where it did not understand,
And with a superstitious eye of love.

So passed the time; yet to the nearest town
He duly went with what small overplus
His earnings might supply, and brought away
The book that most had tempted his desires
While at the stall he read. Among the hills
He gazed upon that mighty orb of song,
The divine Milton. Lore of different kind,
The annual savings of a toilsome life,
His School-master supplied; books that explain
The purer elements of truth involved
In lines and numbers, and, by charm severe,
(Especially perceived where nature droops
And feeling is suppressed) preserve the mind
Busy in solitude and poverty.
These occupations oftentimes deceived
The listless hours, while in the hollow vale,
Hollow and green, he lay on the green turf
In pensive idleness. What could he do,
Thus daily thirsting, in that lonesome life,
With blind endeavours? Yet, still uppermost,
Nature was at his heart as if he felt,
Though yet he knew not how, a wasting power
In all things that from her sweet influence
Might tend to wean him. Therefore with her hues,
Her forms, and with the spirit of her forms,
He clothed the nakedness of austere truth.
While yet he lingered in the rudiments

Of science, and among her simplest laws,
His triangles—they were the stars of heaven,
The silent stars! Oft did he take delight
To measure the altitude of some tall crag
That is the eagle's birthplace, or some peak
Familiar with forgotten years, that shows
Inscribed upon its visionary sides,
The history of many a winter storm,
Or obscure records of the path of fire.

And thus before his eighteenth year was told,
Accumulated feelings pressed his heart
With still increasing weight; he was o'erpowered
By Nature; by the turbulence subdued
Of his own mind; by mystery and hope,
And the first virgin passion of a soul
Communing with the glorious universe.
Full often wished he that the winds might rage
When they were silent: far more fondly now
Than in his earlier season did he love
Tempestuous nights—the conflict and the sounds
That live in darkness. From his intellect
And from the stillness of abstracted thought
He asked repose; and, failing oft to win
The peace required, he scanned the laws of light
Amid the roar of torrents, where they send
From hollow clefts up to the clearer air
A cloud of mist, that smitten by the sun
Varies its rainbow hues. But vainly thus,
And vainly by all other means, he strove
To mitigate the fever of his heart.

In dreams, in study, and in ardent thought,
Thus was he reared; much wanting to assist
The growth of intellect, yet gaining more,
And every moral feeling of his soul
Strengthened and braced, by breathing in content
The keen, the wholesome, air of poverty,
And drinking from the well of homely life.
—But, from past liberty, and tried restraints,
He now was summoned to select the course
Of humble industry that promised best

To yield him no unworthy maintenance.
Urged by his Mother, he essayed to teach
A village-school—but wandering thoughts were then
A misery to him; and the Youth resigned
A task he was unable to perform.

That stern yet kindly Spirit, who constrains
The Savoyard to quit his naked rocks,
The free-born Swiss to leave his narrow vales,
(Spirit attached to regions mountainous
Like their own steadfast clouds) did now impel
His restless mind to look abroad with hope.
—An irksome drudgery seems it to plod on,
Through hot and dusty ways, or pelting storm,
A vagrant Merchant under a heavy load
Bent as he moves, and needing frequent rest;
Yet do such travellers find their own delight;
And their hard service, deemed debasing now,
Gained merited respect in simpler times;
When squire, and priest, and they who round them dwelt
In rustic sequestration—all dependent
Upon the PEDLAR's toil—supplied their wants,
Or pleased their fancies, with the wares he brought.
Not ignorant was the Youth that still no few
Of his adventurous countrymen were led
By perseverance in this track of life
To competence and ease:—to him it offered
Attractions manifold;—and this he chose.
—His Parents on the enterprise bestowed
Their farewell benediction, but with hearts
Foreboding evil. From his native hills
He wandered far; much did he see of men,
Their manners, their enjoyments, and pursuits,
Their passions and their feelings; chiefly those
Essential and eternal in the heart,
That, 'mid the simpler forms of rural life,
Exist more simple in their elements,
And speak a plainer language. In the woods,
A lone Enthusiast, and among the fields,
Itinerant in this labour, he had passed
The better portion of his time; and there
Spontaneously had his affections thriven

Amid the bounties of the year, the peace
And liberty of nature; there he kept
In solitude and solitary thought
His mind in a just equipoise of love.
Serene it was, unclouded by the cares
Of ordinary life; unvexed, unwarped
By partial bondage. In his steady course,
No piteous revolutions had he felt,
No wild varieties of joy and grief.
Unoccupied by sorrow of its own,
His heart lay open; and, by nature tuned
And constant disposition of his thoughts
To sympathy with man, he was alive
To all that was enjoyed where'er he went,
And all that was endured; for, in himself
Happy, and quiet in his cheerfulness,
He had no painful pressure from without
That made him turn aside from wretchedness
With coward fears. He could *afford* to suffer
With those whom he saw suffer. Hence it came
That in our best experience he was rich,
And in the wisdom of our daily life.
For hence, minutely, in his various rounds,
He had observed the progress and decay
Of many minds, of minds and bodies too;
The history of many families;
How they had prospered; how they were o'erthrown
By passion or mischance, or such misrule
Among the unthinking masters of the earth
As makes the nations groan.
This active course
He followed till provision for his wants
Had been obtained;—the Wanderer then resolved
To pass the remnant of his days, untasked
With needless services, from hardship free.
His calling laid aside, he lived at ease:
But still he loved to pace the public roads
And the wild paths; and, by the summer's warmth
Invited, often would he leave his home
And journey far, revisiting the scenes
That to his memory were most endeared.
—Vigorous in health, of hopeful spirits, undamped

By worldly-mindedness or anxious care;
Observant, studious, thoughtful and refreshed
By knowledge gathered up from day to day;
Thus had he lived a long and innocent life.

The Scottish Church, both on himself and those
With whom from childhood he grew up, had held
The strong hand of her purity; and still
Had watched him with an unrelenting eye.
This he remembered in his riper age
With gratitude, and reverential thoughts.
But by the native vigour of his mind,
By his habitual wanderings out of doors,
By loneliness, and goodness, and kind works,
Whate'er, in docile childhood or in youth,
He had imbibed of fear or darker thought
Was melted all away; so true was this,
That sometimes his religion seemed to me
Self-taught, as of a dreamer in the woods;
Who to the model of his own pure heart
Shaped his belief, as grace divine inspired,
And human reason dictated with awe.
—And surely never did there live on earth
A man of kindlier nature. The rough sports
And teasing ways of children vexed not him;
Indulgent listener was he to the tongue
Of garrulous age; nor did the sick man's tale,
To his fraternal sympathy addressed,
Obtain reluctant hearing.
Plain his garb;
Such as might suit a rustic Sire, prepared
For sabbath duties; yet he was a man
Whom no one could have passed without remark.
Active and nervous was his gait; his limbs
And his whole figure breathed intelligence.
Time had compressed the freshness of his cheek
Into a narrower circle of deep red,
But had not tamed his eye; that, under brows
Shaggy and grey, had meanings which it brought
From years of youth; which, like a Being made
Of many Beings, he had wondrous skill

To blend with knowledge of the years to come,
Human, or such as lie beyond the grave.

So was He framed; and such his course of life
Who now, with no appendage but a staff,
The prized memorial of relinquished toils,
Upon that cottage-bench reposed his limbs,
Screened from the sun. Supine the Wanderer lay,
His eyes as if in drowsiness half shut,
The shadows of the breezy elms above
Dappling his face. He had not heard the sound
Of my approaching steps, and in the shade
Unnoticed did I stand some minutes' space.
At length I hailed him, seeing that his hat
Was moist with water-drops, as if the brim
Had newly scooped a running stream. He rose,
And ere our lively greeting into peace
Had settled, ''Tis,' said I, 'a burning day:
My lips are parched with thirst, but you, it seems,
Have somewhere found relief.' He, at the word,
Pointing towards a sweet-briar, bade me climb
The fence where that aspiring shrub looked out
Upon the public way. It was a plot
Of garden ground run wild, its matted weeds
Marked with the steps of those, whom, as they passed,
The gooseberry trees that shot in long lank slips,
Or currants, hanging from their leafless stems,
In scanty strings, had tempted to o'erleap
The broken wall. I looked around, and there,
Where two tall hedge-rows of thick alder boughs
Joined in a cold damp nook, espied a well
Shrouded with willow-flowers and plumy fern.
My thirst I slaked, and, from the cheerless spot
Withdrawing, straightway to the shade returned
Where sate the old Man on the cottage-bench;
And, while, beside him, with uncovered head,
I yet was standing, freely to respire,
And cool my temples in the fanning air,
Thus did he speak. 'I see around me here
Things which you cannot see: we die, my Friend,

Nor we alone, but that which each man loved
And prized in his peculiar nook of earth
Dies with him, or is changed; and very soon
Even of the good is no memorial left.
—The Poets, in their elegies and songs
Lamenting the departed, call the groves,
They call upon the hills and streams to mourn,
And senseless rocks; nor idly; for they speak,
In these their invocations, with a voice
Obedient to the strong creative power
Of human passion. Sympathies there are
More tranquil, yet perhaps of kindred birth,
That steal upon the meditative mind,
And grow with thought. Beside yon spring I stood,
And eyed its waters till we seemed to feel
One sadness, they and I. For them a bond
Of brotherhood is broken: time has been
When, every day, the touch of human hand
Dislodged the natural sleep that binds them up
In mortal stillness; and they ministered
To human comfort. Stooping down to drink,
Upon the slimy foot-stone I espied
The useless fragment of a wooden bowl,
Green with the moss of years, and subject only
To the soft handling of the elements:
There let it lie—how foolish are such thoughts!
Forgive them;—never—never did my steps
Approach this door but she who dwelt within
A daughter's welcome gave me, and I loved her
As my own child. Oh, Sir! the good die first,
And they whose hearts are dry as summer dust
Burn to the socket. Many a passenger
Hath blessed poor Margaret for her gentle looks,
When she upheld the cool refreshment drawn
From that forsaken spring; and no one came
But he was welcome; no one went away
But that it seemed she loved him. She is dead,
The light extinguished of her lonely hut,
The hut itself abandoned to decay,
And she forgotten in the quiet grave.

'I speak,' continued he, 'of One whose stock
Of virtues bloomed beneath this lowly roof.
She was a Woman of a steady mind,
Tender and deep in her excess of love;
Not speaking much, pleased rather with the joy
Of her own thoughts: by some especial care
Her temper had been framed, as if to make
A Being, who by adding love to peace
Might live on earth a life of happiness.
Her wedded Partner lacked not on his side
The humble worth that satisfied her heart:
Frugal, affectionate, sober, and withal
Keenly industrious. She with pride would tell
That he was often seated at his loom,
In summer, ere the mower was abroad
Among the dewy grass,—in early spring,
Ere the last star had vanished.—They who passed
At evening from behind the garden fence
Might hear his busy spade, which he would ply,
After his daily work, until the light
Had failed, and every leaf and flower were lost
In the dark hedges. So their days were spent
In peace and comfort; and a pretty boy
Was their best hope, next to the God in heaven.

'Not twenty years ago, but you I think
Can scarcely bear it now in mind, there came
Two blighting seasons, when the fields were left
With half a harvest. It pleased Heaven to add
A worse affliction in the plague of war:
This happy Land was stricken to the heart!
A Wanderer then among the cottages,
I, with my freight of winter raiment, saw
The hardships of that season: many rich
Sank down, as in a dream, among the poor;
And of the poor did many cease to be,
And their place knew them not. Meanwhile, abridged
Of daily comforts, gladly reconciled
To numerous self-denials, Margaret
Went struggling on through those calamitous years
With cheerful hope, until the second autumn,
When her life's Helpmate on a sick-bed lay,

Smitten with perilous fever. In disease
He lingered long; and, when his strength returned,
He found the little he had stored, to meet
The hour of accident or crippling age,
Was all consumed. A second infant now
Was added to the troubles of a time
Laden, for them and all of their degree,
With care and sorrow: shoals of artisans
From ill-requited labour turned adrift
Sought daily bread from public charity,
They, and their wives and children—happier far
Could they have lived as do the little birds
That peck along the hedge-rows, or the kite
That makes her dwelling on the mountain rocks!

'A sad reverse it was for him who long
Had filled with plenty, and possessed in peace,
This lonely Cottage. At the door he stood,
And whistled many a snatch of merry tunes
That had no mirth in them; or with his knife
Carved uncouth figures on the heads of sticks—
Then, not less idly, sought, through every nook
In house or garden, any casual work
Of use or ornament; and with a strange,
Amusing, yet uneasy, novelty,
He mingled, where he might, the various tasks
Of summer, autumn, winter, and of spring.
But this endured not; his good humour soon
Became a weight in which no pleasure was:
And poverty brought on a petted mood
And a sore temper: day by day he drooped,
And he would leave his work—and to the town
Would turn without an errand his slack steps;
Or wander here and there among the fields.
One while he would speak lightly of his babes,
And with a cruel tongue: at other times
He tossed them with a false unnatural joy:
And 'twas a rueful thing to see the looks
Of the poor innocent children. "Every smile,"
Said Margaret to me, here beneath these trees,
"Made my heart bleed." '

At this the Wanderer paused
And, looking up to those enormous elms,
He said, "'Tis now the hour of deepest noon.
At this still season of repose and peace,
This hour when all things which are not at rest
Are cheerful; while this multitude of flies
With tuneful hum is filling all the air;
Why should a tear be on an old Man's cheek?
Why should we thus, with an untoward mind,
And in the weakness of humanity,
From natural wisdom turn our hearts away;
To natural comfort shut our eyes and ears;
And, feeding on disquiet, thus disturb
The calm of nature with our restless thoughts?'

He spake with somewhat of a solemn tone:
But, when he ended, there was in his face
Such easy cheerfulness, a look so mild,
That for a little time it stole away
All recollection; and that simple tale
Passed from my mind like a forgotten sound.
A while on trivial things we held discourse,
To me soon tasteless. In my own despite,
I thought of that poor Woman as of one
Whom I had known and loved. He had rehearsed
Her homely tale with such familiar power,
With such an active countenance, an eye
So busy, that the things of which he spake
Seemed present; and, attention now relaxed,
A heart-felt chillness crept along my veins.
I rose; and, having left the breezy shade,
Stood drinking comfort from the warmer sun,
That had not cheered me long—ere, looking round
Upon that tranquil Ruin, I returned,
And begged of the old Man that, for my sake,
He would resume his story.
He replied,
'It were a wantonness, and would demand
Severe reproof, if we were men whose hearts
Could hold vain dalliance with the misery

Even of the dead; contented thence to draw
A momentary pleasure, never marked
By reason, barren of all future good.
But we have known that there is often found
In mournful thoughts, and always might be found,
A power to virtue friendly; were't not so,
I am a dreamer among men, indeed
An idle dreamer! 'Tis a common tale,
An ordinary sorrow of man's life,
A tale of silent suffering, hardly clothed
In bodily form.—But without further bidding
I will proceed.
While thus it fared with them,
To whom this cottage, till those hapless years,
Had been a blessed home, it was my chance
To travel in a country far remote;
And when these lofty elms once more appeared
With pleasant expectations lured me on
O'er the flat Common!—With quick step I reached
The threshold, lifted with light hand the latch;
But, when I entered, Margaret looked at me
A little while; then turned her head away
Speechless,—and, sitting down upon a chair,
Wept bitterly. I wist not what to do,
Nor how to speak to her. Poor Wretch! at last
She rose from off her seat, and then,—O Sir!
I cannot *tell* how she pronounced my name:—
With fervent love, and with a face of grief
Unutterably helpless, and a look
That seemed to cling upon me, she enquired
If I had seen her husband. As she spake
A strange surprise and fear came to my heart,
Nor had I power to answer ere she told
That he had disappeared—not two months gone.
He left his house: two wretched days had past,
And on the third, as wistfully she raised
Her head from off her pillow, to look forth,
Like one in trouble, for returning light,
Within her chamber-casement she espied
A folded paper, lying as if placed
To meet her waking eyes. This tremblingly
She opened—found no writing, but beheld

Pieces of money carefully enclosed,
Silver and gold. "I shuddered at the sight,"
Said Margaret, "for I knew it was his hand
That must have placed it there; and ere that day
Was ended, that long anxious day, I learned,
From one who by my husband had been sent
With the sad news, that he had joined a troop
Of soldiers, going to a distant land.
—He left me thus—he could not gather heart
To take a farewell of me; for he feared
That I should follow with my babes, and sink
Beneath the misery of that wandering life."

'This tale did Margaret tell with many tears:
And, when she ended, I had little power
To give her comfort, and was glad to take
Such words of hope from her own mouth as served
To cheer us both. But long we had not talked
Ere we built up a pile of better thoughts,
And with a brighter eye she looked around
As if she had been shedding tears of joy.
We parted.—'Twas the time of early spring;
I left her busy with her garden tools;
And well remember, o'er that fence she looked,
And, while I paced along the foot-way path,
Called out, and sent a blessing after me,
With tender cheerfulness, and with a voice
That seemed the very sound of happy thoughts.

'I roved o'er many a hill and many a dale,
With my accustomed load; in heat and cold,
Through many a wood and many an open ground,
In sunshine and in shade, in wet and fair,
Drooping or blithe of heart, as might befall;
My best companions now the driving winds,
And now the "trotting brooks" and whispering trees,
And now the music of my own sad steps,
With many a short-lived thought that passed between,
And disappeared.

I journeyed back this way,
When, in the warmth of midsummer, the wheat
Was yellow; and the soft and bladed grass,

Springing afresh, had o'er the hay-field spread
Its tender verdure. At the door arrived,
I found that she was absent. In the shade,
Where now we sit, I waited her return.
Her cottage, then a cheerful object, wore
Its customary look—only, it seemed,
The honeysuckle, crowding round the porch,
Hung down in heavier tufts; and that bright weed,
The yellow stone-crop, suffered to take root
Along the window's edge, profusely grew
Blinding the lower panes. I turned aside,
And strolled into her garden. It appeared
To lag behind the season, and had lost
Its pride of neatness. Daisy-flowers and thrift
Had broken their trim border-lines, and straggled
O'er paths they used to deck: carnations, once
Prized for surpassing beauty, and no less
For the peculiar pains they had required,
Declined their languid heads, wanting support.
The cumbrous bind-weed, with its wreaths and bells,
Had twined about her two small rows of peas,
And dragged them to the earth.
Ere this an hour
Was wasted.—Back I turned my restless steps;
A stranger passed; and, guessing whom I sought,
He said that she was used to ramble far.—
The sun was sinking in the west; and now
I sate with sad impatience. From within
Her solitary infant cried aloud;
Then, like a blast that dies away self-stilled,
The voice was silent. From the bench I rose;
But neither could divert nor soothe my thoughts.
The spot, though fair, was very desolate—
The longer I remained, more desolate:
And, looking round me, now I first observed
The corner stones, on either side the porch,
With dull red stains discoloured, and stuck o'er
With tufts and hairs of wool, as if the sheep,
That fed upon the Common, thither came
Familiarly, and found a couching-place
Even at her threshold. Deeper shadows fell
From these tall elms; the cottage-clock struck eight;—

I turned, and saw her distant a few steps.
Her face was pale and thin—her figure, too,
Was changed. As she unlocked the door, she said,
"It grieves me you have waited here so long,
But, in good truth, I've wandered much of late;
And, sometimes—to my shame I speak—have need
Of my best prayers to bring me back again."
While on the board she spread our evening meal,
She told me—interrupting not the work
Which gave employment to her listless hands—
That she had parted with her elder child;
To a kind master on a distant farm
Now happily apprenticed.—"I perceive
You look at me, and you have cause; to-day
I have been travelling far; and many days
About the fields I wander, knowing this
Only, that what I seek I cannot find;
And so I waste my time: for I am changed;
And to myself," said she, "have done much wrong
And to this helpless infant. I have slept
Weeping, and weeping have I waked; my tears
Have flowed as if my body were not such
As others are; and I could never die.
But I am now in mind and in my heart
More easy; and I hope," said she, "that God
Will give me patience to endure the things
Which I behold at home."
It would have grieved
Your very soul to see her. Sir, I feel
The story linger in my heart; I fear
'Tis long and tedious; but my spirit clings
To that poor Woman:—so familiarly
Do I perceive her manner, and her look,
And presence; and so deeply do I feel
Her goodness, that, not seldom, in my walks
A momentary trance comes over me;
And to myself I seem to muse on One
By sorrow laid asleep; or borne away,
A human being destined to awake
To human life, or something very near
To human life, when he shall come again
For whom she suffered. Yes, it would have grieved

Your very soul to see her: evermore
Her eyelids drooped, her eyes downward were cast;
And. when she at her table gave me food
She did not look at me. Her voice was low,
Her body was subdued. In every act
Pertaining to her house-affairs, appeared
The careless stillness of a thinking mind
Self-occupied; to which all outward things
Are like an idle matter. Still she sighed,
But yet no motion of the breast was seen,
No heaving of the heart. While by the fire
We sate together, sighs came on my ear,
I knew not how, and hardly whence they came.

'Ere my departure, to her care I gave,
For her son's use, some tokens of regard,
Which with a look of welcome she received;
And I exhorted her to place her trust
In God's good love, and seek his help by prayer.
I took my staff, and, when I kissed her babe,
The tears stood in her eyes. I left her then
With the best hope and comfort I could give:
She thanked me for my wish;—but for my hope
It seemed she did not thank me.
I returned,
And took my rounds along this road again
When on its sunny bank the primrose flower
Peeped forth, to give an earnest of the Spring.
I found her sad and drooping: she had learned
No tidings of her husband; if he lived,
She knew not that he lived; if he were dead,
She knew not he was dead. She seemed the same
In person and appearance; but her house
Bespake a sleepy hand of negligence;
The floor was neither dry nor neat, the hearth
Was comfortless, and her small lot of books,
Which, in the cottage-window, heretofore
Had been piled up against the corner panes
In seemly order, now, with straggling leaves
Lay scattered here and there, open or shut,
As they had chanced to fall. Her infant Babe
Had from its Mother caught the trick of grief,

And sighed among its playthings. I withdrew,
And once again entering the garden saw,
More plainly still, that poverty and grief
Were now come nearer to her: weeds defaced
The hardened soil, and knots of withered grass:
No ridges there appeared of clear black mould,
No winter greenness; of her herbs and flowers,
It seemed the better part were gnawed away
Or trampled into earth; a chain of straw,
Which had been twined about the slender stem
Of a young apple-tree, lay at its root;
The bark was nibbled round by truant sheep.
—Margaret stood near, her infant in her arms,
And, noting that my eye was on the tree,
She said, "I fear it will be dead and gone
Ere Robert come again." When to the House
We had returned together, she enquired
If I had any hope:—but for her babe
And for her little orphan boy, she said,
She had no wish to live, that she must die
Of sorrow. Yet I saw the idle loom
Still in its place; his Sunday garments hung
Upon the self-same nail; his very staff
Stood undisturbed behind the door.
And when.
In bleak December, I retraced this way,
She told me that her little babe was dead,
And she was left alone. She now, released
From her maternal cares, had taken up
The employment common through these wilds, and gained
By spinning hemp, a pittance for herself;
And for this end had hired a neighbour's boy
To give her needful help. That very time
Most willingly she put her work aside,
And walked with me along the miry road,
Heedless how far; and, in such piteous sort
That any heart had ached to hear her, begged
That, wheresoe'er I went, I still would ask
For him whom she had lost. We parted then—
Our final parting; for from that time forth
Did many seasons pass ere I returned
Into this tract again.

Nine tedious years;
From their first separation, nine long years,
She lingered in unquiet widowhood;
A Wife and Widow. Needs must it have been
A sore heart-wasting! I have heard, my Friend,
That in yon arbour oftentimes she sate
Alone, through half the vacant sabbath day;
And, if a dog passed by, she still would quit
The shade, and look abroad. On this old bench
For hours she sate; and evermore her eye
Was busy in the distance, shaping things
That made her heart beat quick. You see that path,
Now faint,—the grass has crept o'er its grey line;
There, to and fro, she paced through many a day
Of the warm summer, from a belt of hemp
That girt her waist, spinning the long-drawn thread
With backward steps. Yet ever as there passed
A man whose garments showed the soldier's red,
Or crippled mendicant in sailor's garb,
The little child who sate to turn the wheel
Ceased from his task; and she with faltering voice
Made many a fond enquiry; and when they,
Whose presence gave no comfort, were gone by,
Her heart was still more sad. And by yon gate,
That bars the traveller's road, she often stood,
And when a stranger horseman came, the latch
Would lift, and in his face look wistfully:
Most happy, if, from aught discovered there
Of tender feeling, she might dare repeat
The same sad question. Meanwhile her poor Hut
Sank to decay; for he was gone, whose hand,
At the first nipping of October frost,
Closed up each chink, and with fresh bands of straw
Chequered the green-grown thatch. And so she lived
Through the long winter, reckless and alone;
Until her house by frost, and thaw, and rain,
Was sapped; and while she slept, the nightly damps
Did chill her breast; and in the stormy day
Her tattered clothes were ruffled by the wind,
Even at the side of her own fire. Yet still
She loved this wretched spot, nor would for worlds
Have parted hence; and still that length of road,

And this rude bench, one torturing hope endeared,
Fast rooted at her heart: and here, my Friend,—
In sickness she remained; and here she died;
Last human tenant of these ruined walls!'

The old Man ceased: he saw that I was moved;
From that low bench, rising instinctively
I turned aside in weakness, nor had power
To thank him for the tale which he had told.
I stood, and leaning o'er the garden wall
Reviewed that Woman's sufferings; and it seemed
To comfort me while with a brother's love
I blessed her in the impotence of grief.
Then towards the cottage I returned; and traced
Fondly, though with an interest more mild,
That secret spirit of humanity
Which, 'mid the calm oblivious tendencies
Of nature, 'mid her plants, and weeds, and flowers,
And silent overgrowings, still survived.
The old Man, noting this, resumed, and said,
'My Friend! enough to sorrow you have given,
The purposes of wisdom ask no more:
Nor more would she have craved as due to One
Who, in her worst distress, had ofttimes felt
The unbounded might of prayer; and learned, with soul
Fixed on the Cross, that consolation springs,
From sources deeper far than deepest pain,
For the meek Sufferer. Why then should we read
The forms of things with an unworthy eye?
She sleeps in the calm earth, and peace is here.
I well remember that those very plumes,
Those weeds, and the high spear-grass on that wall,
By mist and silent rain-drops silvered o'er,
As once I passed, into my heart conveyed
So still an image of tranquillity,
So calm and still, and looked so beautiful
Amid the uneasy thoughts which filled my mind,
That what we feel of sorrow and despair
From ruin and from change, and all the grief
That passing shows of Being leave behind,
Appeared an idle dream, that could maintain,
Nowhere, dominion o'er the enlightened spirit

Whose meditative sympathies repose
Upon the breast of Faith. I turned away,
And walked along my road in happiness.'

He ceased. Ere long the sun declining shot
A slant and mellow radiance, which began
To fall upon us, while, beneath the trees,
We sate on that low bench: and now we felt,
Admonished thus, the sweet hour coming on.
A linnet warbled from those lofty elms,
A thrush sang loud, and other melodies,
At distance heard, peopled the milder air.
The old Man rose, and, with a sprightly mien
Of hopeful preparation, grasped his staff;
Together casting then a farewell look
Upon those silent walls, we left the shade;
And, ere the stars were visible, had reached
A village-inn,—our evening resting-place.

'An unimaginable sight'

A SINGLE step, that freed me from the skirts
Of the blind vapour, opened to my view
Glory beyond all glory ever seen
By waking sense or by the dreaming soul!
The appearance, instantaneously disclosed,
Was of a mighty city—boldly say
A wilderness of building, sinking far
And self-withdrawn into a boundless depth,
Far sinking into splendor—without end!
Fabric it seemed of diamond and of gold,
With alabaster domes, and silver spires,
And blazing terrace upon terrace, high
Uplifted; here, serene pavilions bright,
In avenues disposed; there, towers begirt
With battlements that on their restless fronts
Bore stars—illumination of all gems!
By earthly nature had the effect been wrought
Upon the dark materials of the storm
Now pacified; on them, and on the coves

And mountain-steeps and summits, whereunto
The vapours had receded, taking there
Their station under a cerulean sky.
Oh, 'twas an unimaginable sight!
Clouds, mists, streams, watery rocks and emerald turf,
Clouds of all tincture, rocks and sapphire sky,
Confused, commingled, mutually inflamed,
Molten together, and composing thus,
Each lost in each, that marvellous array
Of temple, palace, citadel, and huge
Fantastic pomp of structure without name,
In fleecy folds voluminous, enwrapped.
Right in the midst, where interspace appeared
Of open court, an object like a throne
Under a shining canopy of state
Stood fixed; and fixed resemblances were seen
To implements of ordinary use,
But vast in size, in substance glorified;
Such as by Hebrew Prophets were beheld
In vision—forms uncouth of mightiest power
For admiration and mysterious awe.
This little Vale, a dwelling-place of Man,
Lay low beneath my feet; 'twas visible—
I saw not, but I felt that it was there.
That which I *saw* was the revealed abode
Of spirits in beatitude: my heart
Swelled in my breast.—'I have been dead,' I cried,
'And now I live! Oh! wherefore *do* I live?'
And with that pang I prayed to be no more!—

'Things eternal'

'POSSESSIONS vanish, and opinions change,
And passions hold a fluctuating seat:
But, by the storms of circumstance unshaken,
And subject neither to eclipse nor wane,
Duty exists;—immutably survive,
For our support, the measures and the forms,
Which an abstract intelligence supplies;
Whose kingdom is, where time and space are not.

Of other converse which mind, soul, and heart,
Do, with united urgency, require,
What more that may not perish?—Thou, dread source,
Prime, self-existing cause and end of all
That in the scale of being fill their place;
Above our human region, or below,
Set and sustained;—thou, who didst wrap the cloud
Of infancy around us, that thyself,
Therein, with our simplicity awhile
Might'st hold, on earth, communion undisturbed;
Who from the anarchy of dreaming sleep,
Or from its death-like void, with punctual care,
And touch as gentle as the morning light,
Restor'st us, daily, to the powers of sense
And reason's steadfast rule—thou, thou alone
Art everlasting, and the blessed Spirits,
Which thou includest, as the sea her waves:
For adoration thou endur'st; endure
For consciousness the motions of thy will;
For apprehension those transcendent truths
Of the pure intellect, that stand as laws
(Submission constituting strength and power)
Even to thy Being's infinite majesty!
This universe shall pass away—a work
Glorious! because the shadow of thy might,
A step, or link, for intercourse with thee.
Ah! if the time must come, in which my feet
No more shall stray where meditation leads,
By flowing stream, through wood, or craggy wild,
Loved haunts like these; the unimprisoned Mind
May yet have scope to range among her own,
Her thoughts, her images, her high desires.
If the dear faculty of sight should fail,
Still, it may be allowed me to remember
What visionary powers of eye and soul
In youth were mine; when, stationed on the top
Of some huge hill, expectant, I beheld
The sun rise up, from distant climes returned
Darkness to chase, and sleep; and bring the day
His bounteous gift! or saw him toward the deep
Sink, with a retinue of flaming clouds
Attended; then, my spirit was entranced

With joy exalted to beatitude;
The measure of my soul was filled with bliss,
And holiest love; as earth, sea, air, with light,
With pomp, with glory, with magnificence!

'Those fervent raptures are for ever flown;
And, since their date, my soul hath undergone
Change manifold, for better or for worse:
Yet cease I not to struggle, and aspire
Heavenward; and chide the part of me that flags,
Through sinful choice; or dread necessity
On human nature from above imposed.
'Tis, by comparison, an easy task
Earth to despise; but, to converse with heaven—
This is not easy:—to relinquish all
We have, or hope, of happiness and joy,
And stand in freedom loosened from this world,
I deem not arduous; but must needs confess
That 'tis a thing impossible to frame
Conceptions equal to the soul's desires;
And the most difficult of tasks to *keep*
Heights which the soul is competent to gain.
—Man is of dust: ethereal hopes are his,
Which, when they should sustain themselves aloft,
Want due consistence; like a pillar of smoke,
That with majestic energy from earth
Rises; but, having reached the thinner air,
Melts, and dissolves, and is no longer seen.
From this infirmity of mortal kind
Sorrow proceeds, which else were not; at least,
If grief be something hallowed and ordained,
If, in proportion, it be just and meet,
Yet, through this weakness of the general heart,
Is it enabled to maintain its hold
In that excess which conscience disapproves.
For who could sink and settle to that point
Of selfishness; so senseless who could be
As long and perseveringly to mourn
For any object of his love, removed
From this unstable world, if he could fix
A satisfying view upon that state
Of pure, imperishable, blessedness,

Which reason promises, and holy writ
Ensures to all believers?—Yet mistrust
Is of such incapacity, methinks,
No natural branch; despondency far less;
And, least of all, is absolute despair.
—And, if there be whose tender frames have drooped
Even to the dust; apparently, through weight
Of anguish unrelieved, and lack of power
An agonizing sorrow to transmute;
Deem not that proof is here of hope withheld
When wanted most; a confidence impaired
So pitiably, that, having ceased to see
With bodily eyes, they are borne down by love
Of what is lost, and perish through regret.
Oh! no, the innocent Sufferer often sees
Too clearly; feels too vividly; and longs
To realize the vision, with intense
And over-constant yearning;—there—there lies
The excess, by which the balance is destroyed.
Too, too contracted are these walls of flesh,
This vital warmth too cold, these visual orbs,
Though inconceivably endowed, too dim
For any passion of the soul that leads
To ecstasy; and, all the crooked paths
Of time and change disdaining, takes its course
Along the line of limitless desires.
I, speaking now from such disorder free,
Nor rapt, nor craving, but in settled peace,
I cannot doubt that they whom you deplore
Are glorified; or, if they sleep, shall wake
From sleep, and dwell with God in endless love.
Hope, below this, consists not with belief
In mercy, carried infinite degrees
Beyond the tenderness of human hearts:
Hope, below this, consists not with belief
In perfect wisdom, guiding mightiest power,
That finds no limits but her own pure will.'

'Admiration, Hope and Love'

'We live by Admiration, Hope, and Love;
And, even as these are well and wisely fixed,
In dignity of being we ascend.
But what is error?'—'Answer he who can!'
The Sceptic somewhat haughtily exclaimed:
'Love, Hope, and Admiration—are they not
Mad Fancy's favourite vassals? Does not life
Use them, full oft, as pioneers to ruin,
Guides to destruction? Is it well to trust
Imagination's light when reason's fails,
The unguarded taper where the guarded faints?
—Stoop from those heights, and soberly declare
What error is; and, of our errors, which
Doth most debase the mind; the genuine seats
Of power, where are they? Who shall regulate,
With truth, the scale of intellectual rank?'

'Authentic tidings of invisible things'

I have seen
A curious child, who dwelt upon a tract
Of inland ground, applying to his ear
The convolutions of a smooth-lipped shell;
To which, in silence hushed, his very soul
Listened intensely; and his countenance soon
Brightened with joy; for from within were heard
Murmurings, whereby the monitor expressed
Mysterious union with its native sea.
Even such a shell the universe itself
Is to the ear of Faith; and there are times,
I doubt not, when to you it doth impart
Authentic tidings of invisible things;
Of ebb and flow, and ever-during power;
And central peace, subsisting at the heart
Of endless agitation. Here you stand,
Adore, and worship, when you know it not;

Pious beyond the intention of your thought;
Devout above the meaning of your will.
—Yes, you have felt, and may not cease to feel.
The estate of man would be indeed forlorn
If false conclusions of the reasoning power
Made the eye blind, and closed the passages
Through which the ear converses with the heart.
Has not the soul, the being of your life,
Received a shock of awful consciousness,
In some calm season, when these lofty rocks
At night's approach bring down the unclouded sky,
To rest upon their circumambient walls;
A temple framing of dimensions vast,
And yet not too enormous for the sound
Of human anthems,—choral song, or burst
Sublime of instrumental harmony,
To glorify the Eternal! What if these
Did never break the stillness that prevails
Here,—if the solemn nightingale be mute,
And the soft woodlark here did never chant
Her vespers,—Nature fails not to provide
Impulse and utterance. The whispering air
Sends inspiration from the shadowy heights,
And blind recesses of the caverned rocks;
The little rills, and waters numberless,
Inaudible by daylight, blend their notes
With the loud streams: and often, at the hour
When issue forth the first pale stars, is heard,
Within the circuit of this fabric huge,
One voice—the solitary raven, flying
Athwart the concave of the dark blue dome,
Unseen, perchance above all power of sight—
An iron knell! with echoes from afar
Faint—and still fainter—as the cry, with which
The wanderer accompanies her flight
Through the calm region, fades upon the ear,
Diminishing by distance till it seemed
To expire; yet from the abyss is caught again,
And yet again recovered!

'Sunset'

ALREADY had the sun,
Sinking with less than ordinary state,
Attained his western bound; but rays of light—
Now suddenly diverging from the orb
Retired behind the mountain-tops or veiled
By the dense air—shot upwards to the crown
Of the blue firmament—aloft, and wide:
And multitudes of little floating clouds,
Through their ethereal texture pierced—ere we,
Who saw, of change were conscious—had become
Vivid as fire; clouds separately poised,—
Innumerable multitude of forms
Scattered through half the circle of the sky;
And giving back, and shedding each on each,
With prodigal communion, the bright hues
Which from the unapparent fount of glory
They had imbibed, and ceased not to receive.
That which the heavens displayed, the liquid deep
Repeated; but with unity sublime!

'Conclusion'

THIS vesper-service closed, without delay,
From that exalted station to the plain
Descending, we pursued our homeward course,
In mute composure, o'er the shadowy lake,
Under a faded sky. No trace remained
Of those celestial splendours; grey the vault—
Pure, cloudless, ether; and the star of eve
Was wanting; but inferior lights appeared
Faintly, too faint almost for sight; and some
Above the darkened hills stood boldly forth
In twinkling lustre, ere the boat attained
Her mooring-place; where, to the sheltering tree,
Our youthful Voyagers bound fast her prow,
With prompt yet careful hands. This done, we paced
The dewy fields; but ere the Vicar's door

Was reached, the Solitary checked his steps;
Then, intermingling thanks, on each bestowed
A farewell salutation; and, the like
Receiving, took the slender path that leads
To the one cottage in the lonely dell:
But turned not without welcome promise made
That he would share the pleasures and pursuits
Of yet another summer's day, not loth
To wander with us through the fertile vales,
And o'er the mountain-wastes. 'Another sun,'
Said he, 'shall shine upon us, ere we part;
Another sun, and peradventure more;
If time, with free consent, be yours to give,
And season favours.'
To enfeebled Power,
From this communion with uninjured Minds,
What renovation had been brought; and what
Degree of healing to a wounded spirit,
Dejected, and habitually disposed
To seek, in degradation of the Kind,
Excuse and solace for her own defects;
How far those erring notions were reformed;
And whether aught, of tendency as good
And pure, from further intercourse ensued;
This—if delightful hopes, as heretofore,
Inspire the serious song, and gentle Hearts
Cherish, and lofty Minds approve the past—
My future labours may not leave untold.

FROM LATER VOLUMES

EDITOR'S NOTE

The Farmer of Tilsbury Vale was first published in a newspaper in 1800 and belongs in style and thought to the *Lyrical Ballads* period. It first appeared in book form in the 1815 collected edition.

For *The White Doe of Rylstone* see Introduction p. 59. *The Force of Prayer* was both written and published at the same time as *The White Doe*. *Yew-Trees* probably dates from about 1812, and 'Surprised by joy' is later than Catherine Wordsworth's death in that year. Both were published in the 1815 collected edition, as was *Laodamia* on which see separate note.

To the Poet, John Dyer and *Composed upon an Evening of Extraordinary Splendour and Beauty* were both first published in 1820. The two *Ecclesiastical Sonnets* here given were first published in 1822 (see Introduction p. 68); *To a Skylark* (written 1825), *To —* (written 1824) and 'Scorn not the Sonnet' in 1827; *On the Power of Sound* in 1835; and the poem on the death of Hogg and others (written in 1835) in 1837.

The text of all poems in this section is the final one.

FROM LATER VOLUMES

The Farmer of Tilsbury Vale

'Tis not for the unfeeling, the falsely refined,
The squeamish in taste, and the narrow of mind,
And the small critic wielding his delicate pen,
That I sing of old Adam, the pride of old men.

He dwells in the centre of London's wide Town;
His staff is a sceptre—his grey hairs a crown;
And his bright eyes look brighter, set off by the streak
Of the unfaded rose that still blooms on his cheek.

'Mid the dews, in the sunshine of morn,—'mid the joy
Of the fields, he collected that bloom, when a boy;
That countenance there fashioned, which, spite of a stain
That his life hath received, to the last will remain.

A Farmer he was; and his house far and near
Was the boast of the country for excellent cheer;
How oft have I heard in sweet Tilsbury Vale
Of the silver-rimmed horn whence he dealt his mild ale!

Yet Adam was far as the farthest from ruin,
His fields seemed to know what their Master was doing;
And turnips, and corn-land, and meadow, and lea,
All caught the infection—as generous as he.

Yet Adam prized little the feast and the bowl,—
The fields better suited the ease of his soul:
He strayed through the fields like an indolent wight,
The quiet of nature was Adam's delight.

For Adam was simple in thought; and the poor,
Familiar with him, made an inn of his door:
He gave them the best that he had; or, to say
What less may mislead you, they took it away.

Thus thirty smooth years did he thrive on his farm:
The Genius of plenty preserved him from harm:
At length, what to most is a season of sorrow,
His means are run out,—he must beg, or must borrow.

To the neighbours he went,—all were free with their money;
For his hive had so long been replenished with honey,
That they dreamt not of dearth;—He continued his rounds,
Knocked here—and knocked there, pounds still adding to
pounds.

He paid what he could with his ill-gotten pelf,
And something, it might be, reserved for himself:
Then (what is too true) without hinting a word,
Turned his back on the country—and off like a bird.

You lift up your eyes!—but I guess that you frame
A judgment too harsh of the sin and the shame;
In him it was scarcely a business of art,
For this he did all in the *ease* of his heart.

To London—a sad emigration I ween—
With his grey hairs he went from the brook and the green;
And there, with small wealth but his legs and his hands,
As lonely he stood as a crow on the sands.

All trades, as need was, did old Adam assume,—
Served as stable-boy, errand-boy, porter, and groom;
But nature is gracious, necessity kind,
And, in spite of the shame that may lurk in his mind,

He seems ten birthdays younger, is green and is stout;
Twice as fast as before does his blood run about;
You would say that each hair of his beard was alive,
And his fingers as busy as bees in a hive.

For he's not like an Old Man that leisurely goes
About work that he knows, in a track that he knows;
But often his mind is compelled to demur,
And you guess that the more then his body must stir.

In the throng of the town like a stranger is he,
Like one whose own country's far over the sea;
And Nature, while through the great city he hies,
Full ten times a day takes his heart by surprise.

This gives him the fancy of one that is young,
More of soul in his face than of words on his tongue,
Like a maiden of twenty he trembles and sighs,
And tears of fifteen will come into his eyes.

What's a tempest to him, or the dry parching heats?
Yet he watches the clouds that pass over the streets;
With a look of such earnestness often will stand,
You might think he'd twelve reapers at work in the Strand.

Where proud Covent-garden, in desolate hours
Of snow and hoar-frost, spreads her fruit and her flowers,
Old Adam will smile at the pains that have made
Poor winter look fine in such strange masquerade.

'Mid coaches and chariots, a waggon of straw,
Like a magnet, the heart of old Adam can draw;
With a thousand soft pictures his memory will teem,
And his hearing is touched with the sounds of a dream.

Up the Haymarket hill he oft whistles his way,
Thrusts his hands in a waggon, and smells at the hay;
He thinks of the fields he so often hath mown,
And is happy as if the rich freight were his own.

But chiefly to Smithfield he loves to repair,—
If you pass by at morning, you'll meet with him there.
The breath of the cows you may see him inhale,
And his heart all the while is in Tilsbury Vale.

Now farewell, old Adam! when low thou art laid,
May one blade of grass spring up over thy head;
And I hope that thy grave, wheresoever it be,
Will hear the wind sigh through the leaves of a tree.

from

The White Doe of Rylstone

CONCLUSION

With her Companion, in such frame
Of mind, to Rylstone back she came;
And, ranging through the wasted groves,
Received the memory of old loves,
Undisturbed and undistrest,
Into a soul which now was blest
With a soft spring-day of holy,
Mild, and grateful, melancholy:
Not sunless gloom or unenlightened,
But by tender fancies brightened.

When the bells of Rylstone played
Their sabbath music—'God us ayde!'
That was the sound they seemed to speak;
Inscriptive legend which I ween
May on those holy bells be seen,
That legend and her Grandsire's name;
And oftentimes the Lady meek
Had in her childhood read the same;
Words which she slighted at that day;
But now, when such sad change was wrought,
And of that lonely name she thought,
The bells of Rylstone seemed to say,
While she sate listening in the shade,
With vocal music, 'God us ayde';
And all the hills were glad to bear
Their part in this effectual prayer.

Nor lacked she Reason's firmest power;
But with the White Doe at her side
Up would she climb to Norton Tower,
And thence look round her far and wide,

Her fate there measuring;—all is stilled—
The weak One hath subdued her heart;
Behold the prophecy fulfilled,
Fulfilled, and she sustains her part!
But here her Brother's words have failed;
Here hath a milder doom prevailed;
That she, of him and all bereft,
Hath yet this faithful Partner left;
This one Associate that disproves
His words, remains for her, and loves.
If tears are shed, they do not fall
For loss of him—for one, or all;
Yet, sometimes, sometimes doth she weep
Moved gently in her soul's soft sleep;
A few tears down her cheeks descend
For this her last and living Friend.

Bless, tender Hearts, their mutual lot,
And bless for both this savage spot;
Which Emily doth sacred hold
For reasons dear and manifold—
Here hath she, here before her sight,
Close to the summit of this height,
The grassy rock-encircled Pound
In which the Creature first was found.
So beautiful the timid Thrall
(A spotless Youngling white as foam)
Her youngest Brother brought it home;
The youngest, then a lusty boy,
Bore it, or led, to Rylstone-hall
With heart brimful of pride and joy!

But most to Bolton's sacred Pile,
On favouring nights, she loved to go;
There ranged through cloister, court, and aisle,
Attended by the soft-paced Doe;
Nor feared she in the still moonshine
To look upon Saint Mary's shrine;
Nor on the lonely turf that showed
Where Francis slept in his last abode.
For that she came; there oft she sate
Forlorn, but not disconsolate:

And, when she from the abyss returned
Of thought, she neither shrunk nor mourned;
Was happy that she lived to greet
Her mute Companion as it lay
In love and pity at her feet;
How happy in its turn to meet
The recognition! the mild glance
Beamed from that gracious countenance;
Communication, like the ray
Of a new morning, to the nature
And prospects of the inferior Creature!

A mortal Song we sing, by dower
Encouraged of celestial power;
Power which the viewless Spirit shed
By whom we were first visited;
Whose voice we heard, whose hand and wings
Swept like a breeze the conscious strings,
When, left in solitude, erewhile
We stood before this ruined Pile,
And, quitting unsubstantial dreams,
Sang in this Presence kindred themes;
Distress and desolation spread
Through human hearts, and pleasure dead,—
Dead—but to live again on earth,
A second and yet nobler birth;
Dire overthrow, and yet how high
The re-ascent in sanctity!

From fair to fairer; day by day
A more divine and loftier way!
Even such this blessèd Pilgrim trod,
By sorrow lifted towards her God;
Uplifted to the purest sky
Of undisturbed mortality.
Her own thoughts loved she; and could bend
A dear look to her lowly Friend;
There stopped; her thirst was satisfied
With what this innocent spring supplied:
Her sanction inwardly she bore,
And stood apart from human cares:
But to the world returned no more,

Although with no unwilling mind
Help did she give at need, and joined
The Wharfdale peasants in their prayers.
At length, thus faintly, faintly tied
To earth, she was set free, and died.
Thy soul, exalted Emily,
Maid of the blasted family,
Rose to the God from whom it came!
—In Rylstone Church her mortal frame
Was buried by her Mother's side.

Most glorious sunset! and a ray
Survives—the twilight of this day—
In that fair Creature whom the fields
Support, and whom the forest shields;
Who, having filled a holy place,
Partakes, in her degree, Heaven's grace;
And bears a memory and a mind
Raised far above the law of kind;
Haunting the spots with lonely cheer
Which her dear Mistress once held dear:
Loves most what Emily loved most—
The enclosure of this churchyard ground;
Here wanders like a gliding ghost,
And every sabbath here is found;
Comes with the people when the bells
Are heard among the moorland dells,
Finds entrance through yon arch, where way
Lies open on the sabbath day;
Here walks amid the mournful waste
Of prostrate altars, shrines defaced,
And floors encumbered with rich show
Of fret-work imagery laid low;
Paces softly, or makes halt,
By fractured cell, or tomb, or vault;
By plate of monumental brass
Dim-gleaming among weeds and grass,
And sculptured Forms of Warriors brave:
But chiefly by that single grave,

That one sequestered hillock green,
The pensive visitant is seen.
There doth the gentle Creature lie
With those adversities unmoved;
Calm spectacle, by earth and sky
In their benignity approved!
And aye, methinks, this hoary Pile,
Subdued by outrage and decay,
Looks down upon her with a smile,
A gracious smile, that seems to say—
'Thou, thou art not a Child of Time,
But Daughter of the Eternal Prime!'

The Force of Prayer

OR, THE FOUNDING OF BOLTON PRIORY

A TRADITION

'WHAT is good for a bootless bene?'
With these dark words begins my Tale;
And their meaning is, whence can comfort spring
When Prayer is of no avail?

'What is good for a bootless bene?'
The Falconer to the Lady said;
And she made answer 'ENDLESS SORROW!'
For she knew that her Son was dead.

She knew it by the Falconer's words,
And from the look of the Falconer's eye;
And from the love which was in her soul
For her youthful Romilly.

—Young Romilly through Barden woods
Is ranging high and low;
And holds a greyhound in a leash,
To let slip upon buck or doe.

The pair have reached that fearful chasm,
How tempting to bestride!
For lordly Wharf is there pent in
With rocks on either side.

This striding-place is called THE STRID,
A name which it took of yore:
A thousand years hath it borne that name,
And shall a thousand more.

And hither is young Romilly come,
And what may now forbid
That he, perhaps for the hundredth time,
Shall bound across THE STRID?

He sprang in glee,—for what cared he
That the river was strong, and the rocks were steep?—
But the greyhound in the leash hung back,
And checked him in his leap.

The Boy is in the arms of Wharf,
And strangled by a merciless force;
For never more was young Romilly seen
Till he rose a lifeless corse.

Now there is stillness in the vale,
And long, unspeaking, sorrow:
Wharf shall be to pitying hearts
A name more sad than Yarrow.

If for a lover the Lady wept,
A solace she might borrow
From death, and from the passion of death:—
Old Wharf might heal her sorrow.

She weeps not for the wedding-day
Which was to be to-morrow:
Her hope was a further-looking hope,
And hers is a mother's sorrow.

He was a tree that stood alone,
And proudly did its branches wave;
And the root of this delightful tree
Was in her husband's grave!

Long, long in darkness did she sit,
And her first words were, 'Let there be
In Bolton, on the field of Wharf,
A stately Priory!'

The stately Priory was reared;
And Wharf, as he moved along,
To matins joined a mournful voice,
Nor failed at even-song.

And the Lady prayed in heaviness
That looked not for relief!
But slowly did her succour come,
And a patience to her grief.

Oh! there is never sorrow of heart
That shall lack a timely end,
If but to God we turn, and ask
Of Him to be our friend!

Yew-Trees

There is a Yew-tree, pride of Lorton Vale,
Which to this day stands single, in the midst
Of its own darkness, as it stood of yore:
Not loth to furnish weapons for the bands
Of Umfraville or Percy ere they marched
To Scotland's heaths; or those that crossed the sea
And drew their sounding bows at Azincour,
Perhaps at earlier Crecy, or Poictiers.
Of vast circumference and gloom profound
This solitary Tree! a living thing
Produced too slowly ever to decay;
Of form and aspect too magnificent
To be destroyed. But worthier still of note
Are those fraternal Four of Borrowdale,

Joined in one solemn and capacious grove;
Huge trunks! and each particular trunk a growth
Of intertwisted fibres serpentine
Up-coiling, and inveterately convolved;
Nor uninformed with Phantasy, and looks
That threaten the profane;—a pillared shade,
Upon whose grassless floor of red-brown hue,
By sheddings from the pining umbrage tinged
Perennially—beneath whose sable roof
Of boughs as if for festal purpose decked
With unrejoicing berries—ghostly Shapes
May meet at noontide; Fear and trembling Hope,
Silence and Foresight; Death the Skeleton
And Time the Shadow;—there to celebrate,
As in a natural temple scattered o'er
With altars undisturbed of mossy stone,
United worship; or in mute repose
To lie, and listen to the mountain flood
Murmuring from Glaramara's inmost caves.

'Surprised by joy'

SURPRISED by joy—impatient as the Wind
I turned to share the transport—Oh! with whom
But Thee, deep buried in the silent tomb,
That spot which no vicissitude can find?
Love, faithful love, recalled thee to my mind—
But how could I forget thee?—Through what power
Even for the least division of an hour,
Have I been so beguiled as to be blind
To my most grievous loss!—That thought's return
Was the worst pang that sorrow ever bore,
Save one, one only, when I stood forlorn,
Knowing my heart's best treasure was no more;
That neither present time, nor years unborn
Could to my sight that heavenly face restore.

Laodamia

Laodamia is discussed in the Introduction, pp. 64–6. The text here given is the final one, but the last stanza but one was as follows in the 1815 and 1820 editions:

Ah, judge her gently who so deeply loved!
Her, who, in reason's spite, yet without crime,
Was in a trance of passion thus removed;
Delivered from the galling yoke of time
And these frail elements to gather flowers
Of blissful quiet 'mid unfading bowers.

In the 1827 edition Laodamia's doom is harsh.

By no weak pity might the Gods be moved;
She who thus perished not without the crime
Of Lovers that in Reason's spite have loved,
Was doomed to wander in a grosser clime
Apart from happy Ghosts, that gather flowers
Of blissful quiet 'mid unfading bowers.

In 1832 and subsequent editions the permanent doom was modifie to 'to wear out her appointed time.'

'WITH sacrifice before the rising morn
Vows have I made by fruitless hope inspired;
And from the infernal Gods, 'mid shades forlorn
Of night, my slaughtered Lord have I required:
Celestial pity I again implore;—
Restore him to my sight—great Jove, restore!'

So speaking, and by fervent love endowed
With faith, the Suppliant heavenward lifts her hands;
While, like the sun emerging from a cloud,
Her countenance brightens—and her eye expands;
Her bosom heaves and spreads, her stature grows;
And she expects the issue in repose.

O terror! what hath she perceived?—O joy!
What doth she look on?—whom doth she behold?
Her Hero slain upon the beach of Troy?
His vital presence? his corporeal mould?
It is—if sense deceive her not—'tis He!
And a God leads him, wingèd Mercury!

Mild Hermes spake—and touched her with his wand
That calms all fear; 'Such grace hath crowned thy prayer,
Laodamía! that at Jove's command
Thy Husband walks the paths of upper air:
He comes to tarry with thee three hours' space;
Accept the gift, behold him face to face!'

Forth sprang the impassioned Queen her Lord to clasp;
Again that consummation she essayed;
But unsubstantial Form eludes her grasp
As often as that eager grasp was made.
The Phantom parts—but parts to re-unite,
And re-assume his place before her sight.

'Protesiláus, lo! thy guide is gone!
Confirm, I pray, the vision with thy voice:
This is our palace,—yonder is thy throne;
Speak, and the floor thou tread'st on will rejoice.
Not to appal me have the gods bestowed
This precious boon; and blest a sad abode.'

'Great Jove, Laodamía! doth not leave
His gifts imperfect:—Spectre though I be,
I am not sent to scare thee or deceive;
But in reward of thy fidelity.
And something also did my worth obtain;
For fearless virtue bringeth boundless gain.

'Thou knowest, the Delphic oracle foretold
That the first Greek who touched the Trojan strand
Should die; but me the threat could not withhold:
A generous cause a victim did demand;
And forth I leapt upon the sandy plain;
A self-devoted chief—by Hector slain.'

'Supreme of Heroes—bravest, noblest, best!
Thy matchless courage I bewail no more,
Which then, when tens of thousands were deprest
By doubt, propelled thee to the fatal shore;
Thou found'st—and I forgive thee—here thou art—
A nobler counsellor than my poor heart.

'But thou, though capable of sternest deed,
Wert kind as resolute, and good as brave;
And he, whose power restores thee, hath decreed
Thou should'st elude the malice of the grave:
Redundant are thy locks, thy lips as fair
As when their breath enriched Thessalian air.

'No Spectre greets me,—no vain Shadow this;
Come, blooming Hero, place thee by my side!
Give, on this well-known couch, one nuptial kiss
To me, this day a second time thy bride!'
Jove frowned in heaven: the conscious Parcæ threw
Upon those roseate lips a Stygian hue.

'This visage tells thee that my doom is past:
Nor should the change be mourned, even if the joys
Of sense were able to return as fast
And surely as they vanish. Earth destroys
Those raptures duly—Erebus disdains:
Calm pleasures there abide—majestic pains.

'Be taught, O faithful Consort, to control
Rebellious passion: for the Gods approve
The depth, and not the tumult, of the soul;
A fervent, not ungovernable, love.
Thy transports moderate; and meekly mourn
When I depart, for brief is my sojourn—'

'Ah wherefore?—Did not Hercules by force
Wrest from the guardian Monster of the tomb
Alcestis, a reanimated corse,
Given back to dwell on earth in vernal bloom?
Medea's spells dispersed the weight of years,
And Æson stood a youth 'mid youthful peers.

'The Gods to us are merciful—and they
Yet further may relent: for mightier far
Than strength of nerve and sinew, or the sway
Of magic potent over sun and star,
Is love, though oft to agony distrest,
And though his favourite seat be feeble woman's breast.

'But if thou goest, I follow—' 'Peace!' he said,—
She looked upon him and was calmed and cheered;
The ghastly colour from his lips had fled;
In his deportment, shape, and mien, appeared
Elysian beauty, melancholy grace,
Brought from a pensive though a happy place.

He spake of love, such love as Spirits feel
In worlds whose course is equable and pure;
No fears to beat away—no strife to heal—
The past unsighed for, and the future sure;
Spake of heroic arts in graver mood
Revived, with finer harmony pursued;

Of all that it is most beauteous—imaged there
In happier beauty; more pellucid streams,
An ampler ether, a diviner air,
And fields invested with purpureal gleams;
Climes which the sun, who sheds the brightest day
Earth knows, is all unworthy to survey.

Yet there the Soul shall enter which hath earned
That privilege by virtue.—'Ill,' said he,
'The end of man's existence I discerned,
Who from ignoble games and revelry
Could draw, when we had parted, vain delight,
While tears were thy best pastime, day and night;

'And while my youthful peers before my eyes
(Each hero following his peculiar bent)
Prepared themselves for glorious enterprise
By martial sports,—or, seated in the tent,
Chieftains and kings in council were detained;
What time the fleet at Aulis lay enchained.

'The wished-for wind was given:—I then revolved
The oracle, upon the silent sea;
And, if no worthier led the way, resolved
That, of a thousand vessels, mine should be
The foremost prow in pressing to the strand,—
Mine the first blood that tinged the Trojan sand.

'Yet bitter, oft-times bitter, was the pang
When of thy loss I thought, belovèd Wife!
On thee too fondly did my memory hang,
And on the joys we shared in mortal life,—
The paths which we had trod—these fountains, flowers;
My new-planned cities, and unfinished towers.

'But should suspense permit the Foe to cry,
'Behold they tremble!—haughty their array,
Yet of their number no one dares to die?'
In soul I swept the indignity away:
Old frailties then recurred:—but lofty thought,
In act embodied, my deliverance wrought.

'And Thou, though strong in love, art all too weak
In reason, in self-government too slow;
I counsel thee by fortitude to seek
Our blest re-union in the shades below.
The invisible world with thee hath sympathised;
Be thy affections raised and solemnised.

'Learn, by a mortal yearning, to ascend—
Seeking a higher object. Love was given,
Encouraged, sanctioned, chiefly for that end;
For this the passion to excess was driven—
That self might be annulled: her bondage prove
The fetters of a dream opposed to love.'—

Aloud she shrieked! for Hermes re-appears!
Round the dear Shade she would have clung—'tis vain:
The hours are past—too brief had they been years;
And him no mortal effort can detain:
Swift, toward the realms that know not earthly day,
He through the portal takes his silent way,
And on the palace-floor a lifeless corse She lay.

Thus, all in vain exhorted and reproved,
She perished; and, as for a wilful crime,
By the just Gods whom no weak pity moved,
Was doomed to wear out her appointed time,
Apart from happy Ghosts, that gather flowers
Of blissful quiet 'mid unfading bowers.

—Yet tears to human suffering are due;
And mortal hopes defeated and o'erthrown
Are mourned by man, and not by man alone,
As fondly he believes.—Upon the side
Of Hellespont (such faith was entertained)
A knot of spiry trees for ages grew
From out the tomb of him for whom she died;
And ever, when such stature they had gained
That Ilium's walls were subject to their view,
The trees' tall summits withered at the sight;
A constant interchange of growth and blight!

To the Poet, John Dyer

BARD of the Fleece, whose skilful genius made
That work a living landscape fair and bright;
Nor hallowed less with musical delight
Than those soft scenes through which thy childhood strayed,
Those southern tracts of Cambria, 'deep embayed,
With green hills fenced, with ocean's murmur lulled';
Though hasty Fame hath many a chaplet culled
For worthless brows, while in the pensive shade
Of cold neglect she leaves thy head ungraced,
Yet pure and powerful minds, hearts meek and still,
A grateful few, shall love thy modest Lay,
Long as the shepherd's bleating flock shall stray
O'er naked Snowdon's wide aërial waste;
Long as the thrush shall pipe on Grongar Hill!

Composed upon an Evening of Extraordinary Splendour and Beauty

I

HAD this effulgence disappeared
With flying haste, I might have sent,
Among the speechless clouds, a look
Of blank astonishment;
But 'tis endued with power to stay,
And sanctify one closing day,

That frail Mortality may see—
What is?—ah no, but what *can* be!
Time was when field and watery cove
With modulated echoes rang,
While choirs of fervent Angels sang
Their vespers in the grove;
Or, crowning, star-like, each some sovereign height,
Warbled, for heaven above and earth below,
Strains suitable to both.—Such holy rite,
Methinks, if audibly repeated now
From hill or valley, could not move
Sublimer transport, purer love,
Than doth this silent spectacle—the gleam—
The shadow—and the peace supreme!

2

No sound is uttered,—but a deep
And solemn harmony pervades
The hollow vale from steep to steep,
And penetrates the glades.
Far-distant images draw nigh,
Called forth by wondrous potency
Of beamy radiance, that imbues
Whate'er it strikes with gem-like hues!
In vision exquisitely clear,
Herds range along the mountain side;
And glistening antlers are descried;
And gilded flocks appear.
Thine is the tranquil hour, purpureal Eve!
But long as god-like wish, or hope divine,
Informs my spirit, ne'er can I believe
That this magnificence is wholly thine!
—From worlds not quickened by the sun
A portion of the gift is won;
An intermingling of Heaven's pomp is spread
On ground which British shepherds tread!

3

And if there be whom broken ties
Afflict, or injuries assail,
Yon hazy ridges to their eyes
Present a glorious scale,
Climbing suffused with sunny air,
To stop—no record hath told where!
And tempting Fancy to ascend,
And with immortal Spirits blend!
—Wings at my shoulders seem to play;
But, rooted here, I stand and gaze
On those bright steps that heavenward raise
Their practicable way.
Come forth, ye drooping old men, look abroad,
And see to what fair countries ye are bound!
And if some traveller, weary of his road,
Hath slept since noon-tide on the grassy ground,
Ye Genii! to his covert speed;
And wake him with such gentle heed
As may attune his soul to meet the dower
Bestowed on this transcendent hour!

4

Such hues from their celestial Urn
Were wont to stream before mine eye,
Where'er it wandered in the morn
Of blissful infancy.
This glimpse of glory, why renewed?
Nay, rather speak with gratitude;
For, if a vestige of those gleams
Survived, 'twas only in my dreams.
Dread Power! whom peace and calmness serve
No less than Nature's threatening voice,
If aught unworthy be my choice,
From THEE if I would swerve;
Oh, let Thy grace remind me of the light
Full early lost, and fruitlessly deplored;
Which, at this moment, on my waking sight
Appears to shine, by miracle restored;

My soul, though yet confined to earth,
Rejoices in a second birth!
—'Tis past, the visionary splendour fades;
And night approaches with her shades.

Note—The multiplication of mountain-ridges, described at the commencement of the third Stanza of this Ode, as a kind of Jacob's Ladder, leading to Heaven, is produced either by watery vapours or sunny haze;—in the present instance by the latter cause. Allusions to the Ode entitled 'Intimations of Immortality' pervade the last Stanza of the foregoing Poem.

Mutability

FROM low to high doth dissolution climb,
And sink from high to low, along a scale
Of awful notes, whose concord shall not fail;
A musical but melancholy chime,
Which they can hear who meddle not with crime,
Nor avarice, nor over-anxious care.
Truth fails not; but her outward forms that bear
The longest date do melt like frosty rime,
That in the morning whitened hill and plain
And is no more; drop like the tower sublime
Of yesterday, which royally did wear
His crown of weeds, but could not even sustain
Some casual shout that broke the silent air,
Or the unimaginable touch of Time.

Inside of King's College Chapel, Cambridge

TAX not the royal Saint with vain expense,
With ill-matched aims the Architect who planned—
Albeit labouring for a scanty band
Of white-robed Scholars only—this immense
And glorious Work of fine intelligence!
Give all thou canst; high Heaven rejects the lore
Of nicely-calculated less or more;
So deemed the man who fashioned for the sense
These lofty pillars, spread that branching roof

Self-poised, and scooped into ten thousand cells,
Where light and shade repose, where music dwells
Lingering—and wandering on as loth to die;
Like thoughts whose very sweetness yieldeth proof
That they were born for immortality.

To a Skylark

Ethereal minstrel! pilgrim of the sky!
Dost thou despise the earth where cares abound?
Or, while the wings aspire, are heart and eye
Both with thy nest upon the dewy ground?
Thy nest which thou canst drop into at will,
Those quivering wings composed, that music still!

Leave to the nightingale her shady wood;
A privacy of glorious light is thine;
Whence thou dost pour upon the world a flood
Of harmony, with instinct more divine;
Type of the wise who soar, but never roam;
True to the kindred points of Heaven and Home!

To——

O DEARER far than light and life are dear,
Full oft our human foresight I deplore;
Trembling, through my unworthiness, with fear
That friends, by death disjoined, may meet no more!

Misgivings, hard to vanquish or control,
Mix with the day, and cross the hour of rest;
While all the future, for thy purer soul,
With 'sober certainties' of love is blest.

That sigh of thine, not meant for human ear,
Tells that these words thy humbleness offend;
Yet bear me up—else faltering in the rear
Of a steep march: support me to the end.

Peace settles where the intellect is meek,
And Love is dutiful in thought and deed;
Through Thee communion with that Love I seek:
The faith Heaven strengthens where *he* moulds the Creed.

Scorn not the Sonnet

SCORN not the Sonnet; Critic, you have frowned,
Mindless of its just honours; with this key
Shakespeare unlocked his heart; the melody
Of this small lute gave ease to Petrarch's wound;
A thousand times this pipe did Tasso sound;
With it Camöens soothed an exile's grief;
The Sonnet glittered a gay myrtle leaf
Amid the cypress with which Dante crowned
His visionary brow: a glow-worm lamp,
It cheered mild Spenser, called from Faery-land
To struggle through dark ways; and, when a damp
Fell round the path of Milton, in his hand
The Thing became a trumpet; whence he blew
Soul-animating strains—alas, too few!

On the Power of Sound

ARGUMENT

THE Ear addressed, as occupied by a spiritual functionary, in communion with sounds, individual, or combined in studied harmony.—Sources and effects of those sounds (to the close of 6th Stanza).—The power of music, whence proceeding, exemplified in the idiot.—Origin of music, and its effect in early ages—how produced (to the middle of 10th Stanza).—The mind recalled to sounds acting casually and severally.—Wish uttered (11th Stanza) that these could be united into a scheme or system for moral interests and intellectual contemplation.—(Stanza 12th) the Pythagorean theory of numbers and music, with their supposed power over the motions of the universe—imaginations consonant with such a theory.—Wish expressed (in 11th Stanza) realised, in some degree, by the representation of all sounds under the form of thanksgiving to the Creator.—(Last Stanza) the destruction of earth and planetary system—the survival of audible harmony, and its support in the Divine Nature, as revealed in Holy Writ.

I

Thy functions are ethereal,
As if within thee dwelt a glancing mind,
Organ of vision! And a Spirit aërial
Informs the cell of Hearing, dark and blind;
Intricate labyrinth, more dread for thought
To enter than oracular cave;
Strict passage, through which sighs are brought,
And whispers for the heart, their slave;
And shrieks, that revel in abuse
Of shivering flesh; and warbled air,
Whose piercing sweetness can unloose
The chains of frenzy, or entice a smile
Into the ambush of despair;
Hosannas pealing down the long-drawn aisle,
And requiems answered by the pulse that beats
Devoutly, in life's last retreats!

2

The headlong streams and fountains
Serve Thee, invisible Spirit, with untired powers;
Cheering the wakeful tent on Syrian mountains,
They lull perchance ten thousand thousand flowers.
That roar, the prowling lion's *Here I am,*
How fearful to the desert wide!
That bleat, how tender! of the dam
Calling a straggler to her side.
Shout, cuckoo!—let the vernal soul
Go with thee to the frozen zone;
Toll from thy loftiest perch, lone bell-bird, toll
At the still hour to Mercy dear,
Mercy from her twilight throne
Listening to nun's faint throb of holy fear,
To sailor's prayer breathed from a darkening sea,
Or widow's cottage-lullaby.

3

Ye Voices, and ye Shadows
And Images of voice—to hound and horn
From rocky steep and rock-bestudded meadows
Flung back, and, in the sky's blue caves, reborn—

On with your pastime! till the church-tower bells
A greeting give of measured glee;
And milder echoes from their cells
Repeat the bridal symphony.
Then, or far earlier, let us rove
Where mists are breaking up or gone,
And from aloft look down into a cove
Besprinkled with a careless quire,
Happy milk-maids, one by one
Scattering a ditty each to her desire,
A liquid concert matchless by nice Art,
A stream as if from one full heart.

4

Blest be the song that brightens
The blind man's gloom, exalts the veteran's mirth;
Unscorned the peasant's whistling breath, that lightens
His duteous toil of furrowing the green earth.
For the tired slave, Song lifts the languid oar,
And bids it aptly fall, with chime
That beautifies the fairest shore,
And mitigates the harshest clime.
Yon pilgrims see—in lagging file
They move; but soon the appointed way
A choral *Ave Marie* shall beguile,
And to their hope the distant shrine
Glisten with a livelier ray:
Nor friendless he, the prisoner of the mine,
Who from the well-spring of his own clear breast
Can draw, and sing his griefs to rest.

5

When civic renovation
Dawns on a kingdom, and for needful haste
Best eloquence avails not, Inspiration
Mounts with a tune, that travels like a blast
Piping through cave and battlemented tower;
Then starts the sluggard, pleased to meet
That voice of Freedom, in its power
Of promises, shrill, wild, and sweet!

Who, from a martial *pageant,* spreads
Incitements of a battle-day,
Thrilling the unweaponed crowd with plumeless heads?—
Even She whose Lydian airs inspire
Peaceful striving, gentle play
Of timid hope and innocent desire
Shot from the dancing Graces, as they move
Fanned by the plausive wings of Love.

6

How oft along thy mazes,
Regent of sound, have dangerous Passions trod!
O Thou, through whom the temple rings with praises,
And blackening clouds in thunder speak of God,
Betray not by the cozenage of sense
Thy votaries, wooingly resigned
To a voluptuous influence
That taints the purer, better, mind;
But lead sick Fancy to a harp
That hath in noble tasks been tried;
And, if the virtuous feel a pang too sharp,
Soothe it into patience,—stay
The uplifted arm of Suicide;
And let some mood of thine in firm array
Knit every thought the impending issue needs,
Ere martyr burns, or patriot bleeds!

7

As Conscience, to the centre
Of being, smites with irresistible pain,
So shall a solemn cadence, if it enter
The mouldy vaults of the dull idiot's brain,
Transmute him to a wretch from quiet hurled—
Convulsed as by a jarring din;
And then aghast, as at the world
Of reason partially let in
By concords winding with a sway
Terrible for sense and soul!
Or awed he weeps, struggling to quell dismay.

Point not these mysteries to an Art
Lodged above the starry pole;
Pure modulations flowing from the heart
Of divine Love, where Wisdom, Beauty, Truth
With Order dwell, in endless youth?

8

Oblivion may not cover
All treasures hoarded by the miser, Time.
Orphean Insight! truth's undaunted lover,
To the first leagues of tutored passion climb,
When Music deigned within this grosser sphere
Her subtle essence to enfold,
And voice and shell drew forth a tear
Softer than Nature's self could mould.
Yet *strenuous* was the infant Age:
Art, daring because souls could feel,
Stirred nowhere but an urgent equipage
Of rapt imagination sped her march
Through the realms of woe and weal:
Hell to the lyre bowed low; the upper arch
Rejoiced that clamorous spell and magic verse
Her wan disasters could disperse.

9

The Gift to king Amphion
That walled a city with its melody
Was for belief no dream:—thy skill, Arion!
Could humanise the creatures of the sea,
Where men were monsters. A last grace he craves,
Leave for one chant;—the dulcet sound
Steals from the deck o'er willing waves,
And listening dolphins gather round.
Self-cast, as with a desperate course,
'Mid that strange audience, he bestrides
A proud One docile as a managed horse;
And singing, while the accordant hand
Sweeps his harp, the Master rides;
So shall he touch at length a friendly strand,

And he, with his preserver, shine star-bright
In memory, through silent night.

10

The pipe of Pan, to shepherds
Couched in the shadow of Mænalian pines,
Was passing sweet; the eyeballs of the leopards,
That in high triumph drew the Lord of vines,
How did they sparkle to the cymbal's clang!
While Fauns and Satyrs beat the ground
In cadence,—and Silenus swang
This way and that, with wild-flowers crowned.
To life, to *life* give back thine ear:
Ye who are longing to be rid
Of fable, though to truth subservient, hear
The little sprinkling of cold earth that fell
Echoed from the coffin-lid;
The convict's summons in the steeple's knell;
'The vain distress-gun,' from a leeward shore,
Repeated—heard, and heard no more!

11

For terror, joy, or pity,
Vast is the compass and the swell of notes:
From the babe's first cry to voice of regal city,
Rolling a solemn sea-like bass, that floats
Far as the woodlands—with the trill to blend
Of that shy songstress, whose love-tale
Might tempt an angel to descend,
While hovering o'er the moonlight vale.
Ye wandering Utterances, has earth no scheme,
No scale of moral music—to unite
Powers that survive but in the faintest dream
Of memory?—O that ye might stoop to bear
Chains, such precious chains of sight
As laboured minstrelsies through ages wear!
O for a balance fit the truth to tell
Of the Unsubstantial, pondered well!

12

By one pervading spirit
Of tones and numbers all things are controlled,
As sages taught, where faith was found to merit
Initiation in that mystery old.
The heavens, whose aspect makes our minds as still
As they themselves appear to be,
Innumerable voices fill
With everlasting harmony;
The towering headlands, crowned with mist,
Their feet among the billows, know
That Ocean is a mighty harmonist;
Thy pinions, universal Air,
Ever waving to and fro,
Are delegates of harmony, and bear
Strains that support the Seasons in their round;
Stern Winter loves a dirge-like sound.

13

Break forth into thanksgiving,
Ye banded instruments of wind and chords;
Unite, to magnify the Ever-living,
Your inarticulate notes with the voice of words!
Nor hushed be service from the lowing mead,
Nor mute the forest hum of noon;
Thou too be heard, lone eagle! freed
From snowy peak and cloud, attune
Thy hungry barkings to the hymn
Of joy, that from her utmost walls
The six-days' Work by flaming Seraphim
Transmits to Heaven! As Deep to Deep
Shouting through one valley calls,
All worlds, all natures, mood and measure keep
For praise and ceaseless gratulation, poured
Into the ear of God, their Lord!

14

A Voice to Light gave Being;
To Time, and Man his earth-born chronicler;
A Voice shall finish doubt and dim foreseeing,
And sweep away life's visionary stir;
The trumpet (we, intoxicate with pride,
Arm at its blast for deadly wars)
To archangelic lips applied,
The grave shall open, quench the stars.
O Silence! are Man's noisy years
No more than moments of thy life?
Is Harmony, blest queen of smiles and tears,
With her smooth tones and discords just,
Tempered into rapturous strife,
Thy destined bond-slave? No! though earth be dust
And vanish, though the heavens dissolve, her stay
Is in the WORD, that shall not pass away.

Extempore Effusion upon the Death of James Hogg

WHEN first, descending from the moorlands,
I saw the Stream of Yarrow glide
Along a bare and open valley,
The Ettrick Shepherd was my guide.

When last along its banks I wandered,
Through groves that had begun to shed
Their golden leaves upon the pathways,
My steps the Border-minstrel led.

The mighty Minstrel breathes no longer,
'Mid mouldering ruins low he lies;
And death upon the braes of Yarrow,
Has closed the Shepherd-poet's eyes:

Nor has the rolling year twice measured,
From sign to sign, its steadfast course,
Since every mortal power of Coleridge
Was frozen at its marvellous source;

The rapt One, of the godlike forehead,
The heaven-eyed creature sleeps in earth:
And Lamb, the frolic and the gentle,
Has vanished from his lonely hearth.

Like clouds that rake the mountain-summits,
Or waves that own no curbing hand,
How fast has brother followed brother,
From sunshine to the sunless land!

Yet I, whose lids from infant slumber
Were earlier raised, remain to hear
A timid voice, that asks in whispers,
'Who next will drop and disappear?'

Our haughty life is crowned with darkness,
Like London with its own black wreath,
On which with thee, O Crabbe! forth-looking,
I gazed from Hampstead's breezy heath.

As if but yesterday departed,
Thou too art gone before; but why,
O'er ripe fruit, seasonably gathered,
Should frail survivors heave a sigh?

Mourn rather for that holy Spirit,
Sweet as the spring, as ocean deep;
For Her who, ere her summer faded,
Has sunk into a breathless sleep.

No more of old romantic sorrows,
For slaughtered Youth or love-lorn Maid!
With sharper grief is Yarrow smitten,
And Ettrick mourns with her their Poet dead.

BIBLIOGRAPHY

1 Publications in Wordsworth's Lifetime

An Evening Walk (1793).
Descriptive Sketches (1793).
Lyrical Ballads (1798, 1800, 1802, 1805).
Poems in Two Volumes (1807).
The Excursion (1814).
Poems—first collected edition (1815).
The White Doe of Rylstone (1815).
Peter Bell (1819).
The Waggoner (1819).
The River Duddon (1820).
Miscellaneous Poems—second collected edition (1820).
Memorials of a Tour on the Continent, 1820 (1822).
Ecclesiastical Sketches (1822).
Third Collected Edition (1827).
Fourth Collected Edition (1832).
Yarrow Revisited, and other Poems (1835).
Fifth Collected Edition (1836–7, reissued 1840).
Poems, Chiefly of Early and Late Years (1842).
One volume Edition (1845).
Last Collected Edition (1849–50).

2 Publications after Wordsworth's Death

The Prelude, or Growth of a Poet's Mind (1850).
The Prose Works, ed. by A. B. Grosart (1876).
The Recluse (1888).
The Prelude—1805 version (1926).
Collected editions of the Poems:
Ed. T. Hutchinson (1904).
Ed. Nowell C. Smith (1908).
Ed. E. de Selincourt and H. Darbishire (1940–9).
Correspondence of Henry Crabb Robinson with the Wordsworth Circle, ed. by E. J. Morley (1927).
Letters of William and Dorothy Wordsworth, ed. by E. de Selincourt (1935–9).

Letters of William Wordsworth—World's Classics (1954).
The Journals of Dorothy Wordsworth, ed. by E. de Selincourt (1941).
Letters of Mary Wordsworth, ed. M. E. Burton (1958).
William Wordsworth: The Prelude, ed. by E. de Selincourt, revised by H. Darbishire (1949).

3 Biographical and Critical Studies

Memoirs of William Wordsworth by C. Wordsworth (1851).
Preface (*Golden Treasury Wordsworth*) by M. Arnold (1879).
The Early Life of William Wordsworth by E. Legouis (1897).
Concordance to the Poems by L. Cooper (1911).
William Wordsworth, His Life, Works, and Influence by G. M. Harper (1916).
William Wordsworth and Annette Vallon by E. Legouis (1922).
William Wordsworth, His Doctrine and Art in Their Historical Relations by A. Beatty (1922).
Wordsworth by H. W. Garrod (1923).
Wordsworth by H. Read (1930).
The Lost Leader by H. I. Fausset (1933).
The Later Wordsworth by E. C. Batho (1933).
Dorothy Wordsworth by E. de Selincourt (1933).
The Mind of a Poet by R. D. Havens (1941).
Wordsworth's Formative Years by G. W. Meyer (1943).
A Study of Wordsworth by J. C. Smith (1944).
The Poet Wordsworth by H. Darbishire (1950).
The Art of Wordsworth by L. Abercrombie (1952).
Wordsworth and Coleridge, 1795–1834 by H. M. Margoliouth (1953).
Wordsworth's Prelude. A Study of its Literary Form by A. F. Potts (1953).
Wordsworth, A Reinterpretation by F. W. Bateson (1954).
The Egotistical Sublime by J. Jones (1954).
William Wordsworth, A Biography, The Early Years (1770–1803) by M. Moorman (1957).
The Early Wordsworthian Milieu by Z. S. Fink (1958).
Wordsworth (in "Writers and Their Work" series) by H. Darbishire.
Study of Wordsworth by J. C. Smith (1958)

Portraits of Wordsworth by F. Blanshard (1959).
Simple Wordsworth by J. F. Danby (1960).
Wordsworth and Schelling (in "Studies in English" series) by E. D. Hirsch, Jnr. (1960).
Discussions of William Wordsworth ed. by J. Davis (1964).
Wordsworth's Poetry, 1787–1814 by G. H. Hartman (1964).
William Wordsworth, a Biography: The Later Years, 1803–50 by M. Moorman (1966).
Wordsworth and The Artist's Vision by A. King (1966).
Wordsworth (in "Literature in Perspective" series) by M. Drabble (1966).

INDEX OF TITLES AND FIRST LINES

First lines of extracts are not included